BLIGHTED

T0384289

BLIGHTED

A Story of People, Politics, and an American Housing Miracle

MARGARET STAGMEIER

NewSouth Books

an imprint of
The University of Georgia Press
Athens

NSB

Published by NewSouth Books
an imprint of the University of Georgia Press
Athens, Georgia 30602
www.ugapress.org/imprints.newsouthbooks/

Paperback edition, 2024

Printed and bound by Sheridan Books, Inc.

The paper in this book meets the guidelines for permanence and durability of the Committee on Production Guidelines for Book Longevity of the Council on Library Resources.

Most NewSouth/University of Georgia Press titles
are available from popular ebook vendors.

Printed in the United States of America
24   25   26   27   28   P   5   4   3   2   1

Library of Congress Cataloging-in-Publication Data
Names: Stagmeier, Margaret, author.
Title: Blighted : a story of people, politics, and an American housing miracle / Margaret Stagmeier.
Description: Athens : NewSouth Books, an imprint of the University of Georgia Press, [2022] | Includes bibliographical references and index.
Identifiers: LCCN 2022945958 | ISBN 9781588384713 (hardback) | ISBN 9781588384843 (ebook)
Subjects: LCSH: Housing—Georgia—Atlanta. Urban renewal—Georgia—Atlanta—Citizen participation. | Minorities—Housing—Georgia—Atlanta.
Classification: LCC HD7304.A7 S73 2022 | DDC 363.509758231—dc23/eng/2022945958
LC record available at https://lccn.loc.gov/2022945958

ISBN 9781588385277 (paperback)

To John—my champion
I thank God for you every day

Exhibits

Demographic Detail Report, 2010 Census / 6

911 Service Call History, 2013–2017 / 12

Top 10 and Bottom 10 Ranked Georgia School / 31

2017 Cost of City of Atlanta Municipal Services / 33

Cost of Capital, Interest Rate Burden / 60

2019 Star-C Students Georgia Milestone Scores / 306

Rent Burden of Permitting Costs and Delays / 310

Analysis of Cost of Evictions from Summerdale / 319

911 Service Call History, 2013–2021 / 326

Contents

Preface / ix

Acknowledgments / xvii

I — INVESTING IN BLIGHT TO REMOVE IT

1 The Bombed-Out Cleveland Avenue Neighborhood / 5

2 The Science of Blight / 20

3 Blighted Communities and the Value of Political Will / 35

4 A Walking Tour of the Community Chaos / 45

5 Capital Stack Gymnastics—How We Raised $9.6 Million to
   Purchase Summerdale / 55

II — EFFECTS OF BLIGHT ON THOSE WHO LIVE AND WORK IN IT

6 Virginia Humphries—The Longest Surviving Tenant / 64

7 Sharon Allen—The Phantom Tenant in Apartment D-12 / 79

8 Melinda Wyatt—the Blighted Tenant / 86

9 The Atlanta Police Lieutenant and the Drug Kingpin / 94

10 Dr. Payne—Cleveland Avenue Elementary School / 104

11 Kingston Humphries—The Traumatized Tenant / 114

III — RE-SIFTING THE COMMUNITY SOCIAL CAPITAL

12 The Physical Inspection / 124

13 Purchase and Management Takeover / 148

14 Lucy Hamby and the Wild West—the First 30 Days / 155

15 Taming the Drug Kingpin in Unit D-12 / 170

16 The Federal Compliance Burden of Equitable Housing / 178

17 The Management Office / 192

Eight pages of photographs follow page 182.

18   The Toxic Community Culture / 207

19   Kristin Hemingway—The Children and Star-C After-
         School Program / 214

20   'I Have Lived Here for 22 Years' / 220

21   Pest Infestations Management / 227

22   Crime and Security / 233

23   Melinda Wyatt and the Blighted Mentality / 240

24   Jeff Miller and the Tedious Permitting Process / 246

25   Education and the Star-C After-School Program / 259

26   The Eviction of Melinda Wyatt / 267

27   The Replacement Criminals—Crime and Security / 272

28   Rebuilding Social Capital / 279

IV — EPILOGUE

29   Change Gonna Come / 288

30   Summerdale Survives the COVID-19 Pandemic / 328

31   Solutions / 345

         Notes / 360
         Index / 367

Preface

A brilliant Wall Street future awaited Doug Avryn at his family-held investment banking firm. Educated in Ivy League schools, he looked the part of a young, successful investment banker—smooth olive skin, thick curly dark hair, intense brown eyes, and a chin cleft worthy of a movie star. He was on his way to join the lucrative family business when he decided to take a career sabbatical and devote his talent to teaching poor kids in the rural South. He signed a contract with DeKalb County, Georgia, to teach in Stone Mountain, a backwards suburb of Atlanta with a lingering history tied to the Civil War. A year later, I landed in his sixth-grade classroom.

Mr. Avryn was an anomaly among the faculty at Hambrick Elementary. He made up his own rules for teaching, and with a vast bank account at his disposal he spared no expense in his innovative teaching methods. If the geography topic was Hawaii, he outfitted the entire class in grass skirts and leis, and we hula danced and drank juice from straws in real pineapples with little umbrellas. He took the time to listen to us and treated us like important people who mattered. We loved Mr. Avryn.

When the time came to teach about capitalism, Mr. Avryn purchased ten Monopoly games and hosted a class championship. What better way to explain risk, profit, and loss to a group of eleven-year-olds living in functional poverty? We played Monopoly for the entire week and the winners of each game advanced to the next round and the next until it was just me and John Burke in the final. I had a big crush on John but didn't let that deter my pursuit of capitalism. I won after an intense hour where I purchased almost every property on the Monopoly board. After that lesson in finance, I was hooked. That night I announced to my family at the dinner table that when I grew up I planned to be a landlord. My parents and sisters listened and smiled and encouraged me.

When I was fourteen, my father advised me to become a CPA. He wasn't sure what being a CPA entailed, but a young lady accountant had visited his office, and she drove a luxury car and knew about taxes and business and impressed him. I took his advice and graduated from Georgia State University, studied for a year to pass the CPA exam, and pursued my career as a landlord. I've been fortunate to work for smart, supportive people in the business, and over my career I have owned and/or managed more than ten million square feet of office, retail, hotel, and apartment space.

Legacy housing, or older apartment communities, has always been my favorite class of investment because you are dealing with the lives of real people and their community. Landlords of large apartment communities can make or break entire neighborhoods. It is one of the few for-profit investment models that brings out the best of community building and profit if sequenced correctly. It is the triple bottom line.

SEVERAL YEARS AGO, MY real estate business partners and I purchased a large, severely blighted apartment community in Cobb County north of Atlanta. The Madison Hills apartment complex had everything wrong. Mold, high crime, transient tenants, pest infestation, exasperated municipal leadership, and a failing elementary school. It was challenging to turn around this blighted property in the face of a community that was hostile and a municipality that stigmatized the property and sabotaged our efforts to restore the complex to health. In the process, I learned the impact of housing on people, municipal leaders, educators, community volunteers, healthcare systems, churches, and more.

Everyone of influence was operating in their respective narrow lane and the lack of resource coordination perpetuated the blight. We refused to accept defeat and demonstrated that you can build community capital around education and housing, in a sustainable for-profit model. With virtually no government subsidies, we did turn around that blighted property and provided affordable housing for 446 working-poor families. The local failing elementary school eventually became a Title I school of distinction, and the neighborhood started to thrive.

We wondered if what we had done could be a formal model where apartments are treated as "Communities" versus "Commodities," thus solving the affordable housing, healthcare, and education crisis that is presently festering in so many cities and neighborhoods. My partners and I asked ourselves this question and decided to host a hundred meetings with community leaders, volunteers, nonprofits, foundations, homeless people, mayors, school superintendents, police officers, and just about anyone who would meet with us and allow us to share our experiences and theories. The feedback to the case-study results of our model indicated strong political and community support.

That led to our next project, the subject of this book. While I have owned and managed more than three thousand apartment units in my career, Atlanta's Summerdale Apartments was the first blighted apartment community in which we deliberately set out to apply and document the community capital model. Our goal was to take a severely blighted 244-unit apartment complex and improve the marginalized living conditions and educational outcomes of the families living at the property.

We succeeded. So can others.

Landlords play a critical role in apartment communities. A very critical role. They are the de facto mayor and can make or break an impoverished family, school, government, and neighborhood with the stroke of a pen to raise rents or cut expenses. In reality, the social capital of the community truly belongs to the residents, and the work to be done is not all about exclusively using one's talents as a landlord to convert social capital into one's own short-term personal profit.

I think Mr. Avryn would agree.

THIS BOOK WAS WRITTEN to share the Summerdale Apartments story, giving readers an inside look at the challenges we faced, the people we impacted, and how we made the model work. At the start, the visual of Summerdale was intimidating and scary. I often had to often remind myself that dignified families lived at the property and called Summerdale their home, despite the high crime and toxic stress associated with its blighted structures. Ironically, my understanding of these facts had been expanded through a very different experience.

On one beautiful October Saturday evening in the middle of Buckhead, one of Atlanta's wealthiest and most fashionable neighborhoods, I patiently waited behind a long line of luxury automobiles to turn into the swanky Ritz-Carlton Hotel. My husband John sat next to me, handsomely attired in a crisp tailored tuxedo and keenly focused on the black Maserati inching ahead in front of us.

We were in our undistinguished white Jeep Cherokee, and I joked to John that we should have arrived in our 1990 Mitsubishi truck. That humble vehicle gave us—having grown up as middle children in working-class families—a sense of nostalgic pride. It grounded us in a comfortable shared reality that neither of us had expectations other than to work hard, raise a family, and save our modest paychecks. Both accountants with resumes crowded with Fortune 500 corporations, we started dating in our thirties in the Mitsubishi truck in a period when I was dirt-poor trying to build my real estate company.

At the time, neither John nor I anticipated in our wildest dreams that we would be attending a high-society fundraising event that put us in the same circle as distinguished doctors, Buckhead socialites, multi-millionaire business owners, trust-fund babies, and a little glamor. The Crystal Ball for Arthritis was a much-anticipated social event expected to raise more than $500,000, a nice sum in the early 2000s. Nine months earlier, two neighbors had cornered me at a community event asking me to chair the fundraising ball.

I had been on the board of the Atlanta Community Food Bank for years, attending its rather modest fundraisers, but had never considered a large society event. I was amused to be asked but more than a little intimidated by the prospect. But the neighbors persisted, and I researched the cause. I came to understand the urgent social needs and costs of an autoimmune disease that affects healthy tissue in children and adults and leaves them debilitated from the more than a hundred types of arthritis including lupus, gout and eczema. No matter how gut-wrenching it would be to take on the effort, I recognized there was a dire need for the money from the fundraiser, and the time commitment to chair the event was worthy of my time. I said yes. Nine months of planning later, here were John and I, about to attend the sold-out ball.

Inside the Ritz-Carlton's grand ballroom, Arthritis Foundation director Christine Lennon had everything organized, with dozens of volunteers
guiding guests to tables covered in deep blue cloths with flashing gold and
ruby red trim, large flower centerpieces, and crystal glassware. There was
a large stage with a full orchestra warming up. We had "fortune tellers" in
"booths" at the entrance to the ball room—who wouldn't want to get their
personal fortune read at "Your Crystal Ball."

The last nine months had been an interesting time learning the dynamics
of a society event. I grew up in Stone Mountain, Georgia. Our neighbors
were engineers, shoe salesmen, and tradespeople driving Fords, Plymouths,
and Chevrolets and struggling to maintain their working-class lifestyles and
hopes to fund their children's college. Dining at a restaurant was a special
event. The people associated with the Crystal Ball were a sharp contrast.
They drove luxury cars, lived in large expensive homes (many with staff),
shopped at designer boutiques, and amused themselves with extensive
travel or country clubs. They would not be impressed by my Dairy-Queen
upbringing or public school education. My committee members included
a core group of dominating matriarchs who had been involved in high-
society events for years.

Arrogant society ladies were not entirely new to me, having worked for
an international real estate company based in Munich, Germany, with a
client roster including counts and princes who lived private lives in castles
and estates. But my being a young American woman, neither judgmental
nor easily impressed, led those blue-blooded Germans to drop their guards
and embrace me at face value, without expectations to fit within their social
pecking order. Besides, I liked most of them.

It was more or less the same with my fellow fundraisers for the Crystal
Ball in Buckhead. Furthermore, I was actively purchasing severely blighted
apartment communities around Atlanta, in marginalized high-crime areas.
The people living in these toxic apartment properties were toughened by
poverty and daily survival instincts and were not exactly students of fine
etiquette. If I could endure screaming tenants, racial slurs, verbal abuse,
and hostile rudeness from my angry, impoverished tenants, a high society
Buckhead matriarch would be a piece of cake.

The Crystal Ball event was just one of a series of opportunities for me to get out of my comfort zone with people I didn't know or who lived differently than I. The various personalities that came together expanded my understanding of people, and the event seemed to attract generous people with similar ethics. That was comforting to me even as I was aware that many of these people would not come within a hundred miles of the marginalized apartment communities where I invested the majority of my time.

However, most interesting for me personally was the commonality of all the people attending or servicing the event. The majority of the low-wage service workers no doubt left the safety and luxury of Buckhead at the end of their shifts to live in higher-crime marginalized apartment communities. The volunteers lived all over Atlanta—most with better-paying jobs than the service workers—but crime and struggle happened in their neighborhoods too. The wealthy participants had high drama in their lives, but just lived in nicer homes with shorter commutes. Despite their luxury lifestyle and perceived place in society, I learned that wealth and glamour are superficial, and in the end people are just people and everyone is worthy of dignity and respect no matter their income level.

In a word, that is the core of my work and the mission of TriStar as it redevelops blighted apartment communities, and it is what this book is about and why I wrote it.

THE CONTENT IS ORGANIZED to follow loosely the timeline of our process in redeveloping the Summerdale Apartments.

Part I, "Investing in Blight to Remove It," starts with an introduction to the Cleveland Avenue area in south Atlanta where Summerdale Apartments sit just east of I-75. The first chapter reveals what I observed about the conditions of Summerdale and the surrounding neighborhood, including a failing elementary school, high crime associated with drugs, abandoned or deteriorating stores, and other ills of the social ecosystem neighborhood at the time when TriStar purchased the property. The next chapters explain what blight is and show how we approached the purchase of and then the renovation of Summerdale Apartments, including our mission to provide decent housing at affordable rents to lower-income residents.

Part II, "Effects of Blight on Those Who Live in It and Work in It," offers a more personal view of Summerdale, told through the words and experiences of the characters involved. These include Virginia Humphries, an elderly long-time resident, and her grandchildren; Sharon Allen, a phantom tenant who facilitated crime on the property; Anthony Fowler, a drug kingpin; Melinda Wyatt, a blighted tenant; Joe Pulaski, our police officer; and Dr. Anyeé Payne, the heroic principal at Cleveland Avenue Elementary School. Plus many others, from staff to contractors to security personnel to tenants. While the visual of Summerdale at the start was intimidating and scary, I realized that dignified families lived at the property with their children and called Summerdale their home, despite the high crime and toxic stress associated with blighted structures. Note also that the events and individuals described in this book are based on personal observations, business and legal records, and interviews with the persons named, networks around the persons, or the administrative files. Some names have been changed for privacy reasons. I did not interview the criminals identified and portrayed, but they are depicted based on court records, social media, and observations of tenants, staff, police and security, and other people familiar with the criminals and their behavior.

Part III, "Re-Sifting the Community Social Capital, 2017–2018," outlines the purchase and planning associated with the structural environment, including the initial physical inspection of each unit, meeting the tenants, and taking over the daily management. It shows the demarcation between the prior slumlord owners and TriStar's efforts to start the community turnaround. We document the day-to-day challenges of realigning the social, structural, and legal environments. We follow property manager Lucy Hamby, construction chief Jeff Miller, and Star-C after school program director Kristin Hemingway as they take on the drug dealers, blighted tenants, regulatory inspectors, and community culture to bring order to Summerdale. It is especially encouraging to see the positive impact of the work on the children including the Star-C intervention. By this time we have control of Summerdale and are focused on improving the social capital including the after-school program, evicting toxic tenants, addressing the crime, and organizing the KABOOM! playground event where the community comes together to build a beautiful playground and safe community space in which the residents can interact with their neighbors and build trust.

Part IV, "Epilogue," discusses the effects of our four-year effort on the community and the people portrayed in the book. What happens to Virginia Humphries, Sharon Allen, Dr. Anyeé Payne, the rents, evictions, and criminals? Were our goals met? Did our efforts bring about positive social change? We were nearing the conclusion of the renovation of Summerdale when the COVID-19 pandemic hit, which dramatically altered TriStar's course and our tenants' lives. We returned to interview our tenants impacted by COVID-19 offering transparency on the damage caused to our families and efforts to rebuild the social order in an environment impacted by viral chaos. This section outlines thoughts and potential solutions for other apartment communities, nonprofits, businesses, and municipalities interested in learning more and bringing our model to their communities.

Acknowledgments

I had to step out of my landlord-comfort zone and dig deep to write this book—real deep. Without the desire to tell the story of the thousands of lives impacted by a single marginalized, blighted and dangerous apartment community, I would have never joined tenants in their living rooms, principals in their classrooms, police officers on their beats, volunteers doing their impactful community work, municipal workers enforcing complex rules during their watch, and brave management staff rebuilding community from chaos. I would have had no clue of the profound, inter-generational impact of drug dealers and their toxic, illegal, often violent business model. I would have had no idea that children living in roach-infested apartments suffered from asthma and other major health issues that stunt brain development. I would have never fully grasped that marginalized, toxic, blighted apartment communities generally leads to traumatized, blighted, unhealthy humans . . . and this trauma passes down and many families never recover. I would have had no idea that generous investors would accept a modest (or zero) investment return in favor of creating strong, equitable communities.

Through this journey, I was overwhelmed by the grateful assistance of so many friends, family, and colleagues who invested their valuable time and talent to see the evolution of Summerdale published into a meaningful unique story.

I express my sincere thanks to my family. My sister Kathleen Boring generously volunteered countless hours reviewing, editing, counseling, and urging me to tell the story. My sister Raina Kant, thank you for your encouragement and rallying your friends to review the many manuscripts and provide excellent feedback. My parents Peg and Michael Morton—thank you for your constant support, not only of me as your daughter, but of Star-C and the families.

I thank my TriStar business partners Audrea Rease and Duncan Gibbs and my assistant, Keya Oates. Without their sage leadership or encouragement, Summerdale would have never achieved community success and the families certainly would not have much hope for a productive future. I thank the team at TI Asset Management and Star-C Communities, who orchestrated our Eduhousing[1] mission by patiently managing the thousands and thousands of endless incremental steps of that epic marathon to forge community structure from blighted chaos. Visit us at www.blightedapts.org.

A small army of people generously volunteered as manuscript reviewers to ensure the story was being told understandably. Angie Santy, Jody Fay, Jen Christensen, Holly Crenshaw, Karen Gray, Karen Meyers, Liz Blake, Matt Kuehn, Michelle Eaton, Nancy Drummond, Sandra Bowen, Sheila Yarbrough, Terry Kidder, and Audrea Rease—I can't thank you enough for taking time from your very busy schedules to dive into the gritty ecosystem of a blighted apartment community. Your valuable feedback greatly shaped this book.

Karen Gray, thank you for designing the title and cover page concepts. It was one of the best Christmas gifts ever!

I would like to also thank my publishing team of Randall Williams, Suzanne La Rosa, and Drew Plant for having faith in this project.

Finally I would like to acknowledge the thousands of families currently living in blighted apartment communities. It takes courage to maintain dignity and composure when society around you is crumbling and you have no options. God bless you.

BLIGHTED

I — Investing in Blight to Remove It

Summerdale Apartments, Cleveland Avenue Neighborhood

1 Cleveland Avenue
2 Old Hapeville Road
3 Exxon station

4 Summerdale Apts. Phase 1
5 Summerdale Apts. Phase 2
6 Cleveland Avenue Elementary

1

The Bombed-Out Cleveland Avenue Neighborhood

In the southeast corridor of Atlanta—the city "Too Busy to Hate"—Cleveland Avenue intersects Interstate 75, a north-south Michigan to Florida artery of the freeway system launched in 1956 under President Dwight D. Eisenhower. Daily, the drivers of some 140,000 vehicles speed beneath the Cleveland Avenue overpass without a glance at the adjoining area. The cars exiting at Cleveland Avenue are typically older models with faded paint jobs, spewing gas fumes along the long, trashy off-ramp.

The neighborhood, a vibrant commercial district in its 1970s heyday, was by 2017 a dying landscape dotted with an abandoned Kmart, boarded-up apartment buildings, and shuttered fast-food restaurants. Dilapidated cinder-block buildings highlighted by faded commercial signage testified to the neighborhood's stark poverty. On any given day, the chipped and weedy sidewalks were populated with heavy pedestrian traffic, and jobless men lurked aimlessly in the shadows of vacant parking lots or loitered at the popular Exxon station at the corner of Cleveland Avenue and Old Hapeville Road. The U.S. Census recorded the concentrated poverty of the dying neighborhood that crowded this section east of I-75. An estimated 10,714 people lived within a one-mile radius and earned a median income of $26,942 (half the U.S. average), which of course means that roughly half the neighborhood's residents, at least the legal ones that reported to the U.S. Census, earned even less.[2] Despite being within economically booming Atlanta, the population along Cleveland Avenue shrank 15 percent between 2000 and 2015. The unemployment rate for this corridor was 15.8 percent or 168 percent higher than the U.S. average. The high pedestrian

Demographic Detail Report - 2010 Census
2015 Estimates & 2020 Projections
Summerdale Apartments, Atlanta Georgia

	0-1 Mile Radius	1-3 Mile Radius	3-5 Mile Radius
Population			
2020 Projection	11,580	60,238	184,462
2015 Estimate	10,898	59.093	179,764
2010 Census	10,110	57,642	174,768
2000 Census	12,383	70,924	202,348
Growth 2010-2015	7.79%	2.52%	2.86%
Growth 2000-2015	-12.00%	-16.78%	-11.16%
Households by Marital Status			
Married	814	4,705	16,332
Female HH: No Husband	1,535	6,928	18,464
Female HH: Children	692	3,666	9,484
2015 Population by Education	7,236	42,407	129,267
Some High School, No Diploma	1,583 (21.88%)	9482 (22.36%)	24,980 (19.32%)
High School Grad (Incl Equivalency)	2,380 (32.89%)	13.550 (31.95%)	36,878 (28.53%)
Some College, No Degree	1,903 (26.30%)	10,221 (24.10%)	30,933 (23.93%)
Associate Degree	696 (9.62%)	3,399 (8.02%)	10,993 (8.50%)
Bachelor's Degree	527 (7.28%)	4,069 (9.60%)	16,204 (12.54%)
Advanced Degree	147 (2.03%)	1,686 (3.98%)	9,279 (7.18%)
2015 Avg Household Income	$36,224	$39,647	$46,240
2015 Med Household Income	$26,942	$26,594	$31,434
2015 Occupied Housing	3,911	21,529	68,559
Owner Occupied	1,458 (37.28%)	8,807 (40.91%)	30,071 (43.86%)
Renter Occupied	2,453 (62.72%)	12,722 (59.09%)	38,488 (56.14%)

traffic was by necessity—31 percent of the residents in the neighborhood did not own a vehicle.[3]

The saving grace of Cleveland Avenue was its proximity to thriving employment centers in downtown Atlanta and at adjacent Hartsfield-Jackson Atlanta International Airport, one of the busiest in the world. The neighborhood was also convenient to Grady Memorial Hospital, the only Level I trauma center in Georgia. Every day, a parade of ambulances made the short commute between Cleveland Avenue and Grady to deliver the victims of gunshots, stabbings, and other drug and domestic violence. In 2017, you exited I-75 onto Cleveland Avenue at your own risk.

Meanwhile, Atlanta overall was experiencing rapid population growth. For the year ending June 1, 2017, Metro Atlanta added more than 89,000 people, the third-largest population increase among U.S. cities.[4] The demand for housing fueled by rapid population growth created an affordability crisis, impacting impoverished residents such as in the Cleveland neighborhood. According to a housing study by the Cushman & Wakefield real estate firm in January 2018, Atlanta had a deficit of 80,353 affordable housing units.[5] Over recent years, growing numbers of high-wage earners had relocated to the flourishing city, gentrifying many in-town neighborhoods and pushing low-income renters to cheaper housing in the outlying suburbs. The Cleveland Avenue corridor was one of the few remaining neighborhoods within the city limits with a housing inventory affordable for working-poor families who needed access to predictable public transportation. Hourly workers employed in the robust service industry as housekeepers, custodians, baggage handlers, child care providers, and grocery cashiers eventually found their way to Cleveland Avenue in search of affordability, but at a social cost. The high criminal activity and dilapidated aging housing stock kept rental prices in check. A two-bedroom apartment could be rented for $800 per month, affordable for a family living on $15 an hour ($30,000 per year), but tenants risked armed robberies, carjackings, or a bullet in exchange. You got what you paid for, especially when it came to housing in an economically booming market like Atlanta.

The families living along the Cleveland corridor are educated in the Atlanta Public Schools district, commencing with Cleveland Avenue Elementary as the entry point for kindergarten. In 2017, Cleveland Avenue Elementary was ranked 813th of 1,205 elementary schools in Georgia.[6] High poverty and dangerous housing environments manifest in the education system, and Cleveland Avenue Elementary was not immune. Of the 352 students attending Cleveland Avenue Elementary in 2017, every one qualified for the federal free and reduced cost lunch program.[7] Meanwhile, only 27.5 percent of the third graders were tested at a reading level at or above the Grade Level Target[8] (however, the Cleveland Avenue Elementary staff and leadership persevered, and by fifth grade, 73.8 percent of students were reading at or above grade level). The students of Cleveland Avenue Elementary graduated to Long Middle School, which achieved a State Grade of "F" and where 18.5 percent of the students missed more than 15 school days a year. After graduating from Long Middle School, students landed in South Atlanta High School, with a School Grade of "F" and where 30.1 percent of the students missed more than 15 days of school, compared to a state average of 11.2 percent. The educational challenges mirrored the stark reality of the Cleveland Avenue neighborhood.

THE BLIGHTED APARTMENT COMMUNITY

The Summerdale Apartment Community sits two blocks east of the 1-75 Cleveland Avenue exit and one block south of Cleveland Avenue Elementary. The complex is made up of two distinct properties, built in separate decades, neatly divided by Old Hapeville Road. On the east side resides Summerdale Phase I, a mismatched group of partially boarded-up brick buildings containing 144 one- and two-bedroom units that are predominantly townhomes. The decaying apartments were built in the early 1970s at the peak of a development boom fueled by the residual effects of the John F. Kennedy administration's liberal housing policies for low-income families, at a time of unparalleled housing demand by the baby boomer generation then entering adulthood.

Summerdale Phase II sits on the west side of Old Hapeville Road. Built in 1998 by Phase I owner Donald Dressel, this multi-acre property contributed another one hundred modern, spacious two- and three-bedroom units to the neighborhood. The newer apartment community was a strategic move for Dressel, who needed larger units to accommodate the growing families on his tenants roll. Dressel constructed Phase II with a $5 million HOPE VI Program grant[9] administered by the U.S. Department of Housing and Urban Development.

Phase II's more contemporary design of vinyl siding and cleaner brick contrasts sharply with the 1970s vintage brick and boarded-up facade of Phase I. Most people driving along Old Hapeville Road between the two properties would not associate one apartment community with the other. With both properties, Summerdale consists of 244 units with 528 bedrooms and can legally house up to 1,056 people.[10] At illegal capacity, the population of Summerdale could easily top 2,000, if no one was paying attention.

The significant criminal activity in the Cleveland Avenue neighborhood spilled over into both phases of Summerdale. Official 2017 police records document 440 emergency calls from the property, with 275, or 63 percent, from violent crimes such as armed robbery, gunshots (48 calls), car thefts, and fights [see "911 Call History" exhibit, page 12]. Drug dealers had gained control of the environment and openly operated their illegal business, daring anyone to challenge them. Police sirens were a daily presence, and the Fulton County judicial system was a spin-cycle—those arrested rarely got real jail time and usually landed back at Summerdale within 48 hours. The Cleveland Avenue neighborhood was a dangerous, decaying environment of survival, and no one was spared, including the elderly and other long-term residents at Summerdale Apartments. The out-of-state owners were actively trying to sell the property, complete with high violent criminal activity, decaying structures, and community turmoil.

ENTER A NEW LANDLORD WITH A NEW IDEA

I am a partner in TriStar, a mission-based landlord that purchases large older legacy apartment communities near low-performing elementary schools and partners with Star-C—a 501(c)(3) nonprofit organization—to provide wrap-around community services including free after-school programs and summer camps. Reweaving social capital in large, blighted, crumbling apartment communities is my specialty. Along the way, I have developed a profound respect for the hard-working families whose breadwinners are blue-collar laborers or hold hourly wage jobs at Walmart, Home Depot, Starbucks, Delta Airlines, hotel and fast food chains, and other service companies, while trying to raise their families with dignity in a crumbling apartment environment. Many Americans avoid blighted neighborhoods at all costs; few understand that these intimidating communities may be home to many hard-working families with limited or fixed incomes and few affordable housing options. These families are usually stuck in their deteriorating community and just pray things improve as they survive the toxic environment daily.

Summerdale Apartments came across our radar in late 2016. At the time, simply driving through the neighborhood and touring the property was dangerous. Summerdale Phase I was severely blighted and the environment was ominous, with open drug-dealing and criminal activity. You could feel the inherent risk just walking through the gates and into an environment actively populated by groups of loitering men who coldly watched your every move. However, the seller indicated he was willing to take a price that met our business model of providing affordable housing near a low-performing elementary school. That was important. The seller wanted just over $5 million, a sum that after renovation would allow us to offer rents for approximately $730 per month, considered affordable for families living on $12–15 hourly wages.

TriStar submitted a purchase offer in January 2017 and was informed a few days later that the seller had accepted an offer from another buyer. But this buyer did not complete the purchase, so the seller's agent called us in July 2017, and again we submitted an offer. The HOPE VI grant signed in 1997 as part of the construction of Phase II created an administrative hurdle. The HOPE VI grants are now defunct since Congress has moved on to different housing programs; however, the compliance agreement was recorded in Fulton County records with a mandate that the property comply with complex public housing rules through the year 2037. Those rules would have sabotaged daily operations, and the removal of this agreement was necessary to close the deal and allow us to efficiently operate the property.

In the year between our first offer in 2016 and the second offer in July 2017, the Cleveland Avenue community was visibly spiraling downward. Several more commercial buildings in the neighborhood had closed, boarding up their windows, and the drug-dealing and loitering at the corner Exxon gas station was even more evident, spreading throughout the neighborhood and across the street from Cleveland Avenue Elementary. Gunfire often erupted in broad daylight as the dealers fought to gain control between the McDonald's and Exxon corners.[11]

Apartment landlords typically run from blighted properties with high crime and low-performing elementary schools in crumbling neighborhoods, but we chose to put the Summerdale property under contract in November 2017 and closed the purchase in June 2018.

I then started documenting the transformation of Summerdale Apartments, including the people involved in the process. What does it take to convert a marginalized, crime-infested, blighted apartment community to a healthy, stable environment for low-income families? To understand this transformation, it is important to understand why a perfectly healthy apartment community fails in the first place, with reverberation throughout the community including the local elementary school.

This book unpacks the journey of Summerdale Apartments through the eyes of the individuals who were innocent witnesses to its deterioration and then beneficiaries of the rebuilding. Everyone plays a role in the success of a community, but tragically resources tend to stay in the comfort of their own "lane." Educators focus on education, medical providers focus on healthcare, police officers focus on safety, and foundations focus on their mission. Rarely do these critical resources cross-collaborate and align towards a common agenda to successfully rebuild communities. I have had countless conversations with generous foundations bemoaning the failure of a multimillion-dollar investment in a single low-performing elementary school. Despite their good intentions, the funding of critical programs and investment in the students walks out the door when a local landlord raises rents $100 a month thus forcing the families to move their children out of the school to other neighborhoods in search of affordability. Landlords have the capacity to bring these resources together as a catalyst for community building. I am sharing my story so communities around the country have a sample benchmark to blend the resources of their community partners to improve families. It is all there in plain sight.

NEXT STEPS
The families and people portrayed in the book—and living in your communities—need our help. Housing is at the core of human stability and impacts life quality well beyond a roof and safety. Housing matters. It influences occupants' health, education, and finances and can make or break human success.

Housing or the "structural environment" is just one part of an interconnected ecosystem that links many societal issues. Let's start with housing and education. Landlords of large apartment communities can dramatically impact the local elementary school. Large rental increases or high criminal

Summerdale Apartments — 911 Service Call History
For the Years 2013–2017

Call Code	2013	2014	2015	2016	2017
Violent Crimes					
Burglary/Armed Robbery	24	19	6	8	73
Shots Fired	6	13	3	28	48
Fights/Stabbing	45	49	46	103	107
Sex Assault	1	1	0	5	2
Stabbing	1	1	0	0	0
Armed Person	1	1	1	9	7
Stolen Autos/Goods	1	5	0	16	37
Suicide	1	3	1	1	1
Violent Crimes Total	**80**	**92**	**57**	**170**	**275**
Nonviolent Crimes					
Disorderly Per/Simple Assault	18	18	11	10	18
Drugs	5	0	1	12	48
Theft	14	4	10	12	16
Person Injured	5	5	4	5	2
Dead Person	1	1	2	1	1
Suspicious Person	3	4	2	18	40
Trouble/Vandalism/Theft	1	5	3	4	3
Miss Person	1	3	0	0	2
Loud Music	4	1	1	6	27
Domestic	1	6	4	3	0
Silent Alarm	0	0	7	0	0
Person Located	2	0	0	4	1
Criminal Trespass	2	0	0	1	7
Fire	0	1	0	1	0
Child Abandonment	1	0	0	1	0
Nonviolent Crimes Total	**58**	**48**	**45**	**78**	**165**
Crimes Total	**138**	**140**	**102**	**248**	**440**
Other 911 — Clerical Service Calls					
Officer Information	27	19	30	30	50
Total All 911 Service Calls	**165**	**159**	**132**	**278**	**490**

Source: Atlanta Police Department Public Records.

Note: TriStar purchased Summerdale in June 2018

activity usually trigger families to move from the apartment community in search of affordability or safety. This movement is also known as "mobility" or "transiency," and educators are well aware of the impact on their school. Transiency is so critical that many states require individual schools to report student mobility. The high level of tenant transiency initiated through large rental increases or criminal activity at apartment properties destroys schools and communities, contributing to a vicious circle of poverty. Research has proven that when children transfer schools, they lose approximately three months of learning, and this "churn" is a crisis. As children who experience high transiency fall further and further behind their stable peers, their low performance on federal test scores negatively affects the performance of their school. I have spoken with dozens of educators who are powerless to address the impact of transiency. Imagine starting the school year with twenty students and only having eight of the original twenty still in your classroom at the end of the school year. It is stressful for educators to maintain standards in a revolving-door classroom. There is no "plan" to teach through transiency since it is beyond an educator's control. However, landlords of large apartment communities can influence transiency by maintaining a safe property and affordable rents.

It is well documented that single-family home prices and neighborhood desirability are impacted by school rankings. Children who move two or three times a year while their parents chase affordable housing are now a common occurrence, especially in low-income neighborhoods; TriStar certainly sees these families in our own apartment portfolio. As a child moves, it requires considerable effort for the new school to evaluate learning status and make sure the student is caught up to his or her peers.

Meanwhile, the success of local schools is a large factor in the choice of destination neighborhoods. Evidence of this is in a comparison of the home prices near low-performing and high-performing elementary schools. In 2017, I surveyed the home prices of the five top-ranked and the five bottom-ranked elementary schools in Atlanta. The average home price of the zip codes with the top-ranked schools was $863,000, compared to the average home price of $51,900 in the zip codes with the bottom-ranked schools. Families that could afford it were willing to pay a significant premium to live near higher-ranking elementary schools. Housing directly impacts school performance, and school performance directly impacts demand for housing, and all of it impacts property tax collections which obviously affects education funding. This is true not just in Atlanta but across the nation.

HEALTHCARE IS THE NEXT noteworthy social interconnection within the housing ecosystem. The toxic impact of lead or asbestos is well documented, but a poor-quality housing environment also harbors conditions such as roaches or mold and can trigger cancer, asthma, headaches, and blood issues. Landlords can control structural environmental factors that influence tenants' health. Sound windows and roofs, functioning appliances, and adequate heating and air conditioning are the responsibility of the landlord. However, the quality of the interior is a collaboration between the tenant and landlord. Tenants can easily destroy interiors as they play out trauma and anger issues that are commonly seen in marginalized apartment properties. We also see the strong relationship between tenant housekeeping practices and family health.

Households with major pest issues or mold—often created by not running air conditioning during the humid summer months—create toxic environments for children, triggering asthma and other illnesses. When I set out to document this journey, I wasn't aware that roaches were a trigger for asthma. Roach infestations at Summerdale were almost epidemic, and not surprisingly the majority of the children living there were asthmatic—many in households with dismal housekeeping. Hence, a consequence of poor housekeeping is sick children, creating academic challenges. How can children learn if their education is frequently interrupted by absences or even hospital visits to address asthma attacks or poor health issues? Health issues triggered by substandard housing are expensive in many ways. How can parents support their families under the burden of medical bills and lost wages from missed work to care for a sick child? The healthcare industry is starting to take notice of the interconnection of housing as a social determinant of health. Children's Healthcare Atlanta, a hospital specializing in children's medical services, realized that many of its young asthma patients were recurrent visitors to the emergency room, and many of these children lived in roach- or mold-infested housing. The dedicated doctors could treat the patients, who then returned to their toxic housing environment only to return to the emergency room in a short time. In an effort to reduce the causes, Children's Healthcare partnered with Atlanta Legal Aid, which is now part of the intake process in the emergency room. Advocacy is provided to families of asthma patients in substandard housing. The object is to enforce the law and hold the landlord accountable to provide clean, decent housing. The result was an improvement in the home environment and a dramatic reduction in repeat hospital visits.

The strong relationship between psychiatric illness and criminal activity is also well-documented; many victims of violent crime later experience mental health challenges. The families living at Summerdale before we purchased the property were at the mercy of a drug kingpin who ran a regional drug hub from within one of our apartment units. The resulting violent criminal daily activity included random gunfire, armed robberies, fighting, intimidation, late-night loud music and carousing, and loitering. The children living at Summerdale at this time were exposed to this activity, and high levels of toxic stress that directly affect brain development and general well-being. Ten types of childhood trauma are measured by the CDC's Adverse Childhood Experiences Study. The study uncovered a stunning link between childhood trauma and the chronic diseases people develop as adults—including heart disease, lung cancer, diabetes, depression, violence, and suicide, as well as social emotional problems. We are raising the next generation of poverty through substandard housing communities. We observed the impact of high stress on Summerdale's children. Many were depressed, low-proficiency readers, or exhibited trauma symptoms. Our Star-C after-school programming was engineered to provide relief to these children and assistance to their working parents.

AS PART OF TRANSPARENCY in the interconnection in the housing environment ecosystem, I have not omitted my personal struggles in executing TriStar's model of improving a local elementary school and the surrounding neighborhood by stabilizing a toxic apartment community. Summerdale was mired in high violent crime, drug dealers, traumatized tenants, exasperated municipal workers, dysfunctional federal regulations, and truculent capital markets. The dysfunctional ecosystem led to the collapse of the social order of Summerdale. Reversing the situation faced many, many challenges.

The first challenge was raising sufficient capital to purchase and renovate a blighted apartment community, at an interest rate low enough to keep our rents affordable for families living in the neighborhood. As you will read, every percent we had to pay in interest required $33 per month in additional rent for our tenants, which is a significant amount of money for our tenants living on $13–$15/hour. We ultimately raised our capital by relying on the strength of our business model, the market dynamics around the affordable housing crisis, some generous mission-based investors, and some major luck.

Our second challenge was creating order within the social hierarchy. When we purchased Summerdale Apartments, we knew we were buying the entire social hierarchy associated with blight. Many tenants we inherited were model citizens, but many others (or their illegal guests) were criminals, or were traumatized, or exhibited a blighted mentality. The latter ignored the community rules, fought with their neighbors, fired their guns, had terrible housekeeping, or refused to pay their rent. However, we were determined not to displace the honest, hardworking families. We know from experience that reversing the established social hierarchy of a blighted apartment community is a risky, dangerous, tedious effort that can take years. It would have been much faster and easier if we focused our efforts solely on rebuilding the structural environment of Summerdale Apartments and ignored the social environment, neighborhood, and Cleveland Avenue Elementary School. We could have wiped out the established hierarchy by simply evicting everyone—the long-term legacy tenants along with the drug dealers, prostitutes, car thieves, and illegal tenants. Once the property was completely vacant, we could have renovated the interiors, repaired the exterior to improve the appearance, and remarketed the newly renovated units at monthly rents $200–$300 higher than before, then enjoyed the profits from operating a healthy apartment community. If we had chosen this approach, the legacy tenants you will read about could not afford higher rents and could not afford to move; some would have joined Atlanta's growing homelessness problem.

But this was not our business approach. We did not want to uproot the valuable tenant population who followed the rules and, just as importantly, disrupt the adjacent public elementary school that already had a high transiency rate. Many of the residents living at blighted Summerdale Apartments and in the neighborhood were full-time workers, dedicated and loyal to their employers, or retirees living on social security. These minimum-wage workers and retirees need safe, decent, affordable housing. A major increase in rents would cause relocation to other neighborhoods in the pursuit of affordability, usually at the cost of a longer commute from the suburbs where rents are more affordable but public transportation is almost nonexistent. The affordable housing crisis is a major contributing factor to the growing traffic issue in many cities. The renovation of older apartment communities by opportunistic landlords is a popular trend right now. Unfortunately, many of these landlords earn their profit by displacing low-income tenants. Very few of these landlords, in their eagerness to make an almost sure and quick profit, take a community approach to carefully build the social capital to the benefit of the entire neighborhood. This trend of fast profit is destroying the social hierarchy at many of these low-income apartment communities and fueling the affordability, transiency, and homelessness crises.

Our third challenge was associated with the built environment. Rent affordability for working-poor families was the core of our business mission. We diligently studied the market and potential operating efficiencies and carefully designed an executable business model that delivered on our mission. Based on the acquisition cost, renovation costs, anticipated operating expenses, and debt costs, we set a goal to offer rents at an affordable monthly cost. However, there were two challenges. First, our direct operating expenses had to allow this rental rate. If our annual operating expenses (excluding debt and capital expenses) for property taxes, property insurance, salaries, administration, repairs, landscaping, security, utilities, and trash removal exceeded our budget, then we would have no choice but to raise rents. Second, tenants have a major impact on expenses. They can run up the complex's water bill by leaving faucets flowing, damage their apartments, not pay rent, run their cars through the security gates, break security cameras, and trash the community—all leading to higher, much higher, operating expenses.

The final cost of the capital renovation was another major component of our rent affordability goal. We budgeted for renovation of the entire property, including compliance with mandated federal housing requirements. The renovation was not a large job for our company, but we were rightfully concerned with the cost to comply with the burdensome federal regulations. Furthermore, timing was important. If the permitting and construction process took longer than six months, then we would have to fund the operating expenses of any units that were vacant and not generating income. Again, we would have to borrow money to fund the additional costs of the renovation including the costs associated with delays. As you will read, the federal and City of Atlanta permitting process increased our renovation budget. Sadly, we had no choice but to raise our monthly rents —to the chagrin of our tenants. We were able to help some tenants through creative rent subsidy arrangements.

Our final challenge in the housing ecosystem was the regulatory environment. A complex web of laws at the federal, state, and local level is associated with the components of the housing ecosystem. When we purchased Summerdale Apartments, we inherited parts of this environment. There are thousands of pages of rules and regulations, and I have to confess that I have never owned an apartment community exposed to the complex rules associated with subsidized housing. At the state (Georgia), county (Fulton) and city (City of Atlanta) level, there are myriad laws around evictions, criminal activity, code enforcement, permitting, and construction. As you will read, the City of Atlanta permitting process bogged down and delayed the Summerdale renovation for over a year, adding more than a million dollars to our costs and forcing us to raise rents higher than we had projected or wanted to. Many of these delays reflected a dysfunctional permitting and inspection process with many misinterpretations of the rules by municipal employees who didn't seem to care about affordability.

There were also challenges and delays caused by the criminals who for years had commanded the playgrounds and other common areas. We followed the law around public safety; unfortunately, some of our tenants and their guests (and customers) did not. The criminals know the law and how to evade it, which makes it frustrating, time-consuming, and difficult to relocate them to their new housing—the Fulton County jail. And when we finally got the drug dealers arrested, the prosecutor's office was so dysfunctional that the criminals were released within a day or two and they returned right back to their illegal business at Summerdale. I count my blessings that tenants or their children were not physically harmed before we could eradicate the criminal activity, although the physiological harm cannot be accurately measured.

WHILE THERE WERE SIGNIFICANT challenges realigning the structural, education, healthcare and legal environments at Summerdale, there are positive efforts and outcomes which you will see unfold through the following pages. I am still learning about this business and anticipate that this book will stimulate a lively discussion of best practices. However, this is the story of Summerdale, and I hope you find it educational. It certainly was for me.

2

The Science of Blight

As part of our effort to build community partnerships at Summerdale Apartments, we began hosting informational tours to showcase our Eduhousing model and inform the public on the topic of blight. We were pleasantly surprised when a diverse group of about twenty-five investors, lenders, government leaders, nonprofits, tenants, vendors, and employees registered and attended the first tour. Transparency is important to TriStar's moral framework and for an hour our guests experienced the reality of the deteriorated social and structural ecosystem at Summerdale. Our property manager Lucy Hamby, our contractor Jeff Miller, and the leasing staff escorted the guests across parking lots and sidewalks littered with broken glass, extensive trash, drug paraphernalia, and evidence of vandalism. As the visitors walked past the boarded-up windows, overgrown weeds, loiterers, and graffiti, we explained our plans to rebuild the structural and social capital of the community. We were showing the "vision" and inviting the community to be part of the transformation. The experience was emotional for many of our guests who lived in safer, privileged neighborhoods and had never encountered the stark reality of a large, blighted apartment community.

People are fascinated with a business model that uses equitable housing to improve education. Summerdale was demonstrating in a live case study the critical social connection between housing and education—a symbiotic relationship most of our property tour guests had never considered. People tend to stay in the comfort of their specialized lanes and seldom have an opportunity to link how private and public sectors contribute to a blighted community. Educators are rarely exposed to the daily challenges associated with apartment ownership, and landlords generally do not concern themselves with the challenges of delivering quality education. But the interdependency of education and housing is significant, and Summerdale was giving the community an opportunity to funnel their areas of expertise into one focused lane. It was encouraging to see our guests embrace the vision and understand this critical interdependency. We answered many questions during these tours but the most common one was: "What happened to make Summerdale a blighted community?" With such a strong demand for affordable housing in Atlanta, it was inconceivable that a seventeen-acre property, housing 244 families at below-market prices, could crumble into such disrepair. For many of our guests, this was a socially awakening experience. Giving them that experience was a key part of our effort to ensure there would be local political will to tackle the social problem of blight in the Cleveland Avenue/Summerdale community.

We had learned the value of municipal political will the hard way while renovating two other seriously blighted apartment communities in DeKalb and Cobb counties, adjacent to the Atlanta city limits. That is how I began to understand how municipal governments stigmatize low-income housing, creating barriers for well-intentioned landlords wanting to improve such properties. In Cobb County, the local elected officials simply wanted the Madison Hills apartment property demolished and its debris put into the landfill. I strongly disagree that bulldozing blighted apartments and replacing them with newly constructed units is a solution to affordability. We purchased and renovated Madison Hills for less than $45,000 per unit, whereas a demolition and new construction would have cost more than $130,000 per unit, or two-thirds more. At renovation costs of $45,000 per unit, the landlord can rent them at $725 per month, versus $1,300 per month for newly constructed units. Renovating blighted apartment communities is a much better solution.

THAT BRINGS US TO TriStar's purchase of Summerdale Apartments. Summerdale's story, and that of many other blighted apartment communities across the United States, is predictable for properties built in 1971. From 1960 to 1979, some 6.2 million, or 30 percent of existing apartment units in the United States, were built, making these two decades into what the U.S. Census refers to as one of the most robust construction eras in the history of apartment housing; 1968–1973 were the peak years as developers catered to the baby boomers entering adulthood and forming households. The majority of these legacy apartment communities are still offering vital housing at rents affordable for working-class families. You only had to drive around the immediate Cleveland Avenue neighborhood to see evidence of the construction boom of these decades. Five competitive apartment communities near Summerdale were built during the 1960s and 1970s. The surge in construction met a growing housing demographic of post–World War II baby boomers as they entered adulthood and formed households. Today, for many reasons, this aging apartment inventory is rapidly disappearing from the supply pool.

Over the past decade, major cities like Atlanta have experienced explosive population growth, creating significant housing demand. Developers are meeting this demand by tearing down aging apartment communities in prime locations and replacing them with higher-density construction allowing more units. Municipal zoning laws and construction codes have evolved since Summerdale was constructed. The municipal code in place in the 1970s when Summerdale Phase I was built generally allowed twelve apartment units per acre. A developer could build 240 units on a twenty-acre site. However, it is now legal to build twenty to thirty units per acre in prime locations. If a metro-Atlanta developer could locate twenty unencumbered prime acres today, she could easily rezone it into a mixed-use development to include four hundred-plus apartments and multiple retail storefronts. The City of Atlanta, like other municipalities, is certainly interested in higher-density construction since it ultimately benefits from the higher tax base generated from the new project. An older 244-unit property like Summerdale could have an assessed tax value of $8 million. If Summerdale were torn down and replaced with a new apartment community, the assessed value might increase to $60 million, or the cost of new construction, creating not only a stronger tax base for the city but more modern housing for the community.

Unfortunately, the removal of affordable older apartment communities is disruptive, as many cities are learning after the fact. Children displaced from the local public school system cause transiency throughout the school district, and low-income wage earners have fewer affordable housing options, forcing them to outlying areas. In neighborhoods with expensive housing, it is common for more than 90 percent of the labor pool to commute from outlying neighborhoods, creating not only a traffic and air quality nightmare but also labor scarcity.

Physical decline due to poor maintenance and management is also reducing the supply of older apartments. Most complexes built in the 1960s–1970s era are now fifty to sixty years old and arguably at the end of their useful life (for depreciation purposes, the IRS allows 27.5 years as the useful life of residential real property, including apartments[12]). Housing structures and systems require continuous maintenance, and if ownership is not vigilant the structures eventually become compromised. Plumbing and roofs are prime examples of structural components that need continuous maintenance. Over time, drain lines and roofing materials deteriorate, creating water leaks, and repairs can be tremendously expensive. Repairs do not add value to the profit bottom line since a landlord cannot increase rental rate charges to pay for the cost of maintenance. Ignoring failing roofs and plumbing systems can quickly escalate into mold and water damage. Eventually the cost of repairs will exceed the value of the property, creating economic obsolescence. The next step is to board up or tear down the apartment community, removing units from the housing supply. This is a dramatic example of how poor maintenance can lead to the structural obsolescence of housing, but we often see this where capitalistic landlords, in the pursuit of short-term profit, don't prioritize maintenance, eventually causing blight.

THE HISTORY OF SUMMERDALE is typical for an apartment community built in 1971. The sequence of events that transforms a healthy community with high occupancy and financial profitability into a blighted eyesore is a drama decades in the making. The collapse of once-vibrant communities is caused by various yet collaborative influences. Every apartment community, regardless of its age or location, can fall victim to blight due to external or internal influences; both contributed to Summerdale's decline.

External influences are outside the control of the landlord. Examples include the economy, unemployment rates, increased mortgage interest rates, municipal events like rezoning or increases in municipal costs such as property taxes and water rates, high crime, and environmental events like weather. There is a clear relationship between these external influences, and a single unforeseen event can significantly impact the economic viability of an apartment complex, especially for landlords who cannot quickly adapt or absorb losses, including damage costs. Mortgage interest rates are one example of an external influence that can quickly impact the economic viability of an apartment community. Let's say an owner secures a $10 million property loan at a 5 percent interest rate. After ten years, the loan matures and the owner must replace it with another loan. Only this time the interest rate is 2 percent higher. The higher rate costs the landlord $200,000 more in annual mortgage payments, or $68 per unit per month assuming all 244 units are rented.[13] If the landlord can't pay the additional costs, he increases the rent and the $68 monthly burden falls on the tenant.

When rental increases are not possible or a landlord can't reduce expenses, then the property is not economically viable and may be at risk of foreclosure. I have canceled apartment acquisitions because interest rates increased before we closed our loan, and the market could not support the rental increase required to fund a higher mortgage. In one example, the increased mortgage payment associated with the higher interest rate would have required us to charge an additional $75 rent per month per unit. The average household income for renters of these nonsubsidized units was less than $30,000 per year. My partners and I knew this particular property was not economically feasible; we decided not to purchase it.

Another type of external influence, an economic recession, usually triggers the sequence of events that destabilizes a healthy apartment community. Economic recessions challenge the financial viability of any property to produce a profit. Apartment communities are in the business of renting the physical unit in exchange for money. When a recession occurs, tenants lose jobs and their ability to pay rent. If Summerdale is short on collections due to a recession, it has no choice but to reduce expenses to equal rent collections or find other sources of income. The monthly expense to operate Summerdale is approximately $130,000, or about $533 per unit. This includes standard expenses such as utilities, property taxes, staff salaries, repairs, landscaping, and administration[14] but excludes the monthly mortgage expense. If Summerdale does not collect $130,000 per month plus the monthly mortgage payment, then we have no choice but to reduce expenses to equal collections.

WHEN MONTHLY COLLECTIONS ARE insufficient to fund monthly expenses, smart landlords start prioritizing their outlays. If Summerdale only collects $110,000 monthly and has $130,000 in monthly expenses, we must decide who gets paid and who does not. Payment of the monthly mortgage and property insurance has priority, since we do not want our lender foreclosing, and property insurance is a required expense for a lender to protect the collateral of their loan against losses. Utilities are the second priority bucket. We cannot legally operate apartments if the water or electricity is shut off for lack of payment. Tenants cannot live in an apartment community or pay their rent without essential utilities. Usually, utility companies will allow a few months to pay delinquent bills and, more importantly, a utility company cannot foreclose. Usually, its only option is to shut off the water rendering the property functionally obsolete.

That leaves other expenses like staff payroll, repairs, maintenance, and landscaping at the bottom of the priority list. Once a landlord starts cutting back on staffing and maintenance, the operating capacity is compromised, rendering the property at risk to start the downward spiral towards blight. A property cannot operate without sufficient staff to oversee leasing and maintenance. The general rule of thumb is one maintenance staff and one management staff employee for every one hundred apartment units, depending on the age and condition of the property. Older properties like Summerdale, which have older appliances and other elements, typically have a higher number of maintenance staff to address leaks, broken appliances, broken gates/fences, and plumbing leaks. A leaky toilet in the City of Atlanta can easily cost $1,000-plus per month in additional water usage.[15] As a landlord, I am highly motivated to repair leaky toilets and faucets to avoid large unexpected water bills.

A landlord can reduce maintenance staff and attempt to maintain a property like Summerdale with just one person, but the results can have immediate consequences. Summerdale employs three maintenance employees to address routine work orders, preventative maintenance, and grounds landscaping. Since Summerdale averages fifty-plus maintenance work orders per week, ranging from broken appliances, leaks, or unit turnover for a new tenant, it would be difficult for one maintenance person to timely and efficiently address all the work orders. A backlog of more than three hundred maintenance work orders greeted us on the day we closed the Summerdale purchase, and that did not include the work orders never reported by the tenants, which arrived by the thousands after word got out that we promptly addressed maintenance repairs. After years of neglect, Summerdale tenants had learned to endure with their leaky toilets, roaches, broken air conditioning units, and malfunctioning appliances. The rent was so low—where else could they pay $650/month for a two-bedroom unit in an $850/month market? A culture of open communication is important at apartment communities, and a landlord must be responsive to maintenance work orders to maintain structural integrity and avoid long-term expensive repairs which can render the property structurally and functionally obsolete.

The second influences that can jeopardize the viability of an apartment community are internal, generally controlled by the landlord and their action or inaction. Examples include the selection of management staff, execution of critical repairs and maintenance, structural upkeep, rental rates, and marketing. Day-to-day property management is a skill set which can strongly impact operations and profits. The manager needs to wear many hats and use a vast array of business skills. Accounting, lease negotiation, fair housing laws, human resources, marketing, public relations, administration, software and maintenance are just a few skills a competent property manager should master. The hiring of incompetent management, or if the staff is competent but does not follow standardized management practices such as fair housing laws, or if the staff embezzles money from property operations—these circumstances can render the operations insufficient to fund the expenses and put the property at risk of foreclosure.

The establishment of rental rates is another internal influence directly under the control of the landlord. Setting monthly rents is not an exact science as much as an ongoing test of supply and demand. If a landlord sets the rates too high for the market, it could be at the risk of income loss though increased vacancies. I have seen this happen many times where an ambitious landlord raises rents $100 to $200 per month and drives away good tenants who cannot afford the increase. I recall a recent example at a property we were managing for a third-party owner and our client-landlord insisted we raise monthly rents by $100. We advised our client against this sudden rent increase because it was above the rents charged by our competitors, and the existing tenants simply could not afford it, thus the property would be at risk of losing good long-term tenants. This client insisted on the rent increase, with devastating consequences to the economic viability of the operations. The first week after the increase went into effect, eight tenants turned in their keys and moved out. Within a month, twenty-three tenants vacated. A total of $18,975 in monthly collections walked out the door the first month, and the property was not in a physical condition to attract replacement tenants at the higher rents. The landlord did not invest in the maintenance or landscaping, and part of the property had unrepaired fire damage. Within three months of pushing the new higher rental rates, the owners surrendered and lowered the rents; however, by this time they had lost 20 percent of their monthly revenue and could not make the monthly mortgage payment. We had no choice but to start cutting back on expenses, and the spiral to blight was launched. It is a hard lesson for landlords to learn and even harder for the property rent collections to recover from.

THE VISUAL DETERIORATION OF a property is evidence of a downward spiral to blight. When a landscaping contract is canceled or reduced, weeds, trash and balding landscaping appear. The staff hours may be reduced, and prospective tenants show up to an empty office with no one to facilitate the leasing process. A smaller, overworked maintenance staff does not have time to clean the grounds, and trash accumulates. Tenant work orders get set aside, and items such as faulty appliances and leaky roofs escalate beyond a quick and affordable fix.

Once an apartment community starts to visually deteriorate, the next phase is what I term as the great "tenant sift." Many tenants will not tolerate deteriorating apartment communities, and those that have the financial wherewithal to move will promptly vacate when their leases expire. Those who remain usually have limited resources and no choice but to settle for the deteriorating conditions. When financially stronger tenants move out to nicer properties, vacancies rise, collections go down, and cost-cutting measures come into play.

Faced with a growing inventory of non-income producing vacant units, landlords will reduce their qualifications to lease units. Typically, landlords like to lease to tenants with incomes equal to three times their rent. For example, a tenant earning $3,000 per month can qualify for a $1,000 monthly rent. These criteria are at the sole discretion of the landlord. Some landlords require income at four or five times monthly rent. With a growing inventory of vacant units, one trick landlords use to fill apartment vacancies is to reduce the qualification level to income equal to 50 percent of the applicant's rent. A tenant making $2,000 per month can now qualify for a $1,000 per month rental apartment. The downside is that instead of paying 30 percent of income on rent, the tenant is now paying 50 percent of income on rent, a real stressor for low-income families who have utilities, transportation, food, and other basic necessities left to pay monthly. Once a landlord relaxes the income leasing standards, they start leasing to tenants who are financially vulnerable and struggle to pay rent. When unforeseen events happen, like losing a job, they become delinquent, eventually triggering an eviction. And during this time, the unit does not generate income for the landlord. The decline continues as the property becomes a revolving door where the landlord may have all the units occupied—by a growing population of financially stressed tenants—but is only collecting about 75 percent of billable rent.

The "$99 Move-In Special" is another ever-present gimmick landlords used to fill vacant units. The landlord charges $99 for the first month's rent but raises it to a higher market rate during the remaining term. The landlord may have good intentions in reducing the first month's rent; however, in my experience this tactic typically backfires and negatively impacts profitability. An underground contingent of working-poor tenants chases the move-in special. Typically these tenants are not financially viable renters. They usually qualify based on the lower rent threshold, pay the $99 for the first month, then do not pay rent until they are eventually evicted months later. The tenant usually "skips" their lease just before legal eviction happens, and would be recorded on their credit report, and relocates to the next apartment community offering the $99 Move-In Special. I speak from experience because we once advertised a $99 Move-In Special, and a year later, fewer than half of the tenants were still living at the property and faithfully paying their rent. Landlords only have to do this once or twice to learn the true cost of running a move-in special. In many cases, it is better to leave the apartment vacant than to operate occupied but nonpaying units which eventually lead to damage repairs once tenants move out. Meanwhile, educators detest the gimmick because it increases transiency in their schools, as explained by Dr. Amanda Richie at Brumby Elementary School [see Chapter 31].

THE "SPIN CYCLE" OF transient tenants creates significant wear and tear on apartment communities. Tenants who are not economically engaged where they live are usually unmotivated to care for their apartment interior. Carpet is stained and ruined, poor housekeeping attracts roaches, mold grows in unkept bathrooms, windows are broken, and walls get kicked in and vandalized. The landlord is usually not collecting full rent for the many months it takes to evict the tenant, so income is reduced, and expenses increase because the apartment unit is significantly damaged and unfit to re-lease without thousands of dollars in repairs. The result is reduced income and increased expenses, so profit takes a double hit.

The visual deterioration increasingly impacts operations as more and more financially stressed tenants occupy the property, creating a larger percentage of delinquents. Monthly collections go down. Maintenance issues go ignored as the log of work orders accumulates, with overwhelmed and limited maintenance staff falling further and further behind. Eventually the roof leaks, plumbing lines break, and other maintenance items deteriorate the structural components of the property. Worst, the landlord does not have the income to pay for the repairs. Mold follows water leaks and now the unit is technically inhabitable. There are no laws in Georgia regarding a landlord's obligation to lease habitable units, but conscientious landlords remove these moldy units from their inventory. Over time, the mold and decay take over the building, and the municipal code enforcement responds to complaints and issues citations to the landlord. Under the terms of the property loan agreement, the landlord is required to give these municipal citations to the lender, but it rarely happens. But when lenders become aware of code citations, they rightfully become concerned to protect their collateral. A lender has full right to place a loan into default, triggering a higher interest rate and exacerbating economic decline. With the landlord lacking the funds for mold repairs, the municipality may require the buildings to be boarded up, attracting squatters and vagrants. The property has now lost its financial viability, and the loan usually goes into default. Foreclosure is the next step, and the desperate owner loses the property to the bank in an emotionally and economically painful foreclosure process.

Sensing weakness, vagrants and phantom tenants move into the shadows of the property and the criminal activity escalates. Contrary to popular belief, it is difficult for over-stressed police departments to address criminal activity occurring on private property without strong collaboration with the property owner. Based on the state and municipality, the police department may need written permission from the property owner to be on-site. If the criminal activity is occurring inside an apartment unit, then the police will need probable cause and a warrant to gain access. The criminals know the rules and can easily evade arrest for years if they play the game correctly. Catching savvy criminals is time-consuming and expensive. The property owner needs the resources to fund meaningful, effective, and expensive on-site security and the financial reserves to fund their mortgage and other expenses during the long process of removing the criminals.

Meanwhile, the growing toxic environment is contagious and impacts properties in the immediate vicinity, including the local school and businesses. Neighbors complain, and landlords either ignore the complaints or feel helpless as the criminal culture escalates. Home invasions, armed robberies, and car theft are now a daily reality rather than the exception. The neighboring home values are also a victim of the growing criminal activity, as are municipal revenues. Property taxes paid are a function of the property value, which is based on the operating profit. With the operating profits declining, the landlord can validly argue with the municipality for reduced property taxes. Sadly, when a property is in turmoil, it commands additional municipal services such as police, code enforcement, and judicial time. Increased transiency impacts the local schools through lower test scores, and additional funding is required to invest in the growing spin cycle of children who are not at grade levels. The property is now on the path of "blight," and it can happen in as little as five years.

The below exhibit demonstrates the impact of transiency on elementary schools. Note that during the 2019–2020 school year, the ten top-ranked

Georgia School Rankings
Top 10 and Bottom 10 Ranked Elementary Schools (2019-2020)

10 Top Ranked Elementary Schools in Georgia

State Rank 2019 - 2020 (1)	Elementary School	County	Note (2) Transiency	Student Teacher Ratio	%%% Free Lunch	Avg Test Score
1	Kittredge Magnet	DeKalb	1.00	13.20	8.60	99.80
2	Britt David Computer Magnet	Muscogee	2.60	18.60	15.90	99.70
3	Daves Creek	Forsyth	3.50	15.30	3.30	99.50
4	Big Creek	Forsyth	7.10	13.60	4.60	99.20
5	Johns Creek	Forsyth	6.20	16.30	5.00	99.10
6	Sharon	Forsyth	6.10	16.00	3.40	99.20
7	Level Creek	Gwinnett	6.10	15.20	8.30	98.00
8	Lake Windward	Fulton	9.60	13.90	5.70	98.10
9	Creek View	Fulton	18.00	15.30	5.30	95.90
10	Brookwood	Forsyth	5.80	17.40	5.90	98.20
Average			6.60	15.48	6.60	98.67

10 Bottom Ranked Elementary Schools in Georgia

1200	Fairington	DeKalb	51.00	13.20	99.00	8.50
1201	Tuskegee Airman Global	Fulton	35.10	13.60	100.00	17.70
1202	Alice Coachman	Dougherty	13.60	16.20	100.00	6.10
1203	Lewis	Hancock	13.00	13.50	100.00	5.90
1204	W.S. Hornsby (Note 3)	Richmond	33.30	12.80	97.90	11.50
1205	Continental Colony	Fulton	40.10	12.40	100.00	13.20
1206	Michael R. Hollis	Fulton	32.40	10.70	100.00	13.30
1207	Dobbs	Fulton	37.90	11.00	100.00	10.30
1208	Benteen	Fulton	23.30	10.60	100.00	14.90
Average			27.97	11.40	89.69	10.14

Sources:

(1) SchoolDigger.com School Ranking Report

Georgia Elementary School Rankings/School Year: Test Grades: 3rd, 4th, 5th, 6th, Tests: Milestones Assessment Englis Arts, Milestones Assessment Mathematics, Milestones Assessment Science, Schools: Copyright 2022, Schooldigger.com

(2) Governors Office of Student Achievement - Transiency for the School year 2019-2020

(3) Note: score pass rate was blank for W.S. Hornsby so the metric is based on the average math/English test scores on the

elementary schools in Georgia had an average transiency rate of 6.60 percent compared to 27.97 percent for the bottom-ranked schools.

AN EXAMINATION OF SUMMERDALE'S 716-page title history,[16] starting in the year 1935, demonstrates the impact of external influences on this property. As of 1964, the Cleveland Avenue neighborhood including the future site of Summerdale was farmland. That year, the Fulton County records show an easement was granted to develop Old Hapeville Road, giving vehicular access to the undeveloped land. In 1969, the land that would become Phase I of Summerdale was sold to Bob Young Development and the Pendley Brothers, who secured bank loans to build three independent apartment communities. All three were foreclosed between 1974 and 1975 by the respective lenders, possibly because of the rapid increase in federal fund costs rates from a 5 percent rate in 1972 to an 11 percent rate by 1975. The monthly debt service would have increased dramatically, and the property could not generate the income to fund the mortgage.

Between 1975 and 1991, all three properties underwent a "recovery cycle," selling several times at higher and higher prices until the economic bubble burst, causing one of the complexes to foreclose again. The three apartment communities gradually merged into Summerdale Phase I when a local developer, Donald Dressel, purchased them in 1996–97 via an entity called Summerdale Partners. Dressel also assembled the land on the other side of Old Hapeville Road, and the Phase II construction of one hundred apartment was completed in 1998. Both phases were marketed as Summerdale Commons Apartments under one joint ownership.

Dressel held Summerdale Commons for almost ten years until the financial collapse in 2007 led Fannie Mae to foreclose the property in early 2008. Piecing together the records, it is highly likely that external influences—the recession, unemployment, and distressed businesses—caused Dressel's profits to crumble. Approximately 6.0 percent of all U.S. housing units were foreclosed between 2006 and 2016; unfortunately, Summerdale was an innocent and unfortunate victim of the global financial collapse.[17]

Between 2008 and 2011, Summerdale traded three more times to new buyers, including one who paid $3.45 million for the property, then took a 70 percent loss when it sold to Z Summerdale LLC in February 2011 for $1,001,000.[18] Z Summerdale LLC was an out-of-state buyer who owned and operated the property from 2011 until it sold the property to TriStar in June 2018. The previous owners had invested to upgrade fifty-two units in Phase I with new appliances and nice interiors. But due to code issues or a lack of funding, the remaining Phase I units were boarded up and sat unleasable. The overgrown weeds, burned-out roofs, and plywood-blocked windows and doors cast a visible pall upon the neighborhood and attracted a criminal crowd.

Internal influences spurred the continuing decline of Summerdale. After we purchased the property, it was evident that existing management and maintenance were ineffective. Summerdale held the dubious distinction of having one of the highest 911 call rates logged to the Atlanta Police Department for 2017. Tenants living at the property were either long-term residents on low fixed incomes or were engaged in the growing criminal activity. Understandably, the City of Atlanta was exhausted with the crime, the code issues, and the impact of the toxic community on Cleveland

Summerdale Apartments ("SD")
2017 Cost of City of Atlanta Municipal Services

City of Atlanta Service	Millage (*)	City Budget	# Served Budget	Cost/ Unit	SD # Served	SD Usage	Actual Taxes Paid
Police (911 Calls)	2.62	$180,210,202	11,770,765	$15	483	$7,245	$4,899
Fire/EMS	1.16	79,839,317	76,040	1,050	50	52,500	2,170
School	21.74	777,000,000	52,000	14,942	63	941,346	21,122
Other (Court/Etc)	0.20	14,062,478	18,766	749	41	30,709	382
Total	25.72	$1,051,111,997				$1,031,800	$28,574

(*) Note: The 2017 Millage was 8.84 for "General Fund." The 2017 Budget for the General Fund was $607,388,585 broken down as follows:

		Per Page 57 2017 Budget ($)
Police (911 Calls)	2.62	$180,210,202
Fire/EMS	1.16	79,839,317
Other (Court/Etc)	0.20	14,061,478
Subtotal	3.98	$274,110,997
Remainder Services	4.85	$333,277,588
Total 2017 Budget	8.84	$607,388,585

Avenue Elementary School. Fulton County property tax records show that Summerdale paid $28,574 in property taxes in 2017, significantly below the estimated $1,031,800 operating costs of the municipal services associated with the apartment community.

Our interviews and research showed clearly that Summerdale's sad march to blight was launched by the world financial collapse of 2007, followed by years of internal mismanagement, leading to the boarding up of part of Phase I, attracting a growing toxic criminal culture, and eventually overwhelming the ownership. The evolution from a healthy property to blight occurred in less than six years. Sadly, blighted Summerdale served as ground-zero for neighborhood contagion. The dozens of houses along Waters Road bordering Summerdale Phase I were now abandoned and deteriorating with boarded-up windows. Drug dealers and vagrants eventually took over these unoccupied homes spreading the toxic environment that launched at Summerdale. Much to the dismay of nearby homeowners on the outlying borders of Waters Road, the crime and structural blight were spreading like a toxic infection to the adjacent neighborhood housing at large. And sadly, there was little they could do about the contagion.

3

Blighted Communities and the Value of Political Will

The previous chapter mentioned political will as a strength we had deliberately cultivated in advance of our Summerdale project. We were well aware of the necessity because of what we had learned from the first severely blighted apartment community we renovated, Madison Hills Apartments, a 446-unit property with 990 bedrooms in Cobb County, a relatively affluent section of North Metro Atlanta.

Madison Hills was in terrible shape. More than half its units were uninhabitable because of black mold or significant fire damage. The high criminal activity kept the property in constant turmoil that spilled over to the neighborhood. We planned a $7 million renovation budget, but the Cobb County government had politically stigmatized the property and refused to give us the required construction permits on a zoning technicality that had no legal merit. The Cobb County leadership was tired of Madison Hills and its constant criminal activity and turmoil. We appealed the zoning technicality, and several months after purchasing the property I was invited to a public meeting hosted by the local board of zoning appeals. The purpose of this meeting was to present our case to get the construction permits. During my presentation, I was interrupted by a member of the zoning board who loudly condemned any efforts to renovate the property. This hostile reaction took me by surprise. How could renovating Madison Hills, thus improving the neighborhood, be such a bad thing? After the meeting, my partner and I took a deep breath and approached the board member, Robert Ott, to get an understanding of the issue. Were we missing something? He got right to the point and blamed Madison Hills for causing the failure of Brumby Elementary, its local elementary school, to achieve a successful standing in Georgia's public school ranking. Despite owning and managing thousands of apartment units at the time, I had never considered the impact of an apartment community on the performance of an elementary school. (Interestingly, Ott, who eventually became a Cobb County commissioner, called me years later and asked if he could be on the board of our nonprofit, Eduhousing. He apologized for his initial aggressive behavior and has become a big advocate of our model.)

The very next morning I knocked on the front door of Brumby Elementary School. Immediately after introducing myself as the new owner of Madison Hills, I was ushered into the office of Dr. Amanda Richie, then the assistant principal. We exchanged a few pleasantries and then Dr. Richie explained transiency—a new concept to me at the time—and its linkages between apartment communities and elementary schools. The transiency rate of Brumby Elementary was 67 percent when we purchased Madison Hills in 2007, meaning that almost seven in ten of its students registered or exited during the school year. Further, Brumby was in the bottom 25 percent of Georgia public elementary schools on test scores in reading, math, and social sciences.[19] Almost a fifth of the Brumby students lived at Madison Hills, and for this reason the local politicians, parents, and school leaders blamed the turbulent apartment community for the problems in their school. Their consensus was that if Madison Hills remained blighted and operated in an environment that fostered prostitution, drug dealing, and other criminal activities, Brumby Elementary would continue to have high transiency and be a low-performing school. Looking back, they were right.

The municipal leadership of Cobb County was emotional and combative on the topic of Madison Hills Apartments. They were rightfully proud of their standing since Cobb County was perceived as a well-managed, affluent community, home of many Fortune 500 companies and a coveted Triple-A credit rating. At the time, the county had only two elementary schools on the federal watch list of failing schools; Brumby Elementary was one. The commissioners, fire marshal, code enforcement, and business leadership were frustrated by years of promises from previous owners to clean up the Madison Hills Apartments in the hopes of improving the school. The relationship with the previous ownership was contentious even though the owners spent more than $2.4 million[20] to improve the property at the county's request. From September 10, 2003, to October 12, 2006, the Cobb County records indicate forty-six letters between the ownership and Cobb County on the efforts to resolve various code issues. We walked into a hostile, emotionally charged environment when we purchased Madison Hills despite our efforts to show genuine intent to get rid of the criminal element and improve the property.

THE DAY-TO-DAY OPERATIONS OF Madison Hills were challenging from the start. Crime was significant, and we had 103 units occupied and 343 units in unleasable condition due to black mold, fire damage, or vandalism. Permitting delays imposed by Cobb County limited our ability to address the deteriorating condition. We chose to plow ahead despite Cobb County's resistance. We started by hiring local armed police officers with arrest powers to work night shifts throughout the week with two officers scheduled to work weekend shifts. This was expensive, but it was the quickest and safest way to remove the entrenched criminal activity operating at the property.

However, cutting crime also removed some tenants. In one singular week, we lost 13 tenants and went from 26 percent to 23 percent occupancy. This was an alarming business development because the vacated units had provided vital rental income. At one of our Tuesday staff meeting about a month after starting the security program, I looked at the numbers and asked, "What happened to our rent roll?"

Betty Simmons, our property manager, calmly explained, "[The 13 tenants] were arrested by the police blockade at the front entrance."

"What? We had that many criminals with active outstanding felony warrants living at this property?" I asked, stunned by this information. I surveyed the property through the panoramic glass window of the management office. Everything looked peaceful.

"Oh, yes, and the ones that are not in the pokey either skipped on their lease or moved next door."

"Next door . . . are you serious?"

"Yep . . . I waved at one of them just this morning. We saw the U-Haul empty out apartment F-7, and five minutes later it was going up the hill to our neighbors."

I was somewhat shocked that our neighboring apartment community would accept a criminal freshly released after a felony arrest. We were on friendly terms with our neighboring apartment communities, and this particular owner seemed reasonable and a good businessman, not one that would accept tenants with recent felonies. I guess the drug dealing had moved next door.

As the owner of Madison Hills Apartments, we knew we were losing the political popularity contest. However, the real damage was the economic cost associated with the stigmatism of our property by the various departments within the Cobb County government. The strong relationship between housing, provided by us, and services, provided by the various Cobb County municipal departments, played out in our efforts to renovate Madison Hills. Public safety resources must be spent to police the high criminal activity typical at blighted properties. That spills over to the court system which must fund the judicial process and prison facilities. The public school system must deal with the turmoil and transiency associated with the unstable housing that traumatizes their students. Municipal utilities are impacted by landlords who carry arrears due to insufficient rent collections or by vagrant tenants poaching the electricity for free. The code enforcement department tries to enforce the building code, which can involve long and expensive legal action against disinterested absentee landlords. The turmoil of blighted apartment communities can make the municipal provision of services closely tied to housing and education excessively expensive.

To local leaders and officials, it can feel like a losing proposition. The cost of municipal services for Madison Hills the first year we purchased the property was estimated at $1,958,644, and the property paid $154,700 in property taxes. In effect, Madison Hills was utilizing municipal services at 12.65 times its property tax contribution. Municipal leadership is aware of this collection gap, which is one of the reasons blighted apartment communities create tensions with government leadership.

ON THE OTHER HAND, we simply could not renovate Madison Hills without a proactive working relationship with Cobb County to obtain the required permits. Furthermore, Madison Hills was having an enormous impact on the surrounding community and the living standards of individuals and families. We have already discussed how the social capital of a community is disrupted by blight. Scholars have highlighted the breakdown in social capital—crucial to a community's ability to organize and advocate for itself—that stems from abandoned buildings and vacant lots. As social disorder grows and incivilities increase, residents tend to live and work in isolation and become less willing to step in and prevent crime.[21] The dysfunctional relationship between Madison Hills and Cobb County was negatively impacting both parties.

It took almost four years to navigate the hostile political environment and convince Cobb County to issue permits needed so we could invest $7 million, renovate Madison Hills, and move forward. It was an unpleasant experience and one that I never want myself or any conscientious landlord to repeat. The fire marshal and code enforcement department regularly arrived at our management office unannounced and continuously issued citations to stop the basic renovations—all legal—needed to improve the property to leasable condition. Madison Hills was so stigmatized by Cobb County that even a small matter like turning on a water meter was an arduous negotiation requiring months of meetings and various levels of involvement in Cobb County government. No one in Cobb wanted to deal with us at the risk of doing something politically incorrect and potentially losing his or her job.

In the meantime, we proceeded with small renovation projects within the limits allowed by the official building code adopted by Cobb County. We started utilizing TI Asset Management (TIAM), a specialty property management company experienced in stabilizing blighted and low-income apartment communities. (Full disclosure: I am a partner.) We got the crime under control. Unlawful activity was so entrenched at Madison that the first weekend our licensed officers were on site, they requested a valid driver's license and car registration for every car going through the front gate. Strict tenant screening was enforced, weeding out during our first year more than 70 percent of those who filled out rental applications due to extensive criminal backgrounds and poor credit history. We also started enforcing the rules of the community including citations for loud music and bad behavior. Throughout, we strove to keep our rents affordable for the families living in the area.

AFTER A FEW MONTHS, the property was safer, and this encouraged us to open a free after-school program in collaboration with Brumby Elementary School. We started our program in the office of our property manager, and had two children sign up the first week. We partnered with Destiny Church, a local church, to provide family fun events and volunteers for our program. It was through the relationship with Destiny Church that we found Kristin Hemingway (who would eventually come to Summerdale to launch the Star-C program). Kristin took over leadership of the Madison Hills after-school program and was brilliant in her approach. She volunteered at Brumby Elementary as a lunchroom monitor in the mornings which gave her an opportunity to socialize with the students and parents living at Madison. As part of her compensation package, we gave her a free apartment, making her immediately a resident of the Madison Hills community. It took a few years for Brumby to take our efforts seriously, but the after-school program started to thrive, and within five years we had 75 Madison Hills children enrolled. When the CRCP federal testing came around to Brumby, all 75 passed the competency testing. In 2012, Brumby Elementary was recognized by the Georgia Department of Education as a Title I Distinguished School, meaning that it had made Adequate Yearly Progress (AYP) for three consecutive school years.[22]

The Madison Hills after-school program created tremendous social capital and was a valuable win-win for the parents, school, and children. Parents were reassured that their young children were not going home to empty apartments. Instead, the children went to a supervised environment with structured play time, snacks, homework assistance, and tutoring. Delinquency studies are conclusive that "violent crimes by juveniles occur most frequently in the hours immediately following the close of school. Almost 62 percent of violent crimes committed by juveniles occur on school days."[23] The after-school program also expanded to a summer camp that was free for our residents, thus saving parents the average $80 weekly expense of after-school activities. Brumby Elementary benefitted by having an extension of its daily educational curriculum in an innovative, collaborative environment—one that was conveniently accessible within a community housing a large percentage of its students. Kristin, meanwhile, had become an educational advocate for each student enrolled in our after-school program. She collaborated with Dr. Richie on a curriculum plan for each student to excel. Kristin developed trust with the parents and served as a vital link between them, Dr. Richie, and the children to source resources like special tutoring or simply meals to help each them reach their full potential.

The business model of affordable housing and free after-school and summer camp programs at Madison Hills Apartments was delivered at no cost to Cobb County; Madison Hills operated without government subsidies.

THE REVITALIZED ECOSYSTEM ALSO created a financial win for us. As the landlords, we captured the implicit social value of a stabilized community. The predictability of the rental environment, where we did not push dramatic, unsustainable rent increases, combined with the benefits of the after-school program seemed to motivate the residents to renew their leases, saving us the cost burden of apartment turnover. Earlier, I discussed the effect of rent increases on tenant transiency, which then contributes to transiency in the local school. At Madison Hills, we determined that a $100 increase in rents would result in nonrenewal of the leases of up to 92 percent of our tenants depending on their income levels. The average monthly rents at Madison were $578 for a one-bedroom, $626 for a two-bedroom, $765 for the three-bedroom, and $916 for a four-bedroom unit. A family earning near poverty level wages of $30,000 per year could not afford a $100 per month increase and would move at the end of their lease term to other apartment communities that offered affordability.

Meanwhile the average cost of rental turnover varies by the size and condition of the unit as left by the departing tenant, but generally we spent $2,106 for flooring, $350 for painting, $400–1,200 for new appliances, plus $500 in labor and materials for other repairs. This equates to $3,250 to $4,050 or arguably 4.5 to 5.7 months of rent payments. This excludes the downtime when the apartment is not generating rent while the repairs are completed and the lead time for a new tenant to sign a lease and move into the unit—typically another one to two months of rent. It thus makes better business sense to renew a tenant even at a lower monthly rent.

We also noticed that tenants with children in the after-school program took better care of their apartments. We saw a reduction in vandalism typically caused by unsupervised children roaming the property after school. Unfortunately, we did not own Madison Hills long enough to really capture the metrics to document the value of a stabilized community and thriving elementary school. After six years of ownership, we were required to sell Madison Hills as part of a partnership agreement. The day after we sold, the new owners immediately closed the after-school program, raised the rental rates over $100 per unit, and fired our security police officers who had improved the safety of the community.

The dramatic changes by the new ownership impacted Brumby Elementary. "We lost many of our families with children attending Brumby Elementary after the new ownership took over and closed the after-school program," recalls Dr. Richie. "The families no longer had a free after-school program or affordable housing."

These parents simply could not afford the new rents and moved, taking their children out of Brumby. When the next federal testing was administered, within eighteen months after we sold the property, the students tested poorly and Brumby Elementary was again a failing school. The careful work by our volunteers and partners to rebuild the social capital for the families living at Madison Hills and attending Brumby Elementary was virtually erased by the landlord's stroke of a pen to raise rents.

In retrospect, we did not connect the dots between Madison Hills and Brumby and did not know that Brumby Elementary had become a Georgia Title I Distinguished School until after we sold the apartment community. Quite frankly, we did not even know we had an impact with our combined education and housing model until I was invited to give a presentation at the Atlanta Regional Housing Forum about four months after we sold the property. The invitation was from Bill Bolling, the well-respected community leader and founder of the Atlanta Community Food Bank. He held a quarterly regional housing forum in Atlanta for decades as an effort to bring community leaders together to discuss housing issues. I was on the Food Bank board of directors and on a few occasions casually discussed my model of interweaving community programs in our housing community, mainly around food security in low-income communities.

Bill asked me to give a presentation on our work at Madison and another of our communities, Willow Branch Apartments. As part of the preparation, I visited with Dr. Richie to determine if our after-school program had impacted Brumby Elementary. She surprised me by saying that not only did our after-school program have a positive effect on Brumby, but Brumby had become a Georgia Title I Distinguished School. She attributed much of that success to our program. She also shared the historical transiency statistics for Brumby Elementary. From that discussion, my additional research made me realize that the strong symbiotic relationship between low-income apartment communities and elementary schools with respect to transiency.

We purchased the property in December 2006 when the transiency rate was 67 percent and 75 percent of the students passed the reading tests. We partnered with Brumby Elementary in 2008 and started the free after-school program and summer camps at Madison Hills. By 2012, the transiency rate had reduced to 41 percent and the reading pass rate increased to 88 percent. Madison Hills housed approximately 20 percent of the student population at Brumby.

THE PRESENTATION AT THE Housing Forum was well received. We answered numerous questions about our model, but more importantly, we had many generous offers of support by a diverse group of community leaders. Large apartment developers offered financial support. Educators applauded the results of educational efforts and later shared stories of educators in their family who were well aware of the impact of housing on area schools. Nonprofits wanted to partner with us at our apartment communities. The audience gave great suggestions to expand the model. In effect, the audience was enthusiastically supportive of our efforts to interweave housing and education. The experience was a pivotal moment for me personally. If I was to continue to be a landlord of Class-C properties and offer housing to families that typically live on incomes close to the poverty line, then I needed to better understand the role that our apartment properties played in the greater community. I decided to use our Willow Branch Apartment property as a case study to determine the program's feasibility.

The experience at Madison Hills and the uncooperative leadership in Cobb County taught me the value of the political will of the local government as part of owning and renovating blighted apartments in an education model. Cobb's condemnation of Madison Hills and refusal to collaborate cost us four years in holding cost—which proved expensive and jeopardized our business model of delivering equitable affordable housing. However, Cobb County was a financial beneficiary of our model by virtue of the reduced burden on municipal services to Madison Hills. After the renovation was completed, we delivered a stabilized community with significantly fewer 911 calls, commanding fewer law enforcement, judicial, and prison services. We also delivered a stabilized community which reduced transiency at Brumby Elementary and improved the performance of the school. Furthermore, after the renovation, Cobb County increased the apartment community's property tax assessment and collected higher annual taxes. Madison Hills demonstrated that a proactive working collaboration between apartment landlords and municipalities could create a win-win for both parties.

Madison Hills unfortunately did not prove to be a long-lasting success in Cobb County because our purchase was time-limited due to our investors' purchase agreement. After we sold Madison Hills, the community-building focus was not maintained. Nonetheless, I was determined to create the same win-win dynamic in Atlanta's Cleveland Avenue neighborhood as we proceeded five years later with the purchase and renovation of Summerdale Apartments.

4

A Walking Tour of the Community Chaos

On a bright cool November 2017 morning I wound my small candy-apple red electric car south on Interstate 75, passing through the city center of Atlanta with tall skyscrapers fading in my rearview mirror. I cruised past the Interstate 85 split six miles south of the central business district, exited onto the long ramp to the Cleveland Avenue intersection, stopped at the perpetual red light, and patiently looked around. In the summer at that intersection, with school out, two or three boisterous kids loudly hawked $1 cold waters from a dirty cooler. But today the corner was quiet, strewn with smashed plastic bottles and stained cardboard boxes.

I had an appointment to tour the Summerdale apartment community, a 244-unit Class-D complex comprising several severely blighted and boarded-up buildings, adjacent to some newer fully occupied buildings. Apartment complex classifications are from A to D based on age, location, and condition. Properties built after 2000 tend to be Class A; 1980 to 2000, Class B; and before 1980, Class C. Class D properties are uninhabitable or in severe disrepair. Locations in desirable urban or suburban areas are typically Class A; if the location is not very desirable or has a low average household income, it would be Class C. But a well-maintained 1970s Class C complex in a Class A location would generally be Class B, a blend of the factors.

Summerdale was for sale at a price that met our business model of providing affordable housing near a failing elementary school. We had made an unsuccessful bid on the property, then submitted a second offer which the seller accepted. We spent about two months negotiating the purchase contract, and all the details were finalized; we just needed to sign the purchase contract agreement which was neatly organized and sitting on my desk at the office.

My appointment was to tour the property and give it one last look before signing the contract. I drove along Cleveland Avenue and passed the standing scars of a once vibrant middle-class Atlanta community. To my right sat a dilapidated, long-abandoned Kmart adjacent to a struggling Piggly Wiggly. Across the street on the north side was an Exxon station, bordered with tall weeds and trash. Animated young men sat outside drinking from bottles in brown bags and watching the brisk traffic. Everywhere I looked, abandoned buildings bore faded signs that spoke of past business glory. The crisp modern campus housing the Cleveland Avenue Elementary School was a welcome sight at the first major intersection. I took a right at the McDonald's and another right into the Summerdale Apartments. A half-dozen pedestrians were on the sidewalks that linked the thousands of working-class single-family houses to the Cleveland Avenue commercial district. My bright red car stood out, and I received a lot of stares. An outsider cruising the "hood" was noticed. I knew the danger of driving in a high-crime area, hence the value of driving an unusual model. A luxury car driven by a male stranger screamed "drug dealer" in dangerous neighborhoods and was subject to a higher probability of a carjacking, theft, or target of a bullet if perceived as a threat to the local drug trade. My risk was lowered by driving an under-stated EV that no hard-core criminal would want if he valued his reputation.

THE SUMMERDALE APARTMENT COMMUNITY was built in two phases split by Old Hapeville Road. Built in 1971, Phase I's thirteen burgundy brick buildings contained a mix of townhouses and flats totaling 144 units. Phase II's eleven three-story buildings, built in 1998 with a more contemporary design, were clad in burgundy brick and beige vinyl siding, with open breezeways and metal staircases and railings. Despite its fashionable modern construction, the entrance to the newer phase reflected the neglected neighborhood. The grounds were littered with trash, thousands of cigarette butts, fast-food bags, and plastic bottles. The landscaping along Old Hapeville Road was overgrown with large weeds and a hodgepodge of dying bushes, in which large snakes were rumored to lurk, perhaps hindering the terrified maintenance staff from cleaning up discarded trash along the periphery of the property.

I pulled in through the bent, rusted black metal entrance gate and stopped in the parking lot whose striping had faded away. Large oil stains and dirty chipped curbing marked the asphalt. Today a greenish-black mildew covered the siding on the north-facing buildings, and large blown-out holes were probably due to bullets. The once creamy sidewalks and concrete landings in the stairwells were stained with a greasy brownish green sheen and were filthy with trash. The stairwell railings were rusted and rough, and covered with drab brownish paint.

The management staff was expecting me. Sammy Young, the head maintenance technician, was in front of the office, clutching a plastic bucket in one hand and a metal trash picker in the other. He was of Chinese descent, slightly built, and dressed in dirty khaki pants and a cotton shirt. He was busy picking up trash along the interior of the property and did not look up when I approached him. I waited patiently outside the office for Sammy to acknowledge me, but it was clear he wanted me to notice his diligent concern for the cleanliness of the property. I tried to show respect for his efforts, but the amount of trash throughout the property was so overwhelming, the scene was almost comical. It was clear that trash duty had been ignored for years and his superficial efforts were purely for show.

Having met Sammy before, I knew his English was limited. Though I had been told that his understanding of my English was much better than I thought, we still struggled to communicate even basic ideas. Sammy was a major link between the tenants and landlord, and I wondered how the tenants were able to get repairs done when the key maintenance person has limited English skills. Instructions and operational settings for mechanical equipment, electric wiring, toilets, plumbing lines, warranties, and life safety were all documented in English at the property, not to mention work orders. After walking the property a dozen times and observing the residents walking around the parking lot, I was pretty sure that few tenants were fluent in Chinese.

After a few minutes, he put down the bucket and briskly walked over to me. "Gu mernen," he nodded, with no smile and a slight bow, seemingly impatient to get the meeting over with.

"Good morning Sammy," I said smiling.

He looked at me impatiently. "Wha you wanna see today," he spoke carefully.

"I just wanted to walk around and look at the outside of the property."

"Ewe wanna see bothie sides, yeh?"

"Yes, I want to walk both sides. I don't need to get into any units so don't worry about pulling keys."

At the request of the seller, I did not mention the reason for my visits to the property as a prospective buyer, and I did not know if Sammy or Maya Galindo, the property manager, had any suspicions. This was the typical arrangement between buyers and sellers, limiting disclosure to employees of a pending transfer of ownership. Sellers do not want their valuable maintenance and management employees panicking at the thought of a new owner taking over daily operations, only to immediately fire them. However, if the sale was canceled, the owners may have lost talented workers who moved on to another stable job to protect their need for a steady paycheck. As a rule, our company always offered jobs to the existing management and maintenance staff with a ninety-day trial period after closing, to make sure the employees were competent and a good fit. It was always strange to me that more owners did not take this approach and value the technical knowledge and experience of the existing staff rather than new hires having to learn the core operational and structural culture of a property from scratch. Even at a property like Summerdale suffering from severe blight and disrepair, a new owner should not summarily fire the staff on the day of closing the property, unless fraud or incompetence was detected.

My past inspections at Summerdale involved groups of three to five people in attendance with a lot of back-and-forth discussions and distractions. Today I wanted to get the vibe of the property, alone in a quiet uninterrupted manner. It was a chance to understand the operations, tenant profile, and a thousand other small but important details in plain sight that gave a contextual understanding of operations and the tenant/consumer profile. Sammy and I quietly walked around Phase II, and I carefully studied the tone of the property. The parking lot was about one-third occupied with dozens of older cars mixed with a few newer basic affordable models. There were Hondas, Kias, and a mixture of older Jeeps with a fair representation of dented and dilapidated Oldsmobiles and Toyotas. I was also on the lookout for souped-up luxury cars, typically the sign of drug dealers living at the property. There was one new black Cadillac Escalade parked near the common area grass, backed into the parking lot facing the management office, the driver's door open and a big guy sitting inside diligently studying his cell phone. The Escalade stood out among the working-class cars surrounding it. The guy was neatly dressed in an Izod shirt and looked relaxed, like he was patiently waiting for his mother to escort her to the grocery store or hair appointment. This was my first observation of Anthony Fowler—the kingpin who operated the brisk drug trade at Summerdale. I didn't yet know his role, and he was clever at hiding in plain sight; it took almost a year to identify him as a key instigator in the high criminal activity. He often drove the Escalade between his territories carved out in the common-area courtyards of Phases I and II.

As Sammy and I walked slowly and casually around the back section of the property, we met a well-worn path through a broken gate and abandoned road with extensive piles of trash, mattresses, old furniture, and tires at the southwestern border. A cut through to the adjacent Piggly Wiggly grocery store was a quick and easy exit for criminals eager to escape a police chase and other enemies. The stairwells and landings at many of the buildings were strewn with worn-out easy chairs of various colors, and grills indicating a social order of tenants that sat outside and socialized with neighbors. Along the northern section and towards the common area, we came upon what first appeared to be a grape orchard, but after further inspection was filled with unusual growing bushes—not illegal drugs—rather a garden with beloved vegetables possibly cultivated by immigrants. The building exteriors along the common area displayed more physical damage and there was a large group of about a dozen men and teenagers hanging out around the metal picnic tables in the interior. They became quiet and eyed us suspiciously as we walked by their building towards the management office. The property was a mixture of good and bad people, with a culture of mismanagement and a lack of enforcement for the property rules. We ignored the hostile stares and kept walking.

After touring the general exterior of Phase II, Sammy and I silently exited the property and walked across Old Hapeville Road to Phase I. Built in 1971, this side of the complex looks and feels much older than its age.

A gated entrance and tall black metal fence stood as a barrier between the apartments and the traffic on the sidewalk and Old Hapeville. Sammy opened the unlocked metal pedestrian gate and we stepped inside the interior of the property. Unlike the sister apartments across the street, Phase I is divided into two sections—one section was at the front of the property, partially occupied by rent-paying tenants, and the other section located in the back of the property was vacant. We passed by the first of four long red brick buildings in the front occupied section, each containing a row of multiple townhomes surrounding an interior weedy, overgrown courtyard. Altogether, the buildings formed one giant square, and I had to sidestep dozens of gaping potholes as we walked past the D building towards the courtyard.

At the corner of the D building, a group of nine men dressed in dirty T-shirts and sagging pants sat on the front stairs and in various cheap folding chairs. Upon our approach, the group went silent as they studied us, trying to determine if we were customers or a threat. They seemed to relax once they recognized Sammy, except for the two men who turned away to avoid eye contact. I caught a quick glimpse of one of the men and noticed a pair of matching teardrop tattoos under his left eye. While I am not fluent in gangster culture, I was pretty sure that these were some bad dudes. Sammy ignored them and continued walking briskly around the corner with his bucket, trash picker, and me in tow. The units housing these men, D-12 and D-13, faced a large trash dumpster surrounded by heaps of stained mattresses and faded, torn sofas that had probably been there for years. The guys were loitering at the corner of the D building, the only section of the square of buildings that allowed pedestrian access into the courtyard.

As we walked past the group of loiterers, I eyed the courtyard interior to get a feel for the interior common area. In the middle stood a single-story building with boarded-up doors and windows, topped with a sagging roofline. What was once the central community center, was now covered with years of graffiti in various colors, some faded, and some covered up with patches of paint representing a mosaic of whatever color paint was available to an indifferent maintenance staff. I only paused for a moment, politely said "hello" to the nine guys and caught up with Sammy who was clearly on a mission to quickly end our tour. I was surprised when several of the guys politely said "goodbye, ma'am—have a good day." As we kept walking, I passed a shiny penny and could not resist stooping down to pick it up. Shiny pennies are usually good luck, signaling that I was getting ready to purchase another apartment community. We kept walking past Building C, then around the corner to Building B, noting the parking lot was populated with cars indicating three of the courtyard buildings were occupied. Building B had a completely vacant parking lot and showed no evidence of legal tenants, but plenty of rat droppings around the front of the buildings which confirmed a serious vermin problem.

At the corner of buildings B and C, a five-foot-tall chain-link fence separates the front half of Phase I from the vacant back half of the property. We stood for a moment as I looked at the back half of the property which brought me back to earth. I now faced several two-story buildings in various stages of serious blight. A driveway escorted us down a steep hill and deeper into the blighted section, and as we progressed, the decay grew worse and worse. The landscaping through-out this section of the property was a lush green miniature forest of six-foot tall weeds intermingled with large quantities of trash, old toilets, buckets, construction rubbish, bathroom vanities and abandoned household items from departing residents. As we walked, my shoes crunched on sharp slivers of broken glass, which were impossible to avoid throughout the parking lot. Several buildings were boarded up with planks of gray weathered, peeling wood—evidence of handiwork made many years ago. A few buildings were not boarded up, but the broken window glass and doors left dangling on the frames indicated a robust history of vandalism and vagrants. It was eerily silent and something in my gut said there were several pairs of eyes watching us from inside the boarded-up buildings. Suddenly, the hairs on the back of my neck stood up when I realized we were incredibly unprotected and exposed. The thought of hiring an armed escort, other than one armed with a metal trash picker never occurred to me. At 5'4" and slightly built, Sammy strolled the property as if it were a luxury apartment community, oblivious to the blight, criminal activity, and potential danger. You could almost hear a pin drop as we inspected more of the decrepit area. The only noise beside the crunch of glass from our steps, was the faint hum of an airplane flying overhead, on its way to the Hartsfield-Jackson International Airport just three miles west of Summerdale. Despite the bad vibe, I never heard of a woman-landlord in a nice dress being attacked at a blighted apartment community. I try to be logical in every situation, good or bad, and that statistic helped me keep my cool. When inspecting a decaying, potential property, I always wear a nice dress as a courtesy to any of the existing tenants, legal or illegal, I might encounter in hopes that my dress code reminded them of their grandmother, the Avon lady or other situations that encouraged polite behavior.

Ever the optimist, I made a mental note of the few positives that stood out while we finished walking the remainder of the property. The construction of the brick buildings was solid and there were several saving graces such as newer windows on a few units and a solid metal gate surrounding a large portion of the property. The seller had renovated five buildings; Building G was about 90 percent renovated, however, the windows and doors were boarded-up with newer wood coverings. The rebuilding of this section of Summerdale was going to be a lot of work, but if the capital were invested in the appropriate sequence, the property had the potential to be a healthy, affordable community that residents would be proud to occupy, and my patient socially conscious partners would be proud to own.

We finished the walk-through by exiting the second pedestrian gate located at the corner of the A and B buildings, since I did not want to retrace our walk along Building D and through the loitering men. Old Hapeville Road was crowded with cars and we waited a minute before crossing over to the entrance gate at Phase II, quickly running to avoid the speeding traffic. Upon our arrival to Phase II, I turned and thanked Sammy for his time. He wordlessly bowed, ceremoniously turned away from me, and resumed picking up trash around the management office. I went through the Phase II pedestrian gate and decided to sit in my car for a few moments gathering my thoughts. Something associated with the Phase I tour was disturbing me and after a few minutes, the burden emerged from my conscience. I decided to drive back over to Phase I and see if indeed there was a hot pink tricycle on a patio near the drug dealing units, indicative of small children living in the war zone. Seeing the drug activity extend within the ecosystem of an extended family with small children gave evidence of how entrenched the drug business was at Phase I. The dealers had established roots and were growing their families, and it was very likely that their children attended Cleveland Avenue Elementary. While parked in the entrance of Phase I, I noticed a young man in a well-cut gray business suit and tie, briskly walking away from the drug-dealing group and through the suspiciously unlocked pedestrian gate. A newer SUV was waiting for him, parked in the middle of Old Hapeville Road. It was a busy time of day and the SUV sat idling, oblivious to the line of cars going around it. Several cars impatiently honked at the illegally parked SUV, but the young female driver just ignored them. The young man opened the car door and quickly jumped into the front passenger seat. While still parked, the driver pulled out a pipe and through her lightly tinted window, I could see her hand shake as she put a lighter to the pipe and inhaled. She passed the pipe to the man who took it to his lips and breathed in the illicit drug. I watched in fascination, as the couple remained seated in their car, passing the drug pipe back and forth oblivious to the public view of their disgraceful activity. After a few minutes, the car brake lights flashed off and they drove north to Cleveland Avenue, onwards to the affluent jobs that afforded them well-cut suits, drug-induced highs and a nice SUV.

After witnessing the illegal activity, I returned to my notes. There was indeed a hot pink bicycle with sparkles on the wheel spokes casually lying on the ground in front of unit D-5, one of the apartments near the drug zone. I estimated the bike was comfortably scaled for a three-year-old girl. The observations from the tour gave me enough evidence to conclude that Summerdale was severely infested with an entrenched drug culture—one that undoubtedly affected the surrounding single-family houses, commercial district and Cleveland Avenue Elementary. Summerdale was ground zero of the neighborhood blight, but I knew from experience that it took a determined ground zero position to commence the rebuilding of the entire community.

I put my car back in gear and headed south along Old Hapeville to tour the neighborhood bordering the southern edge of the Summerdale property. Not surprisingly, Waters Road, the road curving the southwest property line of Phase I, was riddled with abandoned, boarded-up ominous homes —several completely gutted by fires and covered with graffitti. Waters Road exited Cleveland Avenue and several vacant, boarded up apartment buildings fronted our property line just south of Cleveland Avenue and directly across from Cleveland Avenue Elementary. These vacant buildings were virtually hidden by a forest of overgrown weeds and trees and the perfect spot to foster a criminal environment.

This final inspection completed the initial homework of Summerdale. I knew Cleveland Avenue Elementary was a low-performing school and the teaching staff struggled to improve the outcomes for its 350 students. We also knew that the stark demographics of the Cleveland Avenue neighborhood did not paint a bright future for the elementary school or any school for that matter. Despite the vast resources and best intentions of Atlanta Public Schools, as long as a large percentage of the Cleveland Avenue Elementary students lived in a decrepit housing environment, it was doubtful the families and the school would thrive.

I pulled onto Cleveland Avenue and drove past Cleveland Avenue Elementary to Interstate 75 and back to my office in a nice section of the city. Summerdale provided a challenge to improve social capital by rebraiding the structural, community, and municipal environments. I had a clearer vision of the issues and a better understanding of the strategic plan to revitalize the community and improve Cleveland Avenue Elementary. I signed the purchase contract that afternoon and started the process to acquire Summerdale Apartments.

5

Capital Stack Gymnastics— How We Raised $9.6 Million to Purchase Summerdale

After I signed the contract to purchase Summerdale Apartments, we raced against the clock to close the deal within the allotted time frame.[24] The sellers agreed to a final purchase price of $5.2 million,[25] and we budgeted an additional $4.4 million to fund the closing costs, holding expenses, and construction costs to elevate the property to its highest and best use as an affordable apartment community. Our construction plan included renovation of the 92 blighted units plus general improvements to the remaining 152 units to promote a healthier family environment. We also planned exterior renovations to improve the aesthetics, including new roofs, parking lot sealcoating and striping, and a complete renovation of the central community center (future home of the Star-C after-school and wellness programs). So we had to raise $9.6 million in a relatively short time to buy and rebuild Summerdale Apartments, a property located in an impoverished section of Atlanta with a high violent crime rate, suffering from significant physical blight, surrounded by a large inventory of blighted residential homes, and in a low-performing elementary school district. The money sources and loans for apartment investments typically do not favor projects with such high negatives. It was an understatement that raising $9.6 million for this purchase would be a challenge. We decided to focus on the strengths of Summerdale, stay positive and pray.

Affordable housing was becoming a hot political issue not only in Atlanta, but nationally and internationally. Articles in the daily press highlighted the growing lack of affordable housing in Atlanta, and dozens of "affordable housing" task forces were forming. We knew Atlanta's problem had festered for several years, but the severity was highlighted in the previously mentioned 2018 Cushman Wakefield report. There was evidence that the problem would worsen if not addressed immediately by municipalities. This growing political momentum behind the hot affordable housing issue was presenting funding opportunities for innovative solutions, like our TriStar model, that increased or preserved the affordable housing inventory. An example of the growing political significance of affordable housing was the 2017 campaign announcement by future Atlanta mayor Keisha Lance Bottoms promising to spend $1 billion on affordable housing as part of her leadership platform.[26]

Summerdale had several key strengths we hoped would support our business case to attract a $9.6 million investment from lenders and investors.

• First was the $5.2 million purchase price which would allow us to profitably operate the property at rents affordable for working poor families. The all-in price of $9.6 million when divided by the property's 244 units equaled $39,344 per unit. This is bargain pricing for a fully renovated apartment unit in the city limits. At this price, we calculated that monthly rents averaging $730, excluding water and utilities, could show a reasonable profit after paying expenses, our monthly mortgage, and funding of a capital reserve. We were also able to fund a partnership with Star-C Communities to provide after-school care, affordable healthcare, and other services.

• Second was that supply and demand market dynamics were in our favor. On the demand side, a staggering 50 percent of Atlanta's renters earned less than $38,556 per year, which meant they could afford rent of $964 per month or less, at the HUD formula of paying no more than 30 percent of income for housing.[27] However, average apartment rents in Atlanta in 2018 were $1,350 per month. On the supply side, the Atlanta apartment market lost more than 60,000 affordable apartment units in the five years before COVID.[28] Thus our strategic plan to keep rents at $730 per month and thus affordable for families near the poverty line was strongly supported by market demand in this price category. We would have no problems finding tenants who qualified to lease our apartments.

• Third was Summerdale's location within the boundaries of the City of Atlanta. One valuable and unforgettable lesson we learned from owning other blighted apartment communities was the necessity of broad political will by the local government and community. Large, blighted apartment communities are understandably stigmatized by the local government and community leadership, and navigating the emotional political climate can be tricky if not done with transparency and sensitivity. The future mayor was making affordability a political issue, and the City of Atlanta had a vast lending and financial toolbox of incentives at its disposal to fund affordable housing communities. We were certain that Summerdale would qualify for some of these incentives. (Contrary to popular belief, it is difficult and expensive to navigate the complex bureaucracy associated with affordable housing subsidies. Most landlords avoid subsidies and rely on frequent rent increases to fund expenses and profit. See also Chapter 24, "Permitting.")

OUR TRISTAR EDUHOUSING MODEL was not known by Atlanta leadership, so my partners and I decided to cultivate political will. This involved having 100 meetings with a diverse group of community, government, and nonprofit leaders to showcase our model and seek support. We spent about a year hosting these meetings with Atlanta Public Schools superintendent Dr. Meria Carstarphen; a former CEO of Georgia-Pacific (a Fortune 100 Company); Eloisa Klementich, CEO of InvestAtlanta (the investment arm of the City of Atlanta); Eli Hammer, a former homeless veteran and our community consultant; and many other individuals who had important insights. After these meetings, we had built a good base of support within the city government and community for our model for turning around blighted apartment communities and the process to get the units renovated. We also collected endorsement letters from these community leaders, which we used to market our credibility to future lenders and funders. Our experience with Madison Hills, our project in Cobb County, had come full circle.

We were now ready to find an apartment community in Atlanta and execute our affordable housing and education model, and the property that we landed was Summerdale Apartments. When the purchase contract was signed, we hit the ground running. But attracting the $9.6 million in investment funding proved a challenge despite our good intentions and time spent laying the groundwork.

There came a day when I paused after thanking a listener for his time and hanging up the phone. He was the tenth lender I had spoken to in hopes of securing funding for Summerdale, and we were not having much luck. This traditional lender, who had capitalized more than $10 million in loans over the past few years for shopping centers and office buildings in our commercial portfolio, gave us a hard and fast "no" when asked to look at Summerdale. He justified the decision by claiming to have no experience dealing with apartment properties targeted to low-income families. I found this quite interesting since he, at the time, paid his bank tellers $13 per hour—wages just above the federal poverty line.[29]

It was hard not to get frustrated. I had overseen more than $1 billion in apartment debt over my career and knew how the game was played. If Summerdale was located in a nice, higher-income neighborhood, then we would easily have lenders lined up to provide financing. I routinely got solicitations from lenders interested in financing our apartment properties located in affluent areas. But there was a cold response from these very lenders when approached about financing Summerdale. Financing blighted properties is a challenge because lenders typically do not want to invest in areas of high crime and unemployment, yet the lack of available lender capital is at the core of blighted areas. The lenders who were interested in us wanted to charge an interest rate of 15–20 percent to compensate for the perceived higher risk of a blighted property. But the higher interest rates would force us to increase rents beyond affordability for the neighborhood demographics.

We finally found a hard-money lender who agreed to loan us $7.0 million at an interest rate of 11 percent—more than double the standard bank rate at the time. The lender made it clear he thought we were lucky to get an offer of an interest rate that low. He didn't understand that even an 11 percent interest rate exacerbated the affordability problems and would create a poor business model for us. To put this in perspective, if Summerdale had been located in an affluent area, lenders would be lined up to give us a $7 million loan at 4.5 percent, or $315,000 in interest per year. Because we would have to pay the interest from income (rentals), the annual interest burden would equal a debt burden of $108 per apartment unit per month ($315,000 divided by 244 units divided by 12 months). But if we pursued the easy route with the hard-money lender's 11 percent interest rate, our annual debt burden would equal $770,000 or a debt burden per apartment of $263 per month ($770,000/244 units/12 months). We would thus have to charge our tenants $155 more per month in rent ($263 - $108 = $155) just to cover the debt penalty for being in a blighted area. In effect, our Summerdale tenants would be paying a monthly rent penalty for living in blight, which was simply not acceptable to TriStar.

To finance Summerdale, we had to get creative, and we had only ninety days to raise $9.6 million and close the deal. We politely declined the hard-money lender's 11 percent interest rate despite the loudly ticking clock. We were determined to keep rents affordable for the families at Summerdale, and raising rents just to pay the higher interest for a hard-money loan was not an option we were willing to put on our families.

IT TOOK SEVERAL STRESSFUL months to raise the money to purchase and renovate Summerdale, and we finally closed the transaction in June 2018. We were proud to piece together a committed and innovative group of investors who contributed $9.6 million at an average cost of 2.99 percent per annum including debt and equity, enabling us to offer rents averaging $730 per month, affordable for families earning $13–15 per hour. Our investor group included a $4,904,740 loan from Renasant Bank at a floating rate of LIBOR plus 300 basis points. The date we closed, LIBOR was at 1.11 percent and our interest rate started at 4.11 percent. I once asked Chris Braun, our banker, why Renasant was willing to lend to Summerdale when other lenders were unwilling to take the risk. He said it was a combination of Community Reinvestment Act opportunity and Renasant's belief that community development fostered economic development.

TriStar also organized the TriStar Community Impact Fund, a private social impact fund that offered investment in mission-based Eduhousing communities like Summerdale. Our aim was to purchase blighted apartment communities near elementary schools that ranked in the lower third of state education performance standards. Thirteen investors contributed $1.9 million to the fund to purchase and renovate Summerdale at a reduced interest rate. The fund paid its investors 2 percent on their investment the first year, 3 percent the second year, and 4 percent years three through ten. At the time of closing, a bank loan would be approximately 5.5 percent for this property, but the lower interest rate we had assembled allowed us to reduce our monthly rents by approximately $20.

We were pleasantly surprised to obtain a $1.3 million interest-free loan from a local nonprofit foundation, payable in four years. Finally, we received a 1 percent loan from the Housing-Opportunity Bond offered by

Capital Stack - Cost of Capital - Interest Rate Burden
June 2018 (Acquisition)

	Amount	Interest Rate	Annual Interest Cost
Sources of Capital:			
Loan Renasant Bank	$4,904,740	4.11%	$201,585
Loan from Family Foundation	1,300,000	0.00%	0
Loan Housing Opportunity Bond	1,500,000	1.00%	15,000
TriStar Social Impact Fund	1,894,662	3.70%	70,102
Total Sources of Funding (Avg Cost of Capital)	$9,599,402	2.99%	$286,687
Uses of Capital:			
Purchase Price to Seller	$5,200,000		
Renovation Cost (Est)	3,685,519		
Closing Costs (Purchase)	185,552		
Carrying Cost During Renovation	528,331		
Total Funding Needed	$9,599,402		

Deal Underwriting Terms:	Rents	Affordability Annual Salary	Hourly Salary
Targeted Rents 1bedroom/1 Bath Unit	$595	$23,800	$11.44
Targeted Rents 2 bedroom/1.5 Bath Unit	$695	$27,800	$13.37
Targeted Rents 2 Bedroom/2 Bath Unit	$729	$29,160	$14.02
Targeted Rents 3 Bedroom/2 Bath	$826	$33,040	$15.88
Targeted Avg Rental Rates (After Renovation)	$730	$29,190	$14.03

Estimated Operating Expenses Per Unit Per Year	$5,649
Estimated Capital Reserves Per Unit Per Year	$500
Total Estimated Expenses Per Unit Per Year	$6,149

InvestAtlanta, the development arm of the City of Atlanta (see Chapter 31). This low-cost capital was critical in our ability to offer affordable rents. If our blended cost of capital had been the standard market rate of 8 percent, then we would have been forced to raise our rents by $198 per month to fund the additional monthly capital cost.

With the capital sources organized, we proceeded with the closing of Summerdale and execution of the model. I mentioned earlier that the third strength of Summerdale was its location in Atlanta, which had political will. We worked hard to cultivate that political will because my business partner and I had learned from our experience with Madison Hills Apartments. We decided that if we were going into another area with blighted apartment communities, the local municipal government had to be a willing participant in the model. Without the political will of the City of Atlanta municipal leadership, it was doubtful that we could purchase and renovate Summerdale and deliver affordable rents for the families populating the Cleveland Avenue neighborhood.

II — Effects of Blight on Those Who Live and Work in It

AUTHOR'S NOTE:

The events and individuals in this section are based on interviews with the persons named, networks around the persons, or the administrative files. The interviews were conducted between 2018 and 2021; some of the statements included reflect the speakers' perspectives and recollections of earlier years.

No direct comments are included from the criminals and other undesirables ultimately removed (voluntarily or involuntarily) from Summerdale Apartments. I was advised not to interview the criminals, so the events outlined are based on personal observations, court records, social media, and interviews with people familiar with the criminals and their behavior. The names of some persons have been changed to protect their privacy.

6

Virginia Humphries—The Longest Surviving Tenant

On a clear crisp January afternoon before Summerdale was cleaned up and renovated, octogenarian Virginia Humphries carefully stepped outside her apartment and onto the concrete corridor. She held her neat, slender 5'5" frame erect, with an elegant dignity that commanded respect despite her frail appearance. The years of hard physical labor as a domestic, combined with the stress of working multiple jobs to provide for her four children, were evident in the lines etched in her face. The blaring of the big-screen TV faded as she closed her front door, leaving her daughter and a great-grandson in the fetid apartment. The leaves had long fallen, and the winter air was bitterly cold despite the bright sunlight.

As the chilly breeze hit Virginia's face, she shivered, zipped her light cotton jacket, and then lightly tamped down her black wig. She adjusted her thick glasses and surveyed the Phase II apartment community from her second-floor vantage point. Summerdale was a perpetual war zone where gunshots were fired with and without notice. The all-too familiar loud "pop . . . pop . . . pop" traumatized her family, including great-grandsons Kingston and Joshua, who recently had been waking the household with nightmares. She knew the dangers outside her apartment—most tenants knew the same risks—and only her strong faith in God assuaged her fear and calmed her rapidly beating heart. Still, despite her age and deep Christian faith, she was "all street."

The long-term residents called her "Momma," and she liked that. Virginia had been living at Summerdale for eighteen years, longest of any tenant in the complex. She explained:

A group of us went to pray with a friend who was feeling badly, and we came to her apartment at Summerdale. I didn't even know these apartments was out here, and while we was praying, God told me to sell my house and move to Summerdale, so I did. The Lord put me out here and I've been here ever since.

Her history included:

I was born in the Fourth Ward and raised in Summerhill by my Aunt Ida after my mother was murdered when I was twelve years old. My mother had the most prettiest figure you could have for a lady. She was a doll and ever'body wanted her. And you know how men want you, and then you go with someone else, they get jealous. Her boyfriend stabbed her and he wouldn't let nobody move her and she bled to death. Not anyone wanted no three chil'ren. We went sleepin' from house to house, but my Aunt Ida stepped in. She gave up her young life and raised me, my brother, and sister in the church. I thought she was so good that she took all three of us in and gave us everything. I will never forget she did that for me. Aunt Ida had a ninth-grade education but was smart. She owned a soul food restaurant on Mitchell Street and ran eight cabs with Techwood Flowers Cab, but she always put God first and raised me in the church. I've been a faithful parishioner at Mt. Carmel Baptist Church for over forty years.

I attended David T. Howard High school in South Atlanta. I had five children and four are living. I have worked since I was fourteen years old in restaurants, night work, and then I worked for twenty-two years as a domestic. I had to move into the Carver Homes, and someone told me that I should work nights to raise my own family. I had two jobs, but my father and friend said they would help me get a house, so I was blessed with a brand-new house on Hill Street. I stayed there for over thirty years, after my father and friend gave me the house because they said I worked so hard.

My momma was a cab driver 'fore she got killed. My father was like a hustlin' man. He had to take care of himself, so he had to learn to survive. But he didn't get into our lives 'til I was older.

As Virginia exited down the stairs, pains shooting through her hip and lower back almost took her breath away. She gripped the metal railing and sidestepped the sticky brownish-green stains accumulated over years of neglect by management and tenants. She sighed in frustration at the paper, gum, wrappers, and beer and soda bottles strewn in the stairwell, but she could no longer bend over to pick up trash as she had when younger. Virginia had always been fastidiously neat and clean. The persistent trash so embarrassed her that she had cut off contact with her network of church friends outside of Summerdale. She did not want her friends to see the toxic environment or to put them at risk of getting robbed or worse if they visited (although many lived in equally violent neighborhoods). After years of dealing with violence and neglect, she had resigned herself to the bleak reality that the landlord did not care about the condition of the property. She resolved to accept her limitations, not take the embarrassment of her rental community personally, and focus on the good.

Virginia loved Summerdale's convenient proximity to the schools, grocery store, drugstore, and her church. This connection to the community, combined with the affordable rent, made her determined to survive the dangerous and crumbling environment. She prided herself for being on good speaking terms with many neighbors, at least those who remained. Several had lived in her building for more than ten years. However, the violence and crime were driving them away to safer neighborhoods. This saddened Virginia, especially the loss of caring neighbors like Ms. Zachary, who lived in the unit directly above her for five years, and Mr. Velasquez, who lived next door for twelve years. Virginia's great-grandchildren had played with the two Zachary boys at the community playground, and those boys were missed by the entire Humphries family. As she noted, neighbors are important:

> In the olden days you know it was more activity between neighbors . . . wasn't no drugs. People were more friendly and neighbors were neighbors. I used to take care of a blind lady on our street. But I'm not close to many neighbors anymore cause I don't want their mess. My mother used to always tell us a "dog bring a bone and a dog take a bone." That's what she used to say, like

that. It's not like it used to be between neighbors. You don't have to live here to know this. You could walk outside and know it's active 'cause of the traffic. You just had to know who was dealin' and stay away. Sometimes after school when you go get the chil'ren, you could see it. People going back and forth at Summerdale.

THE OLDER FOLKS WHO moved out were being replaced by residents who were young, arrogant, and unsocial with legacy tenants like Virginia. She noticed these new residents, though younger, seemed hardened by life. They rarely smiled, appeared stressed out, and released anger by yelling at their innocent children. They treated the community like a junkyard, littering the grounds. Virginia tried to reach out to them, but they had little patience for an elderly black woman who just got in their way. Virginia knew her place and kept her peace. The community around her was deteriorating, but her immediate and growing family still lived close to her, and she was not leaving Summerdale.

At two in the afternoon, the property seemed quiet. Most neighbors were at work except for Ms. Sims, who was also retired and safely locked behind her closed door. Most of the drug dealers were in their apartments sleeping off the previous night's activity or relaxing with their families, getting ready for the brisk traffic later in the evening when their customers were home from work. By now, Summerdale had an established reputation as a one-stop shop for crack, cocaine, marijuana, opioids, heroin, and everything in between. Virginia knew that drug addiction did not discriminate based on income, race, or nationality. The constant flow of visitors who discreetly rolled down the windows of their Ford trucks, Honda Civics, Rolls-Royces, Bentleys, and Porsches quietly did their drug buying and promptly exited. Prior to leaving her second-floor landing, Virginia glanced around to ensure that no drug dealers or other riff-raff were obstructing her path to the elementary school. She clutched the cold metal banister and cautiously stepped around the litter in the stairwell and down the steps.

WALKING HER GREAT-GRANDCHILD TO and from Cleveland Avenue Elementary School was one of Virginia's favorite daily rituals. She said walking was "like peace—moving that stress. Walking brings back good memories, like walking to school at David T. Howell High School in Atlanta or putting on a pretty dress and shoes and walk with my aunt and family to Bethlehem Church in Summerhill." Since moving to Summerdale in 1999, Virginia had proudly provided for three generations of family. Of her four children, daughter Simona had lived with her since surviving a heart transplant and becoming disabled. Simona's thirty-four-year-old daughter Ashley and Ashley's two boys also lived in the three-bedroom apartment. Virginia did not mind having a full house, especially since Ashley was saving money to move into her own two-bedroom apartment, also in Summerdale. Ashley was Virginia's pride and joy and in her eyes could do no wrong. She was thrilled that Ashley had chosen to live in Summerdale where she could personally supervise the upbringing of her great-grandsons.

Virginia had supported her family as a domestic worker for a wealthy couple with four children on the north side of Atlanta. For two decades, she provided childcare eight hours a day, five days a week. It was tiresome work, especially when the twins arrived, but Virginia never complained. There was no sick pay or time off for holidays. Her $330 weekly paycheck plus her $546 monthly social security check had left little for extras like movies, clothes, and gifts for her own children.[30] She recalled:

> I worked for an attorney-lady family, raisin their four chil'ren including a set of twins—twins, that's somethin to preach on. I said to my employer, I don't know how to keep no twins, but one day God told me how to do it. I only got two raises in all the years I worked there, but that's where I stayed for twenty-two years and never missed a day of work.

Upon retiring at age eighty-one, Virginia took it upon herself to make the daily walk to Cleveland Avenue Elementary where she fetched her six-year-old great-grandson, Kingston, and personally escorted him back to the apartment. They walked because she had recently sold her 1991 beige Ford at the request of her family because she could no longer drive safely. As the matriarch of the family, she had a strong sense of obligation and felt it was her responsibility to keep the next generation safe, warm, and protected. She made the half-mile round-trip journey every day at 7:45 a.m. and 2 p.m. despite repeated protests by Simona and Ashley that they were happy to assume this dangerous mission. Ashley worked full-time for the Fulton County Sheriff's department. Before bad health forced her retirement, Simona had been a custodial worker at the Fulton County Courthouse—she cleaned eighteen judicial chambers and the law library nightly for thirteen years. The judges and staff did not want her to go because she was excellent at her job, but she had no choice. Simona moved in with Virginia and took care of the grand-babies for Ashley, so it fell to Virginia to accompany Kingston to school. She gladly accepted the obligation. The five-minute walk to Cleveland Avenue Elementary was dangerous, and Virginia wanted to ensure Kingston was safe. Summerdale had the reputation of being one of Atlanta's most crime-infested apartment communities, and Virginia believed it. Loud gunshots were fired below her window just last night, and police sirens were an almost daily event. So every day, she left Joshua, Kingston's five-year-old brother, with Simona in the apartment, looked towards heaven in a silent prayer, and braved the trek to Cleveland Avenue Elementary.

At the foot of the stairwell, Virginia paused as the harsh wind hit her with the rancid stench of urine. She wrinkled her nose in disgust. The drug dealers routinely used the area behind her building as a toilet. They were like a pack of dogs marking their territory, but there was little Virginia or her neighbors could do about it—they were not about to confront a bunch of young male thugs relieving themselves next to their building, or any other building for that matter. She walked on down the stained concrete walkway, leaving the foul smell behind. Tall, weedy grass framed her path. There was no telling what rats, snakes, and other vermin lurked in the grass, and Virginia knew better than to investigate.

NEARING THE MANAGEMENT AND leasing office, Virginia took stock of the partially melted and boarded-up section of the beige, vinyl-clad building. The rumor around the apartment community was that the office had been set afire by teenagers angry over a rent dispute with Maya Galindo, the property manager. Another rumor was that a former maintenance technician, angry over a paycheck dispute, set fire to the building before quitting his job. Regardless of the cause, Virginia and her neighbors had heard the sirens and seen the fire trucks as they barged in front of the management office to quickly extinguish the blaze. Being a devout Christian woman, she was surprised by the arson rumors and did not want to believe that humanity could be so evil. She and her like-minded neighbors were frustrated as to why the management and police let the arson pass and the drug activity persist. Management's feeble efforts at security seemed almost useless. Maya was not popular with the tenants, and the deliberate fire was a warning to everyone in the community, including Maya, who promptly got the message and sequestered herself behind her locked office door. After the fire, it was rare to see Maya venturing outside the rental office.

At the leasing office, Virginia noticed William, the new maintenance technician, walking out of the dented maintenance door with a toolbox. "Hello, Ms. Humphries," he said with a kind smile as she passed by him. William liked Virginia because she rarely complained about the condition of her apartment and kept it in decent shape. She had worried about the growing mildew in her laundry room and bathroom, and William responded with a one-time Kilz application on the walls. Virginia was grateful for his efforts. She smiled and replied but kept walking. The school was prompt in its schedule, and she did not want to be late. Virginia was focused on her task at hand—no time for chitchatting even with a sweet man like William.

Once past the burnt-out leasing office, Virginia sighed. Summerdale was a nice respectable property until it was foreclosed in 2009 during the Great Recession. For the next two years, the property was operated with little supervision on a nonexistent budget. When Summerdale was finally sold in 2011 to an out-of-state buyer, the combination of an absentee landlord and a negligent on-site manager accelerated its decline.

The drug dealing started cautiously at first, but as the business grew, so did the boldness of the dealers and buyers. Virginia kept her nose clean, paid her rent, and vented her frustrations from a cushioned pew at Mt. Carmel Baptist Church. She was not about to give up her home and community when she only paid $670 a month for a three-bedroom unit. Especially when the market was commanding $850 a month or more for a smaller unit.

Her social security check combined with Simona's disability check barely covered their basic living expenses. She prayed that things would improve and wondered if she would live long enough to see better times. She was raising her great-grandchildren in the three-bedroom apartment, and she was sure the mildew that still seeped through the Kilz was not good for them. Joshua and Kingston had breathing issues, resulting in hurried trips to the Grady Hospital emergency room when their wheezing worsened.

VIRGINIA SLOWLY MADE HER way out the bent, rusted, metal exit gate, ignoring the incoming cars and groups of young men carrying brown paper bags concealing liquor bottles. She turned left onto the sidewalk along Old Hapeville Road. The entrance gate to Summerdale Phase I was across the street to her right; she typically avoided looking in that direction. That property also was controlled by drug dealers and festering with violent crime. Recently a woman caught in the crossfire was killed by a stray bullet about ten feet from Virginia's path. Half of Phase I was boarded up and rotting away, and it broke her heart. She loved the Phase I side and had fond memories of when she lived there decades ago.

Two rowdy teenagers walked past, almost pushing her into the grass without a second glance. She turned around and noticed that they were laughing and eating burgers from the local Checkers restaurant. A few moments later, they casually tossed the greasy fast-food wrappers onto the sidewalk. Virginia shook her head but understood that today's young people just did not respect elders. Luckily, her one-block walk was downhill as she continued slowly north towards the entrance of Cleveland Avenue Elementary. Cars zoomed past as she paused at the busy intersection of Cleveland Avenue and Old Hapeville Road. Waiting for the light to change, she glanced at the McDonald's restaurant on her left and wondered if her sixteen-year-old grandson was working today. He was lucky to have the job and could thank one of his old high school classmates for sending the opportunity his way.

An Exxon gas station stood on the opposite corner of the intersection. The grass in front was overgrown with weeds and studded with bottles, cigarette butts, and other trash, courtesy of busy commuters and pedestrians. The faded parking lot teemed with skinny, grown men who had shifty eyes, large tattoos, and to Virginia's embarrassment—pants sagging below their underwear. The Exxon housed more drug dealers than any other business in the neighborhood and suffered constant gunfire, but Virginia ignored the shifty men and kept walking. She reminded herself that she had made her peace with God and had nothing to fear. She said:

> When I first came here, you could tell the drugs was at the Exxon, 'cause you could see the crowd. But when I went by, I would always speak to the young men and ask if they was having a good day, and they would say "Yeah, momma." Over time I saw two guys and they would be so high, it hurt me so bad to be past there everyday and they just laying cross. Oh, that went all on me. I would jes pray to God, "Please let me see them leave Exxon." One of them stayed in the apartments but he died. The other, he used to go to church but I don't see them anymore . . . they gone. You will never stop it all 'cause it is so much easy money in it. You'll never stop the drugs. Every mornin' I wake up and pray the bullets don't get me today and every night I thank God that I'm still alive. You never know when the bullets is going to strike.

The Exxon was directly across the street from Cleveland Avenue Elementary. Despite rumblings around the neighborhood that the gas station was to be shut down for criminal activity, nothing ever happened except more drug dealing, more shootouts, and a surprising amount of gas being sold. Virginia felt a little safer after passing the Exxon station. She took an immediate right and entered the long downhill driveway to the school.

FROM THE OUTSIDE, CLEVELAND Avenue Elementary is exactly what one would expect in a textbook public school design. The building is wider than deep, with a cascading two-tone brick facade. Its flat white metal roof rises in the center, giving the entrance the appearance of a two-story atrium. Three yellow school buses lined up at the entrance, and about a dozen parents patiently waited in the comfort of heated cars to collect their children. Virginia inched her way past the idling lineup, entered the building, and gratefully sat on an empty bench in the lobby, anticipating the end of the school day.

The bright white walls, dotted with vibrant works of art by the schoolchildren, and spotless white tiled floor always made her smile. She appreciated the effort that went into keeping the interior looking polished and new. Virginia knew most of the school staff and was quickly greeted in the hallway by the principal, Dr. Anyeé Payne, who was headed into the office to announce the ending of the school day. When her first grandson, Dallas, attended the school ten years ago, Virginia was an active grandparent who never missed one of his plays, award ceremonies, or teacher meetings. She wanted a better life for her family and stressed the importance of education, reminding them that she did not have the luxury of education since she had to leave school early to get a job and earn money. She liked the fact that Dr. Payne and her staff were dedicated to creating a safe and caring haven at Cleveland Avenue Elementary.

Promptly at 2:15 p.m., Dr. Payne announced over the intercom that the day had ended. With military precision, the teachers and staff, clutching walkie-talkies, took their positions in the hallways and near exit doors. Rows of children filled the wide hallways as the staff patiently directed the 350-plus students to the appropriate exits. The hallway was eerily quiet, despite dozens of children orderly lining up as the staff patiently directed them to school bus lines, parents, and other exits per parental instructions. Many children were stressed and dreaded leaving the safety and comfort of their classrooms for the toxic home environments awaiting them. Virginia watched the children and looked for her great grand-baby with happy anticipation. She had a special love in her heart for children, and the rows of adorable students with their colorful backpacks and clothing brought much joy to her day. She finally saw Kingston and waved him over. There was not a lot of small talk over the active exodus, so Virginia quickly headed for the door.

Before exiting, she turned to Kingston and fondly buttoned up his coat to make sure he was warm. Kingston knew the routine and stood still while Virginia pulled and tugged at his coat buttons. Then she opened the heavy door, and a freezing breeze entered the hallway. Kingston silently followed as they made their way back home.

The school had organized a "human school bus" for the students walking back to Summerdale, and Virginia and Kingston joined the group of about fifteen children. Once the students left the entrance, a few of the older boys broke loose from the group and ran ahead along Old Hapeville Road, past the McDonald's and towards Summerdale. Two tall fifth-graders took a right, past the congregation of loitering men, and into the Exxon station to purchase sodas. Virginia knew a few of the kids and occasionally intervened. In addition to raising her own brood, she knew their friends and the parents who also lived at Summerdale. Despite the drug dealing and criminal activity, Summerdale was a community of many legacy tenants who watched out for each other.

Finally Virginia and Kingston entered Summerdale through the rusted, broken gate and walked down the sidewalk to their apartment building. At the stairs, Virginia grabbed the railing, pulling herself up one step at a time. Kingston quickly bounded past her. But Virginia had to take her time, the pain in her hip and legs reminding her of her age. When she made it to the apartment door left open by Kingston, she went inside, closed the door, and promptly engaged the two locks.

MEANWHILE, REGINALD JACKSON WATCHED from a dirty folding chair, surrounded by a compacted red patch of dirt littered with weeds, plastic soda bottles, Styrofoam cartons, and other trash, in the shadows of the back of Building 1400 along the courtyard at Summerdale. He liked this spot because it offered the best view of the foot and car traffic making its way from Old Hapeville Road, into Summerdale, and along the driveway to the back of the property. The shadows made him nearly invisible, perfect for taking in the action and staying out of the way. At only 5'8", twenty-six-year-old Reginald was not a big dude. He weighed 145 pounds and did not pack enough muscle to protect himself. Instead, he relied on the firepower of a 9mm Glock to raise his stature among his bigger yet equally shady peers. On many occasions, Reginald eased the pistol partway out of his pocket so everyone knew he was in charge when the boss man was not around. The boss man was Anthony Fowler, a bigger dude with a quiet yet intimidating all-business demeanor.

Virginia was unaware that Reginald watched her walk from her unit and through the gate. He laughed and nodded to Bulldog, the homie sitting next to him, when Virginia hit the landing of her stairwell. She was so punctual in her schedule to get her grandchild that Reginald could set his watch by her.

He and Bulldog supervised the day shift, which did not have quite the activity of the weekend and late-night but still was respectable. He had been operating in the Summerdale courtyard for about a year, and after a few months he had known most of the legal and illegal tenants by sight, including Virginia Humphries. He also knew their cars, bus schedules, kids, family, and routines as he silently built a profile of the community around him. An understanding of the local players and their routines was vital to his survival, and he was getting so good that he could spot and quickly size up an intruder as a threat, customer, or resident. He knew a few of the neighbors were aware of his presence, but he tended to mind his own business, coldly turning his head to avoid eye contact if a resident was bold enough to approach him or look him in the eye.

Anthony was the kingpin boss and social liaison to the legal residents and Reginald was good with this arrangement. The social connection between the residents and the drug business was a delicate matter of diplomacy, and Reginald lacked the social finesse to keep everyone and their expectations in line. Anthony instinctively knew how to soothe the volatile personalities of his men, while also flattering the apartment management, staff, and residents in ways that further enabled his illegal, underground business. Offerings of pizza or money were valuable tools he deployed to garner residents' respect. Anthony was happy to shell out cash for overdue electric or phone bills or offer to fund a new tire because it built loyalty among the poor struggling residents.

With Anthony in charge of public relations, Reginald focused on the transactional side of the business. Crack, cocaine, and marijuana were the products, and the traffic was slow but steady at two in the afternoon. Nighttime had the major action, but the daytime traffic was sometimes just as bold. Business flourished if his posse kept the other suppliers at bay. However, often there were territorial challenges. A few bold upstarts recently tried to set up shop in one of the townhomes across the street in Summerdale Phase I. The young cowboys were trying to carve out a territory, and the boss did not like it. The tension between the dealers in the two apartment phases was escalating. Occasionally, Reginald fired his Glock in the general direction of the competition across the street, just as a warning. Reciprocation was usually loud and swift. Reginald had little concern about the fear he caused by shooting a gun in broad daylight in an apartment community that housed families with children.

VIRGINIA HAD BEEN AT the property while Anthony and Reginald commanded the courtyard, but she minded her own business and left them alone. Unlike some other residents, who screamed at dealers or called the police at their own risk, Virginia saw herself as a Christian do-gooder who always had a kind word. Reginald quietly watched as she fed many of his customers who lived in makeshift tents behind the battered back fence of the property. The homeless camp was accessible through a missing panel of the chain-link fence, conveniently ripped away to provide wide-open access in what could be a life-or-death situation if his guys needed to quickly escape the police or the gun-brandishing competition. As soon as management replaced the missing chain link fence, the transients would tear it down. Over time, management just gave up, and the panel remained horizontal and discarded, allowing the dealers and their homeless customers to declare victory.

On occasion, several of Reginald's transient customers would pool enough cash to legitimately rent an apartment. Groups of like-minded comrades would then show up for round-the-clock parties. The attendees were typically young, small-time criminals who would commit random break-ins to fund the apartment and their daily habits. However, most of the thugs eventually wound up back in the homeless camp where fencing divided the areas between the wooded lot, the nearby Piggly Wiggly, and Summerdale. Virginia was one of the few residents occasionally to deliver a breakfast biscuit or a sandwich to the multi-tent camp. She reminded Reginald of his own grandmother, and Anthony had signaled the boys to leave her alone. They were businessmen with a code. Messing with old ladies was not good for "biz," and the police were already called often enough—the occupational hazard of running a successful business.

WHEN REGINALD SAW VIRGINIA walk past the management office and nod to William, the maintenance technician, he transferred his attention to William. William was relatively new to the property and Reginald noticed that he minded his own business while performing his job. William was a hard worker. Reginald saw him everywhere, mowing the lawn, repairing air conditioning units, and readying vacant units for new renters. It was almost a joke how management and maintenance staff ignored Reginald and his dealers, even avoiding eye contact. They were smart. The Summerdale property was part of Reginald's territory and the estimated cash haul was easily more than a million dollars last year. The growing customer base arrived from a thirty-mile radius around Atlanta: local celebrities, millionaires, and businessmen and -women. Reginald felt righteous because he was part of a product line that was in demand by so many affluent people. Summerdale was the ideal location for nurturing illegal activities. It was a block from the Interstate 75 exit, fronted by an intimidating ecosystem of boarded-up commercial and residential buildings that repelled most legally operated businesses.

The residents living around Cleveland Avenue were barely surviving on poverty wages, without the time or social capital to tackle the growing crime. The toxic environment was an unintentional conspiracy between the property owner, city services, and businesses, which created a golden opportunity for Anthony and underlings like Reginald. As Anthony's dealer network expanded and crime ensued, everyone was either too scared, apathetic, or under his influence to challenge the illegal activity destroying the local community.

Unfortunately for Anthony, his success was noticed. As his illegal operation grew, other drug dealers moved in to carve out a piece of the cash flow. In response, the criminal activity escalated. Gunfire became a by-product of territory disputes, and fights occurred more frequently. The criminal element attracted secondary crime and a group of teenagers had started using Summerdale as a parking lot for their lucrative car-theft business.[31] Management noticed but was unable to address the problem, even with their private security guards. Sammy, the Asian maintenance technician, directly confronted the dealers one morning over in Phase I, only to be viciously attacked. Luckily, William was in the area and ran over to rescue Sammy from the hopelessly one-sided fight. The issue had stemmed from a minor cultural misunderstanding; however, it was enough to anger the dealers. Sammy was not fluent in gangster culture. He survived the attack but was clearly shaken. The next day, he returned to his family in New York for a few weeks to heal. He eventually returned to the property, still injured and hurting, but with a new respect for Reginald and his dealers. The warning was clearly communicated to the staff and tenants at Summerdale. The management and maintenance staff were smart to stay out of the dealers' way for their own well-being, thus inevitably becoming part of the conspiracy.

Thirty minutes after Virginia left the property, Reginald saw her slowly return to her apartment. Kingston was skipping ahead, dragging his Spiderman book bag. Both were oblivious to Reginald and Bulldog watching from the shadows. Reginald—always on the lookout for young recruits who could serve as runners—thoughtfully studied the young boy and considered his future usefulness. With many of the single mothers working long hours at one or even two retail and housekeeping jobs at poverty wages, the kids were rarely supervised. These families were constantly starved for any extra money, so recruiting was easy. At first, the kids were assigned to lookout posts throughout the complex. After gaining the dealer's trust and proving their worth, the kids were promoted to "running" between the dealers and buyers. It was the perfect setup because the young boys were juveniles and thus below the punishment radar if they were arrested, which was rare. Even if the boys were booked, they were usually turned over to their parents rather than spend any time in jail. Such boys were a vital buffer that kept Reginald out of serious trouble and jail time. Reginald filed Virginia's great-grandson in his memory. The kid was young now but might be useful one day.

7

Sharon Allen—The Phantom Tenant in Apartment D-12

Sharon Allen knocked on the black metal door of the leasing office at Summerdale Apartments and waited impatiently for someone to answer. She had called earlier and set an appointment to meet Omari Jackson, the leasing agent, to tour a unit. The door was locked, which was strange for four in the afternoon, so she stepped back and looked at the signage which announced 9 a.m.–5 p.m. She knocked again, and after what seemed an eternity a young man cautiously opened the door. He nervously smiled and sized her up for a moment before stepping aside. Sharon flipped her Futura hair weave, secured her fake Louis Vuitton Alma handbag, and strutted inside. Omari promptly locked the door behind them and waited for her to introduce herself.

"I'm Sharon. I called earlier and spoke with Omari about leasing a unit," she said curtly, without a smile, with her arms folded.

"Hey," the young man said, extending his hand, which she refused to shake but rolled her eyes. "I'm Omari. I need you to fill out a guest card," he said, directing her to a stained metal chair. The young lady had a bit of gangster attitude, but he was used to dealing with a tough crowd.

"How did you find out about Summerdale?" Omari asked patiently; this was part of the interview for prospective tenants.

"I got some friends who live here and I like to hang out," she answered impatiently, avoiding eye contact. Sharon quickly filled out prospective tenant card to tour a Phase I two-bedroom, bath-and-a-half unit. She marked that she needed a unit "ASAP." After a walking tour of the property with Omari and seeing a sample unit, Sharon liked what she saw despite the trash and boarded-up buildings next to the renovated units.

The two-bedroom townhomes were recently renovated with new kitchen cabinets, countertops, stylish new black appliances, tasteful tile flooring on the ground level, and hardwood floors on the second floor. At $650 a month, the unit was a bargain.

Sharon told Omari that she was interested and was instructed to fill out the two-page standard "Application for Occupancy" form,[32] attach copies of her driver's license and social security card, and pay the $75 application fee. Her driver's license photo showed an unsmiling, 5'3", 130-pound woman with a head full of well-groomed long hair and large golden almond-shaped eyes. She was attractive in her skin-tight designer jeans, black leather jacket, and large gold hoop earrings, and she knew it. Sharon worked hard to look good and was rewarded with a lot of attention from men. She was living at her mother's home and had a decent-paying job at a day-care in a seedy part of historic west Atlanta; however, she was often at Springview partying with her friends. If her lease application was approved, it would be the first apartment she had leased on her own. Now that she was eighteen, Sharon was excited by the prospect of having her own space and escaping the watchful eye of her mother. The world was waiting for her and she was eager to get started. In secret, Sharon "had the "mind of a hustler and was grinding to die rich." Sharon wanted the "Crown" and worked hard on her image as a Lil' gangster complete with the bullying behavior and rude racist language. She would be quick to tell you: "Glad I'm not nobody baby momma. I refuse to have a kid by these N@$%. You can't keep going to jail and I'm not living off nobody first-of-the-month check, so yeah . . . I gotta get rich first."

Sharon liked Summerdale Apartments because some of her friends lived there and the rent was cheap for its location in Atlanta. Her annual income of $28,000 as a Pre-K assistant pre-qualified her to rent a two-bedroom townhouse unit at $650 per month.[33] The detailed renter's application asked qualifying questions about her rental and eviction history such as:

1. Have you or any person who will be occupying the apartment ever been a defendant in an eviction action?

2. Is any apartment community or previous landlord trying to collect

money from you or any person who will be occupying the apartment community?

3. Have you or any person who will be occupying the apartment ever filed, been discharged from, or is currently under bankruptcy?

4. Have you or any person who will be occupying the apartment ever been convicted, charged, arrested, indicated, plead guilty or no contest or received deferred adjudication or probation to A) any felony; B) any misdemeanor involving a sexual offense, stalking, illegal use or possession of weapons, assault, battery, theft, fraud, bad checks, criminal damage to property, trespass, vandalism, illegal possession, or sale of drugs?

5. Have you or any person who will be occupying the apartment ever been asked to move because of an alleged lease violation of any kind?

6. Have you ever lived in this apartment community before?

7. Are you unemployed?

8. Do you have the legal right to be in the United States?

Sharon could honestly give the correct answers to all these questions, circling "NO" for questions 1–7 and "YES" for question 8. She initialed the form that she "had truthfully answered Questions 1–8 above," signed the application, and attached a copy of her paycheck stub.

MAYA GALINDO, THE PROPERTY manager at that time, later reviewed Sharon's application and ran her profile through ResidentCheck to verify the information on her application. There are different levels of tenant screening software, and ResidentCheck is popular due to its combination of credit and criminal background research, making it simple for a property manager to verify a tenant's application based on a single credit risk score. If Sharon were giving false information, the ResidentCheck system would likely catch it and give a higher risk. Maya entered Sharon's key data and waited for the credit risk score. The screening report corroborated the leasing application with a clear record search for any eviction, criminal felony convictions, or pending misdemeanor and sex offenses. A public record search indicated no delinquent accounts, past due amounts, or outstanding credit balances. The reality was that at eighteen, Sharon was considered credit and criminal history "neutral." She was just entering adulthood and had no credit or criminal history and had a proven steady job. She lacked the credit experience to have developed bad habits, so she passed with flying colors.[34] ResidentCheck gave Sharon a Credit Risk Factor of 39 (meaning she had a 39 percent risk of going delinquent) with an "approved" recommendation to accept her application with one month's rent as a deposit. Maya approved Sharon as a tenant to move into Unit D-12.

Maya called Sharon with the good news, and they agreed that she would come into the office to sign a lease with February 24 as the move-in date. ResidentCheck had recommended a full month's rent as a security deposit, but Maya needed to lease the apartment, so she agreed to accept a lower deposit. With the prorated rent for February, $250 security deposit, and first month's rent of $650, Sharon owed $1,016 upon the execution of the lease. She had a generous gap between her $2,000 monthly paycheck and the $650 per month rent, but $1,016 was a lot of cash to come up with in addition to the cost of furnishing her first apartment. She evidently felt confident about it, posting on Facebook: "Broke people always wanna argue. Like stop it. Get some money . . . My mother makes more than $10 an hour . . . just to clear the air. She's a store manager at [a national restaurant chain]. My father, LOL, well, let's just say your dad not f@&king with him. My bedroom is the size of y'all hos apartments. FACTSSS."

On February 24, Sharon signed the standard 26-page Georgia Apartment Association rental contract. The six-month lease term legally bound her for a monthly rent of $650, water of $35, and her electric bill paid directly to Georgia Power via a separate meter. The lease also clearly stated a late fee of $100 if the rent was five days past due and an eviction fee of $250 if the rent was paid after the tenth day of the month. The popular GAA rental contract is a well-written document that has been used for thousands of leases in Georgia. The contract is thorough, and Sharon not only signed the lease agreement but also a dozen addendums making her and her guests responsible for bed bugs, running the air conditioning, keeping a clean household to avoid mold, complying with the community rules and regulations, maintaining the smoke alarm, and not engaging in illegal activity. By the time she was finished with the lease and addendums, Sharon had signed her name sixteen times and initialed seven pages. The "Other Occupants" section of the contract was left blank.

Maya congratulated Sharon and went with her to inspect the unit to ensure she was satisfied with its condition. The maintenance staff had already inspected Unit D-12 in anticipation of Sharon's occupancy and had corrected any outstanding deficiencies. Maya did not foresee any problems, but it was Summerdale policy that a tenant signed off on the apartment condition before accepting occupancy, to legally document acceptance of the unit. Maya and Sharon walked the unit and inspected the bathrooms, bedrooms, closets, windows, kitchen, and doorways. Everything worked, and Sharon signed off that the unit was in good condition except for a damaged kitchen cabinet drawer. Maya put in a work order with William, who promptly made the drawer repair. The keys were handed over to Sharon after she signed a "Move-In and Move-Out Inspection" form and paid the first month's rent and deposit. Sharon was officially a legal tenant at Summerdale Unit D-12. She posted a celebratory comment on Facebook: "Bitches can work a double shift and pull five hours of overtime, I bet you still don't have more money than me."

LOCATED IN THE PHASE I courtyard of Summerdale, Unit D-12 was surrounded by vacant and boarded-up buildings. Maya assured Sharon that the ownership was preparing for a renovation of the boarded-up buildings and had already started work on the eighteen units in nearby Building G. Maya then requested that Sharon sign an "Extended Special Stipulations Addendum" acknowledging that the Landlord would be renovating Buildings E, F, H, J, K, L, M, and N at some point during the lease. The construction zone for these buildings would be fenced off, and in the addendum Sharon agreed not to trespass or hold the landlord accountable for any personal injury, losses or claims that she may have or claim constructive eviction by virtue of the property rehabilitation of the boarded-up units.

Summerdale office records show that Sharon was prompt with her rental payments during the first few months. However, in July, her past-due payment triggered a $100 penalty. Sharon worried about her credit rating, so she eventually paid. She liked living at Summerdale and enjoyed the growing social environment around her. The units beside hers were occupied by several guys, and the traffic and partying was almost nonstop on the weekends. Every Friday, the next-door neighbors would watch for Maya and the maintenance staff to depart at 5 p.m. By 5:15 the grills, lawn chairs, and beer coolers had appeared in masse. The party was going full throttle by 9 p.m., and the traffic usually did not peak until around midnight—to the dismay of the legal, law-abiding tenants.

Sharon enjoyed the partying and the admiration of the guys coming to hang out with her neighbors. Some of the guys were rough looking, but she had been flirting with a tall, handsome twenty-eight-year-old tough named Andre Webster. They began full-fledged dating after a few weeks. Andre was her first serious adult boyfriend, and she basked in her new love, forgetting to set her alarm and showing up late or hung-over at work. Predictably, Sharon was fired from her day-care job, but Andre told her not to worry about it. The romance was great, and gradually he stayed at her apartment, took over the rental payment, and gave her a little spending money when she asked. Her polished designer nails and new weave gave her the groomed look of a prosperous lady. Over time they added a roommate, Francis McCulver, who took the second bedroom. The lease required Sharon to disclose any other occupants in the apartment, but she had signed without fully reading the complicated lease. Besides, she thought that who was living in her apartment as a roommate was nobody's business. She posted on Facebook: "I'm not about to keep going back to the same kind of relationships, I refuse to be like the rest of y'all, pregnant as hell and unhappy as f#%k. Bitches out here settling for less than less; you bitches scared to be alone, so you live life around a N#@ga you scared to be with because it's better to be scared with someone else than scared and alone."

IN NOVEMBER 2017, A *"Five-Day Notice of Intent to Terminate Rental Agreement for Non-Payment of Rent"* was taped on the front door of Unit D-12, with an amount owed of $745. The management staff was now aware of the after-hours drug activity and noticed the growing groups of men boldly hanging out between Units D-11, D-12, and D-13 during daylight hours. Maya convinced the ownership to pay for increased security. She also started eviction proceedings after Sharon failed to respond, but a friend of Sharon's appeared in the management office on November 27 with several cashier's checks and paid the rent in full. In December, another notice to terminate was posted, and Sharon appeared in late December with several cashier's checks and paid the full outstanding balance. There was still no record in the lease file of any tenant screening for additional occupants in D-12.

In January 2018, the rent was again late, and after Sharon failed to respond, Maya filed a formal eviction. The eviction hearing was in March, and Sharon made no move to fight it or even appear in court. The records show that a Bernice Azar showed up in court on behalf of the "occupants." A judgment of $1,423 was ordered in favor of the landlord and records indicate that a Notice of Abandonment was delivered to the tenant, giving Sharon or the occupants five days to respond or the landlord would take possession of the premises. Another cashier's check for the outstanding balance appeared one morning through the office collection slot, which Maya gladly accepted and deposited into the bank. A Notice of Intent to Terminate was again posted in May. When June rolled around, the rental payments magically appeared in the collection slot. There are no receipts in the records that Sharon ever appeared to make rental payments. At this point, it had been six months since any response from Sharon had been noted in her lease file. In fact, Sharon was no longer a tenant living in her legally rented apartment at Summerdale. Instead, she was fronting a highly illegal drug-dealing business operating in Unit D-12. Sharon was officially a "phantom tenant."

The City of Atlanta crime reports indicate that 911 was called four times in January 2017 for Unit D-12 versus only one time in January 2016. The occupants in Unit D-12 were not as visible to the neighbors and police. Police are required to follow strict rules and procedures, including obtaining a search warrant, before entering a private residence. Operating a drug operation using a "phantom tenant" as a front in an apartment community effectively conceals illegal activity.

SHARON NEVER RESPONDED TO requests for interviews. This account of her is based on the official lease file, interviews with staff, and social media.

8

Melinda Wyatt—the Blighted Tenant

MARTA—the Metro Atlanta Rapid Transit Authority system—is the popular public transportation lifeline for people living and working along the Cleveland Avenue corridor and in Summerdale Apartments. Bus route #78 runs the east-to-west route along Cleveland Avenue approximately every twenty minutes between 4:15 a.m. and 1:20 a.m. that night. Its westernmost stop is the East Point MARTA train station, a commuter connector to major hub-points throughout Atlanta. The bus stop serving Summerdale is at the corner of Old Hapeville Road and Cleveland Avenue, one block north of the property across from the Exxon station. It is rare to drive by and not see people patiently waiting for the #78 to take them to work, shopping, or church.

Melinda Wyatt was panting heavily after walking uphill from the bus stop on Cleveland Avenue and climbing a flight of stairs to her second-floor apartment, her arms loaded with bulky plastic bags of groceries. She was a large, attractive woman, stylishly dressed in tight designer blue jeans, glitter sneakers, a fresh manicure, and carefully coiffed hair. Although both Melinda and her husband worked full-time, they could afford only one car, and because her job was accessible via MARTA, her husband commanded the car keys. Melinda was a familiar sight walking from Summerdale to the bus stop and back on a daily basis, usually hauling a dozen plastic grocery bags.

She paused for a moment at the filthy landing in front of her apartment unit to catch her breath and mentally brace herself for the chaos predictably waiting on the other side of the dented metal door. The Wyatts had four children ages seven, eight, ten, and twelve, and chaos went with the territory of raising three boisterous boys and a pre-teen adolescent girl. Balancing the grocery bags, she found her keys, opened the door and struggled to the kitchen where she dumped the grocery bags on the floor with loud thuds, sending dozens of German roaches scattering in all directions. Melinda ignored the roaches, took off her stylish black leather jacket, and flung it on the table. A subtle aroma of stale urine floated through the warm apartment.

Walking back into the living room, Melinda eyed the cheap velvet maroon sectional, now dissected into several pieces and haphazardly strewn sideways and upside down on the stained carpet. Her middle son, Jackson, was wildly jumping on a cushion and hollering at his younger brother Anthony, who was gleefully perched on an overturned loveseat, with a fake plastic sword pointed at his brother and a Spiderman cape wrapped around his shoulders. Melinda's daughter and older son were probably buried deep in video games and tablets in their rooms, where they tended to retreat after school. The children rarely invited friends to the fetid, stressful apartment.

The Wyatts had lived at Summerdale Apartments for only a few months. Melinda recalled:

> I was actually looking for a bigger place because I was transitioning from the West End Projects. So, you know, me wanting a bigger and safer environment and just be a little more comfortable with the area. I was living in West End Apartments near Oakland City and it is very high crime over there, very. I met a friend at a workplace and she told me about Summerdale. That is how I really came across knowing about it, word-of-mouth. When I tell people I moved to Summerdale Apartments off Cleveland Avenue, they tell me, "Oh . . . . that's bad over there."

On this June day, Melinda was exhausted from her $8 an hour day job at the Goodwill checkout counter. Melinda was a hard and diligent worker. Her husband was employed full-time at the local Wendy's, also earning $8 an hour. Their combined income was just over $2,770 per month.[35] She was grateful for the work and content to get ahead in life for her family. A second job at the courthouse gave her another $12 an hour to fund extras for her children but required her to work seven days a week. She had little time for herself. It was rare for Melinda to have a full day off, but when she did, she declared them "mommy days" and took some time for personal pampering at the salon.

Melinda's mother, Dorothy, clad in her worn lavender robe and white pajamas, was in the doorway of her bedroom facing the living room, arms crossed, stressed, and scowling at Jackson and Anthony. Occasionally Dorothy would strike out at the boys when things got out of hand, but today they ignored her and kept wildly chasing each other in the semi-dark apartment. In addition to being partially deaf, Dorothy had severe asthma and heart issues. She usually stayed in her bedroom with the door closed and the TV volume turned up, drowning out the pandemonium.

Melinda did not mind having Dorothy living with them but understood that she could never bring in any meaningful income to the family due to her health issues, so it would always be Melinda and her husband's burden to provide financially for the family. After losing her only son in 2006, Dorothy feared being separated from her other children so she alternated living with Melinda and her sister. The death of her son hit Dorothy hard, but Melinda and her sister had been taking care of their mother and brother since Melinda was a young girl, so this living arrangement was nothing new. Recalling her childhood, she said:

> My mom being in her condition and a single parent of three children, it was hard because your mom is hearing-impaired and she had asthma. My sister and I shared the responsibility to go to the doctor's office with her to handle the business, which really messed up my school. It was hard to stay focused on school since we had to help her with a lot of things. I did not graduate from high school but went back and got my GED.

Melinda remained close to her sister and accepted her family situation without complaint. It was helpful having her mother at home with the kids while Melinda and her husband were perpetually working and working to make ends meet.

DOROTHY HAD RAISED MELINDA and her sister in an apartment leased by her own mother in the "projects" located in the city of East Point just outside the Atlanta city limits and about three miles west of Summerdale.

As a young girl Melinda learned her survival skills in the tough neighborhood. Summerdale, despite its violent crime and blighted units, was paradise compared to the neighborhood where she was raised. Dorothy had a large extended family of seven siblings, three sisters and four brothers, all living at some point in a crowded two-bedroom apartment unit.

Melinda had to grow up fast. In addition to her mother's health issues, Dorothy adopted her young nephew because her brother and his lady friend spent more time taking drugs than being parents. Dorothy could not care for her nephew and put the burden on Melinda and her sister when they were themselves just children. Melinda remembered:

> When I say it was rough, it was *rough* in those apartments. My grandmother died when I was young so I don't have too much memory of her, but the stories that I've heard . . . the family depended on her, you know. Once situations happened, somebody got put out, or they had no food, she would sacrifice. She had eight children and over time as they got older and had families, they just all kept piling up in that small apartment. A lot of my cousins didn't have the proper family or parents. Some were alcoholics, drug users, and things of the sorts. They had to depend on my grandma, and she was a good person. She just had her own ways with the drinking and things like that. She was opinionated and feisty and sold alcohol out of the apartment. She probably would have loved me as well, given the chance. Three of the eight siblings are dead. So, you know, but everybody is making it. Yeah, keep living.
>
> The family responsibilities was like an ongoing thing. It never stopped and I went from raising myself, to raising my cousin, then raising my brother, you know, and then also having our own children so you know, so that is a big deal and it is a lot of responsibility. It can be stressful at times.

The family members moved from East Point over time and either died rough deaths or dispersed to other impoverished neighborhoods throughout Atlanta. The occasions when the extended family would get together for holiday celebrations were rare, which was okay with Melinda. She had enough time with her own family and liked her space.

AFTER MOVING INTO SUMMERDALE, Melinda promptly enrolled her children in the Atlanta Public Schools district. Two of her children attended Cleveland Avenue Elementary and two attended Crawford Long Middle School. Anthony and Jackson walked a couple of blocks to the elementary school every morning, which was a definite benefit of living at Summerdale. Melinda liked the convenience and neighborhood feeling of having the school close by her apartment, especially since they only had one car. Summerdale was also just a block from the bus stop, so it made it convenient to get around the city.

According to William, Summerdale's maintenance technician, and the paperwork in her lease file, Melinda's apartment was renovated before she moved in. The "Move-In and Move-Out" inspection form in her file indicated that everything was in good condition before Melinda took occupancy. The kitchen and appliances were older but in good working order, the unit was freshly painted, and the carpet was professionally cleaned. After Melinda and her family moved into the apartment, it quickly became clear that Melinda was not domestically inclined. The homey touches that create a warm, cozy environment were absent in her apartment. No curtains were hung lovingly on the windows or family photos proudly displayed on the walls. The sparse furnishings were functional and dark. Raising four children and working almost full-time was exhausting, and cleaning simply was not her priority. It was evident in the heaps of trash in the kitchen and piles of dirty dishes in the sink and on the counters. The carpet showed large stains in the few areas that were not covered with piles of mildewed clothing. Over time, the walls became stained with grimy handprints that merged into one continuous streak down the hallway walls. The floors in the two bathrooms were strewn with towels. Partially filled personal-product containers littered the sinks and floors. The boys often missed the toilets in their aim and consequently the floors and tub tiles were splattered with rank urine. As the trash and moldy clothes accumulated, the roaches arrived. Melinda called the management office requesting a treatment but it did not help. In fact, the infestation worsened. But after seeing the condition of Melinda's apartment, William and Maya had little sympathy for her. Melinda saw it differently:

Every time I called the Maya the manager to complain, she told me well that was the last work order, but you need to put in a new one to record it, it had to be fresh. I showed them the crack in my daughter's room, when you first walked in the door it was right there, but they kept fixing it with repair stuff. I don't know about the last tenant and whatever they had going on, but there were a lot of repairs that needed to be done, even down to the carpet inside of the closet. The dishwasher never worked, they never got around to that. There was a leak in the kitchen ceiling over the sink that was starting to mildew. It was caused by a leak in the kitchen above the unit, and it just seemed to be getting worse and worse. They had people come in and spray for the bugs, but it seemed to make it worse. I did not know what stuff the maintenance staff was using but it was feeding them rather than killing them.

Melinda often complained to management but she did not consider the piles of dirty dishes and mounds of trash as a food source for the roach infestation. Management inspected her apartment, ordering her to clean up the dishes and trash, but Melinda did not comply. After a few months of dealing with management, Melinda eventually gave up the matter and simply ignored the roaches and broken dishwasher.

EIGHT-YEAR-OLD JACKSON CONTINUED RUNNING around the living room chasing his brother and screaming. He tripped and fell, diving face first into the carpet. Within seconds he was upright and chasing his brother, oblivious to his fall. Dorothy yelled at them to calm down and gave Jackson a hard slap on the leg. That got his attention and he slowed down. Melinda sighed. It wasn't safe outside the apartment with all the shooting and fighting. At one time, there was nice playground equipment in the grassy courtyard next to her building, but the young men who loitered around the property tore down the equipment. With the playground gone, there wasn't much for her children to do other than stay sequestered in the apartment and expend their youthful energy on games and playing with each other. Jackson was recently diagnosed with ADHD (attention deficit hyperactivity disorder). He was an unusually energetic and high maintenance kid. The staff at Cleveland

Avenue Elementary recently told Melinda that he was having reading and writing issues, but the school was working with him, and she trusted the teachers and Principal Payne to do a good job. His breathing issues were becoming a concern and recalled Melinda's lifelong experience of dealing with her mother's asthma.

Melinda was determined to give her children a stable life unlike her own unstable childhood. Her face glowed with pride as she talked about her children. She often held serious conversations with them about being courteous, especially to the elderly ladies who lived at Summerdale. "Open doors for adults and be polite" was part of the life lessons she wanted to instill in her children, as she felt this skill was important to keep employment and get ahead in life. Fortunately her children tended to listen. Most of the elderly residents and families at Summerdale considered Melinda's children to be generally well-mannered. Her kids were always willing to take out the trash and do chores for a few dollars. However, the property management staff found Melinda to be confrontational and combative—directly opposite of her self-reported kind persona. They whispered that there were two Melinda's—good Melinda and evil Melinda. Considering the extreme poverty of her childhood, it was not surprising the fighter inside Melinda became instantly ignited when provoked. It was survival of the fittest and fighting was just part of life in her world.

Melinda really did not have time to meet her neighbors or worry about crime. She was aware of the shootings around the Exxon gas station and the drug dealers that operated in plain sight near the elementary school, but work and family consumed all her time and energy. As she put it:

> I know about the situation that happened with the lady being shot, but the crime is from the outside. The things that are around the Exxon and laundry mat, the drug dealers stand there while we going to school. They make friends on the inside of the apartment complex, so they are like in and out and they are bringing in the men and giving them the gate code and you know things like that. So, I think that is the main issue, the connection from the outside and the inside. Management is good, the only thing I can say that can be improved is probably a little heavier security.

The Cleveland Avenue community and Summerdale Apartments were still a major improvement over the East Point projects where she and her mother were raised. Melinda was a survivor and her residency at Summerdale was rooted in resilience. She said:

> I tell people it's not about being knocked down . . . we are all going to be knocked down. It's a matter of not staying down because if you do, then you are where you are supposed to be. So, making the effort and having the self-motivation to do better is awesome. It is."

9

The Atlanta Police Lieutenant and the Drug Kingpin

Lieutenant Joe Pulaski (aka "Ski") drove his dark blue patrol car one late evening through the broken metal entrance gates at Summerdale Apartments Phase II. Out of courtesy for the neighbors and their sleeping children, his blue lights were not flashing, and his sirens were not screaming the announcement of his arrival. At this late hour, Ski was considerate of the residents and his quiet arrival was one way he showed it. Once past the gate and inside the complex, he slowed and surveyed the property. From his vantage point, he could see groups of young men in stained T-shirts, sagging jeans, and thick gold neck chains strolling around the complex or sitting in the dark shadows of the common area. Loud music booming from somewhere deep in the property added to the festive atmosphere.

In wealthier Atlanta suburbs, this scene would be strange at 11 p.m., but this was Summerdale Apartments in the Cleveland Avenue neighborhood, and Ski was a seasoned veteran who knew his beat. As expected, the vibrant underground community was out in full force, partying, supporting the drug trade and other unlawful activity that peaked late in the evening while most law-abiding citizens were asleep or working their late-shift jobs. On any given weekend night, twenty or thirty people would crowd into the small common area at the property, mostly young men, and an occasional young woman. As Ski stealthily drove further into the complex, the underground activity suddenly froze, quickly recovered, and scattered in all directions. A sturdy black metal fence encircled the property, but over the years many sections of fencing had been discreetly detached. The gaps provided escape routes to the north, south, and west. The fencing along the eastern border also would have been compromised except that the thorny green juniper ground cover along the steep bank was rumored to be festering with large black snakes. The thought of encountering a large snake in the dark commanded the respect of even the toughest guys.

The more seasoned criminals scowled and casually took their time disappearing, some shooting Ski the finger in the dark. They were experienced veterans of the Fulton County criminal justice system and understood how the system worked. Most had long rap sheets and nothing to lose at this point. An arrest was no big deal since usually they were back on the street in a few days. To them, Ski was harassment, plain and simple. The 2017 National Survey of Drug Use and Health indicated that 11 percent of Americans had used some illegal drug in the past year and 49.5 percent had in their lifetime.[36] Americans had to get their illegal drugs of choice from somewhere, hence many underground communities like Summerdale's were thriving, keeping the local public safety departments overwhelmed and the neighbors in an uproar. Ski and the law may have arrived at Summerdale, but the structural ecosystem was designed to swiftly respond to any threat, making it easy for the underground community to efficiently vanish through broken gates and missing fencing, into apartments or behind the bushes. Tonight was no exception.

SKI WAS A LIEUTENANT in Zone 3 of the Atlanta Police Department (APD) which includes Cleveland Avenue and Summerdale Apartments. Ski was often tagged for promotions, which he just as often declined. All he really wanted was to police the neighborhood and keep it safe, so he stayed on the beat. He said that being a lieutenant, "I am in a position that can influence a lot of other people and instill the fun that I had as a beat officer. It annoys the hell out my sergeants and some of my officers. They are like, Lieutenant Ski, stay in your office, and I can't do that! No, I can't do it! Let me play." He had fearlessly worked in this zone for many years and knew from experience that Summerdale was one of the most criminally active and violently dangerous apartment communities in the city. Call logs accessed later through APD Open Records indicated that on this Wednesday evening in July, this visit would be the first of four 911 calls logged in for the day at Summerdale Apartments. The previous day there had been five 911 calls, including two for illegal drugs and one each for a suspicious person, shots fired, and loud music. Surprisingly, despite its reputation, it was rare that anyone was seriously injured at Summerdale. The APD had only so many man-hours in the day to address the crime in Zone 3, and the Cleveland Avenue corridor consumed more than its fair share of police resources.

A dedicated officer who loved his job, Ski was in his late thirties with a jovial demeanor and an easy laugh that emerged when asked why he wanted to be a police officer and ended up on the Atlanta force. With a mischevious smile, he said:

> I passed the psychological test. I grew up in New Jersey and my parents divorced when I was young. I was around my uncle a lot. He was a paramedic and a fire fighter, so I got into that. I always wanted to be a cop—it's something I just knew I would do one day. I was about seventeen years old and in high school when a cop came to career day. A typical cop back in the day; he had to be forty-five or fifty years old, gray hair. He said don't become a cop right out of school because you would be too young, and I wouldn't listen to you.

Ski took that advice and worked as an emergency medical technician (EMT) in New Jersey before following his uncle to Charlotte, North Carolina, for an instructor's job. He stayed in the Charlotte area for several years then moved back to New Jersey, but not before submitting applications to police departments in major cities around the South. The City of Atlanta was the first to respond to his application, and he was hired as an officer with the Atlanta Police Department. However, before he could take the job, a national tragedy happened. The morning of September 11, 2001, Ski was sitting in his living room in New Jersey, winding down from an overnight EMT shift. He turned on the TV just in time to see the first airplane hit the World Trade Center. Both his mother and father worked in the Trade Center district. He knew instinctively that this was no simple accident. His gut told him it was a terrorist attack. Ski wasted no time. He immediately put his uniform back on and headed to the Port Authority, where a hospital ship was being prepared to deal with injuries and casualties, which never arrived. "I didn't treat a lot of people on the hospital ship because the attack was so brutal, there were few survivors," he said. "So, I just packed up and came down here and have been here ever since—sixteen years. I love being a cop! Where else in the world can you play real live cops and robbers and get the bad guys!"

IN THE WARM JULY evening in 2017, Ski watched the reaction to his arrival at Summerdale. The chaos before him was challenging, but the experienced and tolerant officer was patient and methodical. At one time, the APD's beat officers would walk their communities and get to know the residents. But policing had changed. The officers no longer really knew the residents and could not differentiate the patterns of the good guys and bad guys. Summerdale was like a lot of apartment complexes after the recession, owned by absentee investors who also did not know the people living in their communities. These investors considered the property just a money game to get people in and get cash out, without considering whether they were providing stable homes for families. The few good tenants were outweighed by transients who would come in for a couple of months, operate in the underground community, and then move on—be it to jail, family, job, or death.

Policing for the decent, family-oriented legacy residents kept Ski motivated. He continued his drive through Summerdale Apartment and contacted the caller who had dialed 911—for the caller's safety, he would only make the contact if requested. He completed his paperwork while sitting in his car, and then he drove across the street to the Phase I apartments to keep the criminal activity there to a minimum. He would probably return to Phase II before the end of his shift. Over at Phase I, the soft air was warm and humid, with the scent of freshly mowed lawn grass. As expected, the underground community was out in full force and noisily disturbing the evening for the law-abiding tenants whose only mental relief was to routinely call 911. He was not scared of the environment; on the contrary, most of the criminals fled when they saw him drive through the entrance gate. Ski and his comrades at the APD were not intimidated by these guys or afraid to enforce the law, but he was aware that for most of the criminals getting arrested was just an inconvenience. Many of the seasoned drug dealers had long histories with various police departments around the South. An arrest was no big deal and usually they were back on the street in a few days. The Fulton County jails were overcrowded with drug dealers and other criminals.

Ski circled the exterior courtyard, looking at the rows of boarded-up, lifeless dark buildings. He wondered when the property owner planned to renovate the remaining derelict units and improve the neighborhood. Around the corner, a large group was gathered in the courtyard between the C and D buildings. A few kids were running around with a ball, and women in lawn chairs sat facing each other and talking. Nothing illegal about families being out at night, even if it was 11:15 p.m. The management did not have a curfew, so Ski left the families alone. The corner usually was teeming with men who had been arrested many times on suspicion of dealing illegal drugs. The watchman at the entrance gate must have warned that Ski was coming, giving the underground ample time to disappear. He circled the property and headed for the exit gates to continue his shift along the Cleveland corridor. It was a routine. As Ski put it, "Policing is 90 percent boredom and 10 percent sheer terror. That's the best way to describe it. You have the front seat to the greatest show on earth—known as humanity."

ANTHONY FOWLER[37] SAT IN his Escalade and supervised the action from the front corner of Summerdale Phase II near the interior common area. In front of him, ten guys wearing matching gold chains with designer crosses gathered around the metal picnic tables, laughing and joking with each other. A steady stream of customers briefly transacted with members of the group, got their fixes, and promptly exited. Several more friends joined the group, and the crowd swelled to fifteen men, surrounded by bright red coolers and trash from fast-food cartons. Anthony would make them clean up most of their trash before the end of the evening in the spirit of community support. There was a jovial air as the friends congregated, high-fived, socialized and earned their incomes. To an outsider, the cheery mood felt almost like a family reunion, an odd contrast to the inherent danger of the criminal congregation. Everyone seemed comfortable in their role in the ecosystem.

Anthony was a good boss and managed a tight ship, but the sociable atmosphere could and often did change in a split second upon the arrival of the competition or if a customer got aggressive. Small crimes such as home invasions and car thefts came with the territory, and Anthony looked the other way. His young men had a lot of energy and anger, and they had to vent it somewhere. However, there were often fights between his guys and customers, and Anthony stepped in if things escalated. He looked in the courtyard where some guys clustered around a black metal table in a swath of compacted hard dirt. A maintenance staffer shared that the area used to be a popular children's playground, but Anthony's guys, responding to a dare, destroyed the playground equipment, which was constructed of sturdy metal and set in concrete. It took a few days and considerable effort for the rowdy, determined men to pull the heavy equipment from its foundation and throw it aside. The playground pieces remained in a sad pile for a few weeks until William removed them like a discarded carcass. Anthony and his workers felt righteous about destroying the popular amenity, favored by the kids and their parents. The underground community declared victory—confirmation that Summerdale was their territory.

Anthony frowned at the commotion caused by Ski's arrival. His appearance temporarily halted the activity while he did his "cops and robbers" routine check, but it was all part of the risk Anthony took to operate in the community. Anthony looked around to see if any neighbors were peeking out of their windows, but the arrival of the police was so frequent that most neighbors just slept through the event and few came out to investigate. The residents knew who was in charge, and it was not the ownership, the management, or the APD. Ski was clearly outnumbered and, from experience, Anthony knew the law was on his side. To him, an arrest was a slap on the wrist because the judicial system was so arbitrarily forgiving and disjointed.

Anthony Fowler was not new to the underground of drugs and violence. His arrest record started in Fulton County (which includes the City of Atlanta) in February 1998 when he was arrested for aggravated assault, shoplifting, and armed robbery. According to a Jail Records Search, he was released in late July 1998 but arrested three weeks later for driving with a revoked license, no insurance, and running a stop sign. He was released again in early September 1998. He then stayed out of trouble in Fulton

County until May 2001, when he was arrested for shoplifting and fleeing the scene with a concealed license plate. He was released again after five weeks in jail. A burglary arrest followed in April 2005, and he was released in May 2005 "to another agency pending charges." Anthony returned to jail for marijuana possession in August 2007 and again in August 2010 when he was transferred to another agency pending charges. A record from 2013 shows "Time Served" for a probation violation (burglary) and transfer to another agency. In December 2013, he was recognized as a "Fugitive from Justice" from the Louisiana State University police department for an attempted rape charge. In May 2017, he was released from the Fulton County Sherriff's office on a $500 bond after being arrested for operating a vehicle without a current license or decal.[38] Clearly, Anthony was not intimidated by the criminal court system, and, despite a long history of arrests, he was thriving in one of the few businesses that rewarded his personality and skill set. With his arrest history, it was unlikely that he would be accepted in a traditional and legitimately operating company, but this was not necessary. Anthony was a survivor and Summerdale was his territory.

ANTHONY TYPICALLY ROTATED BETWEEN Summerdale Phase I and Phase II watching his team, collecting the cash, and running his tax-free business. At 6'2" with a weight that fluctuated between 250 to 300 pounds, he was imposing. His large staff of guys worked under a strict chain of command. He sold everything from girls and drugs to haircuts, if you wanted to drop by Unit D-12 in Phase I (we found a professional men's barber chair in that unit after we evicted its "phantom tenant"). The layout of Phase I was the perfect setup for Anthony's underground community. The courthouse square consisted of rows of brick townhouse buildings. A watchman sat at the secure entrance gate and swiped phantom tenant Sharon's security access card to let in the customers.

The actual drug trading happened in a dark corner between buildings C and D, away from the prying eyes of the public at the entrance. Based on the arrest records, the drug, prostitution, and other illegal activities operating at Summerdale easily generated millions of dollars in annual revenue for anyone willing to take on the risk—which Anthony clearly was willing to do. It was a business with an almost unlimited customer demand, one that afforded a new Escalade and a large lifestyle for Anthony, his superiors, and his colleagues. The row of mint-condition Maseratis and Mercedes-Benzes parked at Summerdale contrasted sharply with the impoverished apartments that commanded a meager $650 a month in rent. The exotic cars served as a disguise, evidence of a false social order intent on misleading the community on Anthony's influence and control.

The typical business model to launch an underground criminal network was simple. Select a blighted apartment community with an absentee owner and poor residents who lacked the social capital to protest in a significant and organized manner. Select young women like Sharon in unit D-12, or family relatives with good credit, to show up at the management office and lease an apartment as a phantom tenant or become a "front" to house the illegal business. The dealers then moved into the unit and established the business, which included paying the phantom tenant's rent and giving her a monthly stipend to retain a connection with the management office. The business model also includes recruiting juveniles who are immune to the adult court system. In Atlanta, a juvenile is defined as under the age of seventeen, while anyone over age seventeen is considered an adult in the criminal court system. The fresh recruits serve as runners who deliver the drugs to the buyers and then pass along cash proceeds to the dealer. Once the kids "age out" of evading adult prosecution, they are usually promoted to a larger role in the enterprise, which might include serving as a watchman at the Summerdale entrance to assist customers and notify leadership when law enforcement or other threats arrived.

The business model thrives on weakness and intimidation. Once entrenched, an underground community is difficult and expensive to dismantle without a large and vigilant community effort. The Summerdale maintenance staff, for instance, told me that Anthony occasionally slept in Unit C-6 and operated his business out of Unit D-12, giving him two places to hide. Initially, drug dealing happens in the shadows where management is not watching or does not have easy access, such as the interior of an apartment. Contrary to popular belief, landlords have limited access to apartment interiors. Landlords must give formal written notice before entering an apartment except in an emergency or life-safety situation. To gain access to suspicious inner activity, a major coordinated police and criminal court effort is required, which can take months and thousands of dollars in police costs.

But as the illicit business grows, dealers have a harder time hiding the obvious traffic and suspicious people attracted to the underground community. On many occasions, Anthony or one of his employees approached management and maintenance with bribes to keep the peace. It would start with a few hundred dollars for community events like "pizza for the hungry kids" living on site and starving for adult attention. It was rumored that the dealers put one of Summerdale property managers on their payroll, with a monthly stipend to stay quiet and "look the other way." Over time, Anthony developed a reputation as the "Godfather" of the property. Tenants approached him with their problems and Anthony responded by offering to pay their rent or utility bills. He worked hard to maintain the persona of a polite and engaged model citizen. He would give candy or cash to the kids and grocery money to mothers who were living a daily battle just trying to survive.

The survival of the underground community was contingent on participation from various parts of the community, and smart manipulative operators like Anthony financially rewarded those who knew their place—whether it was management, hired security, residents, children, or dealers. His carefully designed network provided critical alerts when Ski and the APD got too close. The law-abiding residents rarely challenged Anthony or his underground network. Anthony and his guys had guns and fists to control the community, and they let the tenants know it. After one confrontation with Maya, the property manager, a few of Anthony's guys shot up her car in plain daylight. Witnesses reported that the car was so badly shot up that it was totaled by the insurance company. It did not take many such incidents for word to get out on the street who was calling the shots at the property. As far as Anthony was concerned, Summerdale was his territory.

ANTHONY WATCHED SKI COMPLETE his routine, patiently waiting for him to leave the parking lot. He called his watchman at Phase I to warn him of Ski's presence, but the watchman already knew and had passed on the message to the guys on the front line housed in unit D-12.

Anthony waited for fifteen minutes until his watchman reported that the area was clear. Then he headed his Escalade over to Phase I. His man was waiting next to the open gate. Anthony drove through the complex to D-12 where his guys were returning after temporarily hiding from Ski. Only twenty of the fifty-two available units were occupied on the Phase I side, and Anthony knew most of the residents. He parked in front of Unit D-12 and was greeted by a group of men dressed in dirty T-shirts and jeans returning to their lawn chairs in the parking lot. The chairs were partially hidden by a grove of trees to the north and a large cockroach-infested metal dumpster to the east.

In addition to Anthony's men, some thirty people were assembled in the courtyard, and several other small groups sat behind Units D-12 and D-11, including women with small children. The humid night was active with children running in the courtyard while the adults drank beer and socialized. The perimeter of the courtyard was lined with assorted coolers for beverages and grills for hotdogs and burgers. Everyone in the courtyard was tied to the underground community, through their men, friends, or relatives working for the system or as prostitutes who serviced the visiting clients. The drug activity, noise, and danger usually scared off law-abiding residents who fled the toxic environment for a safer community. One either accepted the status quo of Anthony's underground community or moved on.

10

Dr. Payne—Cleveland Avenue Elementary School

At her school at the corner of Cleveland Avenue and Old Hapeville Road, approximately one block north of Summerdale Apartments, Dr. Anyeé Payne carefully backed out of her front row "Reserved for Principal" spot and slowly navigated her Lexus up the steep driveway toward the street, surveying the parking lot as she went to ensure there were no wandering children or adults. It had been a long day, and she was ready to get home to her young daughter and relax. Her 352 students had departed a few hours earlier via buses, cars, or "the human school buses" that walked to the various apartment communities surrounding the school. To her relief, the parking lot and school grounds were a ghost town; her loyal and dedicated staff had done a good job safely releasing the students for the day.

Idling at the school exit, she weighed her driving options. I-75 conveniently beckoned less than two blocks from Cleveland Avenue Elementary, if she took a left turn onto Old Hapeville and passed through the Exxon-McDonald's danger zone. Or she could take a right and avoid Exxon-McDonald's, but this would add significant time to her commute home, and it was getting dark. Convenience won out.

As she pulled onto Old Hapeville, she glanced to her left and wearily eyed the numerous men, shivering in dirty sweatshirts and sagging jeans, loitering around the Exxon station on the corner. Just two days earlier, gunfire had erupted between McDonald's and Exxon, across the street from each other at this intersection, and the school was locked down for almost three hours. Three hours of disruption as the loud thumping of swat helicopters overhead reverberated throughout the halls and into the classrooms. The danger of the environment surrounding Cleveland Avenue

Elementary greatly bothered Dr. Payne and her staff, but the kids seemed not to pay much attention to the noise and commotion. Her students lived in the reality fashioned by the decrepit and boarded-up apartment buildings and houses around the school. Gunfire was just another reality of the neighborhood—no big deal. Or perhaps they couldn't understand what a big deal it was.[39] The frequent hail of bullets between Exxon and McDonald's, divided by Cleveland Avenue, was well known to the staff at Cleveland Avenue Elementary and to the neighborhood at large. Dr. Payne and her staff worried that they might innocently get caught in the random crossfire and be hit by a stray bullet. Dr. Payne was a single mother with a young daughter and other responsibilities. The Cleveland neighborhood was risky, and she paid attention.

Dr. Payne was the principal of Cleveland Avenue Elementary School in the Cleveland Avenue district that included Summerdale Apartments. At 5'7", with a big smile, even white teeth, and a pert nose, she had the All-American good looks of a Mouseketeer. She had grown up as a student in the Atlanta Public Schools (APS) district and began college in the sports medicine program at Georgia Southern University. As a HOPE (Helping Outstanding Pupils Educationally) scholar, her tuition was paid by the state lottery program for education set up in 1993 to reward top-achieving high school graduates with educations at Georgia universities. Since HOPE's inception, some $2 billion in lottery proceeds has been distributed to some two million scholarship recipients. Dr. Payne's lackluster performance in sports medicine's requisite biology class jeopardized her HOPE scholarship, so she pivoted to English, with her sights on attending law school. She changed her major again after completing some academic internships with children, thus setting her on track to become a third-generation teacher in her family. "I fell in love with the younger ones and decided to change my major again to early childhood education," she said.

Initially, she did not want to follow the career path of her grandmother, mother, and aunts. Her grandmother was a teacher in Augusta, Georgia, and her mother is still a well-respected high school teacher in the APS system. "I saw how hard my mother worked and how much she cared for her students," Dr. Payne said. "She was working days at her high school, then she would teach night school and she would even teach during the summer. However, I was going through my teaching programs and seeing the students who did not know how to read. After nine months in my program, they were readers. It was like a rush for me."

After graduating with her own teaching degree, Dr. Payne researched positions in the APS system. Her former second-grade teacher recruited her to Cleveland Avenue Elementary, where she worked in various roles, becoming a reading coach and an instructional liaison for teachers at nearby Capitol View Elementary. She said, "I really helped the principals evaluate teachers . . . observing . . . and providing feedback. As a reading coach, I thought I would be helping more students, if I were helping the teacher." The educational performance of Capitol View was above average, and Dr. Payne was elevated to the role of a leadership support specialist for the schools in the Capitol View and South Atlanta cluster. She was also part of a three-year $1 million grant to APS which funded professional development, conferences, and research to coach teachers to get students reading by the third grade. Dr. Payne said with obvious pride, "It was a 'Reading First Grant' and after the third year, our third-grade readers did very well, growing from a 30 percent reading pass rate to a 70 percent pass rate." There is a clear correlation between reading proficiency and poverty when it comes to graduation rates. About 35 percent of children who live in neighborhoods of concentrated poverty and are not reading proficiently by the third grade do not graduate from high school on time.[40]

Meanwhile, a principal position had become available in nearby Gideons Elementary, another low-performing APS school, and Dr. Payne talked to her supervisor about taking the job. Recognizing her ambition, he encouraged her to apply. At twenty-nine, Dr. Payne landed a coveted role as principal of Gideons Elementary. She succeeded a beloved principal who abruptly resigned after thirty years of being part of the local community fabric. The sudden change in leadership brought significant challenges for Dr. Payne. Even though under her leadership Gideons Elementary had some of the highest performance growth in the district, she imposed a new environment that did not go over well with all parents and teachers. Dr. Payne said, "Some of the teachers had never had anyone hold them accountable

. . . The community was used to their principal and teachers loving on them and saying, 'you're great, you're wonderful,' but not ever hearing any constructive feedback if their child was not performing."

However, her methodical and systematic approach to education was noticed by district leadership, and she was reassigned to Cleveland Avenue Elementary as an assistant principal. During her time in that role, she decided to advance her career path and pursued a PhD in education. She was going through a painful divorce, but her mother was supportive and agreed to watch her granddaughter two days a week so Payne could attend Mercer University in Atlanta at night. It was a tough couple of years of un-relenting work—taking care of her young daughter, working at Cleveland Avenue during the day and attending Mercer at night, and her mother was a godsend! After three difficult years, she graduated with her PhD. After four years as the assistant, Dr. Payne was promoted to be the principal of Cleveland Avenue Elementary.

THE NEIGHBORHOOD SURROUNDING CLEVELAND Avenue Elementary School was dotted with shotgun houses and derelict apartment communities that teemed with stolen cars, drug dealing, gang activity, and violence. The large, blighted apartment complex called Summerdale Apartments was a block from the school behind the McDonald's and housed about 20 per-cent of Cleveland Avenue Elementary's students. Colonial Square and Steel Street apartments, located directly across the street from the school, housed another 30 percent. Many buildings erected in the 1970s in Summerdale Phase I were by now almost completely boarded up and enveloped in an overgrown forest of kudzu and trees. A little further south was Waters Road, a thoroughfare of abandoned shotgun houses and small apartment buildings, with decaying roofs and other evidence of decades of neglect and poverty. In addition to the simple impact such conditions have on neighborhood schools, it is well documented that poverty affects how children learn. Dr. Payne knew that children who directly or indirectly experience risk factors associated with poverty or low parental education have a higher than 90 percent chance of having one or more problems with speech, learning, and/or emotional development. Children who experience poverty at home often have difficulties focusing at school. Also, the stressors and issues that these children face when they are not in school are often bigger worries than completing their homework.[41]

Dr. Payne and her staff tried to keep the toxic neighborhood at bay and operate the school in a safe zone, a place of peace and caring shelter where the children could thrive in their studies. However, it was a tough environment. Despite the young age of the children, they innocently brought the reality of their home life into the school. When she began her tenure at Cleveland Avenue Elementary, Dr. Payne noticed that many fourth- and fifth-grade students wore red, representative of a local gang affiliation. Just this morning, the panicked father of one of her fifth-graders arrived at the school looking for his son's book bag. He was adamant in demanding to retrieve the bag, which after inspection by the staff was found to be filled with illegal drugs and cash. The child had mistakenly picked up the wrong bag and took his father's stash to school. Other students came to school mistakenly wearing their siblings' pants containing pockets full of drugs. The violence her students experienced at home had a negative impact on their studies.

The students at Cleveland Avenue Elementary were living in a war zone, and the stress level was palpable. In the mornings, the incoming parade of young students offered few smiles, no "good mornings," no eye-contact with the staff and teachers in the hallway who warmly greeted them. These children were honing their survival skills in a home environment that discouraged conversation or any form of human interaction—lay low and avoid eye-contact with any stranger in your path or risk a gun being pulled in your face. Consequently, the children stayed in their lanes and muted their existence. The behavior was not surprising to Dr. Payne and her staff. Contemporary brain research documents that early adverse childhood experiences can harm the development of a child's brain. The prefrontal cortex—associated with the ability to pay attention, exhibit self-control, organize and plan—is particularly vulnerable during childhood development.[42]

The students would slowly unwind during the day as they were drawn into their studies and away from the stark reality of their home lives. Dr. Payne noticed that if there was any reason to stay after school for a special extracurricular activity, the children did so eagerly, looking for any excuse to avoid going home. Cleveland Avenue Elementary offered warmth, nutritious meals, computers, art supplies, and caring adults, in a bright sunny safe environment. Sadly, many of their home lives offered stress, neglect, hunger, and poverty.

DR. PAYNE AND HER staff were acutely aware that the toxic community created unique challenges for the academic performance expected at Cleveland Avenue Elementary. The Georgia Department of Education annually set targets for content for English, math, and a poverty index, based on previous performance and demographics. The majority of children coming into kindergarten had no prior educational experience to prepare them for a formal education. According to Stanford psychology professor Anne Fernald, the lack of at-home preparation crippled the affected children: five-year-old children of lower socioeconomic status score two years behind on standardized language development tests by the time they enter school.[43] The typical five-year-old at Cleveland Avenue was entering kindergarten from a home situation where they were being supervised by their grandmother, aunt, or older siblings while their single parent worked multiple jobs at poverty wages trying to support the family. Many adults in the household were illiterate or low-skilled readers who lacked the ability to encourage reading or promote other basic educational subjects like history or math. This translated into students who lacked communication, vocabulary, and reading materials at home. Dr. Payne knew all too well that her average student entered kindergarten knowing significantly fewer vocabulary words than a child coming from an affluent household. The research is clear that by the age of three, children growing up in poor neighborhoods or from lower-income families may have heard up to thirty million fewer words than their more privileged counterparts.[44]

All American public schools are required to utilize a standardized student measurement as a peer review and to identify students who are not achieving grade level in their studies. The Georgia Milestone is the standardized test developed by the Georgia Department of Education and administered to students from grades three through high school to measure knowledge in English, math, science, and social studies. The students entering kindergarten at Cleveland Avenue Elementary began with such a large learning deficit that it was challenging to get them to a standardized reading level by the third grade, despite the dedicated hard work of Dr. Payne and her staff. The challenge was further exacerbated by the fact that 10 percent of her students spoke and read English as their second language.

CLEVELAND AVENUE ELEMENTARY'S HIGH transiency (or mobility) rate—related to the crime and unstable housing in the surrounding community—also had a significant impact on students' Georgia Milestone test scores. The transiency rate of Cleveland Avenue students was 36 percent in 2017–2018, compared to a statewide average mobility rate of 13.6 percent and an APS mobility rate of 25.4 percent.[45] In other words, Dr. Payne lost 36 percent of her students every year as families responded to the unstable environment or other issues by moving out of the school district. The overall effect was that of the children who started kindergarten at Cleveland Elementary, fewer than 20 percent remained in the school and graduated after the fifth grade. Even after her students finally achieved reading proficiently, she lost many, only to have them replaced by new students with reading deficits.

High transiency thus hurts both schools and students. The children generally lose about three months of reading and math learning each time they switch schools (though voluntary transfers, more likely during the summer, cause less academic disruption and may be associated with academic improvement if they lead to better services for the student). Mobility can be particularly hard on children in the early grades where they learn foundational skills. A 2015 New York University study found that of 381 low-income, predominantly ethnic-minority students in Chicago, 327 changed schools at least once from kindergarten through fourth grade, and forty transferred three or more times. The more often students moved, the lower they scored on both the state standardized math test and on teacher observations of the students' critical thinking.

In Atlanta, one of the reasons behind the high transiency rate was the escalating crisis of housing affordability. Landlords were beginning to purchase large, dilapidated apartment communities like Summerdale at bargain prices with plans to perform minimal renovations and raise monthly rents by $100 to $300. The higher rents were unaffordable for families barely surviving on wages of $12 per hour.[46] Local landlords raised rents which emptied out entire apartment communities within a year as families fled the district in pursuit of affordable housing. Drug dealers, who could easily afford the higher rents, eventually replaced hard-working families, guaranteeing that these apartment communities would plunge into a downward spiral as the drug dealers carved out territories. Very few landlords had the knowledge or inclination to manage the ensuing unstable environments they created. In their dogged pursuit of rent collections, many landlords simply ignored the growing transiency, gunfire, gang graffiti, and maintenance requests for pest control and mold removal. The majority of the student population at Cleveland Avenue Elementary was being housed in just three large apartment communities representing 516 units. The instability of just one of these apartment communities would have a large impact on the transiency of Dr. Payne's school and its performance on the Georgia Milestone scores.

The interior environments of the students' homes also created learning challenges. Many local apartment units and single-family houses were infested with roaches, rodents, and bed bugs, creating health issues that impeded students' abilities to concentrate and learn.[47] Dr. Payne personally performed a daily check of students' clothing, eventually persuading the APS leadership to install a washing machine and dryer at Cleveland Avenue Elementary. Several students from Summerdale had sores from bed bug bites, and their clothing and book bags were also infested. She would ask the family to send in a second set of clothing for their children and the staff would spend a few hours in the morning doing laundry to sanitize the articles. Children were embarrassed for being singled-out with infested clothing, and the sympathetic staff tried to be sensitive and discreet, but they had no other option. Like lice, bed bugs could easily spread to other students who would take them home to proliferate into new infestations. Dr. Payne noticed a high incident of asthmatic students, probably a direct consequence of roach-infested homes. Few landlords and parents understood that roaches are a common allergy and asthma trigger, leading to frequent visits to emergency rooms and learning setbacks.

THE ACTIVE DRUG CULTURE, entrenched criminal activity, and bug infestations did not prejudice Dr. Payne's efforts to ensure that her 352 students received an excellent education. If anything, the starkness of her students' home lives made her and her staff more determined to provide the students with the same resources enjoyed by children in affluent schools. She realistically calculated the challenges her students faced and set out to equalize the resources and teaching environment. Her awareness of the critical role that reading played in influencing the life trajectory of children was confirmed by her years of immersion in professional development as a teacher's coach. She explained it this way: "From kindergarten to the second grade, you are learning to read, but from the third grade throughout life, you are reading to learn. If students are not reading proficiently by the third grade, it is going to take a lot more exposure to effective teachers to get them to the important proficiency level."

Dr. Payne also mandated high-quality teaching from her staff. She knew from her research that a student in kindergarten with an ineffective teacher would need to be exposed consecutively to two to three more effective teachers to get back on track to reading proficiency. Her students were so vulnerable and had so many other overwhelming issues in their personal lives, they needed high-quality, effective teachers to have any hope of success. Dr. Payne accepted nothing less than excellence from her teachers and staff, and she provided the professional development, training, and constructive feedback to ensure that teachers were meeting her strict standards. If a student was not reading at an acceptable level, Dr. Payne would create a professional development plan for the teacher. If the teacher could not successfully complete the plan, then Dr. Payne recommended the teacher for nonrenewal.

Meanwhile, on this blustery November day, the challenges of teaching in a blighted, high-crime community were winding down for the day, and Dr. Payne was now sitting in her car at the intersection of Old Hapeville Road, debating a possible life-or-death choice—risk gunfire for a quicker route, or take the longer but safer way home. The danger of the immediate environment affronted her adult sensibilities, and her heart went out to her brave students who walked home in this volatile environment every day.

As an adult with a middle-class income, she had the resources to choose between numerous safe neighborhoods in which to raise her own daughter. Conversely, the limited incomes of her students' families constrained their choices to the few communities with affordable rents. Two men walked out of the Exxon parking lot and along the sidewalk, eyeing her as they sauntered towards her idling car. Her heart pounded as she made her decision. She took a right on Old Hapeville and left the possibility of gunfire in her rear view mirror.

11

Kingston Humphries—The Traumatized Tenant

Ashley Humphries was nestled in the comfortable fluff of her 300-thread-count king-size cotton sheets in her grandmother's apartment at Summerdale Apartments. Lovely blissful deep sleep had come easy for Ashley after her exhausting work day at the Fulton County Juvenile Court. At the end of her courthouse shift, her next job had started—being a single mother to sons Joshua, Kingston, and Dallas, respectively aged five, six, and sixteen. Her $29,300 annual salary as a security specialist working with the families of children in the court system covered only her basic living necessities. She wanted more opportunities for her family and was also working on a degree in criminal justice through the on-line program offered by the University of Phoenix. Her every waking moment was occupied with the demands of family, work, and school. Thank goodness she lived with her grandmother who was generous in helping with child-rearing and housekeeping. Ashley lived her life in the loving presence of her grandmother, Virginia Humphries, and could not imagine it any other way.

At 1:30 a.m., a high-pitched scream jolted Ashley awake, and for a few moments she was disoriented in the warm, tepid air. She quickly gathered her thoughts as the fog in her head cleared. Her heart was racing as she focused on the noise, trying to place the source. If the scream was associated with gunshots, then this was a life-or-death situation which might require them to flee the comfortable bed and quickly move to the hallway of the apartment, away from the exterior walls and windows. Ashley was not aware of anyone killed by a stray bullet at Summerdale, but she was not about to take a chance and put her children in harm's way. The flimsy vinyl siding encasing the exterior of her building was hardly resilient and showing more and more scars from the bullets that often ricocheted throughout the property.

The silence following the scream was deafening in the darkness and she did not dare turn on any lights to draw attention from the outside. Criminals surrounded her building and she did not have the social confidence to even turn on her light at night. Ashley was naturally a quiet person, but she was also confident and not afraid to be assertive when necessary. She felt sweat starting to gather on her chest and she held her breath keenly listening for the offending noise. A deep moan emerged beside her from her six-year-old son Kingston and he started thrashing under the covers. He was sleeping next to her and having another nightmare. Ashley almost felt relief that the noise was not something more serious. She relaxed.

It was dark outside and the light fixtures in the parking lot provided a faint light through the flimsy window shades. She looked at the outline of her son Joshua on the other side of her, and he was sound asleep with his sweet face relaxed and chest rising slowly with the rhythm of breathing. He was a deep sleeper like Ashley and did not easily awake. Ashley leaned over and gently touched Kingston's arm to slowly wake him back to reality. Reality to what, she ironically thought for a moment as she became fully awake. This was Kingston's second nightmare this week and she was hopeful it was not becoming part of their routine. The boys insisted on sleeping with her a few months ago after a night of particularly loud noise and gunfire. The loud "pop pop pop" noise of gunfire was becoming all too familiar. They were visibly terrified by the violence and adamantly refused to sleep near the walls or windows for fear of being shot. They went through this every night, where they had to shift the bed away from the windows while the boys argued over who got to sleep on the safest side of the bed. Ashley was patient with her boys and looked forward to things calming down. She wanted her children to feel safe so she could enjoy sleeping alone once again.

Children go through stages as part of their social and emotional development, with nightmares and bedwetting being typical phases; however, Ashley was a seasoned parent and was concerned over the recurring nightmares experienced by Kingston. This just was not right. She never had these issues with Dallas, her oldest son, but the property was much safer during his childhood. In recent years, the violent crime at Summerdale was escalating and creating an unsafe and tense environment playing out in the form of children's nightmares. She recalled:

> I grew up with my mother and grandmother on Hill Street in south Atlanta and then moved in with mom when she got her Habitat house on Atlanta Avenue. My grandmother came to Summerdale first and I came right after she did after I had my first child in 2001. It was a nice neighborhood at the time with minimal crime. We knew all our neighbors—a lot of them are gone and a lot of them passed away before they closed down that area that is now boarded up [in Phase 1]. It was a real community and we all looked out for each other. We had family and neighbors get-togethers all the time. It was a nice area. It wasn't bad for the drugs when I moved here. But they started selling and it ended up on the playground where the dealers used to be all the time. The manager was trying to get it under control, but there was shooting back and forth, on both sides of the property. When you walk out you see trash all over the place and people urinating.

Ashley noticed when things started changing. The property was attracting a crowd of teenagers and full-grown adults who were loitering with their liquor bottles, listening to gangsta rap, and trailing trash in their wake. The crowds were clearly supporting a growing drug trade and associated other illegal activity. Robberies were on the rise and fights in the parking lot were becoming a regular occurrence. Mr. James across the hall had his car broken into just last week and Ms. Jennings down the hall had her apartment robbed two weeks ago. The drug dealers and their clients were taking over the property, terrorizing the long-term legal residents and disrupting the social order.

ASHLEY WAS ON GOOD terms with many of her neighbors, and they had conversations about the growing violence and behavior of the newer tenants. Many at Summerdale were paying $650 or less for a two-bedroom unit conveniently located just six miles from the central downtown city district. Ashley was aware that rents were rapidly increasing in the Atlanta metropolitan area, where the population had surpassed seven million and was growing by 150,000 per year. These new residents needed housing, even in neighborhoods festering with crime and blight. Many of her neighbors just did not have the income to move to comparable apartments elsewhere, and they regularly commiserated in the hallways and parking lot. Even the terrible apartment complex around the corner on Cleveland Avenue offered two-bedroom units for $795 per month—a full $145 a month more than at Summerdale. Her neighbors were frustrated by the growing crime, but with no other feasible housing options, they all decided to hunker down and survive the violence.

Ashley and her neighbors were terrified of the drug dealers and people they attracted. However, after sharing a community with them for two years, there seemed to be an informal truce where they avoided eye contact and pointedly ignored each other. The drug dealers seemed to have a code and some were surprisingly polite to Ashley and her neighbors. But Ashley and her neighbors watched out for each other and often debated via text if they should call 911 after a serious crime or frequent gunfire shots. The word on the street was there were crooked cops in the Atlanta Police Department who allowed the drug dealers to do their business at Summerdale. The neighbors did not know who to trust, so for their own safety a public neighborhood watch was out of the question. She did not want to be seen as an agitator which would invite retaliation if the cops tipped off the drug dealers.

Ashley worked in law enforcement for the county and had been exposed to the political reality of crime both inside and outside the police and sheriff's departments. She also dealt with the personalities of the juvenile criminals daily, so she knew the irrational danger. While she could probably afford a higher monthly rent, there was no way she would desert her mother and grandmother who were living on poverty wages of less than $23,000 per year and barely affording the current rents. It was unfathomable to break up the family. "What made me stay," Ashley said, "was my grandma. I wasn't going nowhere if she wasn't going nowhere. We were in this together. We would pray together and know the signs of when to hit the floor and everything. And I said we are going to stick together, and we did."

Ashley's moral dilemma of choosing between safety for her boys and loyalty to her grandmother and mother tugged at her heart. Her grandmother Virginia eased her conscience: "They drugs everwhere these days and young people who are lost. Even in the rich neighborhoods in Atlanta. Nowhere is safe."

Ashley decided to stay at Summerdale.

ASHLEY GENTLY TOUCHED KINGSTON on the arm again. He rolled over and she rearranged the covers in the dark through her familiar mother's touch so he could sleep comfortably. She peered over and looked at Joshua who quietly slept through the entire episode. She smiled as she fondly studied her sleeping son. Like her, Joshua was quiet but not afraid to state his opinion and stand his ground when things got rough. He was a gentle but tough kid and she was proud of him. Ashley listened in the darkness for a few more moments as Kingston's breathing calmed and he settled down. There was the faint hum of people talking in the distance and she could hear a man's laughter and the sharp echo of another man yelling greetings to a friend. The pulsing sound of music was accompanied by a car door slamming shut. Luckily, she did not live near the common area where there used to be a large children's playground and some metal tables with benches. The dealers and loiterers set up camp in the common area, making the noise and traffic even louder. Ashley lived on the quiet side of the property. She usually slept unless there was gunfire or a car chase through the broken front entrance gates. She listened for a few more moments in the darkness, then glanced at the clock which blinked 1:52 a.m. She had set the alarm for 6:30 a.m. to give her enough time to get Kingston ready so her grandmother could walk him to Cleveland Avenue Elementary where he was enrolled in the first grade. Not hearing any immediate threats, Ashley sighed and settled back into the covers. She had time for a blissful four hours of much-needed sleep before she awoke and resumed the daily routine.

KINGSTON WAS SCARED BUT he tried not to let his mother and grandmother know. He wanted to be a big boy and fearless like Spiderman, but he knew the bad men were out there with their guns. He walked home from school every day with his great-grandmother and saw them. They were on the street corners, at the McDonald's, and in front of the Exxon station. They gathered on the playground where he used to love to visit and run around with Danny and Joshua and other Summerdale children. He could hear the gunshots at night and sometimes see gunfights during broad daylight. His mother taught him to run for cover in the bushes or hallways when the loud gunfire erupted in the quiet community during the day. He was often confined in his apartment after school because permission from his great-grandmother and mother to play outside was given less often since the bad men had come to the property. They were all around him and it was only a matter of time before they got into his apartment and shot him or his mother with their guns. The thought of the bad guys getting him made him sick to his stomach. He wished he was bigger so he could protect his mother.

On the rare occasion when Kingston told his mother he was scared, she tried to reassure him and Joshua that things were safe; but despite her loving reassurances, he did not believe her. Kingston could clearly see the outlines of guns the bad men had hidden in their pants pockets. The bad men had bleary, mean, red eyes and looked at him when he was walking past on the way to and from school. He would never look back at them. He just looked at the ground or stared straight ahead. Just yesterday, a sunny day, Ms. Jackson, his kindergarten teacher, told the class that they could not go outside at recess. Kingston was smart and did not believe her story. Ms. Jackson acted cheerful and read the alphabet on the bulletin board just like nothing was happening outside, but Kingston could hear the helicopters overhead for a long, long time. They were looking for the bad men and the noise made it hard to think.

"Kingston, are you listening?" Ms. Jackson asked. Some of the other students turned around and looked his way.

"Yes, ma'am," Kingston said shyly, coming out of his reverie. He tried to focus on the chalkboard but just could not get the bad men out of his mind. One of his few reliefs was the playground at the school yard and he was mad that he could not play today. He also liked his teacher and Dr. Payne, the principal. She always had nice words to say when she saw him, which was often.

"Kingston, can you read the words on the board?" asked Ms. Jackson

"G . . . R . . . E . . . E . . . N" Kingston started slowly reciting the letter and the word. Of course, he knew the alphabet, but he was shy in the class. He wiggled in his chair and continued, "B . . . L . . . U . . . E"

"Good job Kingston," Ms. Jackson said and moved on, asking the next child to read more words.

He spent the afternoon in the class and went through the motions of learning, like his other classmates. Part of him wished the school day lasted forever, so he would not have to go back home. He was anxious and dreaded walking home past the bad men, despite his great-grandmother and neighbors walking with him. After lessons in reading and math, the announcement from Dr. Payne came over the intercom declaring that the school day was over and the children prepare to exit. Kingston started getting his Spiderman backpack ready. He had no homework, only one test paper that he had to get his mother to sign as proof she had reviewed it. It had a "D" on it, and Kingston knew that was not good but he was scared of bigger things than school. His mother sensed his fear and did not yell at him when he came home with a poor grade.

WHEN THE BELL RANG, Kingston joined his friend Danny as they formed an orderly line to leave the class. They silently walked out the door and through the hallway with the other students. Kingston saw his great-grandmother in the front atrium, and she signaled him to follow her outside. Danny fell in line behind them as they joined the human school bus of about fifteen children and adults walking toward Summerdale Apartments. They filed past the Exxon in silence, and Kingston wished his great-grandmother could walk faster. The station was full of cars pumping gas, but there were three bad men sitting nearby holding brown paper bags concealing beer bottles. Kingston's heart pounded and he walked closer to his great-grandmother and Danny, trying to ignore the loitering men outside the Exxon. The school procession walked silently along Old Hapeville Road, ignorning the trash on the sidewalk and in the right of way. The sidewalk was crowded with kids and adults walking to the commercial district along Cleveland Avenue. Kingston's group finally made it to the entrance of Summerdale and through the black metal gate, and he and his great-grandmother walked up to their apartment on the second floor. He said goodbye to Danny who lived in the unit upstairs. His mother and Danny's mother had grown up together as neighbors. Kingston's great-grandmother would let Danny walk home with them and sometimes watch Danny while his mother was working.

Kingston dashed up the metal stairwell and waited at the door for his great-grandmother to come behind. He looked towards the playground area, longing to swing and play on the monkey bars. But all that was left of the playground was a hard red-clay surface with some patches of weedy grass. Two men sitting in chairs in the shadows of the bushes were watching him, and Kingston was sure they were some of the bad men. He was out of breath after reaching the second floor and paused for a moment. He knocked on the door and when his grandmother Simona opened it, he quickly ran through it before a bullet could him. Kingston would stay inside the dark apartment—his great-grandmother kept the window blinds down to block the view of the toxic Summerdale environment—with his grandmother and great-grandmother until his mother came home from work. Occasionally she would take him and Joshua outside to play.

A few hours later, Ashley arrived and was greeted at the door by her grandmother.

"How you doin', Ash?" her grandmother said joyously. Virginia was immensely proud of her Ash and her eyes shined with love. "Boys, your mother is here," she called out as Ashley greeted her with a hug, put her purse next to the couch, and started towards the laundry basket. Ashley's mother did the laundry a couple times a week, and she was grateful for the help. She lifted a large light-blue plastic basket of clean, neatly folded laundry, balanced it on her hip, and turned to face Virginia.

"Tired. Kingston woke me up with another nightmare last night," Ashley answered before Joshua and Kingston came out of the back bedroom. "It's amazing you slept through it."

"Another one . . . poor baby," Virginia said, shaking her head with concern.

"I'm worried and wonder if I need to take him to see a doctor or something?"

Virginia was from a different era and approached problems in simple terms. "We need to pray that ever'thing is gonna be all right," she said simply.

Ashley was not surprised. Her grandmother had been a solid force her entire life, and she approached every problem with prayer.

The boys came running from the back apartment, happy to see their mother. Ashley gave each a kiss and told them that she loved them.

III — Re-Sifting the Community Social Capital

12

The Physical Inspection

"Management!!!," Mr. Hayes barked as he knocked on the dented front door of a first-floor apartment unit at Summerdale Phase II in March 2018. Behind him a group of us stood poised with pencils, clipboards, and paper checklists in hand, ready to document the condition of apartment's interior. Mr. Hayes was a security guard hired to accompany us and provide protection during the inspection. On the sidewalk, with his back to us, another armed guard faced the street and courtyard. The seller and management company had insisted on the armed security when we visited the property. After seeing the open drug activity and vagrants, we gratefully accepted their offer, but it was unsettling and felt like we were in a lawless third-world country. We were unsure which apartments harbored the drug trade, but we knew these tenants were armed, dangerous, and would not want strangers in their apartments. In my long career, I have needed armed security to inspect only one other apartment community. The present instance spoke to the perceived danger of the property.

We had signed the contract to purchase Summerdale and were now in the due diligence phase. Determining the risk of ownership and the likely costs ahead entailed in-depth research on the legal title, the physical and environmental conditions, operating expenses, rent collections, leases, and crime reports. As part of the due diligence, my partners and I, along with a team of our maintenance and management staff, were inspecting the apartment units spread across the two complexes. The eight in our group would walk a few units jointly, compare notes, and then split into three groups. Our completed unit-by-unit checklists would reveal the conditions of the dozens of elements inside each apartment unit. Unusual issues would be documented on a spreadsheet. Stains on ceilings would be evidence of roof leaks. Moisture around windows would suggest the possible presence of mold.

What is the age of the appliances and are they functioning correctly? Is the tenant a poor housekeeper? What is the condition of the tubs and toilets? Does the unit appear overcrowded with non-legal tenants? Holes in the walls could signal violence, drugs, and guns. Does the unit have a pest issue?

Most importantly, the inspection would introduce us to the tenants. The rent roll documented 244 units, of which 130 were officially occupied by tenants with signed leases and 22 were vacant but rent-ready; the remaining 92 were boarded up but we would remove the boards to get inside and inspect them. We could easily complete the inspection of the entire property in two days, allocating 80 units to each team to inspect.

The purchase price of Summerdale was affordable, but the blighted condition of several buildings was so obvious that many "commodity" buyers would simply pass on the arduous and time-consuming inspection process. "Commodity" landlords typically purchase low-income housing apartment communities planning to make a quick and easy sale to the next buyer and then walk away with a large profit. Such investors purchase a blighted property, evict the tenants—legal and illegal—and do cosmetic renovation. They might change the name of the apartment community in hope of wiping its blemished reputation clean, and then they bring out bright balloons, flags, and banners announcing "Under Renovation and New Management." The unofficial term for this process in the apartment industry is "putting lipstick on a pig." The new landlord increases rents by $200 to $500 a month and invites the public to come back and apply for a lease.

Because commodity landlords plan to evict tenants as part of a quick flip, they generally do not care about the physical condition of the property or the welfare of the people living there before they purchase. Unfortunately, legacy tenants also are usually expelled in the process. After the renovation, these tenants are welcome to return and pay the higher monthly rents, which many cannot afford. An unsustainable monthly rental increase is a harsh reality for thousands of low-income communities like Cleveland Avenue where the median household income in 2017 was $26,942.

COMMODITY LANDLORDS PUT PROFIT ahead of community, but our real estate company is not a commodity landlord. TriStar is a mission-based "community" landlord with a business model that values the existing tenant social capital as a neighborhood asset. Despite its blight and high crime, Summerdale was home to many long-term residents who were dedicated to their neighbors and their property and formed a network that enabled Summerdale to function at least partially effectively. They worked hard at their jobs, attended church, quietly raised their children, and timely paid their rent. These were valuable tenants to landlords willing to embrace and expand their dignified contribution to the Summerdale community. Our plan for Summerdale was to sort through the 130 existing tenants and retain those who followed the rules and were good community residents. The tenants who were active criminals (or had guests who were criminals) or did not follow the community rules were ultimately nonrenewed or evicted.

We read the stack of lease files—all 3,600-plus pages—and were familiar with the backgrounds and details of many tenants before we inspected the property. The seller had provided the lease files; however, these files were disorganized and many lease applications were incomplete. About 40 percent of the lease files contained no information on the occupants, their family, criminal history, credit history, or employment. The lease applications only had a name, social security number, and signature of the applicant—no credit check to determine the ability to pay monthly rent. The landlord was in effect giving the tenant possession of an apartment home with virtually no verification of their ability to pay rent or respect community rules. It is the equivalent of handing the keys of an expensive car to a prospective buyer with no information on their credibility to respect the asset and questioning why it was returned wrecked. The lack of proper tenant screening explained the rationale of high crime and illogical social behavior we were witnessing during the inspection.

The paper trail in the lease files documented the strong interconnections within the tenant social network. Several tenant lease applications had similar last names or listed similar employers or both. Several leases were signed by tenants with names like Humphries, Williams, or Thomas or were employed at the same nonprofit, check-cashing business, or national hotel chain. The history of these families was outlined in unusually large lease files. The lease file for Rosetta Williams was more than three hundred pages starting with a lease signed in 1999 for a two-bedroom that listed Breanna, an eight-year-old daughter, as a dependent. The paper trail showed that in 2003 Rosetta moved her family to a larger three-bedroom unit, and a newborn "occupant" appeared in the lease application, indicating a new baby in the household. Fourteen years later, Rosetta's daughter, Breanna, signed her own lease application for a two-bedroom unit in the same building. Breanna was by then twenty-four and had grown up at Summerdale, probably attending Cleveland Avenue Elementary. The application indicated her student loan history and employment information for a Fortune 500 corporation, although she was in an income bracket similar to her parents'. Breanna listed a one-year-old dependent on her rental application, introducing the third generation of this family to reside at Summerdale; with the good fortune of living near grandparents.

The leasing history showed twenty families that had lived on the property for more than five years, including seven for more than ten years. Many of these families scattered throughout the property as their children, sisters, brothers, cousins, nieces, and nephews moved into units over the years. The value of remaining a close family unit helped the families survive the dangerous, crumbling environment. The foreclosures, commodity landlords, drug kingpins and other elements threatened to tear down their community, but they remained. It was morally impossible for me to approach Summerdale as a commodity landlord and summarily evict these long-term tenants from their homes after they had remained loyal to the previous landlords through the good and bad times. As landlords, we valued the priceless community social capital these tenants created, and it was important for us to read the leases and inspect the units. The inspection and tenant interactions helped create a plan to rebuild the community around the legacy tenants.

We also noticed many incomplete leases signed in 2016 and 2017. The files made it clear that in 2016 the word on the street was that you could rent an apartment at Summerdale despite your criminal history or bad credit; management held its nose and signed the lease. Twelve lease files contained credit reports outlining histories of evictions or foreclosures, leaving prior landlords and banks owed thousands of dollars in back rent or mortgages. Sixteen of the available credit reports recommended "Deny" and another ten said "Pending," meaning there was no recommendation. Management had looked the other way and signed leases with all twenty-eight. Three tenants gave false social security numbers, but the ownership still signed their leases and allowed them to become part of the community. The criminal report indicated that nine tenants had prior felonies and many had dozens of misdemeanors.

After reading the leases for all the listed tenants, and some leases for tenants not listed on the rent roll, we knew the details of the majority of the tenants living at the property, their credit scores, families, criminal histories, car makes and models, and employment histories. Of course, this only applied to the tenants who correctly filled out the lease applications and management correctly processed them with credit and criminal background checks. The 2016–2017 profile of new tenants indicated an underlying class of renters who lacked accountability and were comfortable with social chaos.

"MANAGEMENT," MR. HAYES SCREAMED again, knocking louder on the front door while our group patiently waited behind him. The door opened a crack and a tall, three-hundred-pound-plus man, about thirty-five years old, peeked out and scanned the group. He relaxed when he recognized Maya Galindo and Sammy—a member of the current management staff was included in each group with keys to open a unit if the occupant was not home. The staff also had a list of codes for the units with security alarms.

Maya announced, "We are here to inspect your unit, James. I gave you the notice yesterday."

"Yeah, yeah, I got it, come on in." He opened the door and lumbered back to sit on a small maroon sofa, rubbing his eyes with his hands.

We entered the apartment and gathered in the living room. I took a quick inventory, noting the lack of furniture in the living room or dining room except for the sofa and a large, worn, midnight-blue recliner facing an enormous TV. Two bright yellow bean-bag chairs were tossed in a corner with some children's books. A tangle of wires and video game boxes piled at the foot of the wooden TV stand. I noticed no family photos or pictures hanging on the wall, nor did I see any holes in the wall or stains on the paint. Over the big-screen TV hung a lone wood carving of Jesus Christ on the cross.

This was the first unit to be inspected, so I started debriefing the group with the kitchen: "The property was built twenty-one years ago, so pay attention to the appliances. Many are at the end of their useful life, but the owner indicated that several have been recently replaced. The property is 100 percent electric. We can check the HVAC units on the exterior."

The group asked a few questions and then broke up. I walked into the kitchen and went down the checklist, while other members headed back to look at the electrical panels, water heater, and bathrooms. The unit had the original 1998 appliances; the dishwasher appeared to be broken. In fact, James left the sofa and stood near me as I tried opening its stuck door.

"It's never worked since I've been here," he announced.

I turned and smiled at him. "Anything else not working in the unit?"

"Yeah, the disposal don't work."

Garbage disposal analysis was above my pay grade, so I signaled our maintenance tech to look at the malfunctioning appliances. We opened the cabinet doors under the sink, and the floor was filthy with rust-colored water that obviously had been dripping for years. I closed the doors and made a note on the inspection form.

"Have you called in a work order?" I asked James.

"Yeah," James said, looking at Maya, who was in the living room peering at her cell phone. She noticed us watching her, and we repeated the issue with the broken dishwasher.

"I'll get Sammy to look at it," she said a bit defensively while making a note on her pad.

"How is the heat and air conditioning in the summer?" I asked.

James responded, "Not too bad. I don't have any problems with it."

We made notes on our inspection forms. Overall, the unit was in good condition. A replacement appliance package including a new refrigerator, stove, disposal, and dishwasher would cost about $1,800. We saw no active leaks on the ceiling and around the windows. The carpet was worn but clean and we didn't see roaches or bugs. James seemed to take good care of his unit. I went to the small closet housing the water heater and looked closer at its numbers. The unit was original; a few dead roaches lay on their backs around the base. I didn't see any problems with the electrical panel in the main hallway.

James had somehow crammed a king-size bed into the small back bedroom. The bed was unmade, but judging by how long it took James to open his door, I guessed he had been asleep when we knocked. I remembered from reading his application that he worked a second job in security, probably at night. The bedroom and closets had no evidence of ceiling leaks. The bathroom was neat and clean but I spotted an active ceiling leak over the shower. I made a note that the plumbing in the upstairs unit was probably leaking. Luckily, no mold was growing. Because the bathroom fixtures were original, many areas needed to be recaulked. The fixtures themselves needed replacing.

The next bedroom was empty. In the third, two small beds were neatly made, one with a pink floral comforter and the other with a blue sports-equipment comforter. Small toys were in an orderly pile in the corner. A few clothes hung in the closet and on the dresser were framed photos of a smiling lady proudly displaying two newborns, one in a pink cap and one in a blue cap—twins.

James approached me as I walked out of the third bedroom. "I get my children on the weekends. They living with their aunt," he explained.

I smiled and congratulated him on his beautiful family. He looked sad and did not comment.

After the rest of the group completed their inspections, we met in the living room with James following behind to answer any questions. He seemed to want to say something but stopped before speaking. We thanked him and apologized for interrupting his day and being intrusive. We tried to be sensitive to the personal lives of the people when we inspected the interior units.

"No problem, I understand you have a job to do," he said as he gently closed the door behind us and went back to bed. His shift at the Sheriff's office started in three hours. With a little luck, he could get some more sleep.

James Wilkens had needed a break and got one in 2015 when he applied for a lease at Summerdale apartments. He was then twenty-nine and his credit report showed a history of evictions with thousands of dollars owed to numerous landlords. He also owed on eight trade accounts totaling $46,038; six were in collection or had been written off, mainly medical accounts that had "MedServ" as the creditor. James had severe asthma and frequented numerous emergency rooms, racking up large medical bills, including a recent three-day hospitalization with pneumonia. The 132 Accu-credit score in his file summed up an extremely poor credit history predicting that James had a 132 percent chance of defaulting on his monthly rent. Many landlords would deny an applicant with a 132 Accu-score, and the actual recommendation on the report was "Deny." But the ownership of Summerdale had agreed to lease James a unit. The signature on this lease ended with a flourish, like James was pleased to put his name on a lease.

His application gave other information. He drove a five-year-old American car, and his earnings supported a personal vehicle, unlike many of his neighbors who relied on public transportation. Although no criminal background report existed in his lease file, it was comforting that James listed his job as a local correctional officer—the prison system typically does not hire applicants with criminal histories. A second job working security was also on the application. The credit report confirmed both his jobs and an income level of more than $45,000 per year. No spouse was listed on the report, so he may have never married, but two dependents were listed, with the same ages. According to James, the mother of his children left the kids with her sister two years ago and never returned. James took it hard, and his sister-in-law agreed to take the kids during the week. He had them on the weekends. It was a tough situation because his children were his pride and joy.

He knew he was lucky to get into Summerdale but history would catch up to him if he applied at other apartment communities. So he continued his tenancy at Summerdale and elected to be a model tenant and take good care of his unit. The $690 he paid per month for a three-bedroom unit was a bargain for the market. He knew the complex's growing crime was a challenge, and he did not like his kids being exposed to it, so every weekend he took them to other places away from danger. He was a big guy and a prison system employee, licensed and trained to carry a gun and defend himself. The growing contingent of hoodlums taking over the property did not intimidate him, yet he was not interested in a confrontation and kept a low profile. James was a gentle, protective guy and concerned with his neighbors, especially the young single mothers occupying the neighboring units. When there were frequent gunshots, he hunkered down in the bathroom until the shooting stopped. Then he would text his neighbors Ashley and Sheria to verify they were okay.

He knew why there were strangers armed with clipboards in his kitchen and inspecting his unit. Neither Maya nor anyone from property management had been inside his unit in over two years, despite his request to fix the dishwasher. After being ignored, James kept his silence. He didn't want to be perceived as a difficult tenant and subject to nonrenewal. He knew the property was being sold and was extremely nervous about his future housing options if he were evicted or the new landlord significantly raised the rents. With his poor credit report, it was doubtful he could qualify to lease another apartment, much less secure a mortgage to purchase a home. James was stuck at Summerdale.

AFTER SAYING GOODBYE TO James, we moved on to the neighboring unit. Mr. Hayes knocked and screamed "Management." Within seconds, Miguel Valdez answered the door and smiled at the group. He was expecting us. "Come on in," he said with a thick accent, stepping aside to allow us through the door.

The unit's household environment was exactly opposite of the one we had just inspected. The small living room was crammed with dirty, worn sofas and easy chairs. The carpet was covered with large colorful throw rugs. Dozens of photos hung on the walls, and a shelf stuffed with soccer trophies and a large TV competed for space among the chairs and couches. The noise of screaming fans blared from a televised soccer game between Mexico and Argentina. There was not enough room for all of us to comfortably stand in the living room, so we split up. I headed to the kitchen. A young woman wearing a traditional apron stood in front of the stove, noisily frying beef in an oversized pan. Bags of flour tortillas, cartons of meat, cans of beans, and other spices and ingredients, many with labels in Spanish, covered the counters and kitchen table. Two large pots were boiling on the stove, and something in the oven smelled wonderful. My stomach growled.

It was hard to inspect the appliances and counters with food and dishes scattered everywhere. Miguel spoke to the cook in Spanish and she moved aside so we could look in the refrigerator, stove, and oven. The dishwasher was rusted but full of clean dishes. There was an active leak on the ceiling above the sink but no mold. After noting my findings on the checklist, I joined the others in the hallway to inspect the three bedrooms. One of the rooms had a padlock and Maya asked Miguel to unlock the door.

"Sorry, but I don't have the key," he said, avoiding eye contact.

"You need to get the door open," I said firmly, "so we can look in the room."

He promptly started searching for a key.

The larger master bedroom was in total disarray, with an unmade king-sized bed and piles of dirty clothes strewn all over the floor. In a crib in one corner, a baby laid on her back, soundly sleeping among the chaos. The mess spilled into the bathroom where half-used personal products crowded the limited sink space, and wet towels piled on the floor. While I saw no signs of leaks, there was no evidence of regular cleanings either. I walked out into the hallway to see that Miguel had magically opened the second bedroom door. Four small mattresses, in various stages of tidiness, lined the floor. Heaps of clothing gathered in the corners, possibly contributing to the room's musty odor. The third bedroom was a little neater, with three mattresses on the floor and a small refrigerator in the corner. The closet held hangers with men's shirts and several nice business suits, probably for church. Shoes were neatly organized on the floor. As soon as I exited the third bedroom, Miguel closed the door and locked the deadbolt.

The Phase II units had washer/dryer connections and both appliances were running at full speed with piles of clothes stacked in the laundry room and hallway. My mental count of the beds added up to nine adults and one child living in a three-bedroom apartment. Miguel was running an illegal rooming house, and the woman at the stove was the chef and laundress but certainly not the housekeeper. Based on the occupancy, the business was brisk and very profitable. At $100 per week per occupant, Miguel was pulling in more than $3,000 per month by renting to seven others—probably immigrant construction workers.

Summerdale did not have individual water meters for each unit, and I grimaced at the thought of the water consumption and cost for Miguel's crowded apartment. Atlanta has one of the highest water rates in the country; with ten adult occupants, the water bill would easily be over $400 a month. However, Miguel only paid $600 a month rent and a flat fee of $45 to cover his share of the water bill. This unit was operating at a loss to the landlord.

Miguel's slim lease file contained little information other than that he was from Nicaragua. A copy of a valid social security card accompanied his Accu-score credit report of 39, with a recommendation to accept with one month's rent as a security deposit. Since Miguel had no American credit history, nothing would disqualify him from leasing an apartment. Miguel listed "Construction" as his occupation with an annual income of $36,400—but he made a nice living running a profitable illegal boarding house. No criminal background check or evidence of income was in his file. Later in the day, Miguel would greet us at a different three-bedroom unit where six occupants appeared to be living. "Construction" must have been Miguel's side job.

I thanked Miguel as we walked to the door, and Maya stayed behind and spoke to him in Spanish. Our group stood on the small landing outside the door and waited for her to join us.

"Does everyone feel comfortable about the process?" I asked.

Heads nodded. They knew the routine.

"Okay, let's split up into groups. A maintenance tech should accompany each group to look at the water heaters and electrical panels. Benny [Glover], you come with me. Robert [Jennings], you go with Lucy, and David and Shawn can go together. Who wants to inspect buildings 100–300?"

"We'll take them," said Shawn Jackson, our VP of operations. I handed him the pre-filled inspection forms with the unit number, tenant name, rent, and other notes from a review of the lease files.

"We will take buildings 400–700," Robert volunteered.

I looked at my watch "Okay, that leaves buildings 800–1100 for me and

Benny. Maya, why don't you join us?" I turned to the group. "How about we meet in three hours for a lunch break?"

TWO YOUNG WOMEN SAT nervously in the corner and on the floor of the next unit we inspected. Mr. Hayes had knocked on the door several times with no response and finally Maya stepped forward to open the door with her key. "Management," Mr. Hayes called out as he entered the unit. We waited a few minutes on the concrete landing until he came back and confirmed it was safe to enter. A warm, rancid smell wafted from the open door. I looked at my inspection sheet and noted the two-bedroom unit was leased to a Denise Shepherd at $690 a month, with an additional $35 charged for water.

"There are two women in there with a baby and they wouldn't answer the door," Mr. Hayes warned us, shaking his head in disgust.

The window blinds were drawn shut and the unit was dark when we entered. We were greeted with the heavy smell of body odor, stale diapers, and rotten trash. In the dim light, I made my way to the kitchen and discovered a dozen plastic garbage bags of rotting garbage, spilling over to the floor. Pizza boxes and fast-food containers crowded the countertops along with piles of dirty dishes and glasses. Roaches crawled everywhere and seemed to emit a low hum. My shoes stuck to the floor while I tried avoiding several smashed ketchup packets with sticky red trails streaming in their wake. One of the young women sat in the corner, facing us with her back to the wall, next to heaping piles of dirty laundry interspersed with plastic children's toys and stuffed animals. A dingy-colored infant car seat sat in the middle of the floor, but there was no furniture. A toddler crawled eagerly to where I stood, navigating across the floor and through the gluey ketchup. He was not used to strangers in his apartment. The women did nothing to retrieve the baby as it sat up and started cooing at me.

"Hello there, gorgeous," I said to the baby who smiled and chuckled at me.

"Tatos," one of the women yelled to the baby, "get over here."

"Is this your baby?" I asked.

"Tatos, get over here," she repeated, ignoring me.

"He is a cutie," I said.

She did not say anything or even acknowledge me as she got up from crouching in the corner, roughly retrieved the baby, and quickly returned to the same spot. She was young, maybe twenty or twenty-one, and rolled her eyes at me and the other woman sitting in the corner facing her. Tato's clothes were filthy.

I continued the inspection and noted the condition of the apartment and the roaches. The back bedrooms were equally messy with piles of clothes covering the carpet. A mattress sat on the floor in the master bedroom and alongside it was a metal cage, probably for a medium-sized dog. The closet door was open, and while there were hangers on the rods, most of the clothes were on the floor. Dozens of women's shoes were strewn everywhere, and I had to negotiate around the clothing and shoes to get to the master bathroom, which was overwhelmed with women's makeup, shampoo, hair care bottles, wigs, curling irons, and feminine products covering the counter or on the floor. The toilet and bathtub were covered in a dark sludgy grime and had not seen a cleaning in years. I exited to the second bedroom. It had a small mattress on the floor next to a sleeping bag. Shoes, socks, shirts, and baby clothes covered the floor. An open bag of diapers was in the corner. In the dim light, I could see roaches crawling on the walls and ceiling.

We had seen enough, and I made my notes.

"Thank you for your time," I said to the two young women who had not moved from their positions the entire five minutes we were in the apartment. They did not acknowledge me or get up to close the door. Tatos cooed as we left.

As we waited for Maya to lock the door, Benny and I looked at each other silently, thinking the same thing. What do you do in situations like this? Do you call DFCS, the Department of Family and Children Services? I did not understand how people could provide a filthy environment for a baby, especially two physically capable women who just sat there without making a move to live a better life.

Denise Shepherd's lease file was complete with a criminal background check and credit report. She had leased the apartment in 2011 and listed two dependents ages fourteen and sixteen on the lease application. At the time, her credit report showed eighteen delinquent trade accounts with several "write-offs." I did not see other past landlord debts on her record, mainly medical and credit cards. Her Accu-score was 74 and the software recommended "Deny." She worked in the housekeeping department of a large hotel chain for $10 per hour, just above poverty level at the time, but she clearly didn't use her cleaning skills in her own household. Her files had several lease amendments renewing the term of the lease, but the monthly rent stayed at $690 with each renewal. Denise had had no rent increase in six years, and it was doubtful she had had any inspection by the current management—typically performed during a renewal. My records showed Denise was current on her rent, and there were no delinquent notices in her file. As long as she paid her rent on time, management did not seem to care about the condition of the unit. Given his exposure to the filthy conditions and roach infestation, there was a high probability that Tatos would develop asthma.

WE FINISHED INSPECTING THE ten apartments in Denise's building and headed to the next to get started with the third-floor units. Marilyn Moore opened the metal exterior door to her unit and greeted us before Mr. Hayes could knock. "I was expecting you," she said with a smile while leaning on a walking cane. "Heard you coming up the stairs and have been looking out for you."

I liked her immediately.

She was about five feet tall, in her mid-seventies with thick, braided hair organized in a neat bun. Her freshly manicured nails flashed with silver glitter.

"Come on in," she said cheerfully, waving us through the door.

Benny and I entered while William, our escort with the current management company, stayed outside with Mr. Hayes. We stood in the living room. The apartment was beautifully decorated with expensive heavy wood furniture and quality designer fabrics. A crystal chandelier hung over the polished dining room table which was completely dressed up with Royal China, freshly pressed linens, and green candles in tall crystal and silver candelabras. A framed picture of Barack Obama hung on the wall. I was not expecting to be greeted by so much elegance, a stark contrast to the slimy green mildew on the exterior siding and concrete stairwell. The interior could have comfortably fit in a luxury apartment in Buckhead, one of the most expensive and exclusive neighborhoods in Atlanta. Marilyn watched our reaction with pride. She was looking forward to showing off her unit. After walking the previous apartment, it was refreshing to be in a dignified household that respected order and cleanliness.

"Your apartment is just beautiful," I said, obviously impressed and enjoying the visual.

She smiled and her eyes twinkled. "Please look around," she said, noticing my inspection sheet and pencil.

I went into the kitchen while Benny opened the closet door to inspect the water heater. Marilyn followed us slowly limping with her cane. "It's my knees," she said after I noticed the cane and asked if she was all right.

The kitchen was immaculate, with black appliances indicative of a more recent replacement. The original appliances installed during the 1998 construction were white, and black appliances came in vogue about ten years ago. I looked in the refrigerator and freezer to make sure they were working properly.

"Are your appliances functioning correctly?" I asked, pulling down the door to the dishwasher.

She said, "The owners before the foreclosure upgraded the unit with black appliances and vinyl wood plank flooring and I've been working hard to keep them nice. My air conditioning has not worked properly for almost ten years. I hope it works this summer. It gets so hot in here I could pass out and no one would know. I have been knocking on the door of the worthless maintenance guy, Sammy, for years and his work is very poor."

I noted her comments on my inspection sheet. A new HVAC unit would run around $1,600 if Benny and Robert Jennings installed it.

"Do you want to see my spice cabinet?" she asked, limping over to the cabinet and opening a door to expose neatly organized rows of generic-brand spice jars and cans. They were in alphabetical order.

"Wow!" I said studying her cabinet. Now I was truly impressed. "You are organized and many people, including myself, could take some lessons from you!"

"I was a domestic housekeeper for twenty-seven years for Mr. Charles

Brady, and I took good care of him and he took good care of me too. I got most of this furniture from him over the years except that chair over there," pointing to a beautiful designer chair. "Lord, it took me almost a year to pay that off, but I did it."

Benny and I went to the back bedroom and bathroom while Marilyn followed, obviously in a talkative mood. I got the impression she did not have much company and was looking forward to meeting us after receiving the notice from Maya. Legacy tenants like Marilyn knew the "inspection drill." It usually meant the property was for sale and the new owners were taking a look. In the bedroom a tall four-poster bed sat composed with a stylish coverlet. A wood vanity was draped with lace and held many framed photos of family members. I saw no signs of pest issues or ceiling leaks. The rest of the apartment was as neat and clean as the kitchen and dining room. I wished all tenants were as conscientious as Marilyn.

"Has the current ownership offered you a unit on the ground floor?" I asked, noticing how she struggled to walk with her cane. Marilyn lived on the third floor and had to navigate two floors of stairs without an elevator.

"Lord no, I would not live in one of those handicapped units on the ground floor. Not me! It's too dangerous and I don't like those units. I don't worry about it though, because I have good neighbors who take care of me if I need anything. The Mexican guys next door are good guys and the ladies in my church drive me on my errands and help me around. I like this unit and want to stay."

"Too dangerous?"

"Yeah . . . all these fools with their gunfire and drugs, it's not safe to live on the first floor."

We chatted for a few more moments, and I thanked her for her time.

"Anytime you want to come visit me, you're welcome to come right over," she said as I walked through the metal security screen and door. She quietly closed and locked both doors.

Marilyn Moore's lease file showed that she was seventy-eight and had lived at Summerdale for a decade. She listed her occupation as a housekeeper and had worked numerous jobs in the service industry including security at the local university and in hospitality catering for a national hotel chain. She bragged that this particular hotel catered events which included civil rights legends. She met many during her tenure and shared that her favorite was Hosea Williams—"He always recognized me and had a kind word to say."

Marilyn moved into her unit in 2009, at a time right after the property foreclosure when management did not require a criminal background or credit check. There was no Accu-score in her file, but there was a paycheck stub indicating that Marilyn was living on social security payments of $1,007 per month or an annual income of $12,084 per year. Her $550 monthly rent for her two-bedroom unit plus $35 for water was the same today as it had been in 2009—now easily $250 below market. To her credit, there was not a single late notice in her large lease file; despite living on extreme poverty income, Marilyn always paid her rent on time. But she obviously could not afford a rent increase. Marilyn was part of the 27 percent of households in Atlanta that had income of less than $20,000 annually. In 2016, 89 percent of these households were "rent-burdened," meaning they paid more than 30 percent of their monthly income on rent. In fact, Marilyn was paying 58 percent of her gross income on rent, leaving less than $422 per month for groceries, utilities, and living expenses.[48] Her health was also failing, which would have limited her employment options even if she were younger. "I have five adult children, but they have their own struggles and rarely come visit me," Marilyn said, acknowledging that she could not rely on her family for financial support.

When asked about her opinion of Summerdale, Marilyn responded, "I just love it! I love my apartment. I take good care of it and was always that way. I always took care of other people's property. I keep telling young people that you got to get out there and work. The world doesn't owe you nothing. You have to go out and get it! That's what I had to do, sometimes two or three jobs at a time. If you want a life . . . get out there and get it the honest way."

She knew the reason for our inspection and was nervous that if the property sold the new landlord would raise the rent forcing her to move. On her monthly income, Marilyn had few housing options. Like James, Marilyn was trapped at Summerdale.

OUR TEAM RECONVENED AT lunchtime in the leasing office, closed the door, and over sandwiches discussed the results of the morning inspections.

"It's an older property and there is *a lot* of opportunity," our maintenance tech Robert said first. He was known to use the word "opportunity" instead of "problems" when discussing maintenance issues. We all laughed.

I asked, "Are you seeing evidence of crime?"

Everyone was silent. How do you see crime inside the units? The presence of the security guards throughout the property kept the drug dealers temporarily at bay. They knew something was up and stayed away. They also knew better than to keep their drug stash and guns in plain sight of their apartment units; at least the smarter ones knew this.

I continued, "We know it is there, but I can't see it in the units. No drug paraphernalia or guns or anything like that. We do see a lot of housekeeping issues." I wondered aloud if the majority of the drug dealing was conducted by nonresidents who don't live at the property. We had ordered a crime report from the Atlanta Department of Records, but they were about five weeks behind delivering on the list of the 911 calls reported at each separate address for Phase I and Phase II. I was expecting a very long report. (The longest I had seen in my career up to that point was 78 pages documenting 1,872 calls to 911 in 2015 at another severely blighted Atlanta apartment community—166 units, and the only other one I have ever walked with armed security guards.)

Everyone nodded in agreement.

"Some of the units have roaches."

"We inspected one that was so disgusting. It had garbage and trash in the kitchen and a significant pest infestation. They had a toddler crawling through the unit," I said.

"Are there any other units having issues we should know?"

"One of the units in Building 500 has a candy store operating in the unit."

"A candy store?"

"Yeah, she is a real nice lady, and her nephew is in a wheelchair and living with her. Her unit is in decent shape and would qualify for the upgrades required for handicapped people. I noted the unit as a candidate for the handicap standard so we can make sure it is comfortable for her nephew."

"That's good to know. A candy store? I guess that is the way this tenant makes extra money?"

We had performed inspections for about three and a half hours, with Benny Glover and me taking notes on thirty units. We had worked out a system where Mr. Hayes entered the unit to make sure there were no threats, and then went on to open the next unit while we were still inspecting the first, saving a lot of time. At the break we had inspected a hundred units in Phase II. The management did not have keys for ten apartments so we would have to come back to inspect those once Maya retrieved a key or passcode from the resident. I was suspicious about the ten units, but it was not that unusual given the high crime in the community. The lease agreement mandates the tenants must provide the landlord with access to their units, yet many changed their keys and added alarm systems without approval from management. With a hundred inspections in Phase II completed, we prepared to inspect the 144 units in Phase I including the 92 units that were boarded up. With any luck, we could inspect about half the units that afternoon and come back tomorrow to finish.

AS OUR GROUP APPROACHED the entrance to Phase I, a young man sitting in a car parked outside the closed gate was intently watching us. As we passed by, I said hello, and he did not respond. Maya ignored him and used her card to gain access through the secured gate. I determined he must be employed as the official lookout guy to ensure customers had access to their drug dealers.

Benny and I went over to Building A and started walking the two-bedroom townhouse units, while the others took the inspection sheets for buildings B and C. The first five units in Building A were quiet because the occupants were at work. We found the interiors to be in good to poor housekeeping conditions, but looking past that we were surprised that the seller had recently renovated the units. Each apartment had newly installed hardwood floors on the second floor and large tile floors on the first floor. The black appliances and solid wood kitchen cabinets were new and in good condition.

As we walked over to Building D, the next on our inspection list, I noticed a group of men loitering at the corner of buildings C and D. I recognized them as the same group I had encountered with Sammy, the maintenance tech, during an earlier inspection. We watched as a couple of cars drove slowly through the property, stopped for a moment to interact with the loiterers, and then exited back to Old Hapeville Road. When the loiterers saw we were accompanied by Mr. Hayes and a second armed security guard, two of the guys jumped into a new, freshly polished white Mustang with a New York license plate and quickly sped toward the exit. The remaining men quickly disappeared into Units D-10, D-11, and D-12. Robert and Shawn inspected the interiors of Building D, including the "drug active" units and reported that they were a mess. The notes on the report were "Nasty" with bags of garbage in the kitchen and bathrooms that had not been cleaned in years. The walls were covered with graffiti and large holes in the sheetrock, where someone had punched the wall or because of fights, leaving the electrical wiring and insulation exposed. The sheetrock in the ceilings had also been removed, creating an overhead tunnel between the units. Shawn recommended we evict the tenant listed as Sharon Allen for D-12 and renovate the units including the replacement of all the doors. Units D-10 and D-11 were listed as "vacant" on the rent roll.

MR. HAYES KNOCKED ON the door of Unit D-5 and a young lady in a cotton dress and hair rollers answered the door, flanked by two small children who stared at the group.

"Yeah?" she said rudely.

"We are here to inspect the unit," I said. "You were given notice."

A young man sitting on a worn brown couch rose and slightly staggered as he came to the door. He was tall, malnourished, very skinny, with blotchy grayish skin. He looked concerned and was ready to argue when Maya stepped in and reiterated the inspection notice. His pupils were unusually large and he looked off balance like he was on drugs.

After a long pause as he gathered his thoughts, he asked softly, "Can you give us a few minutes?" We were immediately suspicious, and the hair raised on the back of my neck.

"Sure," Maya replied. "We'll inspect your neighbor and then come back."

I had peered inside the unit and seen piles of substances and drug paraphernalia on a table in front of the couch. The guy looked familiar. After a moment I recognized him as part of the corner crowd of loiterers. So this guy was part of the drug-dealing crowd, but he lived on site and was raising his family—the pink bicycle with the sparkle wheels that I noticed during a prior inspection was in the hallway.

We inspected the neighboring unit but returned about ten minutes later and again knocked on the door of Unit D-5. The woman answered and wordlessly stepped aside so the group could enter. Mr. Hayes blocked us and entered first to inspect the unit and make sure there were no security threats. A few minutes later he came back and told us it was clear. He stayed close as we inspected, and I was grateful for his presence. Maya looked unconcerned and stood next to the front door while we made our way through the townhome apartments. The drug paraphernalia and substances were gone from the table and the man was outside on the back porch, sitting in a lawn chair with his back to us surrounded by the two children. The woman accompanied us as we walked through the unit, closely watching our every move. We wordlessly entered the kitchen and checked the appliances before heading upstairs. Upstairs, the bedrooms were neat with mattresses on the floor next to a newer-looking crib filled with children's toys and stuffed animals. Children's clothes were neatly hanging in the open closet and a changing table had a stack of diapers and baby wipes. We were pleased that the structural elements were in good condition. After a few minutes of checking everything including the tidy bathroom, we headed towards the door thanking the woman for her time. She wordlessly slammed the door after the group exited. I looked at Mr. Hayes and we both shook our head. The unit was clearly drug-active, and it was likely the substances I had noticed were tonight's product inventory.

The lease files showed the unit was leased to Dane Williams and Shercia Dummond, with only one child listed on the application. The couple had moved from Missouri and paid $1,412 a month for an apartment in North Atlanta when they arrived, but that was clearly too expensive for the $3,000 per month he listed as his salary for employment as a store manager at a national retail chain. Shercia's application showed she was unemployed with no income. They both listed the purpose of moving was "needed more space," and both signed the lease for the unit at $650 per month or less than half of their rent at the previous apartment. Their credit checks listed ten trade accounts at least seven years old owing $53,700, of which two were delinquent. The majority of the outstanding trade accounts were for student loans outlined on Shercia's credit report. Shercia had no outstanding criminal records but the crime report listed "pending" for Dane. ResidentCheck gave them a 20 percent chance of delinquency and recommended a regular security deposit. It was not uncommon to see struggling college students succumb to easy money through dealing drugs. Given the large responsibilities of a young family and significant debt, Shercia and Dane had a lot of stress in their young lives. The drug kingpin Anthony Fowler made it so easy to be part of his profitable underground conveniently operating right next door to their unit. Shercia, meanwhile, had the rest of her life to finish her college degree.

EXCEPT FOR UNITS D-10, D-11 and D-12, the inspection of buildings A, B, C and D showed the units were in relatively decent condition and confirmed the renovation claim by the seller. We would not have to put a lot of money into the units in these four buildings after the purchase. We decided to call it a day and return to our offices to summarize the day's notes and prepare for the inspection of the remaining boarded-up buildings.

A smaller group of us returned the next morning to inspect the boarded-up units, including the ten units we could not access the day before. We were joined by Mr. Hayes and other security while Sammy removed the wood boards covering the entrance doors. It was a laborious process and he was moody and not eager to show us what was inside the ominous-looking buildings. If the interiors were anything like the exterior—a jungle of overgrown weeds, broken glass scattered on the sidewalks, and abandoned appliances, toilets, clothing, trash, and other junk everywhere—we were in for a rough day.

The team started with the eighteen two-story townhomes in Building G. After removing the boards on the doors, we were pleasantly surprised by their interior condition. The seller had completed about 80 percent of the interior renovations only to abandon the progress and seal up the units to sit empty for about two years. The units had the same renovation as the townhomes in buildings A, B, C and D with the identical floor plans. The kitchen cabinets and countertops were new, the bathroom tubs and toilets were new, and the seller had installed hardwood flooring upstairs and large tile throughout the downstairs. The appliances and doors were the only things missing, but we estimated we could finish the renovations for $3,000 per unit and get them leased.

As we continued the inspection, the remaining buildings of this section told a different story. The boards on the windows and doors were warped and rotting away due to age and exposure to the elements. A vagrant could easily remove the wood on a door entrance and gain access, and many wood slats were removed and laying in the parking lot or grass. Sammy was not doing a good job of keeping the units secure. We had no idea who or what we would find, so we made sure the security guards entered the dark units first and gave clearance before we went in. Several of us used strong flashlights as we entered the warm humid interiors which smelled of rotting wood and dirt.

The interior of the first unit was in decent condition but had been vandalized by thieves who tore apart large sections of the gypsum wallboard in search of copper to steal, leaving behind exposed wooden beams, wiring, and plumbing. On the black market or at a salvage yard, the street value of the copper from one unit was $6, but the damage caused by the thieves' efforts was more than $6,000. The unit was crawling with bugs and rodents, as evidenced by copious droppings. We dodged spiderwebs throughout the unit, and in the middle of the graffiti and torn gypsum board sat a single mattress and small nightstand. Someone had been living in the unit at some point, although not recently judging from the condition of the bed. The next unit was in similar vandalized condition, except it was full of abandoned furniture, clothes, old video cartridges, and tons of trash. The refrigerator was full of petrified food that we elected not to inspect too closely.

Two dozen more units on the boarded-up side of the property were in the same condition. Copper theft and tons of abandoned furniture, clothing, and trash were evident throughout the buildings. The scene indicated an order was given to vacate the property and the occupants complied, leaving their households behind in the haste to leave. Pans of food were still on the rusted-out stoves, clothing hung in the closets, and more food was petrifying in the refrigerators. We did not see many televisions, computers, or valuables; the interiors had long since been picked over by vagrants looking for anything of value to sell.

We inspected the remaining units and ended the day before noon. I thanked everyone for joining us and collected the inspection sheets to tally the results. We only accessed six of the ten units that did not have keys and all six were in very poor condition with roaches or other issues. The tenants or management did not want us in the remaining four units, but I was determined to get into them to understand their status. It was likely we were getting blocked by Maya or Sammy because the units had major housekeeping issues, mold, or were drug-active, and they were being paid by the tenant to stay away. Two of the units had large lease files due to long-term tenants, and I suspected there were major housekeeping issues.

I noted that one of the units was leased more than ten years ago to a Ms. Humphries, who listed "domestic" on her original lease application. While it was doubtful that a domestic housekeeper would have poor housekeeping habits, experience often told me otherwise. I told Maya we expected to inspect the remaining four units and would return tomorrow to see them. It was not to be. After dozens of requests, Maya stalled and never gave us access to the remaining four units.

However, nothing we saw changed our intent to purchase Summerdale, and many of the tenants I personally met were much better than expected. The positive manner in which several maintained their units indicated strong social capital. The property and the Summerdale community were worth saving.

13

Purchase and Management Takeover

We completed the Summerdale purchase in June 2018 and were the official owners. It took several stressful months to raise the capital to fund the purchase and renovation (see Chapter 5 for how we did it). We were proud to have pieced together a group of committed and innovative investors who provided low-cost capital critical to our ability to offer affordable rents averaging $730 per month for families whose breadwinners earned $13 to $15 per hour. We calculated that every percent of our capital cost added $33 per month to the rent we would have to charge.[49] Our capital cost was 2 percent below market, saving tenants about $66 a month. That is a significant amount of money for folks living at or below the poverty level.

After signing the paperwork and transferring the money to the sellers to close the deal, my partner and I immediately drove to the on-site management office where we were met by the new operations team including property management, our contractor, and a team from the Atlanta Police Department. We fully understood the challenge to renovate the broken Summerdale community and bring back social order for the legal residents. Despite our numerous inspections of the buildings, study of the administrative records, and meetings with maintenance staff, the many still unknowns made it difficult to predict a management path in the chaos. However, we knew that rebuilding a blighted apartment community required in effect a reversal of the sequence of its decline. Social capital is generally seen as a form of capital that produces public common good through shared identity, values, trust, and relationships. But Summerdale's social capital had come to be controlled by drug dealers who exploited the community for personal profits from illegal activities. The thriving drug traffic was a one-way street at the expense of the residents. Virginia Humphries and James Wilkens, for example, were not free to socialize with their neighbors, enjoy cookouts or chats on the front porch, or enjoy the peace of mind of a safe and predictable community. Instead, they were subject to exploitation and potential physical harm if they disturbed the network created by drug kingpin Anthony Fowler, his employees, and customers. Understanding this helped us articulate our goals to create social capital for the entire community. Removing the criminal element was the first step in the management plan. It could take a few months to years subject to the cooperation by the police department and courts.

Once the criminal element was removed, our second step would be investing the millions to improve the physical structures. We could have started renovating the boarded-up units immediately. But the installation of new windows, air conditioners, and appliances would present an opportunity for theft or destruction by the criminals who had no respect for the community. We had to secure the area before investing millions of dollars.

The third step would be to invest in community programs that help tenants improve their personal social capital and build critical community trust. I knew from experience that trust is the foundation of relationships in society, streamlining people to focus on common goals. Effective apartment community programs are designed to help tenants improve their personal skills by providing tutoring, homework assistance, and medical services to stabilize their lives. The Star-C program (see Chapter 19) that we implemented was vital because many children living at Summerdale exhibited signs of severe trauma from the blight and violent crime they had been living with.

WE SET OUT TO rebuild Summerdale by carefully sequencing the steps necessary to support the social hierarchy of a healthy, sustainable apartment community. However, we decided to take our plan one step further and rebuild the social capital of the entire Cleveland Avenue neighborhood. Our business goals were:

1. Offer affordable rents on 50 percent of the units for families living near the poverty line;
2. Sustain low transiency, meaning high legacy tenant retention and leasing to new tenants who would be committed to the community;

3. Positively improve Cleveland Avenue Elementary School (see Chapter 10);

4. Build community partnerships offering healthcare, after-school care, and other social services.

Our reality was that Summerdale was not in a healthy neighborhood, and until the Cleveland neighborhood improved, it was unlikely that Summerdale would. Evicting 100 percent of the tenants would be totally disruptive for the sixty-plus legal tenants who had lived at Summerdale for more than five years, surviving the bullets, poor management, and deteriorating conditions due to their limited choice of rental options. Many of the elderly residents could become homeless or end up in shelters. Our business model set out to carefully grow Summerdale's social capital and redistribute it between the tenants, the neighborhood, Cleveland Avenue Elementary, and the landlord, so we would create a "win-win" for all partners. Yes, a rising tide lifts all boats.

We easily could have raised rents by $200 to $300 per month. But as we have already discussed, Cleveland Avenue is a poor neighborhood. Such a rent increase was unsustainable and would create a costly revolving door of tenants and evictions. We were familiar with this scenario. TriStar is often presented with apartment communities to purchase after the landlord has raised rents. A review of the apartments' rent roll and monthly operating statements tells the story. Many of the existing tenants will have lived at the property "for a few months" and the income statements will show a disproportionate amount of "uncollectible write-offs," "vacancy," or "below market rents." It is common for the income loss by these categories to be 20–30 percent of the total collectible rent due to unaffordability.

If we forced higher rents at Summerdale, we might be able to lease the entire property, but realistically many tenants would fall behind on rent, eventually facing eviction, unless the community at large was improved and attracted higher earners. A festering cycle of unsustainable rent increases and evictions is why so many low-income families and community schools are in turmoil today. The typical annual turnover of an unsubsidized low-income apartment property is 60–70 percent, escalating transiency in the local school. The typical cost to turn (or rehab) a vacated apartment unit is $4,500 to $10,500 in new carpeting, appliances, repainting, damage repairs, and down time.[50] Furthermore, when operating in an unsustainable rental rate environment, the landlord can lose some 30 percent of total billable rent due to bad debts and vacancies. This is a dirty little secret that many landlords who own low-income properties tend to ignore unless it becomes a crisis. If we raised our rents from $647 to the market of $778, the turmoil associated with unaffordability could negatively impact our bottom-line profits.

WHEN WE ARRIVED AT the Summerdale leasing office after the closing, representatives of TI Asset Management (TIAM), a property management company, greeted us. TIAM worked with us through the due diligence phase and organized a "Management Takeover Checklist" of essential actions required to operate the property. We discussed the various line items including the turnover of the utility accounts in the name of the new ownership, rekeying the management offices, and selecting new vendors for landscaping and security. TIAM was also supervising the $3.7 million property renovation, interviewing subcontractors, and conducting pre-meetings with the City of Atlanta planning department to apply for construction permits. Blighted apartment communities harbor so many unknowns associated with the administration, records, and tenant profiles. We were prepared for chaos.

Our second official meeting on closing day was with the Atlanta Police Department (APD), Atlanta Police Foundation (APF), and our management team to address the rampant criminal activity. It is virtually impossible to completely eliminate crime even in luxury apartment communities, not to mention low-income apartments in blighted neighborhoods. Summerdale was an egregious case. Our immediate goal was to get the crime reduced as much as possible to ensure realistic safety of the residents and staff. My partner sits on the APF board of directors and is well-known for his fundraising skills to support the Atlanta police. His commitment to working behind the scenes to improve the safety of the APD is why the APF leadership was willing to help us. A safe environment is a critical component of a stabilized apartment community. We knew from experience that the entrenched criminal culture at Summerdale could easily sabotage our leasing to new law-abiding tenants who would be intimidated by the on-going traffic, gunfire, noise, and loitering.

The APD and APF proposed several security tools to fit our budget, including private security and cameras at strategic locations for 24/7 videotaping throughout the property. The APD agreed to increase assigned police hours and patrols at their cost. Our management team agreed to carefully screen all new tenant applications, enforce a curfew, and evict tenants with behavioral issues or who did not comply with the rules of their lease. Repairs to the security gates and fencing would help control access to the property. We thought it might take a year to make a major dent in crime, especially the rampant drug activity. For every drug dealer arrested by the APD, another was eagerly ready to take his (or her) place. Customers needed their narcotic fixes and the drug lords delivered whether a dealer was jailed or killed. The business was lucrative, and ample dealers were willing to take the risk.

In this environment, we were rightfully concerned about the safety of our tenants and our employees once they started enforcing the rules at the property. Our budget included 24/7 security escorts for property management and maintenance staff. Private security is expensive but it was necessary to maintain safety while we gained control of the property. Our new security team started the day we purchased the property.

PLANS WERE IN THE works to renovate the units as soon as possible. Renovating a blighted property is much harder than demolishing and rebuilding it. My partners and I were set to hire a project manager who could fill a role much bigger than your typical construction supervisory position. This person had to oversee the complex construction of a severely dysfunctional property and deal with all the red tape associated with federal housing subsidies. But the real challenge was how to outsmart the vagrants, vermin, and drug dealers. It was a tall order.

Jeff Miller is a calm, soft-spoken, 6'2" former Marine with combat training including a tour of Afghanistan under his belt. His honed weapons and survival skills instilled a formidable confidence that would not be intimidated by aggressive drug dealers and loitering characters. His military experience had exposed him to much worse human behavior. Jeff used his GI Bill benefits to obtain a construction degree from Georgia Tech and a master's degree in business administration from Emory University. Jeff was prepared for a career in construction. His fluency in Spanish, in a trade dominated by Hispanic workers was just icing on the cake. His wife is also a construction manager for a large apartment developer and is well-versed in supervising multi-million-dollar projects. Jeff was the ideal manager for our project. He recalled his thoughts upon first touring Summerdale:

> When I see a blighted property, I get excited because I know the potential as a construction guy. When people see blight at the level of Summerdale, they usually run in the other direction, but I saw the roofs about 95 percent structurally sound and a real opportunity to create something special for families in need of housing. I have renovated twelve single-family homes in an impoverished area in West Atlanta and I think of the woman who rented and then eventually purchased one of these houses. After a few years, we decided to sell the house and did not take the highest offer, rather sold it to her, who was a schoolteacher who could walk to work. She was super happy to be able to walk to her job at the school a few blocks from the house. That house had bullet holes and broken windows when we purchased it.

Jeff had the perfect personality for renovating a blighted apartment community in a high crime area. He understood the importance to get the crime under control while simultaneously obtaining renovation permits from the City of Atlanta. If the stars aligned correctly, we hoped to reasonably secure the property about the same time we received the renovation permits. Two months after his hiring, Jeff was at the city planning department to obtain the permits to commence the renovation.

WHILE JEFF WAS WORKING on permits, we signed a partnership contract with Star-C Communities, a 501(c)(3) nonprofit offering wrap-around community services to apartment communities near high-needs elementary schools. Collaborating with Star-C enabled us to offer free after-school programs and summer camps for the younger children living at Summerdale.

The success of Star-C depended on partnering with the Atlanta Public Schools and Cleveland Avenue Elementary. Our earlier meeting with the principal and her leadership staff, before we purchased the property, opened the door to a strong working relationship. To onboard a Star-C program, certain requirements must be met, including a safe and secure environment, a facility to house the programs, and a free-apartment for the new Star-C program director. We also contributed $3,000 a month to fund half of the operational costs.

Once the educational components were in place, Star-C planned to ask Morehouse Healthcare, the clinical service arm of the Morehouse School of Medicine, to serve as our medical partner and provide free or affordable healthcare services to our residents. Morehouse Healthcare is one of the largest physician groups in Georgia; its focus is providing quality medical care to Atlanta's multi-cultural community. Star-C also had connections to affordable dental care and community gardening—all of which contributed to stabilizing the community and improving educational opportunities for families. When we closed on the Summerdale purchase, the resident children were out of school on summer break, but until Summerdale was deemed safe, there was nothing Star-C could do for them while they hung out without a playground or other community amenities to keep them entertained. We would work on that.

Between the TIAM staff, the security team, the commitment of the APD, and Jeff, we assembled a great team to renovate the units and stabilize the community. The workload was significant, but everyone was excited and up to the task. On the day we closed on Summerdale, Phase I was 32 percent leased and Phase II was 95 percent leased. Level-setting these numbers in the months ahead would prove more daunting than anyone expected.

14

Lucy Hamby and the Wild West—the First 30 Days

Lucy Hamby navigated her forest green Mini Cooper off Old Hapeville Road and pulled into one of two open parking spaces outside the Summerdale leasing office. She turned off the engine, said a blessing, and stepped out. She briefly surveyed the property and was relieved to see that everything looked as it had when she left the night before. No burning buildings, no crime scene tape across front doors, and no fist fighting between young teenage girls, which happened all too regularly. Just yesterday two girls got into a fight in the parking lot right outside her office window. They were apparently dating the same seventeen-year-old male resident in unit 805 and were viciously staking their claims. The two-timing male resident was on federal probation and had invited some friends to the property. His mother kicked him out of her apartment, ankle monitor and all, but he regularly returned to gamble and drink with his buddies in one of the breezeways when mom was not around. Even if she was at home, he did not care. He had a terrible attitude and was often aggressive with Lucy, the maintenance staff, and security officers. His mother finally confessed to Lucy that she was terribly afraid of him. When he acted out, our on-site security officers, Edward and Mr. Hayes, called the police to escort the teenager off the property and remind him not to return. Everyone was getting impatient with this kid who dropped the F-bomb to anyone who spoke to him. His hostile attitude and behavior were contributing to the toxic environment at Summerdale.

Lucy was the newly minted property manager at Summerdale Apartments. The daughter of a Methodist minister, she had raised two children as a single mother and held an MBA. She was experienced in managing "challenging" apartment communities. She had the business smarts, compassionate maturity, and religious faith to help motivate people and rebuild a broken community. Lucy is 5'6" with glowing light brown skin, short-cropped hair, and a perpetual big toothy smile. After a few minutes with Lucy, people trusted her and felt like they were talking with their favorite cool aunt. This skill was used much to her advantage, especially when dealing with Summerdale's volatile, chaotic human ecosystem. Lucy smiled, even when all hell was breaking loose.

Within her first week, she was not surprised to find that Summerdale was operating with virtually no standardized management policies and practices. The results of this mismanagement were evident in the poor condition of the available records and the even poorer condition of the property and dysfunctional environment. Apartment complexes operating in a standardized, well-funded, and effective property management environment rarely fall into extreme blight. In a sale, the previous management company typically provides the new ownership with the tenant ledgers, rental payment history and administrative history. In Summerdale's case, the previous management provided little but utility bills and a hand-typed tenant ledger showing delinquencies with no backup documentation. This put us at a disadvantage with the tenants, vendors, and understanding of rent collections. We did not know if Summerdale was operating at a profit or a loss.

Lucy set out to recreate the administrative and maintenance policies and procedures from scratch and take control of the property from the drug dealers, felons, and slack tenants. She had to figure out who was living in the apartments, which units were housing the drug dealers and prostitutes and which had good tenants who kept their apartments clean and obeyed the law. She judiciously believed everyone living at the property was innocent until proven guilty, but the sparse management records gave little information to classify the tenants either way.

LUCY DECIDED TO START fresh by enforcing the rules and regulations outlined in the tenant leases, including a 10 p.m. curfew. Many tenants refused to cooperate and verbally let her know it. They wanted to pay cash for their rent (unacceptable for security and accountability reasons), hang out in the parking lot with oversized beer bottles wrapped in paper bags, haphazardly park their stolen vehicles, play loud music, and fight with the neighbors. They also sold drugs to customers who had seemingly unlimited appetites. The property was operating like the wild west—complete with prostitution, gunfire, fistfights, and domestic violence. The previous management did not tell them what to do and they were not about to give up control of the community without a fight. A war was about to be waged. Lucy was determined to prevail.

Dealing efficiently with the toxic ecosystem of blight requires a vast toolbox, including 24/7 security to protect the management staff, a sufficient budget to correctly address repairs, a great staff team to do the work, and a fearless tough skin. In the first short month after taking over management at Summerdale, Lucy learned a lot about how much she knew and did not know about property operations. She learned that anything and everything could go wrong and that she should arrive every day prepared for constant surprises. Summerdale did not disappoint. The residents and their invited and uninvited guests supplied constant twists and turns, and the surprises kept coming.

There was the conservatively well-dressed man who came into the office to lease an apartment. Lucy pulled out the unit application and enthusiastically started her marketing pitch about the quality of the property. The gentleman politely interrupted her. "I only need to rent an apartment for a few hours," he said while smiling and sliding a white envelope stuffed with cash across the desk.

The request took Lucy completely by surprise. "We don't do that here," she said, shocked he would think a unit could be rented on a short-term basis for prostitution or other illegal activity. "What would even make you think that we do that here?"

"I've done this here before," he said calmly.

She handed back the envelope and kindly asked him to leave. Luckily, the security was just outside her office.

ON THIS JULY 2018 day, relieved to see the property had survived the night, she sought out Mr. Hayes, the head of security. He and Edward, his assistant, were a constant and reassuring presence. Their presence was also an absolute requirement to rebuild the property's foundation of safety and stability—a first step in improving the larger community. Mr. Hayes was around the corner and had seen Lucy park the Mini Cooper. He wore a black shirt with "SECURITY" printed in bold white letters, khaki pants, and carried radio equipment to communicate with the other officers. Mr. Hayes was not a big man, but he had a no-nonsense look and a cocky air that garnered respect. Mr. Hayes and Edward had worked in tough neighborhoods before, and they were eager to remove the bad guys and help the property flourish. Mr. Hayes lived on the property and was raising three children who attended Cleveland Avenue Elementary. For him, reclaiming Summerdale was more than a job, it was personal.

Today he and Lucy exchanged pleasantries and he gave a brief update on last night. Mostly quiet in Phase II but considerable activity in Phase I, the 144 units across the street: "Oh, they active over there all right at Unit D-12. All night long, there was a lot of partying and drug dealing activity, but when they see us coming, they go inside and lay low. Any word from the APD?"

"Nothing yet, I have no idea what is going on."

Lucy took in the information and thanked Mr. Hayes. Since day one, TI Asset Management, TriStar and Lucy's team had been working with the Atlanta Police Department to combat the entrenched criminal activity. A detailed crime report sourced from the local police jurisdiction is part of a standard due diligence program to investigate a property before purchasing. The information in the crime report allows ownership and local law enforcement to design an appropriate security plan for a property. A strong collaboration between the ownership and police department is necessary to address crime in blighted apartment communities, with both parties investing time, money, and effort in creating policy to improve safety. The crime report obtained from APD painted a grim picture that was confirmed by on-site security. APD had promised undercover police officers to help address the prostitution, drug dealing, and other illegal activity. These undercover officers would ultimately discover many things, including a car theft ring operated by teenagers. TriStar had agreed to install $45,000 worth of security cameras at strategic locations throughout both phases; this was a program with the Atlanta Police Foundation. The cameras tied into the central police command center, streaming real-time surveillance 24/7. The APD could watch and record the ongoing activity from the air-conditioned sanctity of their offices. It was Lucy's first introduction to the video technology, and she marveled at its potential to keep management informed. To her knowledge, no arrests had been made, but she was grateful for an ownership willing to address the crime and understood it was no quick and easy solution.

AFTER LUCY TALKED WITH Mr. Hayes, she unlocked the leasing office and went through every room, turning on lights and opening window blinds. She twisted her nose and immediately sneezed. Mold in the leasing office. She was asthmatic and could sense mold even if she could not see it. The back office showed evidence of a fire, with scorched ceiling trim that the previous ownership tried covering up with cheap repairs. Not good! The office interior made a bad first impression and was in dire need of a cosmetic makeover. The furniture was old, cheap, and chipped, and the walls had peeling and stained paint. If she and the team were going to turn the property around, they needed a presentable leasing office to make a better first impression.

Lucy usually arrived at 7 a.m. in hope of starting the day with minimal interruptions. Robert, Benny, William and the rest of the maintenance staff liked to arrive between 6 and 7 and tackle the large list of work orders. The rest of her staff arrived before the office officially opened at 8. If all went well, the office closed at 4, sometimes later if the workload was heavy. Her routine was the same every day. She went through the security report and answered dozens of emails and phone messages. She also outlined her plans for the day. There was an enormous workload on her plate to gain control of the daily property operations in an orderly manner. At closing, the seller had provided a list of tenant delinquencies, and Lucy was using this information to get a handle on the monthly rental collections. Since the previous owners did not provide accurate tenant payment histories or delinquent rent receivables, she had to recreate these reports from scratch. She uncovered delinquencies of more than $23,000 and was certain these were for past due base rent, but she could not tell how much was for other charges like late penalties, unit damages, pet fees, and water bills. After scouring the available tenant records, she determined that forty-eight tenants owed more than $100; she sent letters asking them to visit the office and discuss the unpaid balances.

The front door opened, and she looked up from her computer as William, the maintenance technician, stepped through the door. William was about 6'1", with long dreadlocks and kind smiling eyes. He had worked at the property for about two years before Lucy became manager and knew a good deal about its history. William was turning out to be a no-nonsense hard worker and a big sweetheart.

"Good morning Ms. Lucy."

"Good morning Mr. William. How are you this morning?"

"I'm doing good," he smiled.

She handed over a long list of work orders, which William scanned then said, "Okay . . . I took care of unit 1305 and will get on the plumbing issue at unit 710."

"We have an air conditioning unit out in Ms. Moore's unit 1305, but I have Robert and Benny coming over to replace the unit."

Lucy shook her head in disgust at the previous ownership. The poor woman in unit 1305 had not had a reliable air conditioning system since moving to the property almost ten years ago. Upon inspection, it was clear the unit had been broken for years. Robert and Benny were replacing the old unit with a new, energy-efficient model at a cost of $1,800. Expensive, but Ms. Moore was paying for a fully functioning apartment in a city where summer temperatures averaged 95 degrees with 90 percent humidity. Without cool, circulating air, her unit was the perfect incubator for mold. Plus Ms. Moore was a model tenant and a real sweetie. Her apartment was one of the cleanest Lucy had ever inspected.

William looked up and said "okay." He was not certified in air conditioning repairs, but he was interested in learning more about the business.[51]

Lucy continued. "We have some pest issues and we need a plan to address the rodents and infestations in some of the units including units 205 and 1102."

"Ms. Melinda in 205?" William asked, with his eyebrows raised.

"Yes, I know. So can you help out with accessing the unit interiors?"

In Lucy's first week of managing Summerdale, the maintenance staff received more than two hundred repair requests from the tenants, mainly associated with issues existing before TriStar purchased the property. Had the tenants called in all the legitimate repairs, she and the team probably would have been looking at well over a thousand work orders. Faulty ceiling fans, broken appliances, busted windows, and malfunctioning air conditioning units were claimed by tenants who faithfully paid their rent each month. The phone rang off the hook during the first days Lucy came to the property, once word got out that the new owner was legitimate and would fix problems. Tenants came into the leasing office in droves and patiently waited to discuss the problems in their units. Lucy often had one tenant in her office while three or four residents and leasing prospects crowded the small entry room. She needed better office furniture so the waiting elderly residents had a place to sit rather than lean painfully on their canes.

Of the work orders documented by the staff that first week, ninety-six were pest issues, and twenty-six of those were for rodents. Wanting to better understand the pest issues, Lucy knocked on the doors of several units and was surprised by the cold reception she received when the tenants answered the door. The tenants happily shared their maintenance problems in the sanctity of her office, but when William and maintenance staff followed up on the pest complaints, many tenants refused service. At first, Lucy was perplexed, and then she became suspicious. She knew many units were severely infested with bed bugs, roaches, and rodents. Extermination was a necessity, not an option. She concluded that many tenants were hosting felons, conducting illegal activities, or had poor housekeeping and were denying access to conceal their behavior. However, leases allow landlords to access units for maintenance, and Lucy was determined to inspect them. She sent letters to uncooperative tenants. If the tenant continued to refuse access, she followed up with a letter issuing a $25 fine for failure to comply with the lease. If this did not do the trick, a second infraction letter went out with a $75 fine. So far, no one had made it past the $25 fine, and tenants who originally refused to cooperate sent the keys, security passcodes, and permission to access their units. Lucy also requested pest control treatments for neighboring units as a precaution.

Lucy recalled:

> It took us into the first month to find the first mold case. It was Ms. Humphries in Unit 1405. We went into that unit and she had been living there with it but the back of her walls behind the laundry had some mold. When I thought about it later, Ms. Humphries mentioned we never went into that unit during our pre-acquisition inspection. Sammy had controlled the access and would not let us into the bad units with some mold and fire damage claiming "no key." The three units at the south end of the C building were all burnt, but those were the units that his crew was using and they cut the wall between the units. His crew was storing his stuff in those and he would not let us in. When we first got there, he kept saying that his crew was working there. There were guys living there, but they spoke Mandarin. Something was not quite right about this . . . but that is how we discovered there was a hole cut through each of the closets and all three they traveled through. It was horrible housekeeping, but they are all cleaned out now.

Lucy took any mold issue seriously and promptly commenced repairs to the affected units to remove the mold regardless of the cost. She also had the maintenance staff walk the units and check windows for damaging leaks. Meanwhile Jeff was working on bids to replace the roofs in both Phase I and Phase II, and the maintenance team sealed all bullet holes and other damage to walls to secure the interiors against mold and pests. So far, three apartments had some moisture issues, but nothing that Lucy could not handle. In addition to a new roof on her building, Humphries's unit was getting new windows, carpet, and sheetrock to replace the moldy laundry room walls. We noticed high humidity levels in a few of the units, but this is often attributed to the tenant choice of living conditions. To save money, many tenants choose not to run their air conditioning during the day or will hang laundry in bathrooms to dry, choices which contribute to high humidity levels in the unit. Lucy asked these tenants to run their air conditioning to reduce humidity and minimize the risk of mold growth.

High energy costs are another unfortunate challenge of poverty. A Georgia Tech study that I received in 2019 showed that Atlanta ranked third-worst in the country (behind Memphis and Birmingham) in median energy burden levels of low-income households, which on average in the U.S. spend 10.2 percent of their income on utilities. The U.S. Department of Health and Human Services classifies an energy burden of above 6 percent as "unaffordable." Meanwhile, Georgia had the second highest residential natural gas prices in the country and the fifth highest temperature in the country. Many low-income renters simply cannot afford to operate air conditioning consistently in the summer or heating in the winter. When inspecting units during extreme temperatures, we often see evidence of families living in extreme heat or cold due to the inability to pay utility bills. Exacerbating this issue is poor or deteriorated structural components which reduce energy efficiency in older apartment communities.[52]

LUCY WAS GIVING WILLIAM the day's work orders when the phone rang and she picked up. "Welcome to Summerdale, this is Lucy."

"This is Cynthia in unit 417. I know you recently did a lot of work in the vacant unit across from me, but I think people are living in the unit. I think it is the same people who left a few months ago . . . I saw people coming in and out all weekend. Young people."

Lucy remained calm. "Okay, the unit is supposed to be vacant, so I'll get security and we will go take a look. Thank you so much for calling."

She got up from the desk and called Mr. Hayes and Edward on the radio.

"I just got a call from Ms. Cynthia in 417 and she thinks there are people squatting in unit 415. Can you go take a look?"

Lucy hung up the radio and thought for a minute. We had just renovated the unit, and if there was damage due to squatters she wanted to see it personally. She grabbed her keys and walked outside where Mr. Hayes and Edward were suiting up with bullet-proof vests and guns.

"I'm going to join you just to see the unit."

"Isn't this one you just renovated?" Edward asked.

"Yes, I spent over $5,000 getting it cleaned up."

"That's a sad thing if the old tenants broke back in."

When they arrived at the building, Mr. Hayes headed to the back patio while Edward walked to the front door. Lucy unlocked the front door and Edward pulled her aside and said, "Let me go in first."

"Management," he shouted while cautiously scanning the interior before stepping in. They heard a scurrying sound in the back area and saw two young men make a hasty exit out the back door.

Seeing Mr. Hayes in the back patio starting to chase the two squatters, a young woman tried to run past Edward and Lucy and was grabbed by Edward. "Hold on, hold on," he said softly as he grabbed the woman by the arm and pulled her back into the unit. She screamed to let go of her arm. A fight was starting, but Edward handled it beautifully by calmly telling her to calm down. "I ain't gonna hurt you, young lady. Just calm down." She started crying and sat on the floor.

Lucy glanced around the newly renovated unit and saw tons of trash, food cartons, beer bottles, and dozens of used condoms on the floor.

"That's just nasty," she said under her breath.

She headed back to the office, leaving Mr. Hayes and Edward to call 911 and retain the three trespassers until police arrived. It was only eight-thirty in the morning, and she had been at work for less than two hours. Just another morning at Summerdale. She took a deep breath, smiled, and walked past a group of tenants who were standing in the management office waiting to see her.

JEFF MILLER WALKED IN front of the G building at Phase I, studying the fire damage and taking notes. Dressed in an olive-green shirt, canvas military fatigues, and military-style boots, he was a commanding figure, confidently supervising a dozen workers who were busy de-trashing the property. We were eager to start the renovation project at Summerdale. Armed with a hefty budget, we decided on a construction plan which divided the project into three distinct stages that would be executed simultaneously. Our goal was to finalize the entire project by year end; if we were extremely lucky it would be completed in six months. Jeff would be a busy man over the next few months.

The first renovation stage involved the ninety-two boarded-up units spread across nine buildings in Phase I. We estimated these brick buildings sat vacant for more than six years. It was evident the previous owners made little effort to clean out the interiors after the tenants were ordered to vacate and the windows and doors were covered with plywood. When Jeff and his crew finally gained access, he saw that many units had refrigerators stocked with decayed food, dishes and canned food populated the kitchen cabinets, and rooms were furnished with couches, TVs, clothing, and toys. It required a significant effort to clean out the ninety-two units and remove the tons of trash and foliage that had accumulated over the years around the building exteriors. Jeff started by hiring crews of general laborers. The workers were anxious while uncovering the windows and doors, since there was no telling what they would find inside: live or dead bodies, spiders, animals, snakes, or anything else on two or four legs or with wings. The air was noisy as a dozen men and women loudly threw materials out of the second-floor windows into oversized metal dumpsters that were quickly filled, hauled away, and replaced with empties.

The second construction stage was the exterior renovation of Phase II. In addition to replacing roofs and cleaning the siding and stairwells, we planned to update the parking lot and sidewalks in compliance with the federal regulatory requirements of the Atlanta Housing Homeflex program. I was nervous about the compliance requirements after being repeatedly warned by colleagues familiar with the process. With arms crossed and stern looks, they advised that it could easily take a year and be quite costly to achieve federal compliance. Then they shared horror stories about $10-million properties failing their federal inspections because a sidewalk sloped 1:18 degree, or approximately one inch of height per eighteen inches of distance, the equivalent impact of a small pebble versus the compliant slope of 1:20, or one inch of height per twenty inches of distance. Jeff and I walked both phases and warily eyed the hilly terrain of Summerdale situated at the base of the Piedmont region of the Appalachian Mountains.[53]

All eleven buildings in Phase II had to be accessible via parking spaces and ramps that complied with the very stringent regulations of the Federal Fair Housing Act (FFHA), Uniform Federal Accessibility Standards (UFAS), and Americans with Disabilities Act (ADA). Phase I was exempt because it was built in 1971 before many of the federal housing laws were enacted. But even though Phase II had passed the federal compliance requirements when it was constructed in 1998, interpreting the federal code was subject to the politics of consultants and regulators, and some components were vague and difficult to interpret. Furthermore, the hardscape elements of an apartment community are constantly changing since erosion and other natural elements can impact terrain, and parking spaces and sidewalks may sink or rise because of underlying water tables. We had to achieve no more than a 1:20 slope on every handicapped-accessible ramp, parking space, and sidewalk located at each building, which was difficult considering the hilly terrain. We noted that some parking lot sections measured at a 1:08 slope, or a one-inch drop across an eight-inch distance—250 percent steeper than the 1:20 standard.

The third stage was to renovate the unit interiors at Phase II, including the seventy-four Homeflex units that were required to comply with federal regulatory requirements. Of these, all thirty-six of the ground floor units at Summerdale had to comply with FFHA, and six had to be UFAS-certified as accessible by physically handicapped individuals. Jeff and Lucy worked together to identify six UFAS-compliant units. A few that they chose were currently occupied by tenants who would have to be relocated to other units while theirs underwent renovations. Pamela Bates (aka The Candy Lady) in Building 6 was pleased to be the recipient of the UFAS upgrades since her quadriplegic nephew spent several months a year in her apartment.

Atlanta Housing required a letter from a third-party consultant certifying Summerdale's compliance with the federal housing requirements. We eagerly contacted consultants on the list Atlanta Housing gave us, but few would return our phone calls. After we shared our frustration with our Atlanta Housing contact, he told us the U.S. Justice Department recently fined several housing authorities for failure to comply with federal regulations, including Atlanta Housing which spent more than $8 million in repairs to comply. These large fines created a tsunami throughout the consultant community, with many leaving the business for fear of being penalized for faulty reports. We encountered this fear as we tried to find someone to work with us at a reasonable price. The first consultants on the list either did not return phone calls or said they were not interested or were too busy to work at Summerdale. Since we did not have a choice, we undertook a national search and after several months finally engaged a Missouri firm that was acceptable to Atlanta Housing.

With the consultant engaged, the next step was to engage an architect to prepare interior architectural drawings of the forty-two impacted units. Again we reached out to our professional network to recommend a licensed architect familiar with federal housing laws, and again we encountered a tremendous lack of reasonably priced qualified or willing professionals. After several months, we found Lianne Epstein, who had developed a passion about affordable housing after observing homeless people in her neighborhood. Though unfamiliar with the complex federal housing regulations, she was willing to take the time and learn the rules. Her grit and determination turned out to be a godsend! It took her several months to submit the architectural plans to our consultant for review before we could start the required renovations.

The three-stage Summerdale renovation plan was complicated and required a tremendous effort to coordinate the dozens of vendors and suppliers. We also had to follow the federal Davis-Bacon Act rules for paying local prevailing wages, requiring submission of weekly reports documenting every hour of labor utilized in the renovation effort. Jeff met with subcontractors and priced out jobs for the interior and exterior work, including roof replacements on all twenty-two buildings. He interviewed plumbers, electricians, mechanical contractors, and carpenters, then created a timetable for the subcontracts to be completed and documentation to be submitted for payment and Davis-Bacon compliance. My partners and I were also exploring creative ways to make the property more affordable for our tenants through operational improvements. One idea was to install solar panels on the new roofs to reduce electrical consumption from the grid. My husband and I had installed several on our home five years earlier and enjoyed seeing the savings in our monthly energy bill and reduction in our carbon footprint. Jeff and I elected to meet with several solar companies to explore how we could cut electrical usage costs at Summerdale.

Water consumption was another expense we needed to control to keep rents affordable. Since the units were not individually metered, we were directly responsible for the water expense for all 244 units. At the time of acquisition, monthly water bills were averaging $14,955 for Phase II and $3,231 for Phase I, or an average of $150 per month per occupied unit; however, tenants were billed $35–$45 per month for water, far less than their actual consumption. We learned the tenants had been encouraged by previous management to "consume all the water they wanted, since it was free." We realized that the only way to reduce water consumption was to install a water meter outside every unit then bill the tenant for actual usage. Jeff's to-do list kept growing

"WE HAVE MAJOR PEST issues at Summerdale," Lucy declared at one of our early weekly staff meetings. Three weeks had passed since we purchased Summerdale, and six of us were sitting in the TIAM management office in north Atlanta for the weekly meeting to address all management, administrative, or maintenance concerns of the properties. Everyone knew the routine.

I looked over at Lucy, surprised to hear a topic like this make the weekly agenda. Our apartment communities received monthly pest control treatments as part of routine maintenance. A pest issue must be serious to make the management agenda.

"Yes, we know we have some pest issues," I answered patiently. "When we first inspected the units, several clearly had roaches . . . with young children crawling on the floors." It was disgusting to see rotting trash and clothing strewn all over the floor and piles of dirty dishes and food containers in the kitchen sink or cabinets. I wondered if these parents with terrible housekeeping practices even knew that roaches exacerbated children's asthma and breathing issues.

Lucy gave me a direct look and said, "No, we have *PEST* issues. I received over ninety-six work orders the first week and we are getting into some of these units, and Marjy, it's infested."

Lucy was not one to be dramatic unless it was something serious. If Lucy said there was a problem needing to be addressed, I knew to take her recommendations at face value.

"Okay . . . this could be serious . . . what do you recommend?"

"We need to get a major pest plan for the property, and I'm talking about roaches, bed bugs, and rodents."

"Okay, let's get in touch with pest control companies for recommendations and pricing quotes. You know the routine." We had to act fast because the infestation would get worse before it got better. Fortunately, the new budget included money for pest control. I did not want our families, especially with children, living in pest-infested apartments.[54] I also knew that unaddressed maintenance issues could become ticking time bombs. A property-wide infestation that might cost $25,000 to address could escalate quickly to $50,000 if ignored. As conscientious landlords, we believed that tenants deserved decent, roach-free housing. Controlling pests and other costs while keeping rents affordable is a real challenge, but our team agreed it was critical that we address this issue immediately.

Lucy did her homework and a few weeks later presented Massey Services Pest Control as the best option and price. She had previously managed another apartment community handled by TI Asset Management and had enjoyed a good experience working with Massey. After inspecting both Summerdale phases, Massey suggested a tiered approach that would eradicate the problem, starting with how the pests entered and exited the units. She and Eric, the Massey technician, walked around each building to identify holes that would let in rodents. These entry points, along with noting the units exhibiting the most infestation, gave Massey a starting point to work their plan, building by building.

15

Taming the Drug Kingpin in Unit D-12

Anthony Fowler was not having a good month in August 2018. His drug business was thriving at Summerdale based on an intricate underground social order he and his colleagues carefully had built over several years. This was no easy feat since his illegal business was as complicated as any legal capitalistic enterprise. The logistics he dealt with were similar to other industry standards: sourcing and transporting products, maintaining and safeguarding inventory, personnel matters, security, real estate distribution outlets, receivables, payables, and compliance—all within a harsh underground regulatory environment where justice was brutal and swift with no opportunity for appeal. Anthony had large amounts of cash to safeguard, disputes to settle between employees and customers, and perpetual threats from fierce competition. The carefully designed underground reflected his savvy street smarts and business skills and had rewarded him with a handsome income and lavish lifestyle. It began to change when the property was sold and the new ownership started disrupting his carefully orchestrated social order. Their new rules challenged Anthony's underground world.

The day the property sold, new security guards were posted at the entrance. They were fully supported by the Atlanta Police Department's chief commander. The new security team made its presence known by closely watching the daily activities and introducing themselves to tenants and foot traffic. It did not take long for security to zero in on the obvious traffic flow associated with Anthony's underground. It was hard to hide the large groups of disheveled men, with matching gold chains, aimlessly loitering around the property. In the evenings, a constant parade of vehicles, including luxury cars, eased through the broken gates of both Phases, parked for a few minute,s and quickly exited. After a few days of observation, security got the vibe of the property and started questioning Fowler's customers and employees at the entrance, asking them to identify their business at the property. If they did not identify a legitimate reason to be on site, or a specific tenant listed on the rent roll, security politely asked them to leave immediately. At first, some adopted a righteous attitude and challenged security, but only briefly. They backed away after the guards coldly stared them down or called 911. The new security guards were not easily intimidated by Reginald, Bulldog, and the rest of Anthony's underground.

After the first week, Lucy announced a ten p.m. curfew. She notified tenants that loitering around the property after ten was prohibited and anyone questioned by security and not listed on a lease or registered as a guest would be given a trespassing citation and invited not to return. After ten p.m., every person coming through the front gate was confronted by Edward or Mr. Hayes or an APD officer who demanded identification. It was intimidating for tenants and visitors, but the tactic worked. A dozen trespassing citations were issued during the first week. Management also began tagging cars not registered to tenants, and six vehicles were towed in the first week. About a dozen men who had operated the disruptive car theft ring in the Summerdale parking lot vanished overnight.

The most damaging challenge to Anthony's control was repairs to the front entrance gates at both Phases, which functioned correctly for the first time in years. A card key was now required to open the gates. To obtain a card key, you had to register your car license plate with management and be listed as a tenant on a lease. Anthony was neither a legal tenant nor a registered guest. The newly functional gates restricted access by his customers, and his business activity was dramatically reduced. Ownership was disrupting Anthony's social order and taking back control of his territory.

The management, staff, and tenants watched the new security take back control of Summerdale and feared revenge. They suspected certain neighbors were caught up in the drug trade, but the units had so much foot traffic, they could not track all the visitors, or just too exhausted to care. Melinda Wyatt, for example, was fully aware of the loitering men, but having grown up in an equally dangerous apartment community, she was street-smart and ignored them as she went about her daily routine. However, a shooting nearby on Old Hapeville Road got her attention. She kept the boys inside the apartment for a few weeks until things settled down and the area seemed safer.

Anthony may have been challenged, but he was not about to surrender his lucrative territory at Summerdale. He considered himself smarter than any idiot landlord who followed the law and played by the books. In fact, his illegal trade was more profitable than the legal business of owning and operating Summerdale. Anthony's network thrived on poverty, poor management, and fear brought about by blight and deterioration; he used these weaknesses to his advantage. Several families living at Summerdale financially benefited from the underground and gave Anthony their full support. Further, although security was posted twenty-four hours a day, seven days a week, it was virtually impossible to police a multi-unit complex spread across nearly seventeen acres and divided by Old Hapeville Road, a busy street. Security could not stand at the door of every occupied unit to monitor the daily traffic of legitimate tenants and guests, many of whom supported Anthony. He had carefully built his community standing through generous payouts to cash-strapped tenants and using business hubs fronted by phantom tenants. Legitimate law-abiding families unable to pay their rent or utility bills owed him favors, and he did not forget. He was always handing out candy and small cash to the kids as deposits in a social bank account that would be repaid later. Anthony liked playing the role of kingpin and had grown his influence, gradually controlling the community capital of Summerdale.

The new ownership had a formidable opponent in the war to eliminate Anthony's underground world. It would take more than an arrest or two to keep Anthony away from his territory. He decided to use his most reliable tool to maintain control of his territory and increase his financial offerings. The morality of every human's soul has a price, and he tried to turn on the charm with Lucy and Adriane Thompson, the new assistant property manager. They gave him the cold shoulder.

While Anthony was inconvenienced by the new owners, the law-abiding tenants were thrilled to see the new security posted at the front gate. They welcomed Lucy and her new staff and personally introduced themselves to Mr. Hayes, Edward, and the APD officers, expressing their gratitude for the security service. The tenants frequently brought lunch, cakes, and cookies to the office staff and shared stories of the crime. They noticed the late-night partying and drug traffic was slowing, and they held their collective breath that the trend would continue. Many prayers were given in hope that the families and employees at Summerdale would be safe.

SINCE THE INITIAL SECURITY meeting the day of closing, Officer Ski had enthusiastically attended the free monthly breakfasts hosted by TriStar and the Star-C program. He was impressed with our partnership to improve educational outcomes through stabilized, affordable housing. He clearly understood that Cleveland Avenue Elementary was an innocent victim of the community turmoil and was caught up in the toxic criminal activity in the surrounding neighborhood, including Summerdale. Ski watched young kids walk home from school past the loitering drug traffickers and navigate the dangerous turf wars and gun crossfire. Cleveland Avenue Elementary was in a war zone, and significant change was needed to improve the community. The fact that TriStar was willing to take on a large, blighted property to stabilize the community and improve Cleveland Avenue Elementary earned his respect. Summerdale's large footprint could make a major impact on the Cleveland Avenue community if TriStar and Star-C could pull off their business model. He was eager to do his part within APD. He put it succinctly:

> It all really starts with the landlord. If the landlord is willing to step up and develop a relationship with the APD in a meaningful way to improve the safety of their property, then there is a good chance we will be successful. The landlord can reasonably control the activity at the property; you know who comes in on a lease and can hire security.

The surveillance cameras installed around Phase I and Phase II were streaming live coverage of Anthony's round-the-clock narcotics business. Operation Shield, as the program was called, was a big budget item but well worth its cost. We paid over $40,000 to install three cameras and they repaid us by capturing the suspicious activity not seen by our on-site security team. This program was supported by the Atlanta Police Foundation. As of this writing, we understood that the video integration team managed more than 7,200 surveillance cameras and 10,000 private integrated cameras throughout Atlanta. Operation Shield was a good investment for TriStar because reducing criminal activities would increase the Summerdale profitability in many ways. First, revenues would be favorably impacted when good renters remained in a safe community, versus driven away in fear of the criminal environment. The cost of re-leasing units could easily be $1,500–$5,000 depending on the damages to the unit and down time. Second, insurance costs for a property associated with high crime could easily run 20–100 percent higher than for a safer property with fewer insurance claims. Finally, the social capital gained from the peace of mind of our tenants was incalculable. The trauma created by Anthony and his criminal network significantly traumatized our families and their children, lowered their quality of life, and hurt their emotional well-being. We felt strongly that families had the moral right to live in an equitable community that offered both affordability and safety, and the camera investment was one step in maintaining our commitment. While the APD conducted stakeouts on the property, a backup team was watching the criminal activity from the comfort of air-conditioned offices in downtown Atlanta. However, they were not sharing their information with us, under the pretense that their undercover efforts would be futile if discovered by Anthony and his gang. The fewer people who knew about their undercover work, the better chances of success.

Another positive development for the Cleveland Avenue neighborhood was the apprehension of the local "active shooter." During a meeting attended by leadership from Cleveland Avenue Elementary, Star-C, and Summerdale staff, Dr. Payne mentioned that classroom learning was frequently disrupted by level 1 or level 2 active shooter lockdowns.

"What's an 'active shooter lockdown,'" I asked curiously.

"It's when we have notice of an active gun shooter near or on the school grounds," she casually answered and then continued with the meeting agenda.

I interrupted, "How often do these lockdowns happen?"

"We average one or two a month, sometimes even one or more a week. It varies," she shrugged.

I looked at Lucy sitting across the table, and we exchanged surprised looks. We knew Summerdale was a violent apartment community, but to hear how the violence infiltrated Cleveland Avenue Elementary was disturbing. Dr. Payne's calmness in mentioning this indicated that violent crime was the social norm for the staff and children attending a supposed developmental safe haven.

Lucy and I returned to Summerdale with a new perspective. I stopped at the entrance gate and was greeted by Mr. Hayes. He knew the people living in and around the community and the social pattern of the neighborhood, including the drug dealers and other criminals. I mentioned the conversation with Dr. Payne and asked point blank if he knew why Cleveland Avenue Elementary had frequent active shooter lockdowns. I was surprised by his immediate answer.

"Oh, yeah! It's this guy named Dog who likes to randomly shoot his gun, usually at the McDonald's across the street," he said excitedly while pulling out his smart phone and quickly accessing four pictures of the suspect. "He operates at the Exxon station at the corner and deals drugs, mainly marijuana. He lives in those Colony apartments across from the school."

I was stunned. If this was true, this single guy named Dog caused more terror in the neighborhood and more emotional damage to the kids and staff at Cleveland Avenue Elementary than any other person. Mr. Hayes emailed me his pictures of Dog, and they were passed along to Officer Ski. Dog was promptly arrested at the laundromat across from the McDonald's.

AFTER SEVERAL WEEKS, THE APD detective work started to pay off. One late July afternoon, I received a text message from Mr. Hayes with pictures of blue lights and SWAT teams storming Phase I. I barely recognized the property with all the black and white APD vehicles crowding the entrance.

Mr. Hayes asked if I wanted to come see the bust. I didn't. I was thrilled to hear about Summerdale's first drug bust but had no desire to get in the middle of the activity. I was pretty sure that the arrest activity would attract a lot of spectators who were part of the underground and caused trouble from the sidelines. Creating a safe environment was a key objective of our mission, however, part of me was made uneasy. More drug raids followed and ultimately resulted in arrests of at least eleven people. Those eleven probably had grandmothers and siblings, even children. As committed as I was to the employees and tenants living at Summerdale, the arrests of parents, sons, and daughters were not something to celebrate. After observing many of the young adults loitering around the premises, I concluded they were more misguided than evil. These young adults had minimum wage jobs or attended community college, but because they had limited options of affordable entertainment, they ended up hanging out with the wrong crowd in the wrong places: the stairwells, courtyards, and other areas where the dealers preyed. For them, the free-wheeling underground environment was thrilling but they were too young and innocent to fully understand the consequences of how association brings assimilation. Little did I know at the time of the July drug bust that many of those arrested would return to Summerdale within twenty-four hours, right back to their lucrative underground business. Anthony Fowler was one of them, though we didn't know yet who he was and his role at Summerdale. It took almost nine months to obtain the arrest information for us to connect Anthony's criminal record with his activity at Summerdale.

Note that Anthony operated at Summerdale inside two separate apartment units shielded by tenant laws. We did not identify him as the drug kingpin until we finally received police reports after he was arrested again during a second Summerdale drug raid, in December 2018. Police reports from that raid disclosed his correct name, enabling us to get a mug shot identifying him.

By the end of the year, the plan to reclaim Summerdale was working. Crime statistics like 911 calls were down, and arrests were up. Simply repairing the front entrance gate at Phase II improved the residents' safety and netted Ski several arrests. Phase II was an "escape route" for local criminals fleeing the APD and rival gangs. Suspects who needed to quickly disappear along Cleveland Avenue raced over to Summerdale, gunned their cars through the wide-open gates, exited the vehicle (sometimes while it was still moving), and disappeared through the tattered, broken-down fence on the west side of the property. They escaped down a steep bank and through low, rodent-infested bushes toward the Piggly Wiggly and the fringes of I-75. It was particularly rewarding for the Atlanta police, long frustrated with the popular escape route running through Summerdale, to catch the criminals—whether in a car or on foot— when they came to a screeching halt at our new, sturdy, closed metal entrance gate.

Despite the progress, it would take us more than a year of diligent effort to ease the community memory of the criminal underground that greatly contributed to the blighted environment of Summerdale.

16

The Federal Compliance Burden of Equitable Housing

Charles Bishop strode with an air of confidence and purpose towards Building 100 at Phase II. He stopped at the building corner, leaned over, and intently studied the sidewalk, freshly gleaming from its recent pressure washing. He pulled a level from his briefcase and gently laid it on multiple areas of the sidewalk. I was not sure what was going on but sensed the tension.

"Hmm," Charles said, thoughtfully studying the level, oblivious to the brisk morning tenant traffic through the parking lot. "2.05" flashed on the electronic screen when he placed the level on the corner of the concrete sidewalk near the grass. He shook his head wordlessly, avoiding eye contact, and jotted in his notebook. Then he headed to Building 200 and repeated the process. Jeff and I followed with our clipboards and pencils poised, ready to take notes.

"The slope on this sidewalk cannot exceed 2.0," Charles announced. "The corner of this sidewalk has a slope of 2.05 and will need to be torn up and replaced."

Jeff and I looked at each other and at the twenty-foot stretch of concrete sidewalk snaking up to the asphalt parking lot until it sloped slightly to the wheelchair ramp access. From our vantage point, the sidewalk appeared completely flat. I was pretty sure a new sidewalk would cost $10,000.

"What does that mean?" I asked Charles.

"It means that the sidewalk needs to be replaced. The slope of any section of the sidewalk cannot exceed 2.0 percent. The corner of this sidewalk has a slope of 2.05 percent and fails the test." He went on to the next building with his briefcase and level. I looked at my watch. Only 8:35 a.m. and the day was not starting out well. I had a feeling it would be full of bad news and the announcement that we must tear up a concrete sidewalk was a bad omen. Phase II of Summerdale consisted of eleven buildings. At $10,000 per sidewalk, we could easily spend $110,000 to replace concrete that appeared to look flat and accessible to my untrained eye. The funds for this work were not included in the budget.

Charles is an inspector with a Missouri engineering firm specializing in federal housing compliance laws, and we were relieved to have him at Summerdale. It took about nine months and countless discussions with prospective firms around the country to find a qualified engineering firm willing to take the assignment and help us pass this federal requirement, but we had no choice. Our tenants could not participate in the Homeflex program unless a qualified inspector provided a letter verifying Summerdale complied with the layers of complicated federal housing laws. UFAS, ADA and FHA [see box, next page] were vague legal concepts to my partners and me and showed up on our radar when we finalized the agreement with the Atlanta Housing Authority requiring us to set aside seventy-four public housing units. Conversations started several months before we signed the purchase agreement, with AHA politely suggesting we make compliance a priority because it would be the most complicated, difficult, and time consuming component of our Homeflex agreements. Up to this point in my career, I had purposely avoided the red tape associated with the federal housing laws because TriStar did not use federal rent subsidies. Our portfolio up to then had consisted of older apartment communities constructed prior to the adoption of federal housing laws, thus sparing us from finding an inspector willing to ink their name on an AHA contract. But that was where we now were.

The first prospective inspector showed up at the property, poked around, left, and never returned phone calls. The next three prospective inspectors also elected not to return our phone calls. The fifth prospective inspection firm quoted an outrageous fee and said that "no one wanted to work with the government and the complex UFAS, FHA, and ADA compliance rules." The pool of companies willing to work on affordable housing compliance was shrinking.

We were thus thrilled to engage Charles. We contracted with his firm to conduct three on-site property inspections over a three-month period. In exchange, we hoped he would provide a third-party compliance letter verifying that Phase II complied with all federal housing laws. Meanwhile, Phase I was waived from compliance because it was built in 1971 and 1973, prior to FHA, and because some of its units were two-story townhomes with bedrooms and bathrooms on their second floor and thus could not be altered to full accessibility. Further, grade-slope requirements could not be met on its non-townhome units because the property was built on a hill. However, accessibility compliance still would have required upgrades

---

FEDERAL LAWS AFFECTING DISABILITIES IN HOUSING

The Rehabilitation Act of 1973 was the first disability civil rights law enacted in the United States and is better known as the **Uniform Federal Accessibility Standards** (UFAS). It prohibits discrimination against people with disabilities in programs that receive federal financial assistance for properties with more than four units and built after July 11, 1988.

The 1975 Education for All Handicapped Children Act helped states and localities protect the rights and meet the needs of infants, toddlers, children, and youth with disabilities and their families. The law was reauthorized in 1990 and its name changed to the **Individuals with Disabilities Education Act** (IDEA).

UFAS set the stage for the 1990 enactment of the **Americans with Disabilities Act** (ADA) that prohibits discrimination and guarantees that people with disabilities have the same opportunities as everyone else to participate in the mainstream of American life, including in State and local government programs and services. Modeled after the Civil Rights Act of 1964, the ADA is an "equal opportunity" law for people with disabilities.

Section 504 of the Rehabilitation Act of 1973 works with the ADA and IDEA to protect children and adults with disabilities from exclusion, and unequal treatment in schools, jobs, and the community.

Title VIII of the Civil Rights Act of 1968, commonly known as the **Fair Housing Act** (FHA), prohibits discrimination in the sale, rental, and financing of dwellings based on race, color, religion, sex, and national origin. These protections were extended to disability and familial status in 1988 with the passage of the **Fair Housing Amendments Act** (FHAA), establishing design and construction requirements for multifamily housing built for occupancy after March 13, 1991. Violations are regarded as unlawful discrimination.

to six units,[55] so we compromised and made six additional units compliant in Phase II.[56] When Phase II was built in 1998, it complied with UFAS and FHA, so we did not anticipate any issues because the rules had not changed since it was constructed. Both phases were required to comply with ADA.[57]

Charles walked around the remaining buildings with Jeff and me behind him paying rapt attention. We could not afford to miss anything he uncovered. "This isn't an inspection for a DCA [Georgia Department of Community Affairs] Tax Credit deal, is it?" Charles asked anxiously after turning around to face us in front of Building 500. "We don't do inspections for DCA compliance, too complicated and risky."[58]

I reassured him, "No, this is an inspection for compliance with the Atlanta Housing Authority Homeflex program."

"Oh, that's okay then. We can handle that." He seemed relieved but continued, "If this was for DCA, we would have declined the contract."

We completed the exterior inspection and then Charles focused on the forty-two interior units required to be handicapped accessible as part of compliance. In anticipation of the inspection, I had researched the requirements and visited the HUD website to understand the UFAS and FHA elements which predominantly covered the interior elements. After reviewing the checklists, I finally understood the frustration of my colleagues. The ADA, UFAS, and FHA compliance checklists totaled 679 pages summarized in three documents. This was just for the structural elements. There were other requirements for wages and other issues. We were required to pay fair wages per the 1931 Davis-Bacon Act, the federal law ensuring that all on-site construction workers are paid fair wages, benefits, and overtime when they are working on government-funded projects. The Homeflex affordable housing voucher program was creating a significant amount of work for our management staff. Adriane and Jeff held us accountable by filling in the weekly paperwork (in blue ink) to prove that every construction worker earned an hourly wage that the government considered to be fair.[59]

Charles, Jeff, and I inspected the parking spaces, sidewalks, and other exterior elements for several hours. Charles took notes in his computer tablet and pulled out his tape measure dozens of times as he inspected each of the thirty-six ground-floor units. He measured the height of the thermostats, counters, toilets, cabinets, floor barriers, doorways, grab bars, and dozens of other elements. The whole exercise took four hours. Afterwards, Charles spent the rest of the afternoon with Lianne who answered questions about how Summerdale's renovations complied with federal rules. I drove away that afternoon with a sense of doom at the thought of a lengthy inspection report that undoubtedly would be full of challenges with limited but expensive solutions.

A FEW WEEKS LATER, we received the first of three reports summarizing Charles's findings on Phase II. The results were even worse than I had expected. Summerdale failed 139 of 293 federal checkpoints. Our electrical switches measured a half-inch more than the forty-eight-inch compliance height. Some grab bars next to toilets were one-fourth inch higher than the mandated thirty-six inches. A small section of our parking spaces exceeded a 2 percent slope or were not wide enough. The most concerning violation was the bathtubs which, per the report, were configured with the water spigots on the wrong wall facing the wrong direction. To comply, the plumbing in every bathtub would have to be reversed. It took a few moments to absorb all this bad news.

A dejected Jeff reported, "I ran my calculator and estimated the cost at $6,350 per bathroom multiplied by thirty-eight apartments and two bathtubs per apartment, or $482,000." Trying to be helpful, he added, "This is the cost of the outside contractor. We could save some money if we do it in-house."

I took a deep breath that did not ease my panic. "Why so expensive?"

He said, "We have to completely tear out bathtubs, tile, and plumbing fixtures for seventy-six bathrooms, relocate the plumbing lines for hot and cold water to the opposite side of the tub wall, and put it all back together again."

We did not have $482,000 in the budget to flip seventy-six bathtubs. But more than the cost, there was the puzzle that the property had passed federal compliance requirements when it was built in 1998. I could not imagine that in the past twenty years the federal government had changed the rules to require such an expensive repair. Even worse, the financial impact would

Blight destroys not only apartment complexes but entire neighborhoods. Top and left, boarded-up buildings at Summerdale Apartments in 2017. Bottom left, an abandoned single-family house on an adjacent street. Bottom right, the closed McDonald's in the Cleveland Avenue community.

Restoring the boarded-up units to livable and rentable condition was complicated because many had been vandalized and stripped of wiring and plumbing that was sold to scrap dealers.

We assembled a dedicated construction crew, drew up plans, secured permits, cleared out the trash and damage, and got to work, one building at a time.

Renovation required exacting compliance with building codes and regulations. New sidewalks, for example, could not have slopes that deviated from disability standards. Gradually the work was completed and Summerdale took on a fresh, welcoming appearance.

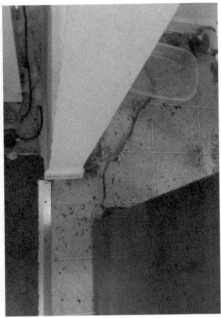

Blight does not apply only to abandonment. Even occupied units that have been neglected for years by absentee landlords and tenants' terrible housekeeping can have rat and roach infestations and mold that make life miserable and cause asthma and other illnesses.

For years, Summerdale had been plagued by crime—drugs, prostitution, car theft, illegally occupied apartments, loud music and partying at all hours, loitering, random gunfire, bullying, and threats. This went on within the apartment community and at the Exxon station on the corner. Residents were prisoners within their units.

We chained gates to restrict illicit traffic. And we hired new security and formed a partnership with the Atlanta Police. Finally, after long investigation and surveillance, there was a raid and arrests:

December 21, 2018 Apt D12 - Undercover Police Raid
Springview Apartments

Renovations included fresh paint inside and out, updated appliances, landscaping, and repaving and striping of the parking areas.

Above left, a Covid-masked team of volunteer tree planters. Above right, Summerdale's children loved their new KABOOM! playground, which was constructed by another tremendous set of volunteers, below, from across metro Atlanta.

Top, with the criminal element arrested and evicted, the outdoor spaces were cleaned up and returned to the legal residents. Left, I'm flanked by City of Atlanta leaders and partners at the ribbon cutting for the newly renovated Star-C facility.

Throughout, one of our key partners was the Cleveland Avenue Elementary School, which benefited from reduced student transiency as Summerdale stabilized. Our Star-C Communities afterschool program served both schoolchildren and their working parents.

In 2017, my TriStar partners and I had purchased Summerdale, a blighted, overgrown apartment community, with the goal of turning it around and making it a decent place for working families to live.

And so we did.

be passed on to tenants, about $80.29 per month in additional rent. We wanted to comply with federal rules, but we needed to balance the compliance costs with our mission to achieve rental affordability.[60]

Jeff and I scoured the UFAS building rules and could not locate language indicating that our existing bathtub configuration was incorrect. We called Charles's boss to discuss the infractions, and he was adamant that if we did not flip the tubs as the report recommended, he would not issue the required Homeflex compliance letter. It was impossible not to be frustrated. We reached out to the Atlanta Housing Authority for advice. Our sympathetic AHA contact shared a similar situation involving another senior apartment community in his portfolio. The owners hired the same consulting firm who also would not sign a compliance letter unless all tubs were flipped. The final cost was more than $1 million.

We did not give up so easily. We hired an attorney who specializes in federal housing law. After a three-week delay to review the housing laws and our design drawings, the attorney concluded that only the two-bedroom "sensory" UFAS units needed the plumbing and tubs reversed. That $12,700 cost was still not budgeted, but it was much cheaper than the $482,000 cost we faced per Charles's report. The attorney agreed to provide a letter to our consultant with the legal opinion that flipping the tubs was not necessary. Charles's firm accepted that opinion, adjusted their report, and removed the requirement to flip tubs in all units except the sensory units.

In September, Lucy gave us a list recommending the six units best-qualified to meet the strict UFAS and sensory compliance requirements. Pamela Bates was on the list. Her quadriplegic nephew lived in Florida and often visited her apartment for several months for specialized care in Atlanta. Pamela enthusiastically agreed to renovate her unit to better accommodate her disabled nephew. Melinda agreed to upgrade her unit 205 to accommodate her deaf mother. We gave the list to Jeff and Lianne so they could outline the scope of work. Jeff assembled a quote and the cost was approximately $7,000 per unit to do the repairs with in-house labor, including new kitchen cabinets and other upgrades. We were ready to get these renovations completed and the compliance requirement behind us.

17

The Management Office

In early September 2018 I pulled up to Summerdale and patiently used my access card to get through the gate. It had been two busy, productive months since we purchased the property. The area outside the management office was crowded—full of parked cars and people walking through the property and going about their business. I was scheduled to inspect the UFAS upgrades with Jeff and to meet with Lucy to discuss a myriad of management items. I noticed that Edward was posted near the entrance gate, keenly eyeing two young men as they walked along Old Hapeville Road. At 5'7", his lean muscular body defied his fifty-two years, and his dark blue cotton shirt boldly printed with "Security" commanded respect. His poise, dress, and cold stare left no illusions—the underground was starting to realize *Edward don't play!*

He was standing under a shade tree outside the leasing office as the two men made a sharp right and nonchalantly approached the front gate. Edward abruptly left his post and approached the pair, who slightly turned from him avoiding eye contact. After sitting vigil at the front entrance during the last two months, Edward knew the vibe of the property and the faces of the residents. He didn't recognize these two.

"Can I help you?" He asked confidently while approaching them.

They slowed down as Edward neared them and tried to size him up. Both appeared to be about eighteen years old, thin, and wearing cotton shirts hanging over their blue jeans with the latest designer Nikes. They looked at each other and then back at Edward.

"Yeah, we here to visit a friend," one said.

"Who your friend?" Edward asked.

"Just a friend. Lives in Unit 204."

"Oh, yeah, what's your friend's name who lives in 204?" Edward pressed.

"What, we gotta have permission to come on the property?"

The teens attempted to look outraged, but Edward was not buying it. He put these two among the crowd that had been coming to Summerdale and smoking weed with their homies in a shady area at the back corner of the property. Afterwards, they would take the shortcut through the broken fence and head to the Piggly Wiggly store for snacks that satisfied their munchies. Edward had seen the game played out many times. For too long Summerdale had been known as the "hang-out" spot to buy dope and mosey over to the commercial district for a little grub from the half-dozen fast-food wings, subs, and soul food restaurants along that stretch.

"Either tell me the name of your friend or keep moving," Edward said, giving them a grave stare.

The teens froze for a moment then realized other people were watching the confrontation. They casually backed up, turned, and walked towards Old Hapeville Road without a backwards glance. Edward returned to the shady post and shook his head.

"You have any idea what that was about?" I asked after witnessing the scene.

"Naw . . . just teenagers, but I know where they was going. They were up to no good and we don't need that at our property. If they was on site, I would have gotten a copy of their driver's license and issued a trespassing warning. That tends to do the trick for uninvited guests."

WE STOOD TOGETHER FOR a few more minutes, comfortably gazing around the apartment community which was now buzzing with construction activity. We had launched the management plan to improve the apartment community's exterior aesthetics, and Lucy, Jeff, and the contractors were busy. We could hear hammers banging in the distance as two dozen workers replaced roof shingles on two buildings in the back section of the property. Six roofs were completed, and only three remained in the queue. Jeff was out in front of Building 900 supervising a crew pouring a new concrete sidewalk required to meet compliance with our Atlanta Housing Authority contract. Freshly poured sidewalks at seven other buildings were smooth and unblemished in the heat. Lucy retained a contractor to remove the trash throughout the property, and a landscaping crew just completed its weekly lawn maintenance, including bush pruning and mowing. The new roofs, freshly poured sidewalks, and recent landscaping gave the property a cleaner, crisp look. Sunbright Pressure Wash was scheduled to remove the brownish green mildew on the siding, followed by a parking lot repaving and striping by Asphalt Enterprises Inc. when the roofing was complete. We looked to have it all completed within a month. The transformation was exciting to watch.

"Yeah," Edward said chuckling after we silently watched the activity for a few minutes, "we was here early yesterday morning and there was a guy at Building 1300 messing with an air conditioner unit trying to steal the copper. We was about to call the police when we learned it was your maintenance guy trying to replace the unit!"

"You mean Robert?" I said incredulously. Robert had been with our company for over fifteen years and was as loyal and hardworking an employee as you could find.

"Yeah, that's him. I guess he was trying to change out an air conditioning unit for Ms. Moore in Unit 1305 and we thought he was trying to steal the unit. I guess things are changing 'round here," he smiled.

Things were indeed changing at Summerdale, but we knew we had a long way to go before the property was stabilized and Cleveland Avenue Elementary was a thriving school. With a few months under our organized approach, the physical changes were visible and encouraging; however, Summerdale's moral culture would be slower to improve. The emotional scars from the criminal violence, roaches, and blight could take years to heal. Community transformation is slow diligent work, but we were steadily making progress.

Ironically, the most noticeable changes were what we no longer had to see. Gone was the unwelcome foot traffic and large groups of loiterers, with their brown bags of beer and liquor and their hostile stares. The combined efforts of the APD undercover officers, our stricter tenant screening, and full-time security were paying off. We also had the full attention of Lieutenant Ski and the APD leadership, which now quickly responded to calls from our security staff. The word was out, and many young thugs found themselves as unwelcome guests with trespassing violations issued by Mr. Hayes and Edward. We had notified tenants they had four weeks to register their car tags at the front office and started towing unregistered cars. A total of eight cars had been towed to date, with many more to go.

Our security plan was a well-organized approach to addressing crime. We understood that a structured, coordinated effort was required by management, maintenance staff, the tenants, and the APD but it could take years to remove the criminal element. For the most part, everyone was tackling the crime head-on. We spent $4,653 repairing the front gates and replacing the bollards, which greatly reduced unwelcome foot and vehicular traffic.

MEANWHILE, LUCY WAS STRICTLY screening new tenant applications, rejecting about 80 percent for reasons such as prior felony arrests (predominantly drug dealers), poor credit, or large balances due to other landlords. When rebuilding a blighted apartment community, landlords must be patient and sensitive to the quality of tenants. We could not have tenants who would jeopardize our efforts around children and family programs to improve Cleveland Avenue Elementary. We also carefully screened existing tenants, leading to eviction proceedings against three who exhibited criminal behavior issues and would not follow our rules and regulations.

Lucy and her team also were inspecting all the units and working with Evan Harris at Massey Services Pest Control to address the pest and rodent infestation. Twelve apartments were found to have major roach infestations, and Evan provided a tenant checklist to follow to eradicate the problem. The checklist included cleaning up trash, removing open food containers, keeping worn clothing and wet towels off the floors, and cleaning kitchen surfaces with disinfectants. Section 14 of our Tenant Lease clearly mandated such basic housekeeping "as provided by law and as provided by the community rules."

Though a dozen units were severely infested with roaches, Units 205 and 1101 stood out. Melinda Wyatt's Unit 205 was infested with thousands of German roaches and bed bugs. Her children probably created havoc at school every day because their uniforms were riddled with bed bugs. The cost of an effective bed bug treatment was $1,600, and under the terms of the lease Lucy billed Melinda for the cost. Lucy and Evan worked with Melinda to clean up the unit and asked her to remove all infested furniture and clothing. She was making an effort but it was not enough to get rid of the infestation despite the treatments by pest control technician Evan. Because Melinda's mother was hearing-impaired and lived with her, the unit was selected to receive UFAS sensory renovations. Many of the apartment elements were original from 1998, and we hoped that new carpet, cabinets, paint, and appliances would help improve conditions for Melinda's family, including her live-in mother, and give them a fresh start in a clean environment. The makeover was so extensive it would practically give Melinda a brand-new apartment.

Unit 1101 was even worse. The unit was occupied by a mother with two daughters and three grandchildren who were respectively three months, two years, and four years old. Evan estimated that more than ten thousand roaches were crawling on the walls, ceiling, and floors, and on the children's toys, clothing, and furniture. Even Evan, a seasoned exterminator familiar with all forms of pests, was appalled when he reported the roaches were swarming on the ceilings and spilling into neighboring units. He handed over the checklist to the tenant with instructions to thoroughly clean the unit, plus remove the furniture, bedding, and clothing so he could start treatments. At first the tenant refused to cooperate and clean up her unit, but when Lucy handed her a letter advising we were starting the eviction process, she changed her mind. The tenant was a working grandmother who told Lucy she simply could not afford to move. The adult daughters who lived with her refused to work, and she had no relatives who could help her financially, so she was left with the choice of cleaning up her unit or becoming homeless.

An overarching goal of our business model was to reduce tenant transiency at Cleveland Avenue Elementary. Eviction was thus something we pursued carefully, especially involving innocent school-age children. We gave tenants time to work out delinquent balances and issued notices of rules infractions, including housekeeping and behavior issues such as loud music. When we uncovered pest infestations, the tenants were given clear written notice and an opportunity to clean up their units and treat the premises. So far, about half the tenants with lease violations were working with us to improve the environment, which was encouraging.

I WENT INTO THE management office to check in with Lucy and paused at the entrance to enjoy the effect of the recent interior renovation. New bleached hardwood-style flooring replaced the old stained and chipped linoleum. Stylish mirrors hung on the fresh mint green walls, complemented by new contemporary polished black furniture. The metal folding chairs were gone, and several inviting, comfortable leather chairs were provided for the tenants and prospects. The staff greeted me with a smile and warm hellos. Everyone was excited with the changes and the office exuded a wonderful positive energy.

I poked my head into Lucy's office and caught her walking towards her chair. "Are you losing weight? Your pants are looking really loose."

"You know, I think I've now lost ten pounds from walking around the property every day. I probably walk up to two to three times a day inspecting units and around the perimeter to get a handle on everything."

I settled into a cushy black leather chair to get an update on how she was doing. I knew she'd been concerned about the the crime and environment. I asked, "Do you feel good about our security program?"

Lucy smiled, "God is really watching me. God is watching the entire property. He truly put his hands on mine, but the other part about it, I don't feel scared anymore. I did in the beginning . . . not for my safety, but the stories because they kept saying Maya, the property manager. You know her car got shot up, right at the leasing office. One of the girls had her car stolen at the leasing office. The leasing office was set on fire by an arsonist by someone who was really mad. But later, God gave me the enlightenment not to be scared. The rumor was that a member from the previous management staff was sleeping with one of the residents and she had different relationships with various people so a lot of things happened that she brought on herself. I don't think it was the environment, rather it was the situation. Mr. Hayes told us she was getting paid by the drug dealers and there was a lot of play with the rent collections."

"How are collections going?" I asked, knowing that it had been a struggle to get a handle on the operations and records for the first few months.

She replied that at the start she had tenants who told her they hadn't paid rent since February and were not going to pay; three of those tenants were now gone. But surprisingly one tenant had not paid since March but suddenly paid the entire six months of past due rent. "He told me you guys are really doing something and enforcing the rules. The kids follow the curfew, there is no hanging out and everyone is trying to comply." She paused and beamed at me.

I looked back at her in wonder at life's pleasant surprises. Imagine a tenant paying six months in past-due rent because we were doing the right thing.

Lucy continued:

> The tenants were never afraid of being evicted because the previous management just didn't care. But also, people were paying in cash. There was a lot of that, and they were looking at me strangely when we told them we can't take cash. It was almost as if it was foreign for them. More than 60 percent of residents were paying in cash. It was strange because this was the first time I've seen this. Everything, from the locks to the rent and gate cards, was paid in cash. I was finally working out the rent payment history for the tenants owing past-due rents. The owners gave us a list of delinquents, but the tenants came in with receipts showing they paid their rent. I had a tenant who showed a $3,700 past-due delinquent balance, but he showed up with eight months of receipts proving he was current on all his rent payments. How was this possible? The previous management was not accurately recording rent payments; there was no consistent administrative record-keeping system. The manager was writing everything down or putting it on a spreadsheet she managed and whatever was on the spreadsheet was the law. A few tenants were trying to figure out [if they were about to be evicted over an unpaid balance] and if management was keeping accurate records of their past payments. So, when we worked it all out with the tenants showing proof of past payments, it was fine. There are still a few tenants with delinquent rent issues we will probably never resolve because they didn't get receipts when they paid the rent in cash, but we are going to just move on and trust them going forward.

You know I sent out forty-two letters to people who had balances more than $100 to say there is a balance on your account and I need you to come current, and the first week, we got thirty-eight responses. And they came in one by one and each one of them, including the ones that didn't speak English, had receipts showing they had paid their rent.

I was aware of the collection issues, but what Lucy was saying made sense. Embezzlement was a common theme in sloppy apartment administration. Furthermore, a blighted apartment community was happy hunting grounds for theft, especially when absentee owners had to rely on management staff to operate the property. I looked at the tenant receivables report, and as of the end of August fifteen tenants still had not paid their monthly rent and eleven were over two months past due. A total of $31,500 was outstanding. Delinquencies seemed to be getting worse, but many tenants didn't pay rent or had an arrangement with the previous management to make payments later than specified in their leases. Our enforcement of a structured, accountable administrative process allowed us to sift through the honest and dishonest tenant-landlord relationships. Had the previous management kept accurate, transparent records, the reported delinquencies probably would have been much higher when we purchased the property.

Lucy added:

There were a lot of tenants who live here and are good people who work hard at their jobs. There were a lot of lease files with felonies, but many were twenty years ago and nonviolent crimes.[61] The only nervous people were the ones without proper legal identification. The people with felonies did not seem concerned about being evicted. The ones we're concerned about don't have background checks or information in their files, if they existed. The ones we are having issues with are the ones knowing they came in illegally, and now we are getting their documents in order, they are afraid we are going to find out about their history.[62]

I have people who transfer apartments all of the time, and I read everything because I want fresh and new information. Tenants were really upset when we did a background check because management has never done this in the past. Why are you doing it now, the tenants asked? I told them I need this information if I ever get audited and don't have anything. The tenants agree it makes sense and eventually came around. Miranda James in Unit 503 in Phase II was upset at first. She is a UPS worker and I knew she would have a clean record. She passed everything, and now she has moved to Phase I and loves it, pays her rent on time. She is not a problematic tenant, she is great. Moved from a three-bedroom in Phase II down to a two-bedroom townhome in Phase I. She got rid of the boyfriend and started taking care of herself and is going great. She is a nice lady. She said there was so much back and forth with the prior management. She had nine to ten outstanding work orders since January and February, and most tenants were like that. Ms. Moore had no heat or air for ten years. Now she has a new air conditioning unit . . . it's done! We are having to find all sorts of bad maintenance repairs.

I asked if we were caught up on maintenance repairs. "I know we have been averaging dozens every day since we purchased the property, mainly due to a large backlog of work orders that were never addressed."

Lucy laughed:

Instead of spending a couple of dollars to get the electrical wires correct, the maintenance guy, Sammy, did wire repair all wrong and caused something that burned everything out, and now we had to replace everything. There were a lot of electric repairs done incorrectly and triggered problems. Some of the windows were leaking and not repaired with water going down walls. Sammy was not making repairs. He did poorly on hot water, HVAC, and ceiling fan repairs. He wired ceiling fans to the lighting so when you turn on the light, the ceiling fans went berserk and popped the breaker. We turned on the ceiling fan at one apartment and the refrigerator blew. Benny Glover, our maintenance tech, started going into every unit and finding interesting "stuff." The guys will find stuff and keep going, but I want to make sure all repairs were done correctly. A lot of kids have asthma at the property. One family has seven children with asthma or bronchitis. That could be tied to the tons of roaches in the units.

When I sent out the forty-two letters to tenants with balances over $100, I found four phantom leases on the Phase II side. At Phase I, there were twelve phantom leases; didn't know the person, had no idea, don't see them. Whenever I go to visit the unit and ask for the tenant by name, those people in the unit are looking at me like "who?" But this is how we ended up with the mess in Unit D-12. There is a woman whose name is on the lease, but there are only guys in there.

I asked, "So who comes first in bringing a functioning apartment community property from healthy to blighted? Is it the building design, the ownership, the tenants or a combination of all three?" I was curious to study the process of how Summerdale Phase II, a perfectly beautiful property when it was built in 1998, would become a community failure complete with entrenched drug activity, pest infestation, hostile tenant behavior and eventually, a failing school, in less than twenty years.

Lucy was thoughtful, "Oh I think the mentality of the tenant makes a property blighted, but on the other hand, the previous landlord just gave up! They didn't invest correctly in repairs and certainly not in the administrative policies and procedures."

"Wow!" I said and stood up to leave. The phone had been ringing almost nonstop and a tenant was outside the door waiting to talk with Lucy. I had taken enough of her time, but said, "Before I leave, we need to get the Star-C after school program started once the property is deemed safe. We are making progress from a security perspective, but we will need to have a facility to start the program. I was thinking about the back of the leasing office. We can hold fifteen to twenty kids between the two rooms. What are your thoughts?"

"I agree," said Lucy. "We won't have the community center in the middle of Phase I ready for at least another ninety days with permitting taking so long, so we can organize in the back. We will have the rooms cleaned out of all the leftover boxes and maintenance supplies. I will go ahead and get it started. When are you thinking about starting the program?"

"Kristin accepted our offer to start the Star-C program at Summerdale, so as soon as we can get the kids enrolled. School starts August 1st so we can't hit that date. We are guessing it will be late August or early September before we can actually launch."

NEXT I WENT TO visit Jeff and see all the construction process. He was standing outside next to his truck talking with a subcontractor about the renovation plans when I approached him in front of Building 500. "'Lo," he said smiling as I approached. "You ready to see something?"

"Sure," I said. "Let's go look at the sidewalks, and you wanted to discuss the concrete pours for the parking lot ramps in front of a few buildings with steep slopes." We had almost completed the sidewalk replacements to get the property in compliance with UFAS, FHA, and ADA.

Jeff said goodbye to the subcontractor and joined me to walk through the parking lot. The project to dig up the sidewalks left large mounds of red clay in front of each building. Empty forms waited to be filled and two sidewalks were curing in the sun, giving the front a fresh, new look. It was a major undertaking to dig up and remove seven tons of thick concrete, but it had to be done for all the sidewalks throughout the property. The crew had also demolished the asphalt in eleven parking spaces and was repaving to comply with the UFAS and ADA checklist. We agreed we needed to do the work right.

We talked for a few more minutes about various issues. The units in Phase I were completely gutted and all the trash, appliances, furniture, and dishes removed. We filled dozens of thirty-yard dumpsters with the trash we pulled out. Jeff was getting bids from mechanical and electrical suppliers to continue the Phase I renovations.

"I have two units we are working on to comply with the UFAS. Unit 401 and Unit 205. Unit 401 has a nephew who is a quadriplegic in a wheelchair and I'm going to work on that one once I get Unit 205 started. You got a minute to see Unit 205? This is the unit that has the roach infestation and I'm having a problem dealing with the tenant. She is being verbally abusive to our workers and I want you to see the condition."

That was Melinda Wyatt's unit.

We walked over to Unit 205 and after a brief knock went inside. A rancid smell greeted us and the interior was in chaos. Furniture was strewn all over the floor. Jeff silently pointed to the kitchen where dozens of roaches crawled over the walls and chipped countertops. The place was trashed and a complete mess.

After a few minutes, we walked outside and talked.

"Wow," I said, disturbed by what I just saw. This was the first time I had inspected Melinda's interior. I had heard rumors, but the abysmal condition of this unit exceeded my low expectations.

Jeff said, "I wanted you to see this unit because I can already tell you it's going to be a problem. Melinda is being combative with my crew and blocking their ability to work and get the unit UFAS compliant, but I'm going to keep going."

I told him to keep moving forward. We did not have a choice at this point in the process since we had started removing her kitchen and bathroom cabinets. "Should we have a talk with her?" I asked. "Is there anything we can do?"

"I think Lucy has been talking with Melinda and I know that Evan, the pest technician, has been working with her as well. She just won't listen to reason."

WE WALKED OVER TO Phase I so Jeff could give me an update on its progress. The property was looking much cleaner with the removal of all the trash and six-foot weeds. As we passed unit D-12, three young men were loitering at the corner between the D and C buildings. They acknowledged Jeff with nods. They clearly knew Jeff but would not make eye contact with me. After we had passed by, I asked Jeff if they were tenants.

No, and they are here every day. They hang out at Unit D-12 and when our security or the police show up, they run inside or jump in their cars and leave. But they are clearly bad actors. They keep offering me cocaine, heroin, blow jobs, stolen stuff or anything I want, and that is obviously not happening. I am 100 percent sure prostitution is going on, and these guys will provide anything illicit; even tattooing and car mechanic work is going on. It took a while, but I finally chased off the guys doing car work in the parking lot. I even had a guy trying to sell me a tool gun, and I'm like "It's mine." He was like "No, no . . . I got this off some other guy." It was brand new—fifty bucks—the cheapest you could buy. I was like "Dude, that's mine, give it to me." He was like "I took this from this guy over there" and I asked him, "So you did steal it?," which of course he did.

I asked Jeff if he ever saw the guy with the teardrop tattoos under his eye.

Oh, yeah. That's Deshawn, the guy hitting me up for damages he claims my construction guy did to his satellite dish. Deshawn didn't murder anyone but he is trying to look the part. Most of the guys try to live the life and act the part, but they are not violent. They are definitely selling drugs and doing things, but they have not crossed the line. Deshawn and his girlfriend have been evicted, but he keeps coming back to smoke weed and hang out. I have told him "You need to leave" but he just blows smoke in my face. I finally texted Edward and asked him to call the police, and the cop immediately comes and eventually Deshawn and the D-12 guys leave. Deshawn is about two inches taller than me but really skinny. I told him, "When I first met you, I thought you were smart," but then he gets into my face and in about two seconds I have him on the ground and the other guys start coming towards me. I confronted all of them and told them "We called 911 and they are on their way." So Deshawn gets up and the guys disperse. The mailman was delivering the mail to the boxes and saw the whole thing. He says, "Why did you do that? They guys could have a gun." But I wasn't worried about a gun. I put him on the ground in a locked-arm hold I learned in the Marines, so he couldn't move once I had him down. I want to keep embarrassing him so he won't come back.

I did not mention that the APD was doing an undercover stakeout, using a boarded-up unit in Building G to house officers and watch the activity at the D building. We intentionally did not disturb the tenants while the APD did their surveillance or broadcast the officers' presence since news travels fast at Summerdale.

Jeff and I made our way to the abandoned small brick building in the middle of the courtyard. The nine-hundred square-foot building was slated to serve as our new Star-C after-school facility. It was a difficult decision to move the after-school program facility after ninety days from the leasing office at Phase II to the building in the middle of the courtyard in blighted Phase I, but I knew we would outgrow the leasing office. The little brick building was boarded up when we purchased the property, but workmen were taking the boards off the windows and installing new floors and a kitchen. The previous owner had tried to renovate the building into a four-bedroom unit with two bathrooms, but construction was never completed. We removed several walls to create an open floor plan that could easily accommodate fifty children. The room was bright and clean with light spilling through several windows. It was going to be a nice, functional after-school program. The new upgrades and Kristen's choice of lilac wall paint would give the children a happy place to be after school.

NEXT, WE HEADED OVER to the back side of the property where boarded-up buildings festered in the sun.

"I forgot to mention we found a gun in the walls of Building K while the guys were trashing out the unit." Jeff said as we approached the building. "It was odd, because it was stuck inside an HVAC vent. The unit seemed to be recently occupied by a vagrant who set up a makeshift camp. I called Officer Ski immediately and sent him a picture. He had one of his patrol officers over to retrieve it in less than ten minutes."

I was not surprised and anticipated we would find more guns given the criminal history of the property.

With the protective plywood removed from the windows, a half dozen workmen were clearing out the units and hauling tons of garbage to the thirty-yard dumpsters positioned in front of the building. The units were open, and without the trash and boarded-up windows, the sun was shining through the open windows and doors so that you could see the interiors. As the light streamed through, you could envision these units as affordable, stable housing. This side of the property had 144 apartments, and Jeff and I were inspecting the buildings housing 36 two-bedroom/two-bath flat units. The remaining units included 100 two-bedroom/bath-and-a-half townhomes and eight one-bedroom/one-bath flat units.

"I really like the layout of these units," I said looking in one of the kitchens. "If we were to open this wall between the kitchen and den area, that would really make the space more family-oriented."

Jeff said excitedly:

I agree and really like the potential with this layout. It has a homey feel, especially if we partially open this wall between the kitchen and den, we can add a small counter and the sink along this wall, so the parents can work in the kitchen but have a visual into the den and supervise their children. I can imagine a Thanksgiving dinner with part of the family in the den while the food is being prepared in the kitchen and everyone is visually connected rather than blocked by the existing wall between the two room. You know what else I found? While pulling out the sheetrock, we discovered washer/dryer connections in all these units. For some reason, they boarded them up several years ago and put laundromats in the basement. I don't know why they did this, but we can bring back washer/dryer capability in all these units, so the families have the option to do their laundry at home.

I replied:

That's a great idea and let us explore a better design. Our model is about education and housing and I like the idea the parents can be in the kitchen supervising the kids in the den while doing their homework. We need to make these unit interiors as comfortable and enjoyable as possible and the layout can play an important role in the quality of life for our future families.

During our inspection, we were constantly interrupted by workers asking Jeff questions. I knew he was busy managing the construction workers, so I left him and headed back to my car. The three guys still loitering at the corner of C and D buildings said hello as I passed them. I did not stop for chitchat, but I noticed this was a different crowd from the guys I saw before we purchased the property. We were patiently working with APD but needed to verify they were tenants or get them removed from the property, especially since they hung around the sidewalk the children would be using to get to the new after-school program facility. There was still so much work to do. I knew from experience that it would be a long process and a test of patience.

18

The Toxic Community Culture

Kandice Kirk marched through the front door of the management office, past a quiet family clustered around a rental application, and confronted Adriane Thompson, Summerdale's assistant property manager. Lucy was out inspecting apartment units and Adriane was alone in her office, engrossed in the rigorous process of inputting data into the Atlanta Housing Authority portal to qualify tenants for the Homeflex program. She was startled when Kandice marched up to her desk and started screaming and waving a finger in her face.

"You motherfuckers . . . y'all sorry," Kandice blared.

Adriane took a deep breath and summoned her patience, aware that the family applying for an apartment was watching. "Can I help you?"

Kandice repeated, "You mother fuckers . . . a piece of ceiling fell in my apartment and it's been like this for three days and you haven't fixed it!"

"I'm sorry, but we were unaware there was a problem."

"That's what you motherfuckers always say, but when it comes time to do it, you'all nowhere to be found."

Adriane looked Kandice in the eye and quietly said. "I'm sorry but you are not talking to me with this type of language and disrespect. You need to leave and come back when you can calmly discuss the problem."

Realizing that she wasn't alone in the office, Kandice turned around with a huff, walked out the door, and stood on the lawn at the entrance to the management office. Adriane watched through the window in her office. Fifteen minutes later, there was a knock on the office door. Adriane opened it and looked out. Kandice calmly asked if she could come in and talk to Adriane about a maintenance issue.

Adriane had a daughter a little younger than Kandice, and her maternal instincts kicked in as she said, "Of course you can if you can talk respectfully."

Kandice burst out crying.

"No need to start crying. Sit down here and let's talk."

Between sobs Kandice shared that her roommate had stolen her money and she couldn't pay her rent. She was now two months behind and was not working. Adriane patiently listened and offered a few solutions including resources that could help Kandice get her rent paid and possibly offer job assistance. Adriane and Lucy had cultivated relationships with nonprofit organizations that could offer rental assistance in emergency situations and had put together an info sheet to hand out. After a few minutes talking with Adriane, Kandice wiped her eyes, took the sheet with the phone numbers, said thank you, and left.

Adriane went back to her thick stack of paperwork. She was not upset by Kandice's behavior. In fact, she was getting used to the confrontational tenants who struggled with the anger issues that came with limited options due to poverty. Adriane knew Kandice was once homeless and had worked with a nonprofit which offered homeless individuals job training and housing assistance to get their lives stabilized. Summerdale agreed to house some participants in this particular program, but the participants often had social and emotional challenges and required a lot of patience. The organization had paid for six months' rent and job training, but Kandice seemed unable to keep a job for more than a couple of months, was currently unemployed, and had fallen behind after the six-month period ended two months ago. Given the behavior Adriane just witnessed, she was not surprised that Kandice could not hold a job. She said, "Kandice just didn't know how to talk with people. She thought that cursing you out and demanding was communicating when all she had to say was 'I have a problem.'"

Adriane was still new working with Lucy in the management office at Summerdale Apartments. She was on a demanding learning curve as she navigated the human and business ecosystem of the property. She understood that the structural elements at Summerdale had been neglected for a long time, which made tenants angry, and many tenants did not have the money to move anywhere else, which also made them angry. When she arrived at Summerdale, she encountered a stressed-out community culture of people who were frustrated and had little patience with management. Confrontations with frustrated tenants such as Kandice were daily occurrences. Kandice was a common visitor in the office with her problems. But so far, no one had pulled a gun on the management staff and Adriane was thankful for the security presence. Summerdale as a community was in a crisis of trust, and until trust was achieved, it was doubtful it would ever build the social capital to fully recover from being a "blighted community." Political scientist Francis Fukuyama defines "trust" as "the expectation that arises within a community of regular, honest, and cooperative behavior, based on commonly shared norms, on the part of other members of that community" and "social capital" as "a capability that arises from the prevalence of trust in a society or in certain parts of it . . . usually created and transmitted through cultural mechanisms like religion, tradition, or historical habit." He argues that the two phenomena are not mutually exclusive. Building both was part of our mission at Summerdale.[63]

Adriane was well qualified for her demanding Summerdale job. She grew up in the "hood" in the New Jersey side of Philadelphia, the daughter of a father who was a career revenue police officer for the Port Authority transit company in New Jersey and a mother who was a registered nurse nicknamed "Sergeant." Adriane was also a single mother of four children; in the tradition of her mother, she ran a tight household ship. She said:

My mother had two sets of eyes and saw everything in front of her and behind her. When I was a teenager, I was nosy and would sneak over to the "Projects" because that's where all the action was. It was one of my favorite places to hang out. One day while hanging out, I was shocked to see my mother come around the corner of a building and catch me at the property. She was completely disappointed and told me she would not pay for my college and I was on my own. I never did drugs but I was curious because I wanted to see life. Having two working parents, we were considered to have money, but my best friend lived in poverty, had roaches in her apartment, and shared clothes with her siblings, so I was able to see both sides of life. Summerdale is nothing new to me—it's actually a piece of cake compared to Philly.

I realized early on after I joined Lucy and the staff, the tenants didn't believe anything we told them until they could see it. They just didn't trust us, but if they gave us some time, they would see that we were getting things done and did what we said we were going to do. When they come in with maintenance requests, I have to say "give me some time," some work requests don't happen overnight. It was just going to take time to build the trust, but once you get the trust, you build a better community."

Adriane wasn't afraid of the drug dealers and tough crowd, and they were starting to respect her. "I used to tell the loitering young men they were going to die or go to jail. They recently started calling me 'Ms. Rent Lady,'" she said, with a twinkle in her eye.

SINCE ACQUISITION OF SUMMERDALE, the TriStar leadership had worked hard to keep the existing tenants, including freezing their low rents for a year and getting them into the Homeflex program. However, Lucy and Adriane had their work cut out to improve the community culture. Many tenants did not know the social norms of being a good neighbor, or they had anger issues, often triggered over minor issues. Adriane would lease apartments to new qualified tenants, but these new tenants moved in with neighbors who played loud music, fought with spouses, tossed their trash throughout the grounds, and screamed at others in the parking lot for the smallest infraction. Adriane continued:

Many of the tenants or their guests have anger issues that come with poverty and limited choices. Take Kevin Howard in unit P-8. He is a delivery guy but doesn't make a lot of money. He moved in as a single father with two young children, and last week I got a call from his neighbor that his car was parked in a way that partially blocked the exit gate in Phase I. So I called to get him to move his vehicle but he would not answer the phone. I called, texted, and emailed him for a few hours, and he still would not respond, so I went over there and knocked on the door. There was no response despite the fact he was probably home since his car was partially blocking the gate. Finally, I left a message that if he didn't move his car within one hour, I had no choice but to tow it.

Sure enough, no response so the tow-truck shows up to remove his vehicle and once the tow truck latched on the car, he and his girlfriend come running out of the apartment and the girlfriend starts threatening me. She gets in my face with attitude and says "I got something for that ass" and starts walking back to the apartment. I told her, "Whatever you are going to your apartment to get, you better use it when you come out." The tow truck guy looked at me and asked if he needed to get his gun.

A few minutes later she returns and launched at me to fight. Mr. Howard pulled her back, and I left to return to the office. They ended up paying $300 to the tow truck guy to drop the car, but a few minutes later, she drove to the management office, parked behind my car and sat there. I went outside because she is now blocking traffic, and she screams, "Bitch, I'm coming back for you next week." She takes a picture of my license tag number and eventually leaves. For the safety of the office, I called the police and decided to file a police report. Later that evening, the neighbor has on video someone with an axe trying to remove the video camera on the neighbor's door. We didn't have 100 percent identity of the person because her face was covered, but we are pretty sure it is the girlfriend thinking the neighbor called me about the car partially blocking the gate, and seeking revenge by removing the video camera. So, I called the police again and started the eviction process. With the time it takes to do an eviction in Fulton County, this could take months and months. It will take six to seven months to evict Mr. Howard and his girlfriend. If we are lucky. But we are trying to figure out a faster way to remove tenants that are a safety concern.

It was bad enough that we had a tenant threatening our office staff, but we had no way to expedite the eviction process in Fulton County Magistrate Court which handled the evictions. Our staff was forced to deal with threats from angry tenants with almost no relief for months while waiting and waiting on the legal process. In the interim, the tenant usually retaliated by refusing to pay rent, damaging the unit, or creating havoc in the leasing office. Many times they did things like punching in walls, stopping up tubs and flooding their unit, or breaking windows, then submitted maintenance requests. Some would get Legal Aid involved, claiming we were not addressing maintenance issues, and demanding large money settlements—all while not paying rent.

AFTER SPEAKING WITH KANDICE, Adriane had returned to her desk and the Atlanta Housing Authority application stack when the door opened and Anthony Fowler strutted in, handed her a rent check for Unit D-12, and put down two heavy plastic bags with take-out food from the local Mexican restaurant.

"I brought you lunch," he said charmingly, smiling at Adriane.

"Oh, thank you, that is very nice of you," Adriane said without smiling. She and Lucy agreed there was something off about Anthony Fowler, but they didn't exactly know what was giving them a bad vibe. He talked too much and was trying too hard to get on their good side, bringing them lunch while commenting on the criminal activity, claiming it was the neighbors and he wasn't involved. Why would someone say that? Lucy recently shared with Adriane that she thought he might be the main culprit in the obvious drug dealing activity, because he was the only tenant that was constantly complaining about the crime. They knew he was dating Sharon Allen in Apartment D-12 and had recently started to come by the office to pay the rent for the apartment, which was preferable to Sharon who showed up to pay the rent but had a terrible attitude. His relationship with Sharon gave him a legitimate excuse to be in the office, but he was not registered on the lease and they had their suspicions. Furthermore, they were told to avoid the characters associated with the drug traffic while the APD did their undercover work, so they stayed out of the activity and focused on the huge task of bringing rationality to the disorganized paperwork and backlog of maintenance orders. The next words out of his mouth confirmed Adriane's suspicions.

Anthony leaned over to Adriane and said, "I interested in leasing an apartment and I'm willing to make it lucrative for you every month."

Adriane didn't know how to respond other than to give him an application and tell him to return it with the application fee. She knew what he was asking—to pay her under the table to hand him keys to a unit with no application and without a criminal background or credit history report.

Anthony stared at her for a moment, took the application, and left the office. He had given Lucy the same "lucrative offer" several times, but she also just handed him an application. He knew that an application would be a waste of his time because he certainly couldn't qualify.

When Lucy returned to the office after inspecting units with Jeff for half a day, Adriane shared the news of the morning, including Kandice, Kevin, and Anthony Fowler. Lucy and she shook their heads but didn't dwell on the tenant issues. The phone continuously rang and the office had a steady stream of tenants with rent checks or maintenance issues and prospective tenants attracted to the low rental rates. The Anthony Fowler situation would work itself out through the APD, and there was nothing they could do but ignore him. Their efforts to bring trust and stability to Summerdale kept them too occupied to dwell on the challenges.

19

Kristin Hemingway—The Children and Star-C After-School Program

It was late August 2018, and the first official day of the highly anticipated Star-C after-school program at Summerdale Apartments was about to begin. Earlier in the month, Lucy had surveyed tenants on what type of community programming they would like TriStar to support. An after-school program was at the top of the responses. The tenants did not know that an after-school partnership with the local elementary school was a part of the TriStar model and that we had been talking with Cleveland Avenue Elementary since we began negotiating to buy Summerdale. Now the Star-C program was taking root.

The sixteen available slots had filled up quickly as the word got out that the management office was accepting applications. Lucy and the staff had done a thorough job marketing the program to the existing residents, and they created a waitlist for future slots that would become available when Star-C moved to its larger facility. That move would take place when renovations were complete on that larger, permanent facility on the Phase I side of the property. But building permits from the City of Atlanta had been slow to obtain, so we decided to start the program at a temporary space in the back of the management office.

Kristin Hemingway taped posters with positive messages on the walls in the temporary after-school program housed in the back rooms of Summerdale's management office, stepped back, and looked at the room with satisfaction. The walls were freshly painted cream, and the floors were new hardwood. Three rows of neatly organized black lacquered metal folding chairs faced the posters. A bookcase full of colorful books reminded the children that reading was central to their daily routine. Kristin was a disciple of social emotional learning, or SEL, an educational process that helps children develop the self-awareness, self-control, and interpersonal skills vital for school, work, and life success. Decades of research show that SEL leads to increased academic achievement, improved behavior, decreased dropout rates, lower drug use, and less teen pregnancy, mental health problems, and criminal behavior.[64]

Kristin had filled the room with positive messaging. Students entering the room would be greeted by "IF YOU CAN DREAM IT, YOU CAN DO IT" and other inspirational messages. She was fully prepared to launch the program. We had signed a contract with her and provided a free apartment as part of her compensation. She had hit the ground running to develop the plan and its partners. She met with Dr. Payne and the staff at Cleveland Avenue Elementary, and she started volunteering at the school to get to know the students and their families. She knew the challenge that faced her as the director of the program, based on the performance of Cleveland Avenue Elementary and the families she had already met.

Many of the children registered in the program had been living in the toxic apartment environment for several years. We already knew from our general survey that approximately 75 percent of the children in the Star-C program were low-skill readers and experienced signs of anxiety associated with trauma. The negative impact of trauma on child development is well documented.[65] The high criminal activity at the property took away their freedom of playing outdoors and feeling safe in their own community and in the sanctity of their own apartments. The drug dealers terrorized the community greenspace, making it unsafe outdoors for kids or adults. As a result, many children went from their apartment to school and back to the apartment after school, otherwise rarely setting foot outside. They remained sequestered in their apartments with the blinds drawn. When we toured the property before the acquisition, the wide, grassy open common areas lacked the laughter and happy screams of playing children that are typical for a family-based apartment community.

FAMILIES STARTED ARRIVING AT the new Star-C room promptly at 2:30 p.m. Within minutes, the room was crowded with eager parents and reluctant children. The adults were festive, appreciative of an on-site facility to socialize their children. But few smiles were exchanged by the children as they shyly looked at the floor, avoiding eye contact with Kristin and the adults. Their social skills were limited to classroom interactions amongst similarly traumatized children who struggled with poverty, crime, gunfire, and hunger. The children's stress was palpable as they entered and quietly sat in any available chair. Their defeated attitudes truly affected me, seeing five through eight-year-olds already stressed out at such young ages.

All seats quickly filled, but parents and children were still pouring through the door. "I didn't realize I was supposed to register my child" was a common answer Kristin heard while checking the arrivals against her list of registered families. It was disappointing to turn families away, but we simply did not have the space to accommodate all the children that were not registered. Once Jeff completed the renovation of the new larger facility in Phase I, we would have the capacity to grow the program.

Eventually the room settled down as the parents said goodbye to the children and headed back to their apartments. Kristin faced her youthful group and smiled. At 6'1", with curly hair, bright purple glasses, and enthusiastic energy, it was virtually impossible for Kristin not to command attention. She began by asking everyone to stand and stretch. The sixteen children looked at each other then quietly stood up and raised their arms overhead, took deep breaths, and relaxed. The official Star-C after-school program at Summerdale had begun.

As described earlier, Kristin Hemingway was not new to managing after-school programs in blighted apartment communities. I had personally recruited her ten years earlier to launch the fledgling after-school program at Madison Hills Apartments in Cobb County, on the opposite and more affluent side of Atlanta [See Chapter 3]. I had stayed in touch with her, followed her career, and sponsored her community work for other nonprofits. I knew she would be perfect to operate the new Star-C program at Summerdale.

KRISTIN IS A WALKING, talking example of SEL success. She was born in Detroit, Michigan, to a single teenage parent. Her favorite photo is of herself, two months old, in the arms of her mother wearing her high school graduation cap and gown.

She said, "I grew up in my grandmother's household with an extended family of uncles and aunts who loved me well. This is where my heart for the community comes from, my childhood and having these other people who invested in me. My mother still lives in the same house. When my grandmother passed away, my mother purchased the house, so I grew up in a very stable environment. I was a naturally curious child and always an avid reader who had an expensive habit of books. By the third grade, I excelled across all subjects and had high test scores at the ninety-ninth percentile and was getting noticed, so my third-grade math teacher suggested to Mom that she enroll me in a more rigorous school. Thereafter, I started going to Bates Academy, a citywide public school for the gifted and talented."

Kristin's first teacher at Bates, Judy Anne McSorley, changed her life, giving her "eighty to a hundred assignments for the week, and you had until Friday at noon to turn in. She taught me responsibility and excellence." Kristin attended Cass Tech High School, where she had the same counselor as her mother had eighteen years earlier. When her grandmother passed away, the staff at Cass Tech said they would take care of her and did. Kristin said, "My network changed my life by showing me how to love students well and stay on track and focus on goals."

After graduating from Cass Tech with honors, Kristin attended Florida A&M University on a full scholarship. She tested well and was a good student because her mother would not accept anything less. She was a National Achievement Semifinalist with the goal of obtaining an MBA. However, her college plans derailed over a bad relationship and subsequent depression. Reflecting on that time when she did not know how to ask for help led her to focus on teaching students in need how to reach out and advocate for themselves. Her strong faith led to her role as an interventionist and life coach for at-risk youth. Though she landed a good job in Tallahassee, Kristin knew it was time to make a move. Good friends and a church were calling her, so she decided to move to Atlanta. Her first stop was Destiny Church where she jumped right in volunteering and networking to find employment. She joined Holy High, a ministry for high school students.

Within a few months, Destiny Church hired her as a preschool teacher to one-year-olds.

Meanwhile, in 2008 I asked our Madison Hills community partners if they could recommend someone to run a new after-school program. The youth minister at Destiny Church introduced me to Kristin, whose energy and passion drew me right in. She was promptly hired. A free apartment was included in her compensation, and she continued networking with Brumby Elementary and her new neighbors. It was a stark lesson in community building.

She gets emotional remembering it: "Many residents living at Madison Hills were basically living in functional poverty. Literally the 'working poor.' We are talking about two-parent households where they were not earning enough to support basic living expenses, and the last thing on the list was food. If these families lose their food stamps, then they simply do not eat. A lot of families with children relied on supportive meals during the summer months when their children were not provided school meals. Again, we are talking about two-parent households where one of the parents diligently worked for a Fortune 500 company. It just tore me up."

RANDOM INSPECTIONS OF THE apartments at Madison Hills disclosed the harsh reality of working poverty. Rooms with no decent furnishings, beds consisting of mattresses on the floor, cabinets with no food (literally, not a single can of food), refrigerators sitting empty and small wardrobes—all sacrificed for rent and car payments. Their full-time jobs barely provided for a decent living and a cheap roof over their heads, and that roof was in the middle of drug dealers and blight.

Dealing with the challenges of families living below the poverty line sometimes shook Kristin. One day her phone rang and the caller, the mother of two gifted students, was crying because she had lost her food stamps. This was not unusual at Madison Hills Apartments. Kristen recalled, "My heart was broken. Here I was a single person with discretionary income and my students and their families were suffering. There was another family— a married couple where the father was working his way through culinary school and the mother worked at Home Depot in customer service. Due to their income, their food stamps were cut, which was the one benefit that they really needed."

The family went for two days without eating. Kristin called a friend at Johnson Ferry Baptist church . . . crying, and within a few hours a trunk full of food was delivered to the family's home . . . along with a month's rent. Kristin reflected on her work with low-income apartment communities: "The face of poverty in America is not what you think. Behind the nice cars in the parking lot and decently dressed kids, the families are facing hard choices every month."

AFTER MY EXPERIENCE RENOVATING Madison Hills Apartments, we expected the same if not worse demographic at Summerdale. Our team was onboard to help stabilize the community and raise educational expectations. Dr. Payne and the leadership of Atlanta Public Schools happily endorsed our model by signing on as active partners. Dr. Payne made herself available to answer any questions and follow up with necessary resources. When the floors in the leasing office needed to be replaced, she generously hosted the Star-C after-school program at Cleveland Avenue Elementary during the renovation, rather than disrupt the program.

We were looking forward to the partnership but knew we faced a serious challenge to improve the literacy and comprehension test scores for the Summerdale children enrolled in the program. Many of the children were low-skill readers, and several had emotional issues associated with the trauma of living in poverty in the toxic environment. Many had asthma exacerbated by mold and pest infestations and their sequestered living conditions.

Given where the Summerdale students started physically and emotionally, well below their peers at Cleveland Avenue Elementary, it would take an incredible effort on Kristin's behalf to get these kids performing at acceptable, grade-appropriate levels. Fortunately, we applied for and were awarded a $7,000 literacy grant for intergenerational reading between grandparents, parents, and children, a part of the curriculum offered by Star-C. We meant to equip the children and their parents with tools to improve their literacy and social emotional skills.

20

'I Have Lived Here for 22 Years'

By October 2018, the exterior renovation of Phase II was completed except for the ramp and sidewalk replacements necessary for UFAS and ADA compliance. We could not stop admiring the results; it looked like a completely different property. The aging black roofs were replaced with light gray shingles and new gutters were in the works. A thorough and complete pressure washing removed the greenish mildew from the siding of the buildings and the accumulated gunk in the concrete sidewalks and curbs. Several chipped sidewalk ramps were replaced with newly poured concrete, and the landscaping had been cut, pruned, and mowed. The parking lot was repaved with a new black sealcoating, and new bright white striping gave the property a crisp look. We had spent more than $300,000 and the effect was remarkable. Several projects awaited completion, but the atmosphere was entirely changed. Summerdale felt cleaner, safer, and more respected. We paused to enjoy the results for a moment, aware there was still a lot to do before the property was stable. We were still working with the City of Atlanta for the required permits to renovate Phase I, and Jeff was diligently working on the UFAS, ADA and FHA compliance.

Even though the criminal element was dramatically reduced, we were still cautious when visiting the property. I was greeted by Edward, loyal and vigilant at his post near the front gate. "Mornin', Ms. Marjy," he said, looking past me at a group of young men walking along the sidewalk outside the gate. I gave him a moment to watch the young men. When they passed, he turned his attention back to me. "How are you doing this morning?" I asked.

"I'm doing jes fine . . . doing jes fine," he said nodding.

He saw me looking around the property with clear appreciation.

"The property is really coming along," I said.

"Yes, it is, I can't believe it sometimes. I tell you that you have really changed the property. Ms. Lucy is amazing. At the beginning, I did not think you could do it . . . there was so much crime and activity, you know, this place was a mess, but it is really coming along. Sometimes, I don't even recognize it . . . all the work that has been done, is making it look really good. And you know Ms. Lucy, she don't play. Anyone get out of order, she is all over it, and you know I'm right behind her."

I laughed in agreement, "Yes, that Ms. Lucy don't play. It really takes a team and Edward, I can't thank you enough for your help with the security and helping us clean up the property."

Edward smiled and modestly said "I'm jes doing my job and you know, it's a pleasure to work on seeing this property improve. Where are you heading?"

"I am on my way to Ms. Humphries's apartment, Building 1405." I was interested in getting a verbal history of the property life from Summerdale's longest reigning tenant who had lived at the property since 1996, through the foreclosure, criminal activity, and blight. She was a walking library of information about the property.

"I know Ms. Humphries!" Edward said. "She walks to the school every day to get her great-grandson. She is a real nice lady. She is right in that building [pointing] on the second floor."

I smiled back, said goodbye and headed over to the building, through the newly paved parking lot and up the clean stairwell to her apartment door.

After one knock, the door opened to a neatly dressed and dignified lady who quietly welcomed me with a warm smile. I held out my hand and thanked her for agreeing to meet with me. She nodded and waved me inside.

The smell of fresh paint hung in the air as she escorted me through her hallway. Piles of furniture and household items took over the middle of the living room. I noted the carpet was brand new and the vinyl in the kitchen and dining room had a new sheen. "Excuse the mess," she said pointing to a couch with a middle-aged woman and a sleeping baby on his back snuggled next to her. "This is my daughter Simona and her grandson." Her daughter looked up and we smiled at each other in silence. I resolved to be quiet and not wake the baby. After we sat down, I jokingly asked, "Are you moving?"

"Oh no, we are staying here at Summerdale!" she said surprised at my question.

While setting up the recorder, I told her how much I was looking forward to hearing about the property from our long-term residents. I said I was curious about her journey to Summerdale and how she found the property. She blinked, paused, and looked at her daughter for reassurance. She began to speak, hesitated, and then started again.

> My father was like a hustlin-man. He had to take care of himself but he was so proud of me. He told me "Ginny, you work two or three jobs, but you find you a house and I'm going to pay to get everything for you" and he did. I hate that I sold my house. I had a beautiful home God has blessed me with. Brand new, I was the only owner that lived there for thirty years. But the drugs, it was the guy up the street was the big drug dealer and they turned it into a nightmare. I had a brick mailbox built and they tore my mailbox up. Every time I looked up, they was in the driveway and it got so out of hand, they came down the street retaliating. I had just walked from the mailbox and that's what made me sell my house and come over here.
>
> I used to have a car, but I have retired. So, I love that this location is so convenient to everything. There is a church, dry cleaning—everything on Cleveland Avenue—everything is so convenient. We have had good management in the past, but they had it hard because of the drugs. But they did everything they could to help the residents. I came over to Summerdale to pray for someone in apartment B and did not know these apartments were out here. I had a house, but when I came to pray for my friend in her apartment, there was something about this community and the Lord told me to sell my house and move to this property. My family thought I was crazy. The apartment has been good to me, but it took twenty-two years for my prayers to be answered.

Simona quietly nodded that indeed the family thought her mother was crazy for selling a perfectly good house and moving into an apartment community. Ms. Humphries continued:

> Well, I started on the other side of the property; it was really nice at the time. I lived in apartment A-10 and my apartment was good and had good

management and good neighbors. There was really no crime and I stayed over there because they (the management) used to have inspections. They remembered me because my apartment was so clean and organized. I then moved over to this side, and I loved the management, but after about ten years, there were a lot of drugs being sold, right outside my door in the common area. For a while after I got over here the drugs wasn't here but then it came in.

The Lord told me to go into [unit] 1405, so I moved here from the other side because I wanted a three-bedroom and that's what I got. And I've been here eleven to twelve years and enjoyed it. But when I first came out here the landscape was different. I used to get letters from the past owner saying that they were in bankrupt. From 2009 to today, there was never anything done to the apartment. Had water coming in some spots, over in the laundry area and we had some electrical problems. Eventually they sold out of bankrupt and I haven't had any problems with management because I attend to my business. I like to be neighborly and attend to my business.

I knew Lucy was responsible for creating trust with the tenants since we purchased the property. I asked, "How has Ms. Lucy been to you?" Tears formed in her eyes as she continued:

Ms. Lucy is the icing on the cake. When you get to a certain age, people don't care. People look over you. Ms. Lucy has restored my faith in God, she has restored my faith about people and me. I asked the Lord for the best, but she gave me the best. She gave me everything and she is so calm. I thank God that I met a manager who loves her work. I hope God sustains her. I always give her a blessing because she has been an inspiration.

You know, I didn't know what mildew was until Ms. Lucy came and told me that we had mildew in our apartment. It was in the laundry room and on the walls around the window. Ms. Lucy told me she was going to take care of me and get rid of the mildew. We got new windows, carpet and paint and they just finished so we are going to get everything back in order."

Ms. [Marilyn] Moore, my humble and good neighbor, has been here a long time as well. I really have had a beautiful life here, in the apartment with neighbors like her, with this side of time. One time it was really bad with drugs. But working with the cops and a group, it got better and better. Nowhere you go, you can't say there is no crime, because that is the time we live in.

She paused and looked at me. I was surprised by her positive attitude despite living through years of neglect, violence, and drug activity. It contrasted with the harsh reality of how the property was just a few months ago. I had to admire the spunk of Ms. Humphries. She had provided a good environment for her family despite all the criminal activity and neglect at Summerdale. The thought that she, her daughter, and great-grandson once lived in an unsafe environment sickened me. She was right, there had been some rough times at Summerdale over the past several years.

One time it was bad—but I did just what I could do—I was taught to just pray because you can't run from anything. You had a lot of activities in the back. You couldn't even sit on the playground it (the drug dealing) was so bad. They just started two years ago. I never called the police, I never did call but before you can call, they would be here, called by a neighbor. The last manager was real sweet because they shot up her car. She did a lot of work on the playground—she did a lot of work getting the drugs off the playground. You would hear shots fired all the time. A person got shot outside the gate.

I asked what she thought of the Star-C after-school program.

I have two great-grandchildren in the program. I love Miss Kristin because she loves the elders. I love her for that and because you never see anything out of order. She is helping the kids. I'm happy. There are quite a few kids that I don't know by name that used to play on that playground [before the criminals destroyed it]. Sometimes they didn't have shoes. The little boy that would play on the playground with his shoes untied, and I would always take the time to tie his shoes. We got to let children know we care for them. You have to show love and show that you care. A lot of the families need help. There are two little boys that don't have coats. That is bothering me. There have been some rough times out here.

She paused and looked at me with a smile. I looked at my watch and it was getting close to two o'clock. Ms. Humphries seemed eager to be on her schedule, so I told her that I should be leaving so she could pick up her two great-grandsons from school.

"Yes, I need to go walk to Cleveland Avenue Elementary to pick up my great-grandbabies."

"Thank you so much for meeting with me Ms. Humphries," I said. "Thank you for sharing your story." She walked me to the door with a lightness unusual for an eight-two-year-old and we said goodbye. I promised to come back and visit again.

WALKING OUT OF HER apartment, I paused for a moment at the landing before heading down the stairs. Ms. Humphries was an amazing lady and I felt inspired after hearing her story. Still thinking about the interview, I headed over to the room in the leasing office which served as our temporary Star-C program.

"I was just over at Ms. Humphries and met her daughter and great-grandson," I told Kristin while entering the room.

"Oh yes, she has two great-grandchildren in the program. A five-year-old and a seven-year-old."

"She was telling me she had mildew in her apartment."

Kristin frowned and shook her head, "And both children have asthma and reading problems, and the seven-year-old is also having some behavior issues. We are taking care of him, though. I have him reading to the first-graders every day and his reading is already improving."

The room grew more animated as the children arrived from Cleveland Avenue Elementary and settled in the room. I watched the children enter, more aware than ever of their personal struggles they faced just from living at Summerdale. Despite being fresh in my mind, the interview with Ms. Humphries exposed me to the reality of these children and their home lives. No wonder very few of them smiled as they entered the program. Their parents were probably dealing with the trauma of juggling jobs at poverty wages that barely covered basic living essentials. We knew many of our residents were late on their rent payments, and the late fees and other costs added to their rent burden.

I also did not understand how a landlord could let a loyal tenant like Ms. Humphries live in such squalid conditions for all these years. She paid her rent and was entitled to a healthy apartment environment. Ms. Humphries raised two generations of children in her apartment and the long-term health effects could not be positive. Lucy organized the repairs on her apartment and the total cost was just over $7,000. The medical and financial impact of living in moldy conditions would not only exceed the thousands of dollars in repairs but would reverberate down through generations of her family. Her great-grandchildren have asthma. The cost to treat this incurable disease is $2,000 a year per the CDC website, so the cost of NOT making that repair easily is $240,000 over a lifetime. This does not include the emotional and physical trauma of not being able to breathe freely. The state of Georgia has no laws mandating a landlord must provide tenants with a healthy, mold-free environment.

The previous landlord could ignore repairs and collect the rent money from good, decent, loyal tenants like Ms. Humphries with no legal repercussions. I started thinking of the other tenants living at the property and the issues they had with their apartments. We had one other tenant that had mold but would never report this to the management for fear of eviction. After Lucy found mold around a window during one unit's inspection, we immediately repaired the windows, replaced the carpet, painted the walls and the roof. This tenant had two small children living in her unit. She ultimately reached out to the Atlanta Volunteer Lawyers Foundation, a nonprofit that works with tenants to resolve legal issues on a pro bono basis. AVLF sent us a letter on her behalf a few months later, and by then, we had already completed the repairs. It was becoming clear to me that until we intervened, the previous owner of Summerdale was raising the next generation of children in a manner that set them up for failure.

21

Pest Infestations Management

I was in the leasing office in November 2018 with Lucy after another community tour, when Evan Harris, our Massey Services Pest Control technician, joined us. At 6'5" and 250 pounds, Evan is a big guy, defying his soft voice and gentle approach. He obtained a bachelor's in biology from Fort Valley State University and a master's in agricultural science with a concentration in etiology from Florida A&M University. To say Evan knows his "bugs" is an understatement. Judging by the serious look on his face, I was about to get lectured on bug infestations.

We were now five months into ownership, and the pest infestation was a hard issue to resolve, taking time and patience. Lucy documented ninety-five pest calls the first week we owned the property, and we started a property-wide treatment. Rodents and roaches were the predominant villains, along with several reports of bed bugs and fleas. Many of the tenants reporting pest issues were cooperative and worked closely with Evan to eradicate the problem. Evan was given access and the tenants completed his checklist of good housekeeping practices.

However, several uncooperative tenants perplexed Lucy. These tenants were downright hostile when Evan contacted them about treating their apartments. Over time, we had sorted the tenants willing to be good, respectful neighbors from the ones that perpetuated a blighted mentality. I was still philosophical on the cause of blight. Was it caused by the management, the tenants, the criminal activity, or all three? But clearly the tenants were part of the problem, because anyone allowing a pest infestation to proliferate over years and spread to their neighbors was an accomplice to a blighted environment. Their selfish actions triggered asthma in small children, bed bug infestations at Cleveland Avenue Elementary, and exposure to various unknown diseases.

Since Lucy had galvanized our attention to infestations, Evan had visited Summerdale's two sections weekly. After his inspection, he would give us a quick verbal report, especially on two apartments that had extreme infestations—Unit 205, occupied by Melinda's family of three adults and four children, and Unit 1101, occupied by a mother, three grown daughters, and three children under five.

Evan began with a report on Melinda's unit:

> I did the bed bug treatment because upon the initial inspection, I was there for roaches, but also noticed they had bed bugs. Now I am pretty sure the bed bugs were brought in from infested furniture. It started in the couches, and then spread to each of the rooms. Each room was bad, literally crawling with bugs, especially the walls. The kitchen was filled with roaches, the living room was probably the worst when it comes to bed bugs. Normally with a bed bug treatment, it is not too difficult, but there must be cooperation between the customer and the pest control technician. In both cases I gave prep tasks for the tenants before the bed bug treatment. So, when we do a treatment, it must be done correctly and orderly because bed bugs are resistant. I prepped Melinda several days in advance, but when I arrived for the treatment, there were a lot of things left undone.

I interrupted to mention that when Jeff and I were at Unit 205 checking up on the UFAS renovations a few weeks ago, it was strange to see Melinda's couches flipped over. Evan replied:

> Yes, I flipped all the couches. I noticed that there was a bigger bed bug infestation under the couch, specifically under the risers of the couch. There are some things that chemicals cannot get through. I tried to treat it but there is only so much that you can get to and bed bugs can live two years without a blood meal. As part of the treatment, we heat the room temperature to above 113 degrees Fahrenheit and that is when they start dying.

I interrupted again to say that Jeff had told me Melinda had been combative while he was renovating her unit. Lucy added that Melinda was usually combative with management. I asked Evan about her demeanor.

> The tenant wasn't combative with me, she just wasn't cooperative. She did not do things that the prep sheet listed. She did not remove furniture in a timely manner. I did a treatment and followed up the next week and there was too much on the checklist that was not done. There were a lot of roaches and there is another infestation of fleas. The unit is being renovated, and the roaches and fleas are coming out. Fleas are not necessarily indicative of her lifestyle. All it takes is a child to run through grass, get the fleas on their clothing, and bring them into the home. Now if you are dirty, fleas are going to thrive more, and you are not going to know what is biting you. If you have both bed bugs and fleas, you are not going to be able to discern which one is biting you. Because of that, what I use to treat bed bugs is also used for fleas, so by one treatment I am able to get rid of both of them.

Evan paused to let this sink in and then continued.

> Massey technicians are trained, and our bosses are trained very well, so we know what to do with stuff, but some things we have to rely on the customer to do the right thing. Like I removed everything out of one closet and came back a week later and I asked her if she treated her clothes, and she was like "no" but I told her you have to wash your clothes to avoid reinfestation, but those clothes were thrown in a bag and put back into the closet. I will go back and inspect, and I can guarantee you that there will be a reinfestation of bed bugs.

This was a serious problem. I changed the topic to Unit 1101, the one we considered to be ground zero of the infestation. Evan had said earlier that he would re-treat Unit 1101 because bugs were moving up its walls and into the adjacent units. He had photos from inside the unit, which he estimated contained ten thousand roaches. In one apartment. How was that even possible? Evan explained:

It is possible, but since we are treating the rest of the building, the problems have been contained to 1101 . . . that is because I have treated 1102–1110 aggressively to make sure we do not have those levels of issues. It is the stack going up. Unit 1103 is having problems because she is directly above the 1101 unit. It really is sad because German roaches have the same properties as fire. They stay in one area and consume as much as they can and when they do not have enough, they move. And it is going to be rinsed and repeated all over again. And it gets to a point that we will have to tent the building because all treatment options have been exhausted. The Unit 1101 tenants need to wash or discard everything. There are some toys that I treated. Make sure you tell them that. I could not move them all. In an occupied unit, I can only do the kitchens and maybe the bathroom. Now if it is extreme, I must make the decision of what infestation I am treating and for this unit, I treated everywhere I could. I did not mess with the couches, but I moved everything out of the way. I did not mess with the car seat, but again, I moved it out of the way. I am a big dude and can move stuff if needed in a safe manner, by myself, without damaging myself or the property. That is a benefit of me being here and in the pest treatment field. I can always do my best to ensure there is a thorough treatment when necessary.

Per the leases, tenants are responsible for the costs of pest treatments. And they could be expensive, especially for bed bugs. Evan explained further:

There is a huge difference between the price of treatments. A heat treatment is $1,200–$1,600 per treatment, but it is usually successful in eliminating the problem. A liquid treatment is $750–$800. It will get rid of the problem, but the tenant needs to cooperate and follow the prep sheet. A roach cleanout depends on if the apartment unit is occupied or unoccupied, and the size of the apartment. [Unit 1101] was $25 because the unit is occupied. But if it were vacant, it would be $75 because I would treat the entire unit, not just the kitchen and bathrooms, or affected areas."

Lucy added that "Melinda paid $250 so far for the bed bugs. She said she was going to pay for the whole treatment, but it didn't happen yet. . . .

I'll get back with both tenants and tell them they have to comply with your checklist, or I'll have to issue a housekeeping violation."

EVAN HAD A FULL day of service calls, so he only stayed a few minutes. Lucy and I discussed the next steps. Our rents were the lowest in the market and we gave long-term tenants the benefit of the doubt and worked with them so they could remain in their apartments. We avoided evictions, especially of families with young children. Melinda had four children living in the apartment; two attended Cleveland Avenue Elementary and were enrolled in our Star-C program, although they had not attended lately. I asked Lucy whether we should evict these tenants based on substandard housekeeping practices that jeopardize the health of their children and neighbors.

Lucy thought for a moment before replying:

> Melinda is the perfect example of a blighted tenant and is horrible. She is nasty, certainly not a housekeeper and is more concerned with her hair, her nails and what she is wearing than making sure those kids are clean, eating properly and that house is clean. Her kids are the sweetest kids in the world, but you can tell they are neglected, dirty and it is one of those times that you just want to call social services so bad, but then you do not want them in the system but trying to figure out what is the better of two evils. They come out and help the elderly ladies with their trash and I do not know what their health is like, but it is sad and scary. If she needs something from you, she swings by, but if you ask anything that is going to be beneficial to her, she is nasty as can be. And if you call and catch her wrong, she will hang up.
>
> Behavior makes a property blighted because no one wants to live next door to someone who lets cockroaches live in their apartment that eventually come through the walls. If you are in your unit and clean . . . that is bad to have all these bugs coming through the walls. Her priorities are not where they should be, and they have nothing to do with her home life. You should see her with her new tennis shoes on every week, her hair is all dolled up every week, her nails are all dolled up . . . but her kids are so filthy, I really want to take them and bathe them. They do not eat three meals a day. The guy was cooking and there were roaches in the pot. That is just too much.

I opened the refrigerator and was done. There were bugs in the refrigerator to escape the filth of the rest of the house. He was just cooking like it was okay. She said that she is married but I did not know the guy because he is not on the lease. He showed up in August, was the first time I have seen him. But he is right in there with her. Unit 1101 is just as bad. You have these kids [ages three months, two years, and four years] in there but there is a new man every time I turn around.

I kept listening since Lucy was so positive and rarely had any negative opinions. She continued, referencing the housekeeping classes we would be mandating for problem tenants:

I just don't understand how you invite yourself into filth. There are two Melindas, one outside the apartment who is groomed and attractive, but then there is Melinda inside the apartment living in filth . . . so a double life. When we call, she does not yell, she just hangs up on you.

We are having problems finding someone to teach the classes, so our management staff may just teach them. We are going to start next Saturday for two hours and are putting together a PowerPoint presentation to show the families. We have a budget for cleaning supplies, right?

22

Crime and Security

The American perception of crime is influenced by the scripted detective shows delivered daily on our living room TVs or handheld devices, which makes crime-solving look so simple. The bad guys commit a crime. The terrified community gets righteous and demands action. The police work diligently to identify and arrest, the efficient judge sentences the perps to prison, and the community is safe again—neatly concluded in under an hour of watching from the comfort of our easy chair.

In real life, removing the criminal activity from Summerdale was much more time consuming and complicated. Drug sales and other illegal activities occurred in plain sight of police, but criminals—protected by fair housing and privacy laws—could easily hide inside apartment units. Once a criminal enters an apartment, the "lawful search" rules make it almost impossible for a landlord or police officer to enter without a warrant, and getting a judge to sign off on a warrant does not happen overnight. These legal roadblocks significantly delayed our ability to create a safer environment at Summerdale. We watched large groups of adults loiter around the property then disappear inside a unit, claiming they were a "guest" of the legal tenant. The criminals were much smarter than we were, and the law was on their side, at least temporarily.

The entrance gates were one of our major weapons to suppress the drug traffic and ongoing crime. But the drug dealers used rocks to prop them open or a "watcher" to physically break the gate latches. Or the watcher swiped a tenant-issued entry card to grant the dealers and customers access. One morning Lucy inspected a pedestrian gate and realized that someone had removed the magnetic security element—no easy feat since the metal gate was made of heavy steel and the magnetic seal was tightly soldered to the metal. Frustrated, Lucy secured the gate with a heavy chain, prohibiting entry without the key to unlock it. An hour later, our police officers reported that someone had called 911 because the gate was chained shut and they were worried the blocked access endangered the community. We silently laughed; it had to be a drug dealer angered by our brazen attempt to block his business. We decided to keep this popular pedestrian gate chained for a few weeks since it blocked the buyers from easy access to their dealers. There were other entry gates, just in inconvenient locations.

Lucy had chased internet providers for months to restore service to Summerdale after years of absence. Internet would have let us put cameras throughout the property and on the gates, to supplement the Atlanta Police Foundation cameras, so we could keep watch from a screen in the management office and on our smart phones. Few internet companies wanted to invest the infrastructure in a low-income blighted apartment community, confirming the digital divide experienced by so many impoverished communities.

Bighted apartment communities are defined by their perceived lack of community capital, which in turn attracts people without the social capital to afford many housing choices. People with poor credit, mental health and behavioral issues, or felonies have records that disqualify them from many apartment housing communities. They thus must choose from the tiny pool of apartment complexes willing to accept such impediments and sign leases. Summerdale's previous ownership accepted risky tenants and then added poor management and an unwillingness to invest the time and money to rebuild the community. The lack of social etiquette at Summerdale was then unsurprising. As Anthony Fowler demonstrated, criminals thrive in areas lacking community capital. Once Summerdale's environment became toxic, tenants with resources departed for safer neighborhoods, leaving behind those who could not afford to move or fight the criminals. The remaining tenants lived in fear and behind locked doors with usually futile hopes of not becoming victims.

SINCE PURCHASING SUMMERDALE, WE had made significant progress removing the visible criminal elements. By December 2018, the car theft rings, prostitutes, vagrants and loitering were almost completely gone from

Phase II. Phase I continued to have issues with loitering and suspected drug dealings in the common areas, but we were advised to hold off disrupting the activity while the Atlanta Police Department performed an undercover surveillance operation. We also had a contingent of disruptive tenants who did not follow the rules despite our written notices. A party would be announced on social media and within minutes forty to fifty people had showed up, spilling out of units into the parking lot and courtyard. The loud music, screams, and fighting kept up all night many tenants who should have been safely asleep. Mr. Hayes, Edward, and our APD officers were significantly outnumbered and could do only so much to quell the crowds without major police backup. Summerdale had a generous security budget, but the removal of the criminal activity took longer than expected and was expensive, and we had to rely on APD backup when large rowdy crowds appeared.

We asked disruptive tenants to follow the rules but they ignored us and continued to party. First, we delivered a written notice outlining the default agreement contained in their lease. If they continued to ignore us, we terminated their leases and gave notice to vacate. The eviction process which followed was no easy process because the legal proceedings were taking months to complete in Fulton County. We also explored the criminal trespass citation process (CO Process), which would give Mr. Hayes, Edward, and Ski more control over illegal guests and trespassers. However, we were told by the district attorney's office to hold off pending review. The DA's office would never respond to our requests for an update nor were we able to use CO as a tool. Even when tenants and their guests were arrested, the Fulton County district attorney ran an incompetent department. Cases would drag out for months if not years. Ski shared that the Fulton County DA had a reputation of being soft on felony criminals, seemingly drawing out-of-state felons to do criminal activity in Atlanta and then return to their homes. I did not fully understand Ski's claim until we researched Fowler's background—a spin cycle of felony arrests.

It was difficult to be patient while we sifted through the tenant list to determine who was legally compliant and who justified eviction. At the same time, we were carefully screening tenant applications and keeping an eye out for those who wanted to move in as phantom tenants to front illegal activity. The property's reputation attracted the criminal culture. Fixing the problem would take more than a few months of armed security and careful screening, but we were in it for the long haul. Several tenants reported desperate buyers standing outside the gate asking for drugs. The drug buyer demand attracted the dynamic supporting phantom tenants. We had plenty of young applicants with valid social security numbers and no disqualifying criminal or credit history. But Lucy continued to carefully screen tenant applications and had a high percentage of rejection. We created a high bar to lease at Summerdale, eventually replacing the lawless tenants with families that had better credit, acceptable criminal backgrounds, and verifiable stable jobs.

AFTER HIS ARREST IN July, Anthony Fowler was released and back on the streets. Given Fowler's extensive criminal history, and as illogical as it may sound, a communications gap exists between the APD, the Fulton County court system, and the owners of properties where crime happens and criminals are arrested. The police could raid Summerdale and make a hundred arrests, and we would probably never know unless a tenant or Ski reported it, or if our security was present and aware of the arrest. Given that Ski was so busy with his precinct and hundreds of other properties, he could only give us so much attention.

During the 2018 stakeout, the APD kept all activity confidential, not trusting how information would be used and the potential that sharing it would interfere with the investigation. The APD and court systems do not share current arrest and court data and sourcing the meaningful information can be burdensome. It could sometimes take months to access criminal records through the APD records process. We were aware of one arrest in July but were under the impression that the arrest was for "Dog," the habitual shooter who kept Cleveland Avenue Elementary in perpetual fear and lockdown. We also assumed that anyone with multiple arrests and arrested as a drug dealer would spend time in jail, but Fowler was deemed innocent and harmless until proven guilty. He posted a $26,000 bond and was out of jail in less than forty-eight hours. We did not have access to the police reports or judicial records for several months after his arrest, and his picture was not part of the arrest report. On paper, we had a name, but we didn't know what the arrestee looked like. We suspected Fowler was the Summerdale drug kingpin, but it takes time to link names and faces, and drug dealers are masters of evasion and intimidation, always ready to pull out their guns and threaten. Fowler hid from Lucy and Adriane, tending to be visible late at night after office hours, or show up when it was time to pay rent.

It was a dangerous undertaking to remove an entrenched criminal element while preserving the rights of the tenants we were trying to retain. The APD was responsive and generously used their limited resources to work with Summerdale, but the post-arrest system was complex and difficult to navigate. For months we offered to house rent-free any APD officer willing to move to Summerdale. No officers responded. They did not want to live at a property with a reputation like Summerdale's.

In December, after four months, the APD completed its undercover surveillance, obtained a search warrant, and conducted a lawful raid on Apartments D-12 and C-6. The APD team found guns in the walls and illegal drugs throughout the apartment and tucked away in a car parked out front. They arrested eleven people including Anthony Fowler. Nine did not live in the Cleveland neighborhood and listed home addresses thirty miles away—indicating that Summerdale was a regional drug hub. Three of the arrested were on social media, having posted pictures of their girlfriends, bass-fishing trips, and family events. One attended Georgia State University, studying business management.

This was our first major blow to the criminal operation at Summerdale, and it made an immediate impact. We promptly boarded up the targeted units after the arrests, but surprisingly we were not allowed to take possession of Unit D-12 despite the drug bust. To reclaim the unit, we needed to legally evict Sharon Allen, the phantom tenant rarely seen by our leasing or maintenance staff. Lucy promptly filed the paperwork in Fulton County. She also filed the paperwork to evict the family living at Unit C-6—a single mother with six children. She had allowed Fowler to use her apartment. This tenant promptly filed an action against us which put her eviction into the federal courts—hence another delay. Meanwhile she stopped paying and on the day of her eviction owed us for almost eighteen months back rent.

AFTER THE ARRESTS, THE word was out on the street and Summerdale's visible vagrant and loitering population dropped noticeably. The winter cold kept everyone indoors, and we suspected some fragments of the criminal network was still here. But we were making it difficult for the criminals to openly operate. In the meantime, the legal tenants provided plenty of challenges. One tenant held a children's birthday party that turned into an adult party, fighting started, and the police were called. A few nights later, another tenant posted about a gathering at her unit, and within an hour sixty people were dancing, screaming, and carrying on in the courtyard.

It took a few tense moments for security to shut the party down and escort everyone out the gate. The party-throwing tenant was promptly given a notice to vacate, but it took almost five months to evict her. She stopped paying rent in the interim but kept the parties going. After receiving her eviction notice, she and her mother confronted Lucy and Adriane in the leasing office, waving her eviction notice. This young lady was a student at a local university and denied having anything to do with the parties despite being presented with evidence that her gate key had been used more than fifty times that night to open the gate. She responded by challenging Adriane to step out to the parking lot and fight.

Another incident occurred one morning while Jeff and the construction workers were inspecting the plumbing system at Building E. During the inspection, Jeff noticed two young men step outside an apartment; one was clothed in nothing but his socks, flip-flops, sweatshirt, and boxer shorts, with a gun hanging out of his boxer shorts. Jeff recognized one of the young men as a tenant but didn't recognize the other one with the gun. Seeing the gun, the construction workers started getting nervous and said they were leaving, but Jeff was already behind schedule and needed to continue the work. He politely confronted the kid asking him to take the gun back inside the apartment. The kid belligerently reacted, claiming the apartment community was dangerous and he needed to protect himself, but Jeff was adamant that he needed to put the gun back into the apartment.

Luckily, another tenant couple was sitting on their porch and witnessed the confrontation. The couple calmly joined the conversation, ultimately telling the kid to leave the property. The kid angrily went inside to put on some clothes, then came out of the apartment and after some choice words to the couple and Jeff, left the property.

Most of the tenants endured the turbulent social structure while security and the APD worked on getting everything under control. Unfortunately, others tenants did not. After witnessing a loud and long night of partying, Mr. Robinson, one of the newer residents living in Phase I, told Lucy he needed to move on. He claimed his tenancy at Summerdale started off okay, but the constant music and younger rowdier neighbors made him uncomfortable. We were all disappointed—so was Mr. Robinson, because he admitted to Lucy that he loved the interior of his newly renovated town-house unit, the affordable rent, and the convenience to his custodial job at Grady Hospital. However, on several occasions he found thugs sitting on his car in the parking lot, smoking a cigarette or selling drugs, and they would be disrespectful when he asked them to move. Mr. Robinson was just one of several tenants who terminated their leases early after moving to Phase I of Summerdale. We didn't challenge these tenants. If they did not feel comfortable living at Summerdale, we let them break their leases without penalty and move out of the property. Re-tenanting Summerdale with good, long-term occupants continued to be a challenge while we went through the long process to remove the criminal element and disrespectful culture.

After six months of patiently waiting, and hundreds of police hours, there was some positive news. A few days after the December arrests, we were rewarded with the noise of kids riding their bikes around Unit D-12 and the areas that were formally populated by brazen drug dealers. The kids and their parents were cautious at first, but after a quiet few weeks without suspicious activity, the families stepped out to explore their safer environment.

23

Melinda Wyatt and the Blighted Mentality

Melinda Wyatt entered the leasing office one day in December 2018 and patiently waited to speak with Lucy, who was occupied with a prospective tenant. Melinda was clutching two documents: a formal infraction notice for housekeeping issues and a $1,200 invoice for a bed bug treatment. Under the contractual terms of the lease, a "Tenant was required to practice good housekeeping and was responsible for any costs associated with pest treatment including bed bugs." After a few minutes of waiting, she entered Lucy's office and got right to the point. Waving the notice and invoice, she demanded, "I need you to show me what bed bugs look like."

"Sure," said Lucy. "Let me show you pictures."

Lucy pulled photos of bed bugs from the internet and showed Melinda, who looked confused.

Lucy took one look at Melinda's face and said, "Okay, let's walk back to your apartment and I'll show you exactly what we're talking about in your notice."

As soon as they entered the apartment, Lucy pointed out the black globs of bugs on the walls. In denial, Melinda said, "That's not what that is, and I don't know what you're talking about."

Lucy, ever patient with tenants, decided to get Evan Harris with Massey to give Melinda an education on Bed Bugs 101. The next week, Evan retrieved a few pests from Melinda's apartment and showed her the living creatures, known as bed bugs, that were crawling around her walls.

Melinda replied, "I thought they were just spots on the walls. There had been so many of them in the past, but they were clearly back and starting to multiply again."

Melinda's continued denial of the problem was no excuse for Lucy. Both Lucy and Evan clearly told her multiple times that she needed to get rid of her mattresses, furniture, and especially the sofa set because her unit was infested. Lucy also invited Melinda to attend the free housekeeping classes that Summerdale now offered the tenants. Evan advised a thorough cleansing of all clothing, sheets, and towels. Melinda eventually removed everything except the severely infested clothing and furniture. A few weeks after Eric's visit, Lucy inspected again and the apartment was again infested with fleas, plenty of roaches, and bed bugs. Lucy gave her a written notice to follow the Massey pest removal checklist. After reading the letter, Melinda grudgingly agreed to remove the furniture. Jeff and his construction crew kindly hauled it to the dumpster.

"Melinda was cooperative at this point because she was concerned," Jeff recalled. "We also helped her put her clothing in black plastic bags. There were piles of clothing throughout the apartment and a lot of it was damp and moldy. Rather than throw out the clothing, we put it in the bags with the assumption that she would wash all the clothes to get them clean and remove any roaches or their eggs. When we tried to have the men remove the mattresses, she refused."

Jeff called Lucy for backup, and Lucy immediately called Melinda. "You do realize that you need to get rid of the mattresses?"

Melinda said, "I know but I don't have any place for my kids to sleep."

"I get that, but you do realize that your mattresses are infested, so if your babies have little bumps on them, that is why."

"Well, I haven't noticed, but I will get rid of them next week."

A COUPLE OF DAYS later, Jeff and Lucy noticed the infested mattresses in the dumpster. Lucy and the staff felt Melinda was at least trying to change her family's unhealthy living situation. Jeff and his team would soon be renovating her unit with new kitchen, bath, and other UFAS-compliance upgrades. Once the makeover was completed, the staff hoped it would improve Melinda's housekeeping. She seemed excited when Lucy called to go over the upcoming renovation and how the apartment would be disrupted for two weeks. She had never lived in a housing unit with new kitchen cabinets, appliances, flooring, and bathroom vanities. When renovation day arrived, Jeff and his team divided the work into phases so Melinda and her family had a functioning kitchen and bathroom during the entire process.

Had the unit been vacant, the renovation work would have easily been completed in a week, but when the crew started dismantling the sink and toilet in the first bathroom, Melinda quickly lost her patience and became noncooperative. Jeff voiced his frustration:

> Melinda was the reason it took over thirty days to renovate the unit. For example, Melinda would slam the door and not let my workers come in her apartment or and she kept making them leave, so things didn't get done on time. The workers are polite and do not push back. They ended up having a big issue with her the weekend before our second scheduled federal compliance inspection with Charles.

Melinda's pushback was happening at a tense time. We were in the middle of UFAS certification and the process was not only complex but the minute details that Charles was demanding were costing time and money. The UFAS checklist had thirty-six compliance items for each of the forty-two units that we scheduled for inspection on Monday, or 1,512 interior elements that had to be 100 percent perfect to pass the inspection. We knew Charles pulled out his white gloves and tape measure, and if we were one-sixteenth of an inch off the height of a thermostat or handrail, then we failed. If Charles had to reinspect the property, it would cost $2,000 to fly him back and could delay the renovations for months if not years. Lucy, Adriane, Jeff, and the maintenance crew was feeling the stress to have the interiors renovated and the UFAS compliance phase behind them. Jeff explained:

> "I told the weekend crew that they have to keep working but they said Melinda was so rude with her racist remarks, they simply refused to work in her apartment. It was the last straw for me that they didn't get everything done before the UFAS inspection.

She is rude and treats Lucy the same. So, to get the work completed in her apartment, I was the one doing it. At first, she said she was not going to let me in, but I told her I have a key and am doing the work. I try to be polite to her and ask how she is doing because I know the construction is disruptive, but if she were cooperative, we would have this done much quicker.

I personally inspected her unit one afternoon to understand the frustration everyone was feeling and immediately felt sympathetic for Jeff and the construction crew on the challenges of dealing with bugs, general filth, and an uncooperative tenant. Jeff summed up the experience:

Her unit was just disgusting. We put in a brand-new kitchen and I had to replace the insulated boot under the kitchen sink. The old one was covered in grease—it was just unwashed and gross. While we were removing the old kitchen cabinets and fixtures, the roaches took off running in all directions. You could see the roach eggs and their poop. I could not work with the doors closed and that was a problem. They were complaining about it being cold and drafty, but I could not breathe. It is moist and musty; you stay in there with the door closed and it just smells. The smell is her living. She has no furniture. There is no mold. It is a combination of greasy cooking and sweaty clothes. When you go to the bathroom you just smell urine. She has three boys, and I understand little boys. I have one myself and know they tend to miss the toilet when they pee, but you have to clean up to keep everything sanitized."

We were patient with Melinda because we did not want her children to be part of the transiency problem at Cleveland Avenue Elementary. Her children had signed up to participate in the Star-C program, Kristin confirmed that after the first day the two boys never returned to the program. I wondered if Melinda had mental health issues.

THROUGH PERSEVERANCE, JEFF COMPLETED the majority of the UFAS work in Melinda's apartment the weekend before Charles arrived. However, several items were not completed. Photos from the inspection report showed piles of trash in front of her newly replaced kitchen cabinets and appliances. Not surprisingly, Charles failed the unit. A month later, the unit was trashed and infested again with roaches.

At our next management meeting, we discussed Melinda's future tenancy at Summerdale. We concluded that her housekeeping practices were jeopardizing the other tenants and she was not going to change despite her unit renovation and our continued invitations to attend monthly housekeeping classes. It was time to start the eviction process.

Lucy delivered the news to Melinda. "Why is your unit infested with bugs again after we just replaced everything with a new kitchen, carpet, and bathroom tile, toilet and fixtures?"

Melinda tried to blame the contractors. "But I've cleaned up, it's not me but their mess."

Lucy went with Melinda to the unit and pointed out the overflowing garbage can in the corner of the kitchen and the clothes strewn all around the apartment. "This is not *their* mess, this your mess. There is a big brown stain in the middle of your brand-new carpet. That is not my contractors, but it is you. *You* have to do something; I can't let you live like this."

Lucy served Melinda with a notice to vacate and later reported, "She was impossible, just unbelievable . . . the situation is not better and now she won't let Evan in there for a new round of pest control treatment. But I told her she has no choice. Her bugs are too bad, and we can't let them spread to other apartments."

After several phone calls and notices, Melinda finally let Evan in to do additional pest treatments. But Lucy said, "It is doubtful that her behavior is not going to change and future apartment units she occupies will have the same problems."

Before finally handing out an eviction notice, Lucy did one last thing to ease her conscience about evicting a family with young children. A City of Atlanta Code Enforcement employee had recently leased a unit and Lucy asked if he would visit Melinda's apartment and advise her off the record. He had seen Lucy and the staff working hard to improve the look and safety of the property, so he agreed. He walked into Melinda's unit and promptly advised us to call social services.

What are the solutions for tenants like Melinda who exhibit a "blighted" mentality? I started thinking that mental health services needed to be part of our Eduhousing business model to remove blight.

24

Jeff Miller and the Tedious Permitting Process

When we purchased Summerdale Apartments, the property was in severe disrepair after years of neglect. More than half of Phase I's buildings were boarded up for more than six years; the roof of one building had collapsed from fire damage. Across the road, Phase II sat with significant maintenance issues, also deferred for years. The neglect attracted loitering, drug activity, and vagrancy—all in plain sight of anyone traveling along Old Hapeville Road. One blighted apartment complex leads to another, spreading like a cancer to nearby properties. Neighbors voiced their anger to various municipal departments, creating frustration and calls for code enforcement. From the outset, we expected code enforcement challenges because Summerdale ranked high on municipal officials' radar. Thus we were not surprised when several code enforcement officers arrived unannounced a few weeks after our purchase. We should have wondered what took them so long.

Jeff and I were inspecting the fire-ravaged Building G on a warm sunny day when the officers approached us in a friendly yet professional manner. After introducing themselves, they requested an update on a code violation citation issued a few months before we closed the acquisition. Jeff and I exchanged confused glances. The previous owner had disclosed no citations. I braced myself for the long list of code violations that were about to be revealed.

"What's the citation?" I asked apprehensively.

The officer replied, "There is some overgrown landscaping around the buildings that needs to be addressed."

Now we were standing in the middle of a boarded-up apartment property, with arguably dozens of serious code violations and suspicious drug dealers loitering around the courtyard, and the officers were only interested in overgrown landscaping. The triviality of the code citation demonstrated the city's exhaustion in dealing with blighted properties like Summerdale.

I hid my surprise and responded, "Thank you for coming and we will get the citation issue addressed immediately. We recently purchased this property and a landscaping contractor is working on a bid to clean up the overgrowth and trash. We will respond to the citation. Is there anything else?"

We went on to explain our education/housing model and renovation plans, and the enforcement officers seemed satisfied. No other citations against Summerdale were delivered. But I asked my good friend Lauren Clayton, an attorney who specialized in code enforcement and zoning in Atlanta, to educate me on the relevant law.

She did not waste words. "To put it simply, the city code enforcement is under-resourced. The city subscribes to the broken-windows theory and the idea that code enforcement violations and graffiti increases the crime levels. However, they shut down part of the jail capacity in the City of Atlanta, so the criminals are not getting locked up for petty crimes."

I learned that the Atlanta Code Enforcement operates within a set of laws strongly favoring the property rights of a landlord over the rights of a community. The laws are so tilted toward landlords that it almost is not worth the cost to cite Summerdale or other blighted properties, despite the diligent and heroic efforts of the city code personnel. Savvy investors shield themselves against fines by placing property ownership in limited liability companies or other legal entities. If a property is cited for a code violation, the legal entity is held accountable, not the individuals who own the legal entity.

Lauren explained, "In the City of Atlanta, a citation for code enforcement is a quasi-criminal charge with the potential for jail time for repeat offenders. It is difficult for code enforcement to break through the liability protection of the 'corporate veil' and get to the human person that owns the corporation to hold them criminally accountable. You cannot put a corporation in jail. Look up *Rick Warren v. the City of Atlanta*, a textbook example demonstrating the complexity of holding code violators accountable."

Warren owned and operated a real estate investment portfolio in the city limits. Over the years, he purchased hundreds of blighted and boarded-up houses in the Vine City neighborhood, one mile west of the downtown central business district. Each property was placed in a separate legal entity. Atlanta Code Enforcement cited him dozens of times for violations, and it took years of complaints by neighbors and forensic legal work to prove that Rick personally owned these blighted properties. On September 22, 2015, Willoughby Mariano reported this in the *Atlanta Journal-Constitution*:

A Buckhead real estate investor facing prosecution for squalid conditions at houses in an impoverished west Atlanta neighborhood faces almost certain jail time after being found guilty on two housing code violations Tuesday. Rick Warren has stood trial in Atlanta Municipal Court three times since May on citations issued during a November 2014 code enforcement sweep on his properties, but Judge Crystal Gaines withheld verdicts on all the cases until Tuesday, when the businessman was scheduled to stand trial on charges related to a fourth house. Instead, Gaines announced guilty verdicts in two of the trials, and found Warren not guilty on three counts relating to the third. Charges for the scheduled fourth trial were dropped because prosecutors think Warren no longer owned that house when he was cited.

As a repeat offender, Warren faces a mandatory sentence of at least 30 days in jail on both guilty verdicts. Sentencing is set for Oct. 20, and Warren is out on $2,000 bond pending appeal.

The convictions are victories for Atlanta's overworked code enforcement division and Mayor Kasim Reed, who made an unusual public appeal for Warren's conviction.

Through a spokeswoman, Reed said Tuesday that Gaines's decision is "a significant step forward in the revitalization of Vine City and English Avenue."

"Rick Warren is an admitted repeat offender of the City of Atlanta's housing code, and he has engaged in a level of lawless behavior with little to no regard for the quality of life of residents in the community," Reed said in a written statement.

Warren and his attorney George Lawson declined comment after the verdicts were read. Warren faces trial again for another property on Oct. 20, the same day he is to be sentenced on Tuesday's verdicts. Warren was found guilty even though the houses were owned by limited liability corporations that were not listed under his name. Lawson argued that his client was not responsible for their conditions because he was not their owner or operator. But witnesses testified that Warren was in charge of day-to-day operations at those businesses, and records showed he had an ownership interest.

Code enforcement officers targeted Warren after an *Atlanta Journal-Constitution* investigation found that he had purchased some 10 percent of the houses in and around the historically black English Avenue neighborhood, leaving many vacant and crumbling. For years, Warren paid fines when he was cited for vacant houses infested with rats and overgrown with weeds, then continued to re-offend. Neighbors complained that drug dealers set up shop inside his properties, undermining attempts to revive the neighborhood. English Avenue, which has been scarred by the heroin trade, was the victim of rampant mortgage fraud during the housing boom. It then became the site of aggressive property speculation because it sits next door to the construction of a new Atlanta Falcons stadium and a planned segment of the Beltline.

Warren became perhaps the neighborhood's biggest speculator. He purchased dozens of properties at a time for as little as a few hundred dollars apiece from other investors who fell on hard times during the housing crisis. While some were kept vacant, he rented some out and tenants complained of unsafe conditions.

The case against Rick Warren was unusual in the fact it went to court and there was a criminal conviction; but the reality is that the current legal process to penalize slumlords is expensive and can easily take years to resolve, if code enforcement can ever get the landlord to court or to pay fines. Faced with the choice of funding repairs, paying fines or just ignoring citations, landlords have very little motivation to choose compliance. Many just ignore the citations or pay the fine after years of demands. The City of Atlanta is not unique either since many major cities have laws that favor nonconforming landlords with a legal process that can take years to achieve code compliance. Unfortunately, the apartment inventory is aging and code violations will only increase.

An "In Rem" proceeding is another tool Atlanta can use against a non-complying property. The City Code allows code enforcement to petition in municipal court to have a blighted property declared a nuisance. If the owner does not respond within thirty days, a judge can issue a demolition order, the city can put a lien on the property for the cost of the demolition, foreclose, and take possession. However, the procedure is unusual because the costs of demolition and foreclosure often exceeds the value of the property.

ON OCTOBER 20, 2015, Warren was sentenced to thirty days in jail. His conviction was rare enough; it would have been even more rare if he had received the maximum six-month imprisonment. Nonetheless, the conviction was significant. The *Journal-Constitution* wrote:

> "What it did psychologically is let people know that the neighborhood is changing," said State Rep. "Able" Mable Thomas. "The people who want to be a part of it, they know they can be. And the people who don't, they know what's coming."
>
> . . . Warren's case came to represent fears in the historically black neighborhood just west of the new Falcons stadium that white, wealthier outsiders would cash in on redevelopment at the expense of locals who spent decades trying to revive it.
>
> "In our area there is a shift," said Thomas. "It's not as big as it needs to be, but there is a shift."
>
> Before Warren's prosecution, absentee investors would mow only half of their overgrown yards to get inspectors off their backs, said Devan Pooler, a community activist and former president of the English Avenue Neighborhood Association.
>
> "People pretty much thought code enforcement was a joke," Peters said. "When this hit the news, I did get a lot of calls from property owners asking how to get their properties into compliance."[66]

INTERACTION WITH SEVERAL CITY of Atlanta municipal departments was a requirement to renovate Summerdale so we wanted the city to know us as good landlords. City Planning (permitting and inspections), Property

Tax Assessor, Public Works (water meters), Public Safety (police), and the Atlanta Housing Authority are just some of the city departments associated with the renovation.

Our most urgent need was building permits authorizing us to renovate the ninety-two units in nine boarded-up buildings: E, F, G, H, J, K, L, M, and N. Jeff had met with the permitting staff before we purchased Summerdale. We held several meetings with Tim Keane, director of the Department of City Planning, who was regarded as innovative and was well-respected by both his colleagues and the Atlanta construction community. Tim was wonderfully supportive of our model and indicated he would be available if we faced roadblocks in procuring permits.

We did not anticipate any structural hurdles. The buildings were constructed of wood framing with a solid brick exterior. Six units damaged by fire in Building G were repairable. After inspecting thousands of older apartment buildings constructed during the 1969–1972 apartment construction boom, I have found the construction quality back then is arguably better than new construction today. The original kitchen cabinets from that era are usually in better condition than standard "pressed wood" cabinets found in newer apartment units. It helped that the older Phase I had received a complete renovation in 1998 as part of the Hope grant funding for the construction of Phase II. This renovation included new kitchens, windows, appliances, and interior elements. We expected a reasonable amount of termite damage, rotten wood, and other issues associated with the recent neglect; however, these issues were easily repaired by our talented construction and service crews. A licensed engineering firm inspected the interior and exterior buildings and confirmed that the buildings were structurally sound.

Phase I's interior sheetrock walls were damaged over the years by thieves in search of copper wiring to sell at scrap yards, but the damage fortunately looked worse than it was. We estimated $1,500 per apartment unit for sheetrock repairs. Since we planned to be long-term owners, we would be replacing the electrical wiring, plumbing, kitchen cabinets, and appliances. We were pleasantly surprised to find that the windows were in excellent condition, possibly newly replaced before they were boarded-up to protect from damages caused by vagrants. Surprisingly, there was little mold in the units despite the buildings being sealed up with limited air circulation. The roofs and windows were durable, so there was little evidence of water infiltration that would trigger mold. We felt we were off to a good start, anticipating permits within sixty days after we applied.

OUR RENOVATION BUDGET WAS $3.7 million for the interiors and exteriors. If this budget held, we would be into the property at a total cost of less than $50,000 per unit, enabling us to keep rents affordable for families living at the poverty line. If we went over our budget, rents would have to increase to cover the cost overage.

We engaged a local architectural firm to prepare the required drawings and paid $25,455 for builder's loss insurance. Everyone was anticipating that the construction phase would take only six months after receipt of building permits. We were wrong—the permitting alone took almost a year.

The City of Atlanta and the International Building Code have three levels of construction permits. Level 1 alterations include the removal and replacement of existing materials, elements, equipment, or fixtures with new materials, elements, equipment, or fixtures that serve the same purpose. In other words, not building anything new but repairing something already existing. Since we were not changing walls or the footprints of the interior units in the boarded-up buildings, we anticipated permits under the Level 1 rules. Level 2 permits applied to construction alterations that reconfigured the space, added or eliminated doors and windows, reconfigured systems (plumbing, hvac, electrical), or installed new equipment. A Level 3 permit applied where the work area exceeds 50 percent of the aggregate area of the building.

In August 2018, we submitted preliminary plans to the city planning office which responded with several comments and suggestions. The plans were revised to reflect the city's requests and a second review was organized where the city requested clarification of our safety plans. A third meeting was held two weeks later, and final comments were voiced by the city planner. The official plans were submitted for the renovation of all nine buildings in mid-September. At the direction of the city planner, we submitted the plans to the Light Commercial Permitting department. This was highly unusual since the property was zoned residential and not commercial (a shopping center or office building). Residential zoning is typically for single-family or multifamily homes like Summerdale. We felt it appropriate to submit plans to the residential department, but we were advised otherwise. The plans were also submitted to the Zoning department for review and passed.

In late September, we received notice the permits were denied, and the city requested a new set of drawings with additional information: an asbestos survey, mold inspection, confirmation of compliance with the Americans with Disabilities Act (ADA), separate floor plans with exit contingencies, plans to provide two-hour fire-rated walls, new roof structural designs, interior finish schedule, fire extinguisher plans, and a dozen other requirements. We were surprised because the requests were unique to renovating an existing apartment community. Our architect was experienced in apartment construction and renovation and had permitted numerous past projects, of similar size and scope, in other local jurisdictions. We had met with the City Planning and Review Department in August and September, and these requests were brand new. Jeff scheduled an on-site visit from the department so we could better understand the additional requirements.

The site visit was in early October, and Jeff toured the property with the inspector. Afterwards the city requested that we provide a structural engineer's evaluation of the nine buildings, including six fire-damaged units. We researched the city ordinance and could find no requirement for a structural engineering report when submitting plans to do a renovation project. Jeff emailed the plan reviewer asking for clarification as to why the structural review was required and what type of report was expected. A week later, my partner emailed his contact within the City of Atlanta saying our renovation plans were delayed and the permitting requirement seemed excessive. One week later, the city posted a "Stop Work Order" at the property. The renovation efforts were officially shut down before they were even started.

We hired another structural engineering firm to help us address the new requests by the city. Although comfortable with the original engineering inspection report, we needed a second opinion that the buildings were structurally sound. A week after the Stop Work order was posted, we reached out to Tim Keane, the city planner who was initially supportive of our model. Tim organized another site visit inspection to ensure the process complied with the city code and international building code. After inspecting the property, Tim determined we could satisfy the city requirements by adopting the 2012 International Building Code.

Jeff said this was the first time in his experience "that a building plan reviewer overwrote an architect and mandated that a specific code be utilized." We resubmitted the plans and waited, fully expecting to receive our permits.

IN LATE OCTOBER, WE received a letter from the city planner requesting an inspection report showing how the property complied with the Americans with Disabilities Act. Given that the property was built in 1971, or nineteen years before the ADA was enacted, we produced a letter signed by a licensed architect stating that the property was grandfathered in; therefore, compliance was waived. This should not be a problem since we had complied with the HUD guidelines required in our Homeflex agreement. The city planner also listed seventeen concerns resulting from the inspection, including broken windows and doors and evidence of vandalism. We seemed to be going backwards. The more information we provided, the more information the city requested.

In early November, our structural engineer provided the "structural observation report" requested by the city. As expected, the report showed damages that we were well aware of including necessary wood replacement, some termite damage, and brick repairs. But overall the buildings were structurally in good condition. The report outlined guidelines for repairs, including wood replacement and brick repairs which basically consisted of reattaching the brick to the building. We planned to remove the damaged brick sections and replace with new brick rather than simply patchwork the problem.

Tim, our architect, and Jeff responded to the city planner's concerns by submitting revised plans that addressed all seventeen points. The planner promised to respond in a week. We asked him to expedite the process because we had scheduled a groundbreaking ceremony with the mayor's office and other city leaders at the end of the month. The Star-C program building had yet to be completed and we were under the gun to have it finished in time for the ribbon-cutting event. After five months of back-and-forth with the city, the plan reviewer finally issued a permit to renovate all the apartment units in Building G. We still needed permits for eight more buildings, but we were relieved to finally start renovation on one!

One week later, we submitted the plans to the city to start the permitting process for Buildings E and F, using the same plan markups as submitted for Building G. A site meeting was scheduled for the city planner to walk the two buildings. It was encouraging to hear the city planner had ideas to "save us money" using the current international building code. As he left after touring the property, he said he needed to talk with his boss about the project.

Under the fire code, if the estimated cost to renovate a building is less than 50 percent of the replacement cost, then any new work shall be brought up to current fire code. If the cost to renovate is more than 50 percent of the replacement cost, then the entire building must be brought up to current fire code. If we had to bring every Phase I unit up to code, it meant new fire-rated walls, sprinkler systems, and other elements that would add extensive costs and make it impossible for rents to be affordable.[67] If the replacement cost to completely rebuild each apartment unit was over $100,000 per unit and our budgeted renovation cost was less than $50,000 per unit, we were easily below the 50 percent threshold.

The city planner ended the on-site meeting by agreeing our engineer could meet with the city and further discuss. Here we went again with more delays. My partner and I reached out again to Tim Keane for clarification. We suspected the City of Atlanta did not have a clear path for renovating blighted apartment buildings in a manner that promoted affordability. We were not clear on which applicable code the City was using, and we were pursuing a Level 1 alteration but the City was requiring that we comply with some provisions of Level 2 such as new fire-rated walls. The current sheetrock on the walls was half-hour fire-rated and the city wanted us to replace 100 percent of all the sheetrock on the walls with one-hour fire-rated walls. If we were to make these repairs, it would add an additional $690,000 in costs or increase rents over $100 per month for each unit.

IN EARLY DECEMBER 2018 we organized a meeting with Tim and the Assistant Director for the Interim Building Official. It was held in the City of Atlanta Building office. In all fairness, Tim and his staff were under tremendous stress preparing for the 2019 Super Bowl that would be hosted by Atlanta. More than 250 temporary buildings and their accompanying permits had to be issued in time for the February event coming up in less than sixty days. In addition to the Super Bowl, a record number of new high-rise buildings—more than fifty—were submitting permit requests. Tim and his team had never been busier.

The meeting went well, with several issues being clarified including ADA compliance and the correct building code. We did not have to add or remove any walls and doors; the footprint of each unit stayed exactly as it was since the 1971 construction. Tim assured us if Atlanta Housing could confirm compliance with the City Planning office, then his team would be satisfied. Our Builders Risk Insurance was coming up for renewal after six months, so we had to pay $25,455 to renew it while we worked through the permitting and renovation process. At this point, the city planning office assigned a new person to review our permits.

"Bad news," Jeff said one morning after the meeting with Tim. "I met with our new plan reviewer and there is still not much progress on permits for Phase I." Jeff was frustrated because the new reviewer was comparing plans submitted in earlier months with the plans recently submitted. He accused us of trying to misrepresent the scope of our work. With each set of drawings, we would get redlined comments or verbal instructions from our meetings, and we would revise the next set of drawings in response to the suggestions and questions. Jeff ultimately had to submit four revised sets of drawings to finally receive permits for Building G. Keeping track of all the written and verbal changes was an effort. The changes from drawing to drawing were simply responses to the questions of our previous plan reviewer. But somehow the new city planner mistrusted our transparency in the submitted plans.

We did receive some good news in December. The city decided we did not have to change our fire alarm system. We could use a one-hour fire-rated sheetrock in Building G's six fire-damaged units—a huge savings versus the two-hour fire rated sheetrock we were originally directed to use. The city also issued a plumbing permit for Building G so we could start the plumbing work. In mid-January, we received correspondence from the city planner summarizing our December meeting and advising that we had a conditional permit to keep working on Building G. We continued to clean out and prep all the Phase I interiors for renovation.

We tried contacting Atlanta Housing to organize a conversation between the ADA compliance officer and city planner, but we were having no luck. We were now six months into the permitting process and it was still not clear when the city would issue final permits to start the Summerdale Phase I renovation. At the heart of the confusion was whether a building qualified as a Level 1 or Level 2 renovation and what code was applicable. We needed the city to agree on one level that was consistent for the entire property. While trying to get all the units ready for occupancy, we were losing $2,150 a day plus paying for security, insurance, and debt service, while generating $0 income.

AT A MEETING WITH the city planners in late January 2019 we outlined the history of the permitting process and questioned why this was taking so long. There seemed to be so much confusion associated with renovating Summerdale. We were not building anything new; we were renovating an existing structure.

In early February, after eight meetings with the city and a dozen plan revisions, we finally obtained Level 1 code permits for Buildings E and F. We jumped on the renovations while simultaneously applying for the remaining six building permits—based on the exact plan drawings submitted for Buildings G, E, and F. This seemed logical since they were basically the same age and construction. The construction staff was in full force and the property hummed with the wonderful sound of progress: hammering, sawing, and large trucks delivering new construction materials to the site. It was exciting to make more units readily available for working-poor families.

There were still more hurdles. Jeff went back to the planning office in March, expecting to pick up the final permits for the remaining buildings. Upon arrival, he was told the city would not be issuing any more Summerdale permits and because of new city planning requirements, they were rescinding the previous permits for Buildings E, F, and G. Once again, our renovation plans were reassigned to a new plan reviewer who demanded a revision of the previously agreed-upon requirements. This included a one-hour fire separation wall between the townhome units consistent with a Level 2 construction. We were now into our eighth month of permit delays, and the office requesting them was just as confused as we were. The city left us with no choice other than to comply with one-hour fire-rated walls. The lack of a clear path was challenging our efforts to provide affordable housing to families living on low wages.

25

Education and the Star-C After-School Program

Kristin Hemingway pulled out her key on a morning in January 2019 and unlocked the door to the newly renovated small brick building housing the Star-C after-school program. The dented black front door easily opened, and she entered and paused a moment as her eyes adjusted, enjoying the beautiful smell of fresh paint and new construction. The interior walls were now pale lilac and she had just decorated the walls with bright happy posters. Kristin smiled . . . she loved her new job as director of the after-school program.

The after-school program was relocated from the leasing office to the small community building in the middle of Phase I, and surrounded by boarded-up apartments. It too had been boarded up for years, serving as a public canvas for artistic expression by the ever-evolving population of drug dealers and drug users who had the urge to paint graffiti and leave their personal brand on something structural. Maintenance was constantly at war with the covert artists. Armed with a limited budget, the maintenance staff randomly selected whatever paint was nearby to cover the explicit words and symbols. To say the courtyard building stood out was an understatement. Despite its squat appearance, sloppy exterior paint job, and low interior ceilings, it was heaven for Kristin.

She had about thirty minutes before the children arrived from Cleveland Avenue Elementary School. The door opened and Iris, her assistant, walked through. It was almost time for one of them to walk across the street to the Star-C meeting spot in front of Phase II. The east side of Old Hapeville Road had no sidewalk, so the children walked on the west side and met with either Kristin or Iris, who escorted them across the street to the after-school program. Parents were not happy about relocating Star-C from Phase

I to Phase II and expressed their concerns for the children's safety. Kristin reassured the parents that the children were personally escorted across the bustling Old Hapeville Road. We were working with the City of Atlanta to get a crosswalk installed between the two complexes. The parents also voiced their concern with the drug activity at the property. They often thanked Lucy, William, and the security team for making Summerdale safer, but understandably they worried the crime could resurface.

After the children arrived, Kristin checked off the enrollment list. The program was offered to families free of charge and attendance was not mandatory.

"Okay kids, let's line up and stretch," Kristin said to the group after they put down their backpacks, took off their coats and got situated. Kingston lined up with the other bigger kids. He smiled and started following Ms. Kristin in the stretching. He was one of the few children with a smile on his face. The twenty other children, ages five to ten, appeared anxious but not at the level I had observed when the program started last August. At least they were making eye contact with each other and forging friendships. All had been under stress due to the toxic environment, but that was changing. The property was much safer, and they were playing outdoors for the first time in years. The mold and pest infestations were almost gone and many of their home environments were much healthier. Their families were continuing to pay below-market rents, and soon some would only be paying only a small portion of their income toward rent, thanks to the Homeflex program. The parents of many Star-C children worked one or two low-wage jobs at incomes of $12,000 to $30,000 per year—near the poverty level, so there was that added stress. If Star-C families qualified for Homeflex, many would continue to live at Summerdale and stay in the after-school program. We hoped that would reduce transiency and keep the children enrolled at Cleveland Avenue Elementary.

Kristin was fully aware of the kids' stress. The stretching exercises helped them relax and reset their minds from a long day in the classroom. Kristin shared:

> My babies don't have coping skills. What I have learned as an adult, myself
> included, as poor children you are not afforded the room to have issues with

mental health or anxiety. Because you are not afforded this space, you are not given the skills to deal with it. I went over to the school yesterday—some of our Summerdale kids were in the fourth- and fifth-grade spelling bee. The tension in the room was so heavy and I said can we do a breathing exercise? The adults in the room agreed and we took a moment and breathed. It worked and the room relaxed!

The high criminal activity at the property motivated parents to sequester the children in their apartment units. Joshua and Kingston at five and seven years old are active boys and their parents really had no choice but to escort them from Cleveland Avenue Elementary to their apartment unit which had issues. The two boys are sweethearts, hilarious babies. But if anybody is holed up all day and cannot be free to express and use their full body, they're going to have challenges. I do not think of that . . . I could walk to the park when I was little. I literally remember flipping in my front yard because we had this huge yard and my friends were running through sprinklers. It was a privilege to use your whole body from an ability standpoint, but I never considered the safety standpoint . . . there is a freedom and learning of self-control by having access to using your whole body and my kids do not have that or the freedom to ask for space to breathe and regroup. Some of them ask when they come to the program, "Can I just sit on the floor away from everyone?" I say, "Sure, do you just need a moment?"

They are asking now, and I don't deny them. Kingston came in the other morning and I let him lay down in the other room on the floor, because he just struggles sometimes, and I could just see it in his face. I asked, "Do you need a moment to just lay down?" And he said, "Yes!" I let him go in the other room, where the lights are low, and closed the door. He came back out after only a few minutes and said, "I'm ready," and we had a good day. But Kingston needed to know that he could do that . . . and it is okay.

Whenever I listened to Kristin, I was always impressed with how she instinctively knows how to communicate with children. She continued:

The rules of the after-school program are very basic. #1 is listen the first time, #2 be kind, and remember rule #1. We have some other rules written down . . . general character ones like try your hardest. When you do not get something, that is one thing. But if you are not trying your best, we need to have a whole different conversation. We have students that have issues paying attention to detail, not reading the whole question. So, you would get this wrong on a test, not because you do not know what you are doing but because you don't read everything. So, we got reading comprehension cards and they have to write down the whole card. Write verbatim and answer the question to work on their study skills. We have a couple of kids in the program that need interventions. There is one kid that was behind last year, so this is his second go around in third grade. We have a kid in fifth grade that tries hard, but he has some learning delays. A lot of kids do not have books at home. You don't realize how many kids don't have age-appropriate books at home, but they need practice reading . . . and opportunities to read out loud.

Scanning the room, I zeroed in on two small bookshelves and noted they were sparsely populated. I asked, "Do you have enough books? You know we can ask our social media fan base to support your kids by donating gently-used books." Kristin said that would be great:

As part of the program, we created opportunities for them to read. The reading part is like "the thing." After four months, the kids are finding there is joy and excitement around reading, and if there is joy and excitement, you will want to do it more. We have sight-word cards that we just made ourselves and we practice with, because they are critical for learning to read. If you struggle over sight words, you break up your ability to comprehend what you are reading. So, in helping with sight words, we help create fluency with the reading, which then creates joys with the reading. It is fun to join words, there is a story here. I read to them every day. Right now, we are reading a chapter book. When we are not reading the chapter book, we will read two shorter books, so we are developing our book hall of fame for the books they really enjoy. The book they love the most is a book they got for Christmas called *I am Enough*. The meaning in it touched them in a deep place, so they literally will ask me to read it three to four times a week.

I asked my Church to donate enough of these books for each kid to take home, because if every kid could take the book home, we have done something magical for them. The kids are reading every day, so now when I read, *I Am Enough*, they finish the lines. I never instructed them to do that, it is something they naturally did on their own, which was to develop this love of reading. I ask questions about the chapter book that we review, and before I read again, I will stop and ask, "what you think this word means?" We are working on vocabulary building, using context clues. We ended up yesterday in a conversation that had nothing to do with the book. Because the mother character pulled on her iceberg outfit. I asked the kids, "Do you know what an iceberg is?" They did not know so now we are looking up icebergs on my phone and looking at the significance of how you might be this little on the top, but there is all this underneath. It's a reminder that you cannot just pay attention to what is on the surface, you gotta always remember there is a whole lot more beneath what you see, that is with everything, not just the iceberg. We also discussed how icebergs form and how they relate to the Great Lakes, and of course we discussed Great Lakes because I am from Michigan. These questions and answers came from kids who are typically not engaged but they are now very engaged in the discussion. So now I am thinking about what the discussion for the day is, because it worked for them.

As I watched the kids stretching and interacting with each other, it occurred to me that it has been four months since the after-school program launched. She had made noticeable progress in the four months. Kristin agreed:

Many of the children like Joshua couldn't write his name; he could not identify all the letters in his name, and he could not identify all the letters in the alphabet. The intervention is letter practice, practice writing your name, and the joy of being able to write and identify your name. Yesterday he wrote something—I said this is a great job of writing your name Joshua, and he just smiled. He just beamed because this was something he could not do, and he did a great job. He is not reading yet; we are still working on phonetics which you cannot fully address without letter recognition. There are steps and there is a process where you must get all the pieces. So, the reality is, he may not be really reading by the end of the year, because he was so far behind, but by the end of first grade, he could be on reading level as we continue to do these things.

Cleveland Avenue Elementary is working hard to help Joshua with his reading but Joshua is not a teacher—only a student. Dr. Payne has said kids that stay from kindergarten to fifth grade, are at the appropriate reading level by the time they graduate. This doesn't say they are on level every year, that's saying over the course of time if you stick with us, we can do all the different things that need to be done to get where you need to be.

After seeing the living environment that some of these tenants had to endure over the years at Summerdale, the challenges of teaching these children made complete sense to someone like me who is a novice in education. The strong interrelationship between housing and education was becoming clearer as I watched the families navigate between Summerdale and Cleveland Avenue Elementary. Dr. Payne shared her daily challenges of trying to educate children living in blighted apartment communities. She had to deal with the environment that came with the children every morning, just before her staff could "teach," and I saw this firsthand as a landlord. We had several families living with roach infestations and raising their children in the middle of a drug and gun zone. These children were coming to Dr. Payne in the morning with bed bugs, fleas, and roaches in their clothing. For some, she had to do their laundry before they could get into the classroom. That is after the gunfire they heard throughout the neighborhood and fear these children expressed that disrupted their sleep. How can a child learn to read coming out of this environment? I asked Kristin, "Do you think there is a direct link between environment and reading?"

There is always a direct link between environment and achievement. I think the environment always plays a role. The kids are very aware, they know who the people are, so this group out there (of loiterers and drug dealers) that we are slowly getting rid of, they know those people. There was a big group of people we had to pass while walking the kids home. Because I am friendly to everybody, I speak to everybody. Some of them were the dealers, absolutely. So, I speak to everybody, and because I am very friendly, they consistently make statements about how nice I am and how welcoming I am. I also explain that the flip side of that is that there is a whole 'nother side of me that you never want to see if it comes to my babies. One day, it was just me walking them and there was a guy sitting on the crate in the middle of the walkway, and the other guy said, "Hey, move." There is a genuine respect for people who work with kids, because you know that I am taking care of the babies. They say, "Get off the sidewalk, the kids are coming." Even if it is people hanging out, I have never seen a drug deal go down, but that can be intimidating for anyone to walk through a group of people standing outside, but the kids know who these people are. So, it is more for me and Iris, like who are you and can you move, but the kids, there has been a familiarity because you have been around. Very interesting times!

I asked Kristin what she thought about the teachers the kids had at Cleveland Avenue Elementary. She smiled and went on:

They have EXCELLENT teachers at Cleveland, excellent programing. The environment that Dr. Payne has built is phenomenal. She had a chat and chew yesterday, and I went for the last thirty minutes, and they provided lunch. I could not go for the entire two hours. There were not enough parents there, only thirty. And there were people coming in and out the entire session. Some came and left before I came. Parents have to be equipped to be advocates for their children and I do not know if anyone is equipping the parents at Summerdale to be advocates. And if you do not have someone in education or come from a family of educators like I did, you don't have anyone helping you advocate. Even if my mother did not know other things, she made sure I had whatever I needed. This is not the case for all these families and students, the parent is struggling to help their child with her homework, so she went to this chat and to see about getting help. One of the things I said is, look, I get it, this stuff is hard—I went to calculus AP, math and reading are my thing. I am an honor roll student and even I do not understand this. But when I asked for help, no one has ever denied me. You have to not be embarrassed, not be scared of thinking it makes you look a certain way because you do not get it. This stuff has changed! And if you ask somebody, can they help you to help your baby, nobody will tell you no. But that was almost like they needed permission to get assistance.

Two years from now . . . that will be the key. Even with the group I have now, next year will be easier because we will have kids that have been in the program guiding the new kids. In this first year, we are building trust. The kids are constantly thinking "can I trust you, can I talk to you, are you serious, will you do what you said." You have to deal with all that because you are dealing with kids that have been disappointed and let down and lied too over and over again. So, I don't know if you are an adult, I can trust because I have met some adults that I can't trust. Now the kids are starting to really trust me and the Star-C program. There is this love, this joy, we are doing fun things, there is a different level of comfort. The parents are starting to trust me more. I had a mom confide in me recently that she lost her job, so there is a comfort that comes with that because you know I care about you and your babies that you would not say before. I helped her out with some Amazon gift cards so she could buy some Christmas gifts. She and her family had a nice Christmas.

26

The Eviction of Melinda Wyatt

"Before you leave, I need to show you the water bills," Lucy said as I stood up to head back to the corporate office in mid-January 2019. My heart missed a beat as she handed me the two water bills—one from the Phase I water meter and one from the Phase II water meter. I read the first bill for Phase II. "$22,274, what!" I yelped as my heart missed three more beats.

I looked at Lucy incredulously and sat back down. I quickly did the math. Phase II had eighty-six occupied units consuming water in Phase II. At $259 per unit, this was a huge loss—we only charged each unit a $35–$45 monthly water fee. At the going water usage rates, the property was not affordable.[68] The second water bill for Phase I's twenty-seven units was $4,783—or $177 per unit and again we were operating at a loss. The water bills indicated there were either severe leaks at both phases or the tenants were taking two-hour showers every day. The average monthly water bill for Phase II for the last year was approximately $11,000, which at $110 per unit was still high for affordability.

I looked up at Lucy and said, "We have a major water leak somewhere!"

"That's what I thought too," said Lucy. "I have already reached out to our plumbers and called in a leak detection company. They will try to get out in the next week."

Looking at the paper bills and trying not to panic, I said, "We need to get Jeff on this as well. He has some plumbers working on the renovation of the blighted units in Phase I, and maybe they can help find the leaks. Let's jump on this immediately." A water bill like this could bankrupt Summerdale since the monthly rent collections were not high enough to pay the mortgage and the water. If leaks were the problem, they were costing us $375 per day in additional water usage, and waiting for a plumber was costing us $2,625 per week. Our goal was to keep our rents affordable and tenants living on $26,000 a year simply could not afford a water bill of $259 per month—which equated to adding 40 percent more to their $674 monthly rent.

"Is the eviction for Melinda in Unit 205 still scheduled for next week?" I asked.

"Yes, 9 a.m. in courtroom 1A."

We shook our heads.

A GUST OF WIND hit me as I briskly walked along Martin Luther King Jr. Drive to the Fulton County Courthouse. It was 8:30 on a frigid Monday morning and the pedestrian traffic was heavy along the sidewalk. I joined the line of people in the warm entrance and waited for security clearance. The hearing to evict Melinda was scheduled in one-half hour and Lucy was joining me on behalf of Summerdale. It had been a rocky road between Melinda and our management staff. We were disappointed we could not work out her tenancy, especially since she had children attending Cleveland Avenue Elementary. With the eviction, her children were at risk of being part of the high transiency problem that our TriStar model was trying to reduce in local schools.

Melinda had been given several chances to comply with her lease, but her continued housekeeping issues were too noxious for her family and the community. Left finally with no choice except an eviction on her credit report, Melinda agreed to vacate but requested an extension while she looked for another place to live. She was delinquent in paying her rent and now owed December and January. The delinquencies, combined with the charge for the pest control treatments, prompted us to start the court process to get possession of the unit and settle outstanding monies we were owed. I had met Melinda briefly while inspecting her unit before the renovation. She greeted us at the door, promptly went into her bedroom, laid on her bed and started scrolling her cell phone because it took priority over our visit. My interaction with her lasted less than thirty seconds.

That all happened a few months ago and today we were meeting Melinda in front of a judge to gain control of her pest-infested apartment unit. Lucy and I waited in the courtroom as the court clerk called the parties for the cases scheduled on the docket. The room was crowded with dozens of landlords and tenants. When our name was called, we answered and so did Melinda, who was standing behind us. Turning around I came face-to-face with someone who hardly resembled the person I had met in Unit 205.

We were escorted into a side room reserved for parties willing to bypass the judge and mediate the case. I was somewhat nervous since this was one of my first evictions in years. Our other property in east Atlanta had few evictions since we kept our rents low and worked with tenants when they could not pay their rent. We did not evict tenants with bad housekeeping or bad behavior but we did "nonrenewals" when their leases expired.

The poised young lady sitting across the table was confident and neatly attired in a leather jacket and pressed blue jeans. Her hair was coiffed into a stylish bun which reminded me of Audrey Hepburn. Sparkly green polish coated her long, slender nails and the makeup on her face was worthy of a fashion model. She had the persona of someone that could have resided in a million-dollar mansion, but we knew better. This fashionable stranger was not the Melinda we knew, with an abusive mouth and filthy apartment.

We quietly smiled at each other before the court-appointed attorney read the charges. The total amount owed by Melinda was $2,461 with back due rent, pest control charges, late fees, and court costs. After discussing the charges with the court-appointed attorneys, it was agreed she would surrender possession of her unit within a week. In exchange, we would accept $1,620 or the outstanding rent due. Melinda asked for more time to pay the amount due because she was getting ready to pay for a new apartment, including a security deposit. We agreed Melinda could pay the $1,620 by March but she had to be out of the apartment by the end of February. Everyone signed the document and it was over in less than twenty minutes.

AS WE WERE LEAVING, Lucy was headed back to the office, but I asked Melinda if I could interview her to understand her story, and maybe get some insight to being a better landlord. I was curious about how she arrived at such a toxic mentality. She agreed and we went to the court snack bar where it was quiet. We talked for about an hour. At first, she was shy and distrustful of my motives. I could not blame her. Her willingness to talk to the person responsible for putting her family on the street showed real honesty and maturity. I was struck during the interview by how determined she was to be a good mother and provider for her four children. She clearly worked hard to make sure that they had everything she and her husband could afford. Life did not deal Melinda good circumstances to begin with, having grown up in the "projects" and being raised by a handicapped mother. She and her husband were hard workers who did not complain about what had been dealt in the past. She mentioned she had worked in the courthouse as a custodian for several years.

While we spoke, people kept interrupting to hug her and ask where she had been lately. One lady turned to me and said Melinda "was a nice lady and a hard worker." Melinda was almost embarrassed by all the attention. She explained that she recently got a better, higher-paying job and left the courthouse position because if she kept both jobs she would have little time for her family. She indicated that Summerdale was a step up from her last apartment and it gave her an opportunity to get "out of the projects" and away from a dysfunctional family. After about an hour, I realized I had taken up too much of her time. As we departed, she agreed to let me follow up and see where she landed. I was hopeful she would find a good apartment, but business was still business, and we had to proceed with the eviction and collection. She seemed to completely understand.

Melinda did vacate the premises on the assigned date but did not pay the $1,620 as agreed on March 1. We took possession of the unit and spent an additional $2,800 to re-treat the unit for pests, perform a thorough cleaning, and replace the contaminated carpet, which at that point was less than four months old. We held off leasing the unit for another thirty days until we were sure that the pest infestation was completely eradicated. The apartment was quickly leased to another tenant who appreciated the UFAS renovations.

THE REGULATORY COMPLIANCE PROJECT was going strong and Jeff was patiently addressing the various issues from Charles's August inspection highlighting 139 failures. Summerdale employed dozens of trade workers, painters, electricians, carpentry laborers, concrete laborers and plumbers, totaling more than a thousand hours to address the concerns and achieve UFAS, ADA and FFHA compliance and get our certification letter from Charles. In November, we had our second site inspection. This time everyone knew the routine. We were relatively confident Charles would pass more elements from this inspection, except for the unit that housed Melinda. Charles arrived early morning and Jeff proudly showed him our work to address the 139 citations in the 42 apartment units.

Unfortunately, the inspection did not go well. Several of our newly poured concrete sidewalks and parking lot ramps still did not perfectly measure the targeted 2.0 slope maximum on 100 percent of the area. About 95 percent of a given sidewalk would comply, and then Charles would put his measure on a corner that would show a 2.07 slope, so he would fail this sidewalk. It was hard to justify this absolute perfection considering that earth does erode, and I was starting to think compliance was impossible. A few days later we received the inspection report and we had whittled down our failures from 139 to 94. Melinda's unit alone had seventeen failures, which we somewhat expected, but the majority of the failures were associated with the sidewalks and walkways. We had no choice but to buckle down and work on the perfection in all the elements. At this point, we had spent more than $150,000 and we still had ninety-four items to address. Our regulatory compliance was starting to get very expensive.

27

The Replacement Criminals— Crime and Security

In May 2019, a 9 a.m. Tuesday staff meeting for TI Asset Management was starting when Jeff came through the door and joined at the last minute. The air was warm with springtime and everyone was in a good mood. Jeff was so swamped with the nitty-gritty logistics of property renovations that his participation in our weekly meeting was rare, especially since we were nine months behind schedule to bring back to life the boarded-up units in Phase I. We enthusiastically hailed his appearance.

"You should know something about what went down at Summerdale this weekend," he remarked while pulling out a chair at the conference table.

My heart sank. I knew from the serious tone of his voice that Jeff was about to deliver some sobering news.

"You know we are allowing workers to live on-site to expedite the workload, since many have transportation problems. I had asked them to keep an eye on the property over the weekends. A few of my workers are living in a C Building unit and told me that there was a big party in the D Building over the weekend. A group of guys actually took the entrance gate off the rollers and opened it up for their friends. It went until early in the morning."

We were lucky to have several vacant apartment units in Phase I, and it was logical that we could rent them to construction workers on a month-to-month basis while the renovation was being completed. This arrangement solved three problems. First, the laborers literally walked across the parking lot to arrive at the job site, so they did not have to worry about driving in Atlanta traffic. Second, they could work flexible hours at their discretion. We were paying them good federally mandated wages required by Davis-Bacon, so they were motivated to work a full eight-hour day. Third, as tenants, the laborers were an important informal security watch—just recently someone had tried to steal a few newly installed HVAC condensing units.

Overall, our security strategy was working, bolstered by the Atlanta Police Department rapid response teams and the security camera surveillance. The APD had made many arrests from undercover stakeouts since we started working with them. Lucy and her staff were helping by carefully screening tenants and refusing to rent to them if they had criminal backgrounds. We had gone over and above what a typical landlord would do to improve the safety of the property and the overall neighborhood. We felt we had turned the corner on the perpetual loitering, partying, and "hanging out." The properties had been quiet for the last few months, so we were not that concerned when we reduced our security hours.

What happened? The incident Jeff reported was simply unacceptable and not fair to tenants deserving of a safe and quiet environment.

We had been under the impression that the property safety was improving. This new incident took us back to last summer when crowds of people with beer coolers and grills partied nonstop over the weekend. At the time our security was almost powerless to stop dozens and dozens of people coming through the gates and fences. Our residents were intimidated by the loud noise, screaming and drinking, which ultimately brought fights, drug dealing, break-ins, traffic, and piles of trash. New keycard entrance gates, 24/7 security, cameras, more policing, evictions of problem tenants—all had brought improvements.

And now this. I was trying not to overreact, but we needed more information to understand why it happened, who was at the property, and more importantly, to develop a new security plan. I was hopeful it was just a large family reunion of some type that got out of hand. But the probable scenario was that the underground was doing a better job of hiding when our security was watching. The lapse of weekend security had been immediately noticed by the underground.

AFTER STRATEGIZING WHAT TO do next, we decided the best plan of action was to collect more data. The APD finally gave us the incident reports for the month of December, including a summary of the successful undercover drug bust. We repeatedly asked to see the police reports from the July raid, but they never materialized. The main haul from the December bust was the confiscation of marijuana and two guns. Also in the report, I found the names and addresses for the eleven men arrested in the raid. I needed more information to understand how we could tackle criminal activity in a safe, sustainable way. We hit a stone wall when requesting more information on the eleven such as mug shots and arrest histories from our sources at the APD.

Fulton County Chief Magistrate Judge Cassandra Kirk is fortunately a good friend and a big fan of our model to turn around failing schools through housing. She is always eager to help. I expressed my frustration at the lack of information from the APD and asked if she would help me find more data on the criminals and the illegal activity to date. She said, "Let me introduce you to your community prosecutor. Fulton County is divided into districts and each district has a prosecutor in charge of felony cases and community outreach. They can get you all the information you need." A few days later, Judge Kirk came through as promised and introduced me to Angie Parker, the Community Prosecutor for District 3 in Fulton County. It turned out my timing was perfect.

The Fulton County District Attorney's office created a citizen's Court Watch in 2004 to engage citizens in the criminal justice system. As community prosecutors track cases involving repeat offenders and those of general interest to the community, court watchers are encouraged to attend proceedings and, when deemed appropriate by the court, offer perspective regarding the impact a defendant's criminal activity has on a community. The District Attorney's office hosts its annual Court Watch training program each spring, where citizens receive a crash course in the judicial processes and felony case proceedings. The idea of citizens following up on criminals was all new to me. When it comes to on-site crime, I have every reason to put my faith in the APD and our security team. But once the criminals were arrested, I had no understanding of the court process. My suspicions were growing that many landed right back in business at Summerdale, but we had no information. We did not have mug shots or photos to verify if criminals were living among our residents or hiding in the shadows.

Angie suggested I attend an upcoming Court Watch program. She was planning to attend, and Judge Kirk would be a speaker. I immediately registered.

In the meantime, our management meticulously sleuthed county records on the internet and compiled the arrest histories and mug shots of the eleven arrested from the December raid. We finally had names to go with the faces of the criminals at Summerdale. At our next management staff meetings, I studied the mug shot of Anthony Fowler and passed it around to the group. "Does anyone recognize this guy?"

Everyone nodded and responded at the same time.

Lucy chirped, "Yep, I always suspected he was the main guy—the Kingpin. I don't see him often but he is the one that is always supervising his guys and telling them what to do."

Jeff followed, "He drives a new Cadillac Escalade and is usually around the place, more after hours. I know this because sometimes I come to the property late at night to check and he is always here, in the middle of all the activity."

Lucy added, "He lives in Unit D-12 and sometimes it is Unit C-6. He is the one who would show up to pay Sharon Allen's rent—the phantom tenant that we could never find. Yep, that's him all right."

I asked, "Is he still around?"

Lucy and Jeff shook their heads. "We haven't seen him lately."

I said, "Interesting because if you look at his court history, he was arrested last month but the record says he was 'detained.' Maybe he is still in prison?"

More was revealed after we compiled a spreadsheet on Fowler's arrest history for the last twenty years. Most recently, he had been arrested on July 25 and again in December—two of the twelve Summerdale drug arrests since we purchased the property.

I asked, "Is he a nice guy? How does he operate in plain sight?"

Lucy shared, "He is always giving the kids candy and paying the rent or utilities for the tenants that need help. He has done a great job networking and developing loyalty within the complex."

I took a closer look at the photo. He was probably in his late thirties or early forties with neatly cropped hair. I recalled seeing him walk by me one day wearing a loose, bright orange Izod shirt that partially hid his paunchy stomach. He was a big guy, clean and manicured, who presented himself well—he could be mistaken for a preacher in a prosperous church. Not what you would expect from your local drug kingpin. But our information only showed arrests, not convictions. For all we knew, Fowler could be completely innocent.

"How does he get out of jail with all these arrests?"

"Actually, I noticed that he would come to the property with a warehouse uniform on, this was probably around late December or early January. Looking back, that was strange, since it was obvious that he had a job somewhere, making minimal wages." Lucy added.

"Ahhh, he must be on parole and required to be gainfully employed and produce evidence of a paycheck." Since the underground did not give out documented paychecks, Fowler's warehouse job could be a new strategy to convince his parole officer that he was cleaning up his act. In fact, he was operating in a parallel universe running the Summerdale underground at night.

We were pretty sure Fowler was still overseeing his underground, even from a jail cell. His photo sent chills up my spine. We needed to all be on the lookout for Fowler since he was certain to return for another round. His illegal underground was way too profitable for him to stay away too long.

I let the staff know that Angie Parker had emailed me with the date of an upcoming preliminary hearing for the December arrestees at the Fulton County Courthouse. We all agreed that we would attend the preliminary hearing and meet the guys who were operating a drug ring at Summerdale.

WE DECIDED TO EXECUTE a heightened security plan. A new security company was hired to provide security after-hours, and Lieutenant Ski was hired on an hourly basis to provide support (police officers were allowed to moonlight). We noticed that new faces were loitering around D-12 and the common area and Lucy asked around to determine where they lived. None could prove residency in any units. Ski discussed with Angie using criminal trespass citations as an option. The criminal trespass citation let us legally document trespassers on the property who are not legal tenants or registered guests. The trespasser is issued a written citation and warned of jail time if caught a second time. But strict compliance with the legal process is required. Angie mentioned that a judge in Florida had ruled in favor of a defendant's challenge of such a citation, and the Fulton County prosecution officer was revisiting the issue. We could not use the criminal trespass process until the review was finished, but she would let us know when it was available. Ski and I waited and waited.

Meanwhile, loitering activity was picking back up, and rowdy tenants didn't help matters. Tenants were organizing large parties, and our only defenses were our security stationed at the gates, calling 911, or eviction. Card readers on our entrance gates recorded the apartment units that allowed access, which enabled us to identify the tenants with multiple guests. Lucy delivered notices to three tenants who were allowing a large number of guests to have access. Those tenants, however, promptly stopped paying rent, but they continued attempting to host large parties until security shut them down. We finally revoked their access cards, forcing them to park outside the gate. After thirty days notice, we started filing evictions.

A few weeks after our staff meeting, I visited Phase I to tour the construction. Five loiterers were standing next to Unit D-12 and I decided to approach them with my cell phone camera. All five started running, but I trailed them with my camera, and one turned around.

"Do you live here?" I asked.

"Yeah, over in unit c-6," the young man replied, catching his breath.

"Unit c-6, huh? Is your name on the lease?"

"I'm a friend."

"A friend? If you are living in the unit, you need to get your name on the lease?"

"I just staying in the unit."

"Are you selling drugs here?"

He chuckled and looked away, avoiding eye contact. "Selling drugs? That's so 1980s."

"We need you and your friends to leave the property," were my parting words.

The next time I was at the property, Ski was there and he approached the guy. Ski later reported, "I had a talk with him and told him the APD was watching the property. I think he is getting the message."

It still took another month of harassment by Ski, Jeff, and our staff for the guys to finally disappear. Jeff reported that he saw one of them in a house about a half a mile south of Summerdale. The drug dealing was moving south.

28

Rebuilding Social Capital

Sporting a big smile and a battered cream canvas hat that had seen better days, Linda Prout walked around the Summerdale courtyard. It was early on an October 2019 morning and more than 220 volunteers were already lining up to start assembling the large KABOOM! playground. The courtyard was stockpiled with unassembled playground equipment, neatly stacked wood planks, and two mounds of fresh-smelling mulch that towered over the tallest volunteers. Young children and their parents were peeking out of apartment windows, in awe of the whirlwind of activity so early on a Thursday morning. The first wave of volunteers had arrived at 6:30 a.m. while it was still pitch dark to start setting up the multiple workstations. Dr. Meria Carstarphen, superintendent of Atlanta Public Schools, was in line to haul supplies from the storage shed. Many other city leaders also showed up—judges, school board members, city council members, lawyers, TI Asset Management employees, Georgia Tech students, and other community volunteers joined about 175 employees from the CarMax Foundation, the official sponsor for the new playground. Each volunteer signed up for an eight-hour shift, knowing that at the end of the day, the Summerdale kids would have a brand-new place to run and play. Linda Prout traveled from New Orleans to help with the effort. This was her eighty-seventh KABOOM! build, and she clearly relished the event.

The rising sun revealed clear blue skies and brilliant fall foliage, creating a perfect setting for the playground installation. The volunteers were assigned to a dozen work teams, each tasked with instructions and supplies to build a specific playground equipment piece. Forty-five days earlier, several children had sat with the KABOOM! architects and designed their dream playground. Now Christopher, Kingston, Joshua, and fifteen other children in the Star-C program could not wait to see what was waiting for them after school.

"The children had a calendar and every day we checked off one day until October 24th, the day they would get their playground. They were giddy with excitement," Kristen reported to the group of volunteers.

The opening ceremony kicked off at 8:30 a.m. with a proclamation by city council member-at-large (and future mayor) Andre Dickens: "I hereby officially proclaim October 24, 2019, to be recognized as "Star-C Day" by the city of Atlanta." He handed me an impressive wood plaque with the proclamation signed by Mayor Keisha Lance Bottoms and sixteen Atlanta city council members. The recognition of the city's hard effort behind rebuilding Summerdale—from physical and criminal, to social and educational—had everyone, including the politicians, beaming with pride.

Within eight hours, the courtyard's oversized patch of red dirt was transformed into a bright new playground with swings, slides, monkey bars, and interactive games. Two large shade structures housing multiple benches faced the playground on opposite ends, and another half-dozen sturdy benches were placed throughout the large courtyard. Lunch and snacks were served by volunteers throughout the day, and over the noise of hammers, shoveling, and banging, a DJ played dance music, prompting spontaneous line dancing by the volunteers. At 3:30 p.m., everyone lined up on the new playground to hear speeches from various leaders, including those from KABOOM! and the CarMax Foundation. Our Star-C schoolchildren arrived just in time to hear the speeches and ogle their new play area. Dr. Payne, Lieutenant Ski, and the Atlanta Housing Authority also converged for the dedication. The KABOOM! playground build day was a tremendous success and brought together the best of many people and organizations throughout the city. After years of neglect and toxic stress, Summerdale had a positive future. As I left the property that day, I was tired but impressed by the broad grassroots community effort to transform a vacant, trashy courtyard into a vibrant place to play.

I VISITED THE PLAYGROUND a few days later and savored the happy sounds of joyful screaming children in the courtyard, replacing the gunshots and drug activity that had ruled for so many years. My visit coincided with Summerdale's very first Tenant Association meeting at the Star-C community center. As I looked at the playground, something did not seem just right. After a few moments, I realized what was missing—the mounds of trash the residents used to mindlessly discard. We typically cleaned the trash in the morning and early afternoon, but within a few hours, a fresh batch of soda cans, snack wrappers, cigarette butts, and other discarded items returned. It was frustrating for maintenance and proof that many tenants simply did not care.

Lucy had recently resigned as manager at Summerdale to take a new position with a technology company focused on building a platform to connect low-income people to housing. The new position let her work from home and have more time with her growing family. We were devastated to lose her but understood it was the best choice for her and her family. Adriane, the assistant property manager, gladly accepted the promotion to Lucy's former position. She was in the community center preparing for the tenant meeting. I asked, "Did you notice the trash is almost nonexistent in the courtyard . . . or am I missing something?"

Adriane said, "Yes, I did notice. And we did not clean up either, other than this morning. One of our Star-C students, a nine-year-old who lives in Building D, has been policing the playground and boldly telling the families to clean up their trash."

"Amazing!" I said. "We need to give her a community award." It had only been a few days and the residents were already policing the playground and taking ownership of her community.

A young man entered the facility and Adriane told him to sign in. He took a seat, and I introduced myself to Johnathan Brewer, a Morehouse College student who worked for Delta Airlines, headquartered just two miles southwest of Summerdale. Johnathan lived in a newly renovated Phase I townhome with an older Mercedes parked out front. He seemed ambitious and eager to get ahead in life. It only took a few minutes for me to appreciate how invested he was in bettering the community.

Adriane later shared, "Johnathan is very active and watches over the property. If he sees something, he will call me. He has already referred several of his fraternity brothers to the property, and if I could get a hundred more of him, I would be happy."

In about ten minutes, the room filled with more than a dozen residents, security officers, maintenance staff, and management. Daylight Savings Time had just started, so lights illuminated the playground, which was crowded with adults, teenagers, and many young children who ran into the community center to check on their parents and back outside to the playground. The meeting had a warm festive mood.

We organized a tenants association to determine if our families were interested in creating the community capital necessary to sustain a healthy community. The capital at Summerdale had been controlled for so long by the drug lords, car thieves, and other illegal tenants. We wanted to honor the legal legacy tenants and saw a community meeting as a way to rebuild trust and community capital.

The meeting started with announcements.

"Congratulations to the students in the Star-C program for their performance on the 2019 Georgia Milestone," Adriane announced.

"What does that mean?" asked Ms. Spencer, a tenant at Phase II.

Adriane looked at me to explain.

I stood up and asked, "Is everyone familiar with the Georgia Milestone?" All nodded except Ms. Spencer. I explained, "Our Star-C students on average outperformed their peers. That is amazing considering where our students started last year. And I would like to thank the families here who have enrolled their children in the program. Just wait until next year!" Many of the original Star-C children exhibited low reading levels, anger issues, anxiety, and high stress associated with living in a high crime, blighted environment.

The parents nodded and clapped.

Adriane addressed the next item on the agenda. "Criminal activity has gone down dramatically, and our security guard is here, Ms. Joyce. If you have any concerns, please let us know. We are having fewer complaints about children since we started the new curfew, so please make sure your children are inside by 9 o'clock."

A new tenant in the recently renovated Building G spoke up, "I had to tell a few kids to get off the HVAC equipment last week. I've had to tell them a few times actually."

It was encouraging to hear her willingness to police the community.

Adriane continued, "Thank you for that and any suggestions to address crime. We are going to start doing pest control on a monthly schedule. Contact me if you have problems."

Ms. Humphries raised her hand "Well, my two boys have asthma. Is the pest control bad for them?"

Adriane didn't have to respond because another resident, Ms. Keisha, answered: "No, it is water-based and doesn't smell. They treat the after-school program twice a month now for a year, and there have been no issues. My children have asthma too."

Ms. Humphries seemed satisfied.

"You are bringing up a good point," I added. "Georgia Tech School of Construction is doing a class and one of the students suggested a different air filter for the HVAC systems, especially helpful for residents with asthma. If you have children or family members with asthma, let Adriane know and we will keep a list to make sure you get this air filter."[69]

Several people raised their hands to get on the list.

"Georgia Tech is having their final exam presentation on December 2nd at lunch time and everyone is invited to attend. They have studied the property and have several suggestions and I wanted to see if you are interested." I paused and looked at the group before continuing, "Would you support a recycling program? How about a community cleanup day, where we join our neighbors and pick up trash?"

Several people said yes, they would be interested.

"How about a Safety to School grant? You know that only one side of Old Hapeville Road has sidewalks and it is very dangerous with the speeding cars, especially since our children walk from Cleveland Avenue Elementary back to Summerdale. There is a $500,000 grant that funds improvements in sidewalks and infrastructure to promote safety. We need to get City support and the students have already spoken with Dr. Payne, principal of Cleveland Elementary, and City Councilwoman Shepherd, who have given their support."

This brought a lively discussion from the group.

"It's just not safe to walk across Old Hapeville between Phase I and II, especially now that it is dark so early," one tenant said. "I'm worried about the kids."

"I take 6–8 kids in my car every day from the after-school program and drive them across the street to their apartment. It's just not safe to walk," Ashley Humphries said. I was impressed by her kindness.

"They need to add speed bumps," Ms. Spencer said, hugging her daughter who was sitting silently next to her.

As the meeting progressed, the tenants spoke up more and became more active in the discussion. Adriane announced that she would like ten members to form the Tenant Association and have monthly meetings with the property management leadership group.

"How much time would I have to invest?" asked Ms. Spencer.

Adriane said, "We want to have quarterly Tenant Association meetings, but monthly leadership meetings so you can give us direction on how we can improve the community and neighborhood. For example, we would like to have job fairs."

Johnathan piped up. "I work for Delta Airlines and they are getting ready to do a massive amount of hiring. Massive. I would really like to organize a job fair here at the property."

A resident responded, "There are so many teenagers at the property who need jobs. My daughter is only fifteen and really wants to work."

"Delta has a partnership with Atlanta Technical College, and they will give scholarships to study mechanics. We are talking about $40,000 worth of education for free and when you graduate, a mechanic's job working for Delta starts at $60,000 per year. That is a life-changing salary."

"Are these part-time jobs, summer jobs or full-time?" Ms. Jeffries asked.

"They can be all of these. Delta hires part-time for peak times of the year, but these part-time jobs can turn into full-time jobs. They are good at working with the employees," Johnathan answered.

Ashley Humphries said, "I work for the Fulton County sheriff's office and they have volunteer programs for teenagers and young adults as well. I would like to see if we could coordinate a leadership program with the sheriff's office and juvenile court. Fulton County is also getting ready to do a lot of hiring, especially for the new libraries they are opening, and it would be nice to have a job fair, I'm sure they would be interested. They also help people get their GED."

Another tenant spoke: "I would like to really see some classes to help me with my credit."

"That's an easy one," I said. "We have had several banks offer to do financial literacy classes, if that is something that you are interested in."

Several tenants nodded yes.

Adriane continued, "I need ten people to sign up for the Tenant Association leadership. Who is interested?." Four people raised their hand.

"I'll be on the committee," said Johnathan. "When is the next meeting?"

"The first week in February. I suggest we serve dinner and the property will cover the cost."

Someone responded, "We would really like that, but don't get pizza, how about BBQ?"

I took it as a sign that the Summerdale Tenant Association was off to a good start. It was another brick in the rebuilding of Summerdale Apartments.

IV — Epilogue

29

Change Gonna Come

In May 2020, a few months after our first Tenant Association meeting, I navigated my new Chevy Bolt south along I-75 and exited the long ramp to Cleveland Avenue. At the stop light, a group of young boys eagerly approached my car and offered a $2 bottle of ice-cold water. "Do you sell a lot of water?" I asked one of the boys, handing him two crisp dollar bills.

"Yes, ma'am," he nodded, cocking his head thoughtfully to calculate. "About four cases a day. I can make good money in a few days, over $400," he said with pride.

"Wow! You're a smart entrepreneur for your age." I smiled and he returned the smile. "Are you at Cleveland Avenue Elementary?"

"Yes, ma'am, fifth grade."

The light turned green and I said goodbye to the young entrepreneur and turned left onto Cleveland Avenue. The Cleveland neighborhood corridor was showing signs of new life. The abandoned Kmart building was newly occupied by a consumer products liquidator neighboring the Piggly Wiggly. The property owner had also signed a parking lease with Amazon and the lot was crowded with dozens of Prime delivery trucks. At the Old Hapeville Road corner, the Exxon gas station was still a hub for loiterers, but today was now the exception rather than the rule. These days I often passed the station and was surprised to see all the cars pumping gas and no sign of loitering men or drug activity. Ski and the APD had a strong presence at Exxon and the loitering was diminishing. Cleveland Avenue Elementary proudly stood at the corner.

Two years had passed since we purchased Summerdale Apartments. The road was long, but the results were spectacular. The renovation of Phase I was approximately 50 percent completed after two years of regulatory delays associated with permitting and construction. The exterior brick was freshly painted with bright-colored doors, and the newly sealed parking areas gave it a neat and crisp feel. The renovation of Phase II was completed a year earlier and quickly leased. In June 2018, we started with 120 leased units in both phases; however, approximately 40 units were leased to tenants who did not follow housekeeping or property rules, were phantom tenants, or operated illegal businesses such as drug dealing or prostitution; these either disappeared or were evicted. We retained 68 of the original 100 legal tenants including Virginia Humphries, James Wilkens, and Marilyn Moore. As I pulled into the parking lot on Phase II and got out of my car, an elderly long-term tenant stopped and asked if I was the lady landlord.

"Yes," I replied, greeting her. She introduced herself and I recognized her name from the rent roll.

"I just want you to know me and my husband appreciate you and the things that have happened around here. I've been living here now for over twenty years and let me tell you they's been some rough years."

"Well, thank you—that's very kind of you to say something. Does your family ever go over to the new KABOOM! playground in Phase I?"

"No, I don't go over there but heard it was nice."

"We are thinking of adding a new playground in the common area of Phase II. What do you think of that?"

She thought for a minute. "Hmmm. Don't do anything that would attract those men drug dealers. They was here too long and I see them sometimes at the Exxon. We don't want them back here, so, no, don't make it easy for them to come back."

"Okay, I hear you. Maybe a playground designed for the smaller children?"

"Yes, that would be okay." She winked, said goodbye, and headed toward the mailbox area.

It was encouraging to see our success reflected through the eyes of our tenants and stakeholders. The families were positively impacted by the stable environment, which translated to a more relaxed property. Families were outside on their porches and happy kids were playing noisily in the common areas. Traffic was pretty constant through the gates, but the flow was tenants going to or returning from their jobs. So many people had contributed to the community transformation, and everyone was a beneficiary. I conducted final interviews with many stakeholders to see where everyone landed.

THE HUMPHRIES FAMILY—VIRGINIA, SIMONA, ASHLEY, JOSHUA, AND KINGSTON

Ashley saved her money and moved with Joshua and Kingston into her own apartment within view of Virginia and Simona's unit. Her sons Kingston and Joshua were still enrolled under the watchful eye of Dr. Payne at Cleveland Avenue Elementary and the Star-C after school program. Ashley's mother, Simona, and grandmother, Virginia, remained a vital part of Ashley's daily life. Virginia and Ashley greeted me at their front door like a long-lost guest. We sat down and everyone was smiling. After some small talk I started by asking, "What are your thoughts about Kingston and Joshua and Cleveland Avenue Elementary now that things around the neighborhood seem calmer?"

Ashley immediately sat up straight and said, "They are doing great in school! I love it! My kids love it! They love this new stuff that they do like planting the garden. They have been interested in new stuff that they have not been able to do until now. It's all an adventure. I tell you that I am so impressed with Dr. Payne. There was nothing good going on with the school before. It was like just there. When Dr. Payne took over, you could see it was totally different. My kids are telling me something new every day! When they got STEM-certified, I was excited and knew this was big! I feel like my children are getting a better education. They are excited to learn new things. My baby son is so excited to learn."

Virginia interrupted, with pride in her voice, "Kingston has that personality and is so observant on everything and they speak so highly of him. He pays attention to everything and just touches my heart to hear him speak so good about the teachers. They let them know that the boys are loved . . . and we are watching them. When I walk down the street every day, I thank God that I can get them, because they keep me going. I am going to sit down now because I'm getting happy. There was this little boy who just ran to me. He doesn't have shoes, so I ask, 'where are your shoes?' He stays in the middle apartment up there [pointing to the unit upstairs] and ever since I tied his shoes, he runs over when he sees me coming."

Ashley said, "She has raised so many in this community. All my kids, some of my son's friends, look up to my grandma and they are teenagers now. A couple of them still live here. One across the hall and one in the back. Just two of them are still here. Quatese . . . used to be around Grandy all the time and we just welcome him, we didn't look down on him, we just welcomed him as one of my son's friends and they were always welcome."

I commented, "It really takes a community to raise children. That is what I just appreciate about the four generations of your family living at Summerdale Apartments since 1996. You tie the community together, but you have witnessed the community and survived. Let's talk about the Star-C after-school program."

Ashley quickly responded, "We love Ms. Kristin. She is so nice, and she is strict with education and I love it. My kids love her. Especially when it was here on this side, it was nice. When they moved to the other side [the blighted Phase I], I was scared. My kids, I had to have a pep talk with them, because they knew that crime happens on that side. And they got used to it. I love her, my kids have improved a lot. Kingston's grades have come up, and his talking skills have improved. He was a preemie baby, but they understand him better at school. He is able to interpret more how he feels and what is going on. He is going through the third grade."

I asked, "Was he having issues, behavioral?"

Ashley responded. "Both were, but more Joshua. Kingston would have outbursts but he has ADHD. He has 'moments.' Ms. Kristin is strict, but it is okay to have your moment, it's okay for you to feel what you feel, and I'm going to give you your time to have that moment, but then we are going to come back down and have our work. She is strict with social emotional issues. And I love that because that has improved Kingston a lot. His reading has improved, and he likes to read now."

I said, "That is the value of the Star-C program. I came the very first day, and then returned in December and the children were so stressed. These are six-, seven-, and eight-year-olds and I didn't think it was natural for them to have so much stress. Kristin told me it was the environment, where the children went from school to home and then back to school, due to the high crime. It is a lot safer now and they are out on their bikes or playing ball. They are happy and helping with their homework and more engaged in their education, and it only took Ms. Kristin eight months to create this positive change."

Ashley smiled, "I love it."

"We are seeing a dramatic improvement in the kid's behavior which should transcend to an increase in academics. When I interviewed Dr. Payne, she was talking about how much happier they are and how their reading grades are improving."

"They are. You can see the transition from when they started."

I asked Ashley. "Anything else you want to tell me about the community?"

Ashley responded, "Everything is so convenient. I like the neighborhood and that's why we haven't moved. If our car breaks down, we have the MARTA. We sometimes walk, I told my son that we are going to walk, and he got his haircut and there is a guy up there that does a good job. The Exxon station has calmed down with the crime. Sometimes there is no one there and thank God, but it's the cheapest gas. The drug dealers are still there in the afternoon. Usually, one or two. But you don't see them every afternoon. The police come out here more often now. I always smile through the bad and good. When I was growing up, my grandmother always told me to treat people how you want to be treated and that is what I stick to. I have an old soul, that's what everyone tells me on my job, meaning I don't think I need to show off to get attention. I don't go out and party, I don't drink or smoke, I am just a homebody. I am very confident and comfortable with myself because of how I was raised."

I commented, "You were also fortunate to be raised in a consistent environment. You didn't move around schools. We don't want people to move . . . we like the fact that the children in this community are supporting the school and you are not having to deal with this constant turnover associated with large rental increases or criminal activity. Education and housing are so interconnected."

Ashley smiled. "I appreciate all the changes you are making to the area and we are glad to be here. I know all my neighbors. My grandma knows her neighbors and they look out for each other and we are just glad to be here."

Ashley and Virginia both qualified for the Atlanta Housing Homeflex program offered at Summerdale and their rents were reduced to 30 percent of their monthly gross income. Virginia's rent was reduced from $670 to $291 per month and Ashley's rent was reduced from $670 to $313 per month. They are now able to comfortably live at Summerdale and raise the fourth generation in an affordable, stable environment. Kingston is no longer exhibiting signs of severe trauma and both Joshua and Kingston are still enrolled in the Star-C program under the careful nurturing of Kristin. Both are now reading at their respective appropriate grade-levels.

SHARON ALLEN—THE PHANTOM TENANT IN UNIT D-12

About a month after the drug bust of Units D-12 and C-6, Ski gave us the green light to start the eviction process and repossess the units. Lucy clearly remembered this day:

> We contacted Sharon and told her about the police raid and drug bust, and that we were starting the eviction process, but she was more concerned about her credit. She didn't want an eviction on her record but she didn't even care about the impact of all the crime on the neighbors! She said she would pay the outstanding rent but didn't seem to care that D-12 was filthy, roach-infested, and there were tunnels through the attic that linked D-12 to D-10 so the dealers could go between the units without going outside. It was clear that no one had lived in the apartment for several years, but it was used to deal with God knows what!

After getting served with the official landlord-tenant dispossessory affidavit by Fulton County, Sharon had seven days to file a written answer with the court. Luckily, Sharon did not answer within the seven days, allowing us to immediately file for a writ of possession of the unit, expediting the eviction process and saving us about five months going through the process. Upon receipt of the writ, our maintenance staff immediately changed the locks. Lucy recalled:

It was disgusting in the totally destroyed apartment. It smelled horrible and the floor was gooey with dirt and walls all torn out. There was very little furniture, an old couch infested with roaches and a salon chair. People were not living there, but a lot of traffic was in and out of the unit. It was their hang out house. It took our maintenance staff about a week to get the floors together, the dirt was so thick.

We decided to board-up the windows, however, someone broke back into the unit about three days later, looking for something, so we decided to trash out the apartment and remove everything because there was obviously something in there the dealers wanted that was not picked up by the police. After the bust, everything was quiet, but the drug activity had moved to unit c-6. We started the process to evict c-6, but this tenant responded to the dispossessory affidavit within the seven-day period and filed additional paperwork in federal court, so it took over a year to complete the eviction.

The impact of Sharon and the systematic practice of phantom tenants to front illegal businesses is an easy trick drug dealers use to disguise their trade, but it is significant to the moral and safety of apartment communities. Sharon leased an apartment as a legal tenant and then invited a drug dealer to pay her rent plus a rumored $2,000 per month to use the apartment as a front. The legal process to remove illegal activity can take months if not years. The Georgia legal system doesn't recognize the phenomena of phantom tenants or hold them accountable for illegal activity in units they leased.

A record check on Sharon indicated she was arrested on other charges in a neighboring county, whose police department declined to share the nature of the arrest due to its "confidential" nature. Sharon has moved on and has not been seen again at Summerdale Apartments. We estimated Sharon's actions as a phantom tenant easily cost over $1 million in lost income, additional security, ADP police efforts, and unit damages. Her actions amplified the blight surrounding the Cleveland neighborhood and Cleveland Avenue Elementary. A meaningful community redevelopment could not commence until the crime was removed, which took us over a year. The emotional cost of the trauma experienced by the children and people living at the community, affected by Sharon's behavior, cannot be measured.

MELINDA WYATT, THE BLIGHTED TENANT

After our court settlement in January 2019, Melinda moved to a competitive apartment property close to Cleveland Avenue Elementary to maintain her kids' enrollment. I knew her new apartment community; it had a high violent-crime rate and was recently on the news after a teenager was killed by a random bullet shot through the floor by the neighbor. This criminal environment was not safe for Melinda's family and I was concerned. I sensed she was honest and had a hard-working moral code, and I enjoyed hearing her perspective on life. She was a street fighter but despite the housekeeping and rude behavior issues we witnessed at Summerdale, she and her husband worked hard to raise well-mannered children. The trauma and stress that comes from extreme poverty seemed to have taken its toll on Melinda, and after "moving up" to Summerdale from her substandard housing in East Point, her new apartment community was a step down. It had been almost a year since I interviewed her and I wanted to get an update on her life after Summerdale.

Since she didn't have a car, we agreed to meet at a location convenient for her, and she suggested Cleveland Avenue Elementary. Dr. Payne graciously offered a conference room for the meeting, and I invited Courtney English to join the meeting. He is director of community development for Star-C and a former chairman of Atlanta Public Schools. He wanted to interview a parent on the impact of Star-C. After Melinda, Courtney, and I were seated in a conference room with her sons Jackson and Anthony, I asked how she was doing.

"Been busy all days," she replied with a smile.

I looked at the two polite and well-behaved boys, who were devouring a freshly opened can of Planters Mixed Nuts and organic chocolate chip cookies that I had offered, with Melinda's approval. "How is school?" I asked.

Melinda fondly looked at each of her boys. "Things are going good. They are making a lot of progress and the school year is almost over."

Courtney asked, "Did you think the Star-C program was helpful?"

"The after-school program at Summerdale was great for me because I was looking for something after school and it seems like an okay environment. I noticed that they helped them with homework which was good since Dad and I work all day. Anthony is a good student and the program helped Jackson go a level-up in reading. At third grade they were saying he was kindergarten but he didn't stay there long. The program started in August and we moved in January. They are currently not in an after-school program and I am looking for a great summer camp."

Anthony spoke up, "I want to go to the GOALS after-school program at Cleveland."

Melinda looked at her boys and said, "Y'all out of school the 24th." Gazing at Jackson, she added. "Now he has to go to summer school. My third son is in middle school. He loves his computer games and he is not active at all, but these two are very active outside."

Anthony stood up and declared. "I've improved my reading. I've gone from second grade to fourth grade. I have to read every question." He sat back in his chair without taking his eyes off his mother as he bit into another cookie.

Melinda ignored Anthony and continued, "I think that the entire Cleveland neighborhood needs to clean out the toxic element. The drug use and hanging out at the corner store, and housing, a lot of people want a house. But they can't reach because they can't afford it. And transportation, the parents can't always get around. [Her children] like sports but because of transportation issues, I can't get there."

I asked, "Have you looked at the houses behind Summerdale? There is one right on Cleveland Avenue. I can pass along the Federal Home Loan Bank first-time homebuyer program information."

Ignoring my offer, Melinda continued. "I want to work in the medical field. I am now at the local hospital and they do help get you through medical services school. But my goal is to own my house, because I don't want to be sixty-seven years old and trying to pick up a short-term job to pay my rent. I want to be set. I just want to own a house and set a foundation and just live."

Jackson interrupted, "I want to go to college."

"What college do you want to attend?" Courtney asked.

"Morehouse."

"Hey, that's my alma mater. There are tons of summer camps at More-house. I used to run one."

Jackson stared at Courtney with complete awe.

I noticed that Jackson had raspy breathing and asked if either of the boys had breathing problems.

Melinda replied that Jackson did. That did not surprise me given the poor housekeeping habits which fostered roaches, a strong trigger of asthma. I was surprised that Anthony, raised in the same environment, didn't seem to have breathing issues.

Anthony announced, "I want to be a lawyer."

Courtney asked Melinda, "Do you feel like you have strong connections in the neighborhood?"

She paused, then said, "School yes . . . neighborhood no. I am a worka-holic. I don't know many of my neighbors. Relationships have changed, and with me, growing up, the neighbors were like a second home."

"Do you feel like you have a place to access resources? Do you know where to go?"

"No, just Google. My mom is my only parent, so I do everything for her."

I looked at the boys. "What about you guys? Do you have friends in the neighborhood?"

Anthony was the first to respond. "A lot of them. We are outside on our bikes the whole year."

Melinda added, "But they stayed in the house for a few days after shooting incidents on Cleveland Avenue . . . I heard it started at that Exxon corner store, and the guy knew people from the apartment, and someone came to get him. It was gang-related or retaliation from a beef. It's just that Exxon gas station . . . and the apartments behind the Checkers. I think that is where all that stuff is happening. They don't hang out at the Chevron. And I've noticed the police is always at the Piggly Wiggly . . . always happen-ing out there. I think part of the thing is trust. People are not trusting . . . everything is just smiley faces. Especially in the black community. I think you should build a relationship, starting off small and try to gain their trust before letting them in. It's hard to break the ice with people who were raised differently, because their parents are aggressive, they are acting out the same way. It is important to break that cycle and I understand that everyone is not trustworthy."

Jackson interrupted, looking at Courtney, "My uncle went to Morehouse College."

Melinda continued, "I say nothing comes easy . . . you have to work hard. It wasn't easy for them, nothing is easy, you have to work for what you want. Reading is very important, going to school is very important. My daughter said, 'I don't want to go to high school,' so I asked her what you want to do, be a doctor?"

Jackson announced, "I want to be a police officer!"

Melinda went on, "Even now when I say I stay in Summerdale or even Cleveland Avenue, they say you still there? I am like, yeah . . . and everyone is like, 'that is bad,' and I say it is not like it used to be, there still a little crime but outside the apartment that is bringing it in, so you know, but like I said I am never home most of the time . . . working, working, working, so and my kids they are at school, they are in the house until I get there. I don't really interact with my neighbors. I was there at Summerdale Apartments for two years and only know one person because I work a lot. And I am to myself most of the time, not saying that I am a nonchalant person like I don't like to communicate, but some people can be trusted, and some can't."

We settled with Melinda in eviction court and she moved out of Summerdale in January owing $1,620 in back rent and fees for the cost of the eviction. By May, working on an installment plan, she had paid off the entire balance she owed to Summerdale. We passed along to her the information for the First Time Home Buyers Assistance Program offered by the Federal Home Loan Bank. Her children are still enrolled in Cleveland Avenue Elementary under the watchful leadership of Dr. Payne and her staff.

KRISTIN HEMINGWAY AND THE STAR-C
AFTER-SCHOOL PROGRAM

There was a knock on the front door of the community center and Kristin called out "Come in." Three students entered and quietly closed the door.

Kristin enthusiastically greeted them, "Hi, Joshua, Kingston, and Quantavious. Do you have any homework?"

"Yes," said Kingston.

"No," said Quantavious at the same time.

"Okay, let's relax until the other children arrive," Kristin replied.

I was in the after-school program building after observing a presentation by fifteen graduate students for their final exam in a "Real Estate Ethics" class that had utilized Summerdale Apartments as a case study in the Fall 2019 semester. The students were in the construction master's degree program at Atlanta's Georgia Institute of Technology (Georgia Tech). The purpose of their case study was to document the community. The presentation produced many valuable concepts to improve the Summerdale environment for the residents and neighborhood.

I noticed that Joshua, Kingston, and Quantavious were engaged and at ease with Kristin as they settled into the program. They seemed eager and comfortable in the Star-C facility—it was their space. These three children had come a long way from our first meeting over a year ago when we first launched the Star-C after-school program. Now the kids were noticeably more relaxed, though Kristin felt they still had progress to make:

> The past year was a building year for the kids. I don't necessarily measure the success of the Star-C program by the Georgia Milestone standardized test scores. My measure of success is social emotional coping skills where the kids have the tools to advocate for themselves and develop self-control. Happy kids that can advocate for themselves, play outside, and build their community. If we can get these things under control, help the kids deal with social emotional and how the child self-views, then the performance in school will take care of itself. We'll get the grades.

The CarMax Foundation and KABOOM! had recently installed a new playground at Summerdale Apartments that the kids personally designed with their parents. I asked if the new playground was helpful in building community capital and self-esteem for the kids in the Star-C program?

The new KABOOM playground is a good thing. The kids LOVE the playground, it has created a sense of community and they help each other. They designed it and they OWN their playground. The older kids push the younger kids on the swings. Star-C and the playground is a blessing for this community.

I asked Kristin what she thought causes a blighted community. Without hesitating, she replied:

Perspective causes blight. If you look in the mirror and the person that you see has no value, then your perspective is of no self-worth, which integrates into the larger community. You could have developed this mentality from your family, the news, your friends, or strangers; but poverty doesn't auto-matically mean you have a blighted mentality or perspective. I grew up in a lower-middle class household, but I was always loved and valued. Every time I looked in the mirror, I saw value in the person looking back at me and if I lost that perspective, then there were several people to remind me that I was valued. Society needs to show kids that they have value and some of that is by investing in the community, some is investing in the schools, their parents, and places for people to get healthy food. The message is: if kids are valuable, then I am going to do everything in my power to make this a safe place where they are valued.

I agreed with Kristin. The Cleveland neighborhood had such little community capital, that an active gun shooter terrorized the community for several years, with very little being done about it other than responding after the shots had been fired. Think of those children who attend Cleveland Avenue Elementary and had the fear instilled by this active shooter who set up shop right across the street from their school at the Exxon gas station. Sadly, no one had the confidence to muster up the community capital to really challenge this social order. No one seemed to understand how to organize the community capital to fight for the kids. Kristin continued:

> We criminalize poverty. We want to penalize people for being poor. The kids growing up in Summerdale have a less than 10 percent chance of moving up the social-economic ladder to the middle class.[70] We treat poverty like it is a human deficiency. You are poor so you can't learn, but the reality is that most of these children are very capable but can't learn because they are dealing with so many other things that they should not worry about at their age. They are worried about if their house is going to be safe when they get home, or if they are going to make it home safely, you know the 1,000-foot walk from the school to their house. They are worried if they will eat tonight and what about their siblings. They worry about more than I worry about as an adult. They are dealing with it at the age of seven or eight and in the meantime, the educators are trying to push long-division on them as the most important thing in their life.

I knew what Kristin was saying based on my own conversations with the families about the community. Many of their children were traumatized and living in fear of stray bullets, and strangers fighting, yelling, and screaming in the middle of their apartment community, a place which is supposed to be the safe haven. Their parents were also dealing with the stress of maintaining a dignified lifestyle, never knowing what challenges awaited them daily. Some days they could wake up and discover their car has bullet holes or was vandalized. Without transportation to their jobs, they might not have a job at the end of the day. I took a moment to share my interview with Joshua and Kingston's mother and the fact that her children have asthma and emotional issues connected with the condition of their community.

After absorbing the information, Kristin responded.

> Joshua just wants to run and play and be a kid. There are times that I can't let him play because it may trigger his severe asthma, and that is not fair. How do you tell a first-grade boy that he can't run on the playground while he watches everyone else run? It's heartbreaking. Kingston had social emotional

issues, but he is really smart and doing much better. My goal for Kingston is to teach him self-control and to have forethought versus afterthought. When we teach kids that you constantly have to be controlled by the outside, versus controlling themselves internally, we are setting them up for prison because that is what prison is, an outsider controlling the day-to-day activity. So, my goal is for the children to know how to handle their anger and problem solve with better outcomes. The opposite of anger is "joy." I tell them that "joy is an inside job." You can upset me, but I don't give you the power to take my joy. You can't control whether or not I have joy. That's a lot of power to give someone else, for them to determine if you have joy in your life.

Behavior is such an important part of learning. Cleveland Avenue Elementary was STEM certified and behavior is one of the criteria to participate in the STEM program. There are kids that have lost opportunities because of their behavior – opportunity to be in an advanced class, additional resources, field trips, programming and they have almost missed it because of coping skills. We don't teach coping skills in school. And these kids are being punished for something that they are not taught and don't understand. There are also times that you need grace. If you are a person that is gracious with others, grace comes back to you. You need to easily forgive. Odds are that none of us are perfect, we all make mistakes. Kingston is learning these lessons and is becoming one of my strongest leaders. He is beyond capable to navigate a successful life. We need to shift the mindset because we focus on pushing through academically, but the kids have to be able to navigate and make decisions and independently self-advocate.

No one is going to hand social capital to a little black boy. You need to always turn in your best work, and if you are lackadaisical or haphazard, you are giving them a reason to reject you and you don't need any more reasons. It is not fair that other people will take their value from you. While we work on fairness, we also have to work on truth, and this is the truth.

I asked if she thought the after-school program was a good investment.

Absolutely, anything you can do to invest in the safety and joy of learning for the kids is a good investment. The kids in the Summerdale Star-C program are developing into community advocates who are excelling in school. Municipalities should invest in after-school programs because not everyone's parents can afford an after-school program. My mother didn't have a car so I couldn't participate in things, if it was something I could walk in my community, it would have been a game changer. I am going to continue working with Star-C until safety is not a concern and the kids can look at themselves in the mirror and see someone worth investing in.

Kristin dropped out of Florida A&M University more than a decade ago, but while working at Star-C she decided to go back through an on-line platform and complete her bachelors' degree in Quantitative Analysis with a minor in education. She does her homework with the kids and said, "We all do homework during homework time. I show them my grades on my chemistry test. The kids are invested in my college education and ask me about it. We all celebrate when I make an 'A' on a test." Kristin graduated in December 2019.

DR. PAYNE AND CLEVELAND AVENUE ELEMENTARY

One day I sat in a classroom at Cleveland Avenue Elementary watching Dr. Anyeé Payne at work in front of a group of fourth-grade students. She was patient and methodical as she walked the kids through a test on the magnetic qualities of Earth. The children were engaged and well-behaved as they earnestly focused on Dr. Payne and then their test papers, brows creased in concentration. Dr. Payne didn't usually teach classes, but the regular teacher was absent and the other staffers were tag-teaming to teach the class for the week. I knew she was busy, but I wanted to meet with her for an update on the partnership between Cleveland Avenue Elementary, Summerdale, and Star-C. After we got settled in her conference room, Dr. Payne and I talked about how things were going.

In a recent conversation, Officer Ski had shared with me that another large apartment community in the neighborhood on Steele Avenue, directly west of Cleveland Avenue Elementary, had experienced a lot of criminal activity. About a year ago, the owners finally hired licensed police officers to provide 24/7 security, and the reduction in criminal activity was having a positive impact. Summerdale Apartments and the Steele Avenue apartment community jointly housed half of the students attending Cleveland Avenue Elementary. In both communities, efforts to remove the criminal element or families that didn't follow the rules on behavior or housekeeping had caused evictions and probably increased the transiency rate at Cleveland Avenue Elementary.

With these two large apartment communities now stable, the transiency rate for Cleveland Avenue Elementary should gradually decrease. From our experience, it takes four to five years of community building to truly make an impact on an underperforming elementary school. Meanwhile, I had noticed that the transiency rate for Cleveland Avenue Elementary increased from 36 percent to 41 percent over the last year and wondered if Summerdale had anything to do with it. If anything, Dr. Payne's job became harder when transiency rose. She pondered the question and said:

> No, I don't think that Summerdale impacted our transiency rate. We have several apartment communities feeding our school, including Summerdale. But as educators, we don't really track transiency rates. Our focus is achievement targets set by the State of Georgia, based on demographics and previous performance. Based on the challenge index, we were "Beating the Odds" in 2017 and 2018, but not for 2019. But the formula changes every year, so it can be challenging to track our progress from year to year. . . . But the transiency rate increasing to 41 percent means [some] students don't have stable homes. Many of our students and their families just live from day-to-day."

I was curious as to whether the stable community had cut down on active-shooter lockdowns at the school. Dr. Payne summarized:

> You know, we haven't had any active shooter lockdowns in the past year. But my students would sometimes complain that there was a guy in the neighborhood who would shoot his gun. It's so nice not to have the active shooter lockdowns. [Before we had too] many to even count, including the

soft shooter lockdowns when we hear the gunfire in the neighborhood. We have to be vigilant and responsible. We lock the doors and don't let anyone have access to the building. We also suspend recess and tell our teachers to be vigilant and observant.

A formal lockdown is when the police call us, and we follow the formal drill. It is considered a Level-4 lockdown where we lock all the doors, turn off all the lights and instruct everyone to stay in their rooms. We shut down the front office so there is no one at the front because of the glass. We can usually hear the helicopters overhead and it can be disruptive. The children and staff are not allowed to leave the campus until the police give us permission. This lockdown can sometimes go on for hours. A soft lockdown is just a tip or intuition. We have had about three formal Level-4 active-shooter lockdowns since I've been here and too many to count the soft lockdowns.

I wanted Dr. Payne's thoughts on the strength of the partnership between Cleveland Avenue Elementary, Summerdale Apartments, and our Star-C program. She said:

We are on the right path. Summerdale is providing a safe, clean and healthy living environment for our families which often is a reason for them moving. You also introduced us to other partners that helped us become STEM Certified [in March 2019] which was valuable. Furthermore, Star-C and Kristin have a growing presence in our school. Kristin is present for many of our programs, the Beta Club, and college and career week. Many of our parents don't communicate well with us, so Kristin has become a strong liaison between the school and our Summerdale parents. She is vested in how the Star-C students are performing at school and is providing a stronger home-to-school bridge where there used to not be one. Kristin can relay information to responsive families. She is helping us establish stronger communication as well because sometimes our parents don't trust the system, but they trust her. Of course, it has been helpful when you look at the safety in general. With the police department involved, the number of incidents has decreased for our students when they walk to and from school. The kids would constantly complain about vagrants and people that made them nervous.

Star-C Students Attending Cleveland Avenue Elementary (CAE)
2019 Georgia Federal Milestone Test Scores

Student Name	Star-C Reading Score	Average CAE Score	Average APS Score	Average Georgia Score	Star-C Math Score	Average CAE Score	Average APS Score	Average Georgia Score
Star-C Student #1	521	468	500	511	522	498	518	525
Star-C Student #2	464	482	502	514	525	487	516	525
Star-C Student #3	447	482	502	514	478	487	516	525
Star-C Student #4	535	482	502	514	496	487	516	525
Star-C Student #5	524	482	502	514	561	487	516	525
Star-C Student #6	461	468	500	511	Note	-	-	-
Star-C Student #7	443	468	500	511	506	498	518	525
Star-C Student #8	483	482	502	514	492	487	516	525
Average	485	477	501	513	511	490	517	525

Note: This information was not provided

The average Georgia Federal Milestone reading test score by Star-C students was 485 versus 477 for their peers at CAE.

The average Georgia Federal Milestone math test score by Star-C students was 511 versus 490 for their peers at CAE.

These scores are for 3rd, 4th and 5th grade Star-C students.

CAE-Cleveland Avenue Elementary

APS=Atlanta Public Schools

The collaboration between Dr. Payne, Cleveland Avenue Elementary, Star-C, Kristin Hemingway, and Summerdale Apartments is creating a win-win for all parties. Summerdale Apartments is benefiting through its proximity to a successful school, and Cleveland Avenue Elementary is benefiting from its students living in stable, healthier home environments, without roaches, mold, bed bugs, and trauma associated with violence. Kristin has become a strong "educational advocate" for the students and families living at Summerdale and has been working diligently with Dr. Payne and her students on social-emotional learning and helping them build their toolbox to develop their individual social capital. One year after we started the Star-C program at Summerdale, Dr. Payne's and Kristin's students in the Summerdale Star-C program outperformed their classroom peers on the Georgia Milestones assessment. These gains are significant considering the reality that the children come from poor families.

Tellingly, when I asked Dr. Payne how my husband and I could make a donation to her PTA, she replied that in her nine years at Cleveland Avenue Elementary, no one had ever made a contribution to the school fund because "our families just don't have the means to make any type of donation."

CONSTRUCTION PERMITTING AND THE CITY OF ATLANTA

In June 2019, approximately ten months after we started the process, the City of Atlanta issued construction permits allowing us to start renovating forty units in the remaining boarded up buildings H, J, K, L, M, and N. Permits were already in place and we had begun renovating buildings E, F, and G totaling fifty-two units. As a condition of granting the permits, the City required that we replace the interior walls of these buildings. To avoid further delays, we had no choice but to comply (even though their decision was not supported by the building code). We originally expected to get the permits in three months and have the construction completed on the ninety-two blighted units within six months, but delays mounted, and lost opportunities piled up for more than a year.

Boarded-up vacant buildings produced no income while increasing blight and thus crime.[71] The permitting delays were costly to us. We funded additional 24/7 security to monitor the criminal element and additional insurance coverage to protect against vandalism and other risks common for vacant units. We were also funding monthly mortgage costs and property management and maintenance staff as the units sat empty. These expenses would continue until the property renovation was completed and the units were leased.

The blight also continued to have an impact on the neighborhood. In a study published in 2015, distressed vacant properties in Atlanta created a measurable spillover effect on single-family property values. The researcher, professor Dan Immergluck, found that single-family homes within five hundred feet of a distressed vacant property lost 3.15 percent of their value per vacant building. Summerdale Phase I had nine vacant and boarded up buildings along its southeastern property line, and the adjacent properties were single-family homes. The spillover effect was visible, and half of the nearby homes were also boarded up and vacant.[72]

PERMITS RECEIVED, BUT IT WASN'T THE END

We were thrilled to finally receive permits, but the delays were not over. Our first priority after receiving permits for buildings E and F was to erect temporary electrical poles and start the rewiring, which required a separate electrical permit. We couldn't start the renovation process without lighting and power for electric power tools, and we needed an inspection for the electrical rough-ins and temporary power poles. The City of Atlanta inspector arrived at the scheduled time on a Friday and passed the rough-ins for Building E. Jeff and the electricians had completed the wiring rough-ins for Building F, but they ran out of time before the building was inspected. The following week the inspector passed the rough-ins for the twelve units in Building F and signed off to start the electrical rough-in work on eighteen units in Building E. Two weeks later, Jeff organized a final inspection of electrical wiring of the twelve Building F units. A new inspector failed them, stating the dining rooms were not correctly wired despite the original inspector having approved the rough-in layouts. This was a typical delay we experienced throughout the renovation. We were renovating entire buildings of twelve or eighteen units, but we hesitated to fund the expense of certain plumbing or electrical components for all units because Inspector #1 would fail the work and make us redo it a certain way, then Inspector #2 would fail the work requested by Inspector #1 and make us put it back the original way. The application of the code was inconsistent, and the project was delayed dozens of times as we navigated different inspectors who interpreting code rules differently. The delays associated with the inspector interpretations added to the project three months of construction and approximately $100,000 in costs. It would have been so much easier if we had the same dedicated inspector for each element. There is a better way, according to Frank Wickstead, a seasoned construction veteran and professor of construction at Georgia Tech:

My suggestion is to have third-party inspectors hired by the general contractor and have them sign-off on the work. We do this for architects and engineers, who carry liability insurance if there is an error. Why don't we do this for building inspectors and take it out of the hands of the city? It will certainly save a lot of time and expense for the city to have to fund the salaries of staffing an inspection department. Of course, the cost of the permits would still be funded by the developer, so the city doesn't lose this revenue source.

Jeff summed up our experience dealing with permitting:

My code library weighs about seventy pounds of paper full of codes and space for interpretation, with no pictures, that makes up the universe of building inspectors, who are expected to enforce this code reliably. The ADA, UFAS, FHA and construction code books have become so complicated that in reality a human being can no longer accurately enforce them.

In July 2020, almost two years after we started the initial meetings with the City of Atlanta permitting office, we received the Certificates of Completion for the original ninety-two units that were boarded-up and blighted. This was eighteen months longer than we anticipated. The delays and new elements such as fire-rated walls resulted in an additional $1,053,000 in costs and $1,355,379 in lost revenue for a total $2,408,379. We unfortunately had to borrow the money from our lender at 4.5 percent. This added $166 per month to our goal of average monthly rental rates of $730 to recover this cost, so our new rents would be increased to a minimum of $896 per month or a 23 percent rental rate increase. To afford this additional $166 per month in rent, our tenants would have to earn an additional $6,640 per year after taxes or obtain a 25 percent salary increase to $17.23 per hour.[73] Knowing the low-income of our tenants and lack of housing options at affordable rents, we were concerned that several tenants that could not afford this increase were at risk of becoming homeless.[74] The high cost of permitting and code compliance is a major contributor to the national affordable housing crisis. One study found that for every $100 increase in rent, homelessness increased 15 percent.[75]

HOUSING AND FEDERAL COMPLIANCE

We were warned that the federal regulatory compliance for subsidized housing would be the most challenging aspect of our Atlanta Housing Homeflex program, and our advisor was correct. As part of the program, we needed a letter from a third-party inspector verifying that the structural elements of Summerdale Phase II met federal regulatory compliance for FFHA, ADA, and UFAS. Our first challenge was just finding a reasonably affordable third-party regulatory inspector that was willing to take the assignment, but after nine months, we signed a contract with a group out of Missouri to provide

The Rent Burden of Permitting Costs and Delays
Analysis of Additional Regulatory Requirements/Cost by City of Atlanta

Demographics 1 mile radius	% Owner	% Renter	Medium Income	Average Income
	36	64	$27,409	$39,551

Unit Type	Original Rental Rates	Affordability Hourly Rate (*)	Annual HH Income (*)
1/1 ba	$595	$11.44	$23,800
2/1.5 ba Townhome	$695	$13.37	$27,800
2/2 ba Flat	$729	$14.02	$29,160
3/2 ba Flat	$826	$15.88	$33,040
Average (Weighted)	$730	$14.04	$29,200

Additional Cost (unbudgeted) Due to Permitting Costs/Delays: **$2,408,379**
Additional Rent Charge per Month Per Unit Due to Permitting Costs/Delays: **$166**

New Rents After Permitting Costs/Delays:

Unit Type	New Rents Increased $166/Mo	Affordability Hourly Rate (*)	Annual HH Income (*)
1/1 ba	$761	$14.63	$30,425
2/1.5 ba Townhome	$861	$16.56	$34,425
2/2 ba Flat	$895	$17.20	$35,785
3/2 ba Flat	$992	$19.07	$39,665
Average (Weighted)	$896	$17.23	$33,545

(*) Based on 30% of Gross Monthly Income Rent Burden per the US Department of Housing & Urban Development guidelines

three site inspections and issue a compliance letter. We did not anticipate additional inspections since Phase I was grandfathered from compliance due to its age and Phase II was built in 1998, and the rules had not changed since this time. We were wrong.

Jeff retained dozens of laborers in preparation for the first inspection which highlighted 139 failures in 293 elements. We invested more than 1,000-man hours to address all these failures, but the second inspection three months later highlighted 94 failures, mainly around sidewalks and interior hardware. We worked hard to address the issues and fine-tune the elements around the reasons why they were failing. By the third and final inspection in February 2019, we had shortened the list to 31 failures. Four of the UFAS units required a specialized washer/dryer combo and the equipment was in the box waiting for installation. This is typical since landlords do not install new appliances until the unit is leased, so that valuable appliances don't sit in a vacant unit subject to vandalism. Because the washer/dryer combo was not installed in the four units, our consultant failed this component. A toilet in another unit was not "exactly 18 inches from the center line closest to the wall"—another failure. But the most challenging aspect of the third inspection report was the failure of 17 sidewalks and parking lot ramps. We re-poured the failed sidewalks from the second inspection. By our measurements, they were perfect; the consultant did not agree. We decided to use another vendor who smelled blood and gouged us $12,000 to achieve compliance for one parking lot ramp which should have cost only $3,000 had it not been a federal compliance issue. Jeff kept throwing labor and materials at the project and in February 2019, after a final inspection, we received the coveted letter stating that Summerdale complied with the federal requirements. What a beautiful piece of paper!

The $238,025 cost of the federal compliance dramatically exceeded our budget. The compliance cost for the six UFAS was $166,442 or $27,740 per unit, adding $175 per month to the rental rate of these units. The total cost of FFHA compliance for the required thirty-six units was $71,583 or $1,988 per unit, adding $13 per month to the rent on these units. We had no choice but to allocate these costs across all rents at Summerdale. We *used "in-house" labor in an attempt to keep rents affordable. A third-party contractor would have probably charged much more. We offered the UFAS units to our handicapped tenants living at Summerdale, but no one was interested. The UFAS unit we renovated for Ms. Boggs did partially accommodate her paraplegic nephew's needs.*

RENT

For the first five days of the month, the Summerdale leasing office now enjoys a constant flow of tenants making the monthly trek to turn over their carefully earned rent checks to property management and report maintenance issues. It is a social time as the staff gets a moment to visit with tenants who they typically see only once a month.

"Is everything okay with your unit?" Adriane asked Mr. Jennings in Unit 1301. "I know you were having problems with your air conditioning, but Robert fixed it a few weeks ago and is everything okay?"

"Yes, everything is just fine. Thank you for asking."

"How is your little granddaughter doing? Is she going to spend this summer with you again? If so, you may want to sign her up for the free Star-C summer camp, do you need the registration forms?"

"Humm . . . that may be a good idea. Let me discuss it with my wife and get back with you."

"Stay blessed," Adriane called as they exited and the next tenant came through the door.

Ms. Moore has a bad knee and cannot walk, but her neighbor drives her to the leasing office and patiently waits in her car while Ms. Moore slowly walks to the management office to hand over her rent check. She is proud of her track record of visiting the leasing office by the fifth day of each month for over ten years. Ms. Humphries typically drops off her check on her way to retrieve her great-grandsons from Cleveland Avenue Elementary. For many of our tenants who barely survive on poverty wages, the monthly trek to pay their rent is almost a pilgrimage, another month of secure housing in their familiar community. If the boss cuts your work hours, your child has a medical emergency and you cannot work for two days, or your nephew is jailed for a petty crime and needs the bail money so he/she can get back to work and pay his/her rent—your bank account quickly empties and you may not be able to visit the Summerdale office to pay on time.

Ms. Pamela is another tenant with almost a perfect record of timely rental payments in her fourteen years of tenancy at Summerdale. But there was one month, she said sadly, shaking her head—she was a proud lady—when she was one day late:

> The fifth day was a Sunday and the leasing office was closed. I tried to put my rent check through the metal drop slot for after-hours rent payments, but the drop slot was sealed shut due to the damages by the arsonist fire a few months ago, so I could not drop off my rent. I returned the next morning after the office was open and personally handed the check to Maya the property manager. Maya took my check but she said, your check is late, and you need to pay a $100 late fee. I couldn't believe she told me this! I explained to Maya that the drop slot was blocked because of the fire, but she would have none of my explanation. I arrived at 10 a.m. to drop off the rent and she told me that if I had been there at 9 a.m., she would have waived the late fee. I told her I'm poor and didn't have the $100 but I would pay her $5 per month until the balance was paid in full. And I paid that late fee. It took me over a year, but I paid it in full.

The first five days of the month is also a festive time for landlords. The rent checks are deposited in the bank to fund the stack of invoices piling up at the office. Landlords also have obligations to pay "rent" to their mortgage companies with severe consequences if they miss payments. Georgia is a nonjudicial foreclosure state meaning our lender can foreclose without filing a lawsuit or appearing in court. If we miss one mortgage payment, our lender can foreclose in less than 60 days. Our mortgage payment is due the first day of the month, with a grace period if we pay by the fifth. We funded Summerdale through several lenders, each with a different payment schedule. Despite the different due dates, the lenders auto-debited our account the first day of the month, so we had to front the mortgage payment before we collected rents for that month. If we did not collect enough rent to pay the mortgage, we were at risk of losing our investment and hard work to improve Summerdale.

After government compliance costs, our second largest impact on rent affordability was our monthly water expense. We spent $150,000 to separately meter the units and replaced the plumbing fixtures with low-flow and water-saving devices. In March 2019, we started reading the submeters and invoicing the tenants directly for their individual water usage for their unit. The readings from the individual water meters let us gauge the water consumption by each tenant. The initial individual water bills ranged from $50 to $600; many tenants were rightfully upset after having been paying a $35–$55 per month flat fee. The new meters revealed the units with leaks and those that were overpopulated and/or illegal boarding houses. Not surprisingly, the water bill for Miguel Valdez that first month was $550. He promptly visited Lucy to voice his concerns. She responded, "What do you expect when you have ten adults living in a three-bedroom apartment?"

We sent maintenance to look for leaking toilets and plumbing lines in units with high usage. Tenants who had continuously running toilets suddenly showed up with maintenance requests. Now that they were responsible for the cost of their water usage, their high bills were suddenly a concern. The $150,000 spent to separately meter the apartment units proved to be a good investment. Tenants started conserving water and calling in leaks. Our total water bills started trending downwards to $11,000 per month, making it affordable for us as a landlord to operate Summerdale.

EVICTIONS AT SUMMERDALE

As mentioned earlier, the overall goal of our TriStar mission-based model is to reduce transiency in the local elementary school. Unsustainable rents are one of the largest contributors to transiency since low-income families simply cannot afford a $50 or $100 per month rent increase, and evictions are one of the few legal tools landlords use to remove tenants for nonpayment. Unfortunately, an eviction becomes part of a tenant's legal record. Once an eviction is filed in the courts, it creates the "Scarlet E" on a tenant's public record profile in Georgia. During a prospective tenant's background check, an eviction is a red flag to landlords,[76] regardless of the final court verdict.

TriStar is often part of the larger policy conversation on community building and economic equality, and when the topic of rents and evictions inevitably arises, I tell listeners that not all evictions are created equal. It is relatively easy for landlords to deal with nonpayers—simply work out a payment plan or find other resources to help tenants reduce their delinquency. However, many tenants are simply disruptive and create a dangerous environment. Sharon Allen, Anthony Fowler, and their criminal activity contributed to the ongoing unrest at Summerdale and the long-term trauma for the sixty-three children living at the property. Kingston and Joshua suffered nightmares and exhibited behavior issues that spilled over to their reading comprehension and possible futures. Melinda and several other tenants refused to follow good housekeeping rules, and their children suffered the consequences of asthma. The health hazard was to their families and the neighbors. In response to the dozens of roach infestations, we included mandatory cleaning classes in our new tenant orientation, to help them understand our housekeeping expectations. It is working. Our housekeeping issues are dramatically reduced, creating a win-win for our families, especially the young children, and for Summerdale.

When we purchased the property, many tenants refused to pay rent or had behavior issues and did not follow the property rules. We went through a tenant "sift" where we retained the law-abiding tenants who paid rent and were viewed as good neighbors and eventually eliminated any tenant who refused to pay rent or follow the rules. We also had tenants who were on the fence, meaning they were good tenants who followed the rules but had temporary problems paying rent. Mr. Gideons was a single father with a young child who developed health issues that led to the emergency room; he lost his job when he prioritized taking care of his sick child, but he was a model tenant who had only temporarily fallen on hard times.

After working with several people like Mr. Gideons, we decided a much broader community engagement was needed for such cases. In 2019, we started an informal "Eviction Lab" to educate the larger Atlanta community on the issue of rent delinquency and evictions. We hoped to develop a toolbox connecting tenants, landlords, nonprofits, and other resources. The community has a limited perception of tenants facing eviction and tends to classify them as lazy or bad people. In my experience, the majority of people facing eviction are experiencing a hardship or temporary financial setback. Summerdale offered a live case study of real people behind rent delinquency and their circumstances. We invited a broad spectrum of interested organizations to the conversation, including representatives from municipal social services, churches, nonprofits, and corporations. The groundswell of support for our Eviction Lab and the outcomes has been strong.

The group started by meeting bi-monthly in the newly renovated Summerdale community center. Adriane brought a list of the delinquent tenants for the month and their balances. We started at the top of the delinquency list and went through each tenant, then held a group discussion on their delinquent balances and status.

Adriane started with Mr. Wilkens: "He had pneumonia and was in the hospital. He is now behind two months but has been to the office to discuss a payment plan to get caught up." The group discussed his case. He had been living at Summerdale for over five years and I recalled meeting him during our inspection before purchasing the property. His records showed he worked for the county and had a history of delinquent medical bills on his credit report. Since we purchased the property, he had been a model tenant and actively participated in our Tenant Association meeting. After much discussion, the group unanimously agreed that we should continue to work with Mr. Wilkens.

"Next on the list is Ms. Evans; she is now behind four months." Adriane continued. "She is a care-giver for her elderly mother in a wheelchair and doesn't have a car. Her mother had an issue with her social security check, and did not get paid for several months, but now has a check that can cover the entire rent balance. The problem is that the rent check is in her mother's name, and they don't have a bank account. How can we get her mother to the bank or the check turned signed over to her daughter's name so they can pay the outstanding balance?"

We had a group discussion, and Robert, a licensed social worker with

Fulton County extension services weighed in. He said he had some ideas and could reach out to the family.

"Next on the list is Ms. Tarantine. She now owes eight months' rent and has never paid since I started working at the property. I've tried on several occasions to talk with her including knocking on her door, but she refuses to come out when she sees me," Adriane said in a frustrated tone. "She has three young kids and works occasionally. I noticed she was letting some of the drug dealers live in her unit."

I said, "Ahhh, a phantom tenant. I know this tenant and have met her unregistered guests."

I told the group. "We have no choice but to evict."

Adriane replied, "I started the process six months ago, but she knows how to game the system. She had the case moved to federal court and we are just waiting to get on the court docket. This trick can delay an eviction for a year." The group agreed Adriane should continue to reach out to Ms. Tarantine but also should continue to pursue the eviction proceedings.

"Unit 120 is Mr. Johnson who is now behind two months and owes $1,620 with late fees. His hours were cut at his warehouse job and he is trying to find a part-time job. I've reached out to Buckhead Christian Ministries and other organizations for help. One has responded and can fund up to $1,000 of the delinquency."

"Does he have children?" my partner asked.

"Yes, he is a single dad to two children, but one is grown and the other is a junior in high school."

"Is he a good tenant?"

"Yes, I rarely hear from him other than to pay rent. He takes good care of his apartment."

The group agreed to work with Mr. Johnson.

After hosting the meetings for a few months, we noticed that the Summerdale delinquencies were progressively dropping. The Homeflex rental assistance program was offering affordability for our tenants with very low incomes, so delinquencies for these families were greatly reduced.

"The collection of monthly rent is getting better, now that many of our tenants are on Homeflex or they know they can come in and talk with me for a payment plan," Adriane told us at our next bi-monthly Eviction Lab meeting. When we started, we were owed about $25,000 in late rent each month, but as we worked through the evictions and more families transitioned to Homeflex, our delinquencies dropped to less than $5,000.

> *In the first eighteen months of our ownership, Summerdale evicted nineteen families who owed a total of $58,500 in delinquent rent. The evictions were due to housekeeping issues, criminal behavior, skipping on the lease, unregistered "guests" and chronic refusal to pay rent. Our average cost for an eviction was $2,186 per unit at Summerdale Phase I and $5,913 per unit at Summerdale Phase II. These costs included lost rent, interior clean-out, and carpet/appliance replacements due to damages. Of the $58,500 owed in delinquent rent, we were able to collect $12,152 after the evictions.*

SKI AND LAW ENFORCEMENT

Removing an entrenched criminal culture from an apartment community is difficult, dangerous, and expensive. The law and judicial system give criminals many tactical advantages as demonstrated by Anthony Fowler and his control of Unit D-12. It took a six-month concerted effort by our security team and APD to arrest him, plus another two months to gain control of the unit through eviction of Sharon Allen, the official tenant on the lease. Privacy laws limited our access to apartment interiors to emergencies or by written notice. Even if the staff saw drugs and guns during a routine inspection, they did not have arrest powers. We could evict Allen and take control of the unit, but Fowler could convince a neighbor to become a phantom tenant and move his illegal business next door.[77] Fulton County has a terrible track record of locking up criminals, and poverty was so prevalent at Summerdale that many tenants would gladly accept $2,000 per month to hand over their door keys to Fowler and disappear.

Removing the criminal element was challenging for us, but more so for Ski and the APD. The Fourth Amendment of the Constitution bars police access to apartment interiors without search warrants, requiring significant police time and resources. Fowler was selling illegal drugs to his "guests"

Summerdale Apartments
Analysis of the Cost of Evictions

Apartment Unit:	101	202	205	501	508	606	802	805	807	1102	Total	Average
5008 Unpaid Rent Write-off	$2,230	$4,201	$2,161	$2,408	$4,091	$2,841	$2,419	$913	$4,831	$2,714	$28,809	$2,881
8042 Dishwashers	0	0	367	0	0	0	316	0	313	356	1,352	135
8044 Garbage Disposal	0	0	0	0	0	0	0	0	0	0	0	0
8046 Refrigerator	684	940	0	0	0	0	771	0	708	902	4,005	401
8048 Stove	0	521	0	0	0	0	0	473	0	521	1,514	151
8049 Washer/Dryer	0	0	0	0	0	0	0	0	0	0	0	0
8052 Carpet	811	0	0	933	1,302	783	0	0	1,349	2,031	7,209	721
8054 Vinyl	427	1,955	0	577	0	721	577	814	678	98	5,847	585
8060 Water Heater	0	0	0	0	0	0	473	0	0	0	473	47
8072 Bath/Sink Hardware	0	0	0	0	0	0	0	0	0	0	0	0
8074 Cabinet/Counter-Other	0	0	0	0	0	0	0	0	3,512	283	3,795	379
8175 Paint	360	355	355	495	520	355	365	960	335	400	4,500	450
6215 Legal Fees	729	602	302	472	241	274	231	141	269	472	3,732	373
Total Paid Costs	5,240	8,573	3,184	4,885	6,154	4,973	5,152	3,301	11,995	7,778	61,235	6,123
Days Vacant	15	134	111	63	23	66	87	132	329	80	1,040	104
Original Tenant Rent	$640	$780	$765	$610	$730	$615	$615	$765	$670	$715	$6,905	$691
Lost Rent During Turnover	$26	$286	$233	$105	$46	$111	$147	$277	$604	$157	$1,992	$199
Total Eviction Cost	5,267	8,859	3,417	4,990	6,200	5,085	5,298	3,577	12,599	7,934	63,226	6,323
Collected After Eviction	0	(2,352)	(1,037)	0	0	0	(2,352)	0	0	0	(5,742)	(410)
Net Eviction Cost	$5,267	$6,507	$2,380	$4,990	$6,200	$5,085	$2,946	$3,577	$12,599	$7,934	$57,485	$5,913
Net Eviction Cost by # Months	8.23	8.34	3.11	8.18	8.49	8.27	4.79	4.68	18.80	11.10	8.33	8.56
Reason	Evicted	Judgement	Pests	Skip	Voluntary	Evicted	Skip	Housekeep	Evicted	Evicted	-	-

in the privacy of Sharon's apartment, and the only way to legally remove him, or so we thought, was through a strong partnership with the APD. We wanted him gone from Summerdale, serving time in jail so he would never return. My partners and I patiently and willingly invested in tools to remove the criminal culture so that we could safely renovate the ninety-two units in the boarded-up buildings. After meeting with various police officials and the Atlanta Police Foundation on the day we closed the property, Officer Ski Pulaski was assigned as the lead of the united team effort. That was two years ago, and I was now interviewing him in the management office at Summerdale to understand our actions to date. Ski started the conversation by summing up our initial meeting:

> I am not going to lie but when I met you, I was skeptical, I really was because I've seen this a million times. You are a landlord in the apartment business and the apartments would typically flip owners or there are mortgage scams and I would just see it. The new owners would come in and say, "we are going to clean up the property.' They may do a little bit here and there, and six months later it would be sold to someone else who would come in and say "we are going to clean up the property" . . . and then six months later it is sold again, and it would never be "cleaned up' of crime."

In hindsight, we knew we were fortunate the APD committed resources to conduct a multi-month undercover operation to document the criminal activity and obtain a search warrant. Despite the warrants, arrests and attention from Ski and APD, the drug activity took over a year to remove. Ski continued:

> You are doing a good job. A big problem for us in apartment complexes has always been a lack of cooperation. Everyone talks a good game until it comes time for the rubber to hit the road. I remember before the raid, calling you to get permission to knock the door off the hinge. You were like "okay . . . have at it." Is the door fixable if you knock it off the hinge? I told you "no," but you were like "okay we will fix it so have at it." You never hear that from a landlord! Police are always up for a good time breaking a door down, that is

not an issue. A lot of people drawn to this profession like to do these things. Especially the narcotics officers and fugitive people. That is why we are here. It's a job but fun catching bad guys, but you get a lot of push back from management because they have budgets, and because they have budgets, you can't go breaking their stuff. But sometimes you have to do some things that you have to do. But we got support from you so getting warrants for people is not difficult if we put in the time and get landlord support.

The cameras helped tremendously. We were able to observe even if we were unable to be on site observing them. We could watch their patterns on who and how they were doing it, just sitting from the desk. So, when it came time to do a buy, we knew who to go for and where they were. The same thing with warrants, we would watch the people who would come out. When we gave the last warrant, I was watching them on the cameras. I watched a guy put a big duffle bag in his car, and then go back into the apartment so we knew to pay attention to that guy. We also got a warrant for the car and that is how we found more dope.

I discussed with Ski what I perceived as a disconnect between the Fulton County judicial system, the APD, and Summerdale that had made removing the criminal activity more difficult. I recalled for him our experience with the December 2018 drug raid, arrests, and court proceedings:

We did not receive the official incident report documenting the raid until months after the arrests. We did not know the names of the men arrested so we could not get mug shots to determine if they were still operating in unit D-12. Considering all the time and expense invested by the APD to get a warrant and perform the raid, we were under the impression that the eleven men arrested were serving time in jail or awaiting their court appearance. Luckily, the judicial system worked equally as slowly for the eleven defendants because their first court appearance did not occur until mid-June 2019. By then, we had the police report and knew the names of the eleven men arrested. We decided to attend the first court hearing.

The eleven defendants were on the docket calendar in June; the case was just one of ninety-four for that morning. Jeff, Lucy, and I showed up at court hoping to identify, finally, the eleven men arrested. When we arrived at 9 a.m. the large courtroom was packed with defendants, attorneys, court employees, and family members spilling out into the hallway. Our case was number 89 on the list, and the bailiff asked us to wait in the hall. When the case was announced, we went into the courtroom and watched as five of the eleven defendants stood up when their names were called. The five stood together and acted like they were at a picnic, laughing and confident with their attorney. The attorney confirmed he represented the five, and he, the judge, and the district attorney conferred to schedule a court hearing in July. The judge continued reading the names in our case and the district attorney indicated that four of the eleven defendants had reached plea deals, so their cases were closed. When the name of Antonio Payne was called, another attorney stood and told the judge that Payne was in jail in neighboring DeKalb County convicted of murder and facing the death penalty. Neither Anthony Fowler nor his attorney was present, and a bench warrant was issued for Fowler's arrest.

Talking was prohibited in court, but after the judge dismissed the defendants in our case and moved on to the next case, Lucy, Jeff, and I eagerly moved into the hallway and huddled in a quiet corner for a conference to discuss what we just witnessed.

Jeff said incredulously, "Those five guys are in front of D-12 loitering all the time. They were just there this morning when I left to come here."

I said, "Yep, they are there all the time and claim they live in other units when I ask them."

Lucy confirmed, "I'm sure they are on their way back to Summerdale and will probably wave at me this afternoon."

"Are they tenants?" I asked.

Lucy shook her head. "I don't recognize any of these names on a lease. I do not think they live on the property. They are there during the day, all the time, but they may be living in another unit."

I said, "None of their addresses are listed at Summerdale, not even Anthony Fowler who is listed in Riverdale, about twenty minutes south of Summerdale."

We left the court elated with our newfound knowledge of the defendants. We now could connect names with faces of the criminals, but more importantly, they had seen us and knew we were aware of their activity. Summerdale management, the APD and our security officers now knew identifications and activities, and the conspiracy was over. Within a week, all five had disappeared from Summerdale.

The reputation of Summerdale as a 'one-stop shop for drugs' lingered even after we legally evicted Allen and Fowler and the other ten had been arrested. The drug business easily generated millions of dollars in annual revenue by offering a craved product to consumers who refused to go away. Long after the drug dealers were gone, would-be buyers still broke down our gates and knocked on doors at 4 a.m., awaking our residents. Summerdale had an entrenched reputation as a regional drug hub, and it took us almost two years of undercover police work, arrests, evictions, private security guards, and cameras to eradicate the brand. It was a slow process.

After the arrests and release of the eleven defendants, things seemed quiet, but we suspected the drug dealing went inside units other than D-12. In the meantime, a second wave of dealers circled the property to capture buyer demand. Prospective tenants, with suspiciously squeaky-clean credit reports and criminal histories, routinely applied to lease. We carefully screened the tenants and rejected eight of every ten applicants for various reasons. It was better to keep units vacant and non-revenue generating than to accept suspicious tenants. We knew we must rebuild the property culture from a position of strength with tenants who followed the rules. Summerdale had a significant number of long-term legacy tenants, and it was worth the effort to retain them, even at reduced rents, recognizing their value to rebuilding the community. The effort paid off despite hiccups including our attempt to use the criminal trespass (CT) law to remove unwanted guests from the property. When I asked Ski about that, he said:

> The criminal trespass process ran off the rails. Too many cooks in the kitchen. I was trying to get Angie [Parker] involved, but after talking with her—she was running up against a lot of roadblocks. There is a system that I have learned from other places. It started to work here, where security has the form and pictures, but now with body cameras, if we have a rep from the property (security and maintenance) and on the body camera, or they have

pictures or recording, they could legally give a criminal trespass citation. So, the lesson here is your security guy should have some way of recording the interaction. Body cams are expensive but cell phones are not so you can use them to record. The loiterers always say they live here, so if we record—can we hand them the CT? Removing them doesn't happen overnight, but you stay the course and eventually they get the message and go away.

In November 2021, the City of Atlanta and Fulton County experienced a significant leadership change which will positively impact the danger of criminal activity at Summerdale and other low-income apartment communities. City Councilman Andre Dickens was elected Mayor of the City of Atlanta and has taken a tough stance on crime. On March 29, 2022, he announced plans to create what he described as an unprecedented Repeat Offender Tracking Unit. The initiative involves partnership with multiple agencies to address the issue of repeat felony offenders. He said, "Every week, 30 percent of the arrests made by APD are of men and women who have already been convicted of at least three previous felonies. We acknowledge right now that any system that allows a cycle of career crime, it is a broken system." The Atlanta Police Department estimates about 1,000 repeat offenders are committing up to 40 percent of Atlanta's crimes. "The goal is to stop the cycle and give agencies better access to data." Also, Fani Willis was elected District Attorney of Fulton County, replacing the former DA who was notoriously soft on crime. Since her election, Willis has fearlessly tackled notorious gang leaders and other repeat violent criminals—some of whom were living in a house along Waters Road south of Summerdale and preying on the neighborhood families. Willis also partnered with Mayor Dickens to relaunch the Atlanta Court Watch Program to engage community volunteers interested in attending court and holding judges, law enforcement officers, and attorneys accountable to prosecution of repeat offenders through the judicial system.

ANTHONY FOWLER—THE CRIME KINGPIN

In July 2020, Adriane noticed a white Dodge Charger parked diagonally, taking up multiple parking spaces, in front of a newly renovated townhouse building. The unit was recently leased to Janet Walker, an attractive young woman who worked for a high-end hair salon, and her moving truck was off to the side. Adriane knocked on the door in anticipation of checking on Janet and asking her to move her car. But the door was opened by a man Adriane recognized as Anthony Fowler.

"It took a minute to register who he was, but it was him. He used to always bring Lucy and me lunch and when he saw me, he realized who I was and slithered behind the door to hide his face while we spoke.

Adriane didn't directly confront Anthony but the next day she went over to talk to Janet and to see if Fowler was gone. She said, "I explained that this guy was dangerous and gave his criminal history at the property. She was surprised to learn he was effectively banned and not allowed on site."

Adriane said Janet was shocked and replied, "My God! I was wondering why he was so interested to help me move in. Thank you for letting me know. I am not interested in hanging out with a guy like him."

We met with Ski and discussed a security strategy.

"This is the kingpin," I said, pushing a mug shot of Fowler across the table.

Ski thoughtfully studied the photo. "I recognize him. He was there just partying. It was his main spot and I know he was keeping another apartment; I just could not figure out which one. There are usually one or two guys who operate within a certain area. Anthony was just a middle- to lower-level guy."

I handed Ski the long report and asked, "What do you think of his rap sheet? He was arrested in July and December at Summerdale but kept returning after bonding out of jail within 48 hours. The Fulton County records alone show 18 arrests since 2000 and the only meaningful jail time was from April to July 2019. It must be frustrating to bust guys and they are right back on the streets within 24 to 48 hours."

Ski studied the report. "Well, Aggravated Assault is not little. Disorderly conduct, burglary, burglary, probation violation, fugitive, probation violation . . . warrant . . . yeah. By the third controlled substance, that is

Summerdale Apartments — 911 Service Call History
For the Years 2013–2021

Call Code	2013	2014	2015	2016	Purchased 2017	2018	2019	2020	2021
Violent Crimes									
Burglary/Armed Robbery	24	19	6	8	73	12	6	4	1
Shots Fired	6	13	3	28	48	12	3	0	0
Fights/Stabbing	45	49	46	103	107	73	52	24	0
Sex Assault	1	1	0	5	2	1	0	0	0
Stabbing	1	1	0	0	0	0	0	0	0
Armed Person	1	1	1	9	7	2	3	0	0
Stolen Autos/Goods	1	5	0	16	37	4	4	0	0
Suicide	1	3	1	1	1	3	3	4	0
Violent Crimes Total	**80**	**92**	**57**	**170**	**275**	**107**	**71**	**32**	**1**
Nonviolent Crimes									
Disorderly Per/Simple Assa	18	18	11	10	18	3	18	4	6
Drugs	5	0	1	12	48	4	1	4	0
Theft	14	4	10	12	16	7	4	0	0
Person Injured	5	5	4	5	2	5	12	8	0
Dead Person	1	1	2	1	1	0	1	4	0
Suspicious Person	3	4	2	18	40	11	4	0	11
Trouble/Vandalism/Theft	1	5	3	4	3	8	2	0	0
Miss Person	1	3	0	0	2	1	0	0	0
Loud Music	4	1	1	6	27	5	4	4	0
Domestic	1	6	4	3	0	1	2	0	0
Silent Alarm	0	0	7	0	0	0	3	0	0
Person Located	2	0	0	4	1	1	0	0	0
Criminal Trespass	2	0	0	1	7	1	5	0	0
Fire	0	1	0	1	0	3	1	0	0
Child Abandonment	1	0	0	1	0	0	0	0	0
Nonviolent Crimes Total	**58**	**48**	**45**	**78**	**165**	**50**	**57**	**24**	**17**
Crimes Total	**138**	**140**	**102**	**248**	**440**	**157**	**128**	**56**	**18**
Crime Reduction (Since 2017)						**-64%**	**-71%**	**-87%**	**-96%**
Other 911 - Clerical Service Calls									
Total	27	19	30	30	50	52	70	28	0
Total All 911 Service Calls	**165**	**159**	**132**	**278**	**490**	**209**	**198**	**84**	**18**

Source: Atlanta Police Department Public Records.

Note: TriStar purchased Summerdale in June 2018

pain pills? Disorderly conduct . . . but two burglary charges with the Agg Assault, burglary, probation violations—two of them . . . and the hits just keep coming."

"What is the solution?" I asked

"The solution is to put bad people in jail."

"Do you think Anthony is a bad person?"

"Everybody deserves a second chance. I am a firm believer that everyone makes a mistake and that's fine. I've made them, you've made them, but by your third, fourth, or fifth time, it just proves that you have no regard for society or the rules. By your second probation violation, it shows you don't care, and your third burglary charge . . .? It's easy to go outside the metro area and see if anyone else has a sheet like that. Rockdale County or south of Atlanta . . . go down there and see if they have any of these problems and then find out why not. They don't tolerate it."

"Why does Atlanta tolerate it?"

"I think volume and then no accountability. The judicial system is a machine. When you get out of the metro area, the judge plays golf with the sheriff . . . who hangs out of the local restaurant. Everyone knows everyone and they get to know each other. Out here (in Atlanta), you are so busy and overwhelmed that even the bad people sneak through. But it goes back to pointing fingers."

I said, pushing over the statistics, "Our partnership with APD and the cameras from the Atlanta Police Foundation significantly reduced crime, especially violence. Summerdale is doing well without Anthony Fowler."

Ski exclaimed, "I think that's awesome!"

The safety and security efforts we implemented after purchasing Summerdale paid off. Crime is down more than 90 percent and violent crime is almost nonexistent. We have learned that we cannot let our guard down, and we have on-site security seven days a week. Ski finally accepted a promotion within APD and has been transferred to another precinct.

30

Summerdale Survives the COVID-19 Pandemic

By March 2020, we were turning the corner in removing the visual and cultural "blight" at Summerdale. After two years of patient listening and encouragement by our staff, our tenants were starting to take ownership of their community. To improve communication, our staff members attended Trauma Certification classes to learn to proactively manage aggressive behavior by many of our tenants, who were starting to calm down. Screaming incidents in the office were less frequent.

We were methodically and timely addressing work orders or other tenant concerns, giving them positive living environment in their apartments. Attendance was growing at the Tenant Association meetings we routinely hosted to build trust between neighbors and management staff. At our last meeting, Johnathan, Tiffany, and Adriane started laying the groundwork for an on-site job fair with companies such as Delta Airlines and Fulton County, giving tenants access to job opportunities that paid $60,000 or more per year. The KABOOM! playground was a popular amenity for children to play and families to socialize.

Our tenants saw our progress to remove the crime and structural blight. We still had on-site security to manage tenants and their guests when emotions flared, but the criminal activity was reduced to random versus daily occurrences. Jeff had a rhythm going to finish renovating the boarded-up blighted units; more than 75 percent were completed and occupied by families who were thrilled with the affordable rent. The remaining units were scheduled for occupancy within a few months for our growing wait list.

Kristin Hemingway and the Star-C after-school program were making progress with the children, who were outperforming their peers academically and were now more relaxed, showing true joy in reading, and bonding with their neighbors who were now friends. Overall, the seeds had been planted, and there was a growing sense of community pride which we knew would improve over time through everyone's collaborative efforts.

Then the COVID-19 pandemic hit.

On March 12, 2020, the leadership of Atlanta Public Schools announced that all APS schools and offices would close on Monday, March 16. On March 18, President Donald Trump declared COVID as a national emergency effective March 1. The same day, Atlanta Mayor Keisha Lance Bottoms shut down City Hall, completely disrupting municipal business operations, including access to building inspections and permits. Over the next few months, the pandemic triggered a sequence of events that significantly impacted Summerdale families.

The financial and emotional impact of COVID-19 directly correlated to the accessibility of resources and trust in the process to access resources. In other words, the COVID-19 experience by the "resource-rich" was substantially different than the experience by the "resource-poor." Access to computers, reliable internet, first-class medical services, safe transportation, and remote digital employment blunted the impact of COVID-19 on many citizens. However, the Summerdale families living without these resources experienced a very different pandemic—reinforcing community, intergenerational, and acute trauma, and exposing many weaknesses that we never considered. The vast community network we developed with partners such as United Way, Atlanta Public Schools, Morehouse Medical and Star-C helped fill the resource voids created by the pandemic. But the crisis of trust reared its ugly head and many of our families were left on the brink of eviction. Even though we are mission-based landlords, we still relied on rent collections to operate Summerdale, hence we had to enforce the leases.

We also had no choice but to prioritize personal health and to pause the human interaction that was so critical to our daily operations and our efforts to remove the "blighted mentality" and rebuild community capital. We had to close the Star-C after school program, suspend the Tenant Association meetings, close the front office, and limit maintenance work orders to emergencies. We continued the renovation but the labor and supply chains were disrupted, causing delays. As a result of these changes, tenants took an economic and social hit, leaving the weak weaker and the strong stronger. Unfortunately, the majority of Summerdale families, living paycheck to paycheck through service-industry employment, were on the weaker social spectrum.

A week after the pandemic became a reality, I visited Summerdale armed with a mask, hand sanitizer, "essential worker" letter, and plans to socially distance from our staff and tenants. I wanted to check on Adriane and the staff to make sure everyone was holding up and thank them for their loyalty to the Summerdale families. Employees associated with facilities and buildings had been deemed "essential workers," and we were following the daily-changing rule book of safety policies, procedures, and protocol recommended by OSHA and various professional management associations. I also checked in with Ms. Moore and Ms. Humphries; both reported they were concerned about the future but otherwise doing well, except Ms. Moore said she needed groceries and asked for assistance. The ladies from her church who typically helped with her errands were safely sequestered in their houses and she had no other support network to help with daily challenges. Luckily, at the onset of the pandemic, the Atlanta Community Food Bank quickly worked with Dr. Payne to set up an emergency mobile pantry at Cleveland Avenue Elementary, distributing free fresh produce and canned goods to any neighborhood family. Adriane arranged for families to visit the mobile pantry where they were rewarded with generous bags of fresh produce, canned foods, and other groceries depending on the household size. Families without cars could walk to Cleveland Avenue Elementary to retrieve groceries, and Adriane assisted the elderly and immobile who were unable to personally visit the pantry.

EDUCATION AND THE DIGITAL AND TECHNOLOGY DIVIDE
On the day I visited Summerdale, the playground and common areas were eerily quiet, empty of the typical robust activity of people and traffic. No children were playing on the playground, no families were getting in and out of their cars, and no tenants were visiting with neighbors on their

porches. Kristin reported the Cleveland Avenue Elementary children were sequestered in their apartments with their newly unemployed parents or grandparents, trying to navigate high stress levels associated with the new digital learning environment and an immediate future without a paycheck. An inventory of usable laptops owned by Star-C families sadly uncovered only two working computers. Since computers were not essential to their jobs, many families just could not afford them and used their cell phones for basic digital commerce. The family stress was further exacerbated in households with multiple children who were exhibiting anxiety after days of being sequestered in their apartments with their siblings.

After we purchased Summerdale, we had spent nearly two years communicating with Comcast to install usable internet at Summerdale Phase II, however, the internet in Phase I was not completely functioning despite repetitive work order requests and the fact some of the units were still under construction. We considered ourselves fortunate to have at least partially working internet system for the majority of our families, because the pandemic demonstrated that reliable internet access was no longer just a luxury, but now essential to virtually everything associated with daily life. Education, access to medications, groceries, unemployment benefits, banking and bill payments now shifted to the internet since almost all traditional channels of human interaction essential to business were disrupted by the pandemic. Reliable internet infrastructure was essential for our families during the pandemic.

After receiving the APS announcement on March 12, Dr. Payne and her staff had only four days to set up the entire infrastructure of laptops and internet to move education to a virtual platform for her students. Dr. Payne shared:

> We had to first exhaust all the technology we had over the years and get a laptop for every one of our students at this time, which was not easy. We were able to provide the laptops, but then realized more and more challenges continued to be revealed about not just the digital divide, but technology in general. We had some apartments or homes that had no internet and realized the internet is just as essential to a student's success as having water

or electricity. Then we had devices get stolen or we would give a device to a child but we would hear "my mom has it." Then it wasn't just here you get a laptop and now we can carry on, we had to teach the children how to use it since many had never been exposed to a computer. For example, we had to teach them about passwords, how you authenticate your account and even how to turn on the computer. That was a whole other level of education we had to provide and we could not do this digitally, so we had to come back to the school and have outside/outdoor workshops for the students and parents. We got over that hump and now our students know what to do, but technology education was a huge piece of the digital component to launching our virtual platform.

Talk about the poverty. Everything was exposed. Poverty was exposed, educations gaps were exposed, family violence was exposed. So many things that we normally deal with and work around when we had classroom settings, we could not work around anymore. When you talk about poverty, you are also talking about nutrition and feeding the kids. At school, they at least get two meals a day from the school and with school not open, now what do we do? We did have opportunities for the school to provide groceries, vegetables, fruits but during home delivery, and through the computer via virtual learning, we were able to see into our students' homes for the first time, and it was a shock for many of us to see the living conditions. We knew our students lived in poverty, but we didn't actually see it, and the opportunities to see in our students' homes just opened our eyes to some of the other issues that our students are overcoming to even come to school every day or log on. Some didn't have functioning lights in their rooms to be able to read at night. There were also instances of abuse. If you are here at school, we can see if a student has a mark on their face, but when you are virtual, how do you connect if the school is supposed to provide a safe haven. So, we developed secret codes for the students to tell us if something was going on and our social worker was able to tap into our partnerships to provide support system for our students. We did have some students move out of state to stay with someone because their parents lost their restaurant job, but they were able to continue with virtual learning. We learned the move was temporary and they did eventually move back into the city, but it was difficult. We had a lot of transiency, a lot of people moving into rural areas and back, and many different scenarios.

Our management staff saw how a lot of the parents struggled to cope with the dramatic disruption in their lives. Overnight, their apartment homes became classrooms and many parents, who were low readers themselves, were not prepared to 'tutor' for their children and did not even make the effort. Dr. Payne reported that less than 70 percent of the students signed into the virtual classroom daily at the beginning of the pandemic. Many of our employed single parents had no choice but to stay home from work, since they had no other options for childcare or their childcare option was closed due to COVID. With reduced or no household earnings, families struggled to prioritize which bills to pay. Do you pay rent, food or utilities given electricity was now a critical component to virtual learning? How do children log-in to school if there was no electricity? Our families quickly realized that Cleveland Avenue Elementary not only provided reliable meals, but day care, water, electricity and school supplies for their children, resources that were no longer instantly available for free. We had many parents report their water and electricity bills doubled the first month since their children were home using both, adding to an already stressful situation.

The partnership of advocacy and resource sharing between Summerdale and Cleveland Avenue Elementary took on a new urgency during the pandemic. With the Star-C program closed, Kristin and Adriane worked as a liaison with the families to provide resources such as the laptops, internet connection, meals, rental and utility assistance. For the first time, we also became more involved on educational issues such as truancy to make sure the children signed into virtual platform, and graduations.

According to Adriane,

A few weeks after the virtual learning started, we started getting calls from Cleveland Avenue Elementary that several Summerdale children had their computer devices but just were not signing on. The Atlanta Police came out and we went to the apartments to find out why the students were not going to school, but some of the kids didn't have internet or an adult to help them do their homework, so we were able to get Star-C and the parents involved to get the children on-line. We also worked with the families and Cleveland Avenue Elementary on meal replacement. There was a meal bus that handed out breakfasts and lunches on Monday evenings to APS families. They would pull up to the corner by the gate and the parents would meet them. We had maybe ten families meet the bus for the entire week and this helped a lot, saving on the grocery bills.

GRADUATION

By May 2020, the families were showing resiliency and learning to cope with the new COVID-19 normal. They were venturing to the playground, ignoring our "Caution" tape, and routinely walking the community and talking with their neighbors. Meanwhile, APS announced that graduation celebrations would be held virtually until the summer or a later safe date. Graduation was a particularly special milestone for our Summerdale students, who have so many hurdles to education, so Adriane and the management staff organized a graduation party outside the office to honor our students who had achieved this important milestone. She explained:

The students and their parents came by the office and we did the whole graduation celebration. We took pictures with the cap and gown, sang, gave graduation certificates, and every graduate received a gift bag. We had about 20 families with a student that had a Milestone graduation from kindergarten, elementary, middle or high school. The students and the parents were very thankful. One senior who graduated often comes back and says "thank you, Ms. Adriane" for helping me. It wasn't easy for her or her mother. She attended South Atlanta High School and if she had a bad day before COVID-19, she would come in to sit and talk to me. She would say "I don't want to graduate and I don't want to college"—but she didn't want to disappoint her mom, who wanted her to go to college. She came in with her cap/gown and we gave her a gift and told her to take her time and figure out what she wanted to do. She ended up enlisting in the Navy and is now doing really well, stationed in Japan! It really does take a village to raise children and she just needed direction and encouragement from another adult."

RENT AND THE EVICTION MORATORIUM

Knowing the impact of COVID-19 on job security and our service industry tenants, we were prepared for many Summerdale families to experience rental delinquency. We came back to our partnership network and started the conversations to develop a list of rental assistance organizations, including Star-C. In April 2020, Star-C launched a $50,000 GoFundMe page to raise money for rental assistance for Atlanta families. The program was widely embraced and by July had raised more than $4 million and was building a network of landlords who offered affordable rents. By this time, Summerdale had more than $76,000 in outstanding rent (compared to $20,000 before the pandemic). We knew many other landlords had much larger delinquencies and were struggling. Adriane shared:

> Once COVID hit, we were okay with rent collections in the beginning until they shut everything down. For the first six months, I can honestly say it affected rent but there were also people took advantage of the situation. Unemployment money started coming—they got an extra $300 for unemployment, but once they were told the moratorium, the rent stopped. I don't think these people understood the moratorium.

On September 4, 2020, the CDC ordered a temporary halt to residential evictions, requiring the tenant to provide a declaration form to their landlord for failure to pay rent. By then we had twenty tenants not paying rent and refusing to work with Adriane. We noticed a strong pattern dividing the tenants that worked with us from the ones that refused to pay rent, and "trust" was the influencing factor. Many tenants just didn't trust us. Johnathan Brewer is an example of a tenant who trusted us from the beginning of his tenancy in 2018 and was able to work with us to access resources to get rental assistance. Johnathan was a supply attendant at Delta Airlines. He shared:

> COVID hit the airline and travel industry really hard. Working was pretty tough since less people were flying, and my hours got cut resulting in a drop in pay. My department took a great hit and the company was trying to save

money in as many areas as possible including offering voluntary leaves to people who could stand it, and for me it was something. I could not take that hit and still be able pay my bills. So, I took a pay cut, and when you are living paycheck to paycheck that puts a significant dent in your plans. I have delayed my graduation from Morehouse until next year and with travel back, I am now working twelve-hour days, every day if I can get the hours. I only have one class to complete before I graduate.

Over time, Johnathan started getting delinquent in his rent. Between car payments, rent, student loans and other expenses, he just wasn't able to pay rent and utilities. He said:

When the Star-C rental assistance program came along and offered rental assistance, that was something. They put flyers on the doors making sure everyone knew about it, saying if you have had your hours cut or impacted by COVID or lost your jobs, come talk to us and we will figure something out to get you some help. That program really saved me. It was a tremendous help and for some people it helped with full rental assistance and others like me, it was part-time and when it got really bad for myself as well, Star-C came through. That was very helpful for myself and other people in the community.

But not all of our tenants trusted us and thus would not take assistance when offered. Adriane diligently worked nights and weekends, advertising the Star-C program and other partnerships with Buckhead Christian Ministries, Chris 180, United Way, Decatur Cooperative Ministries, Project Community Connections Inc. (PCCI), Project Open Doors, and other rental assistance organizations to tenants whom she knew were stressed trying to get their rent and utilities paid. Many tenants were responsive and successfully received rental assistance, sometimes two or three times from various organizations, but others just ignored her. She said:

The moratorium hit and people stopped paying their rent, and now we have a mess. Many of the tenant balances comes from their own negligence since they didn't do their part in getting the help or take advantage of the situation.

For example, there is our tenant Darcy Marshal. I am begging Darcy for documentation to get rental assistance, calling her almost every day. She worked at the Atlanta airport, had her hours cut and just would not provide documentation showing she was impacted by COVID-19. Kandice Kirk has received help from many organizations. She came from PCCI who paid the first six months of her rent and then Star-C paid $1,800 towards her rent. She also received a check from Buckhead Christian Ministries and then from Open Doors. The ones behind now have received at least $5,000 from other organizations to catch them up and then they stopped paying. Kandice is not working and her attitude is nasty and combative until she needs something. She is always saying "I started a new job" but I haven't seen the fruits of her labor. I truly tried to help her and put her on another payment plan and she had to pay $500 every two weeks but she has only paid the payment one time and now she is under eviction.

James Clayton is another who just wouldn't help himself. He was a construction laborer and was out of work. I placed him on the Atlanta Housing Homeflex program after he lost his job and his mother passed away, but he didn't work or get unemployment because he was a contract worker paid under the table, so he was denied unemployment benefits. One thing I like about him, he pays something every month. He brings $300 here or $100, whatever he can bring. It shows me he is making effort. What upsets me is he had an opportunity to get full assistance, but would not bring me the paperwork stating he was out of work due to COVID. I could not understand why he wouldn't do it. I think the moratorium hindered us. I really felt like the rental assistance programs should have only paid 50 percent of the tenant rent. Instead, the government moratorium told tenants they would not be evicted. Now we have a mess with twenty-four tenants that have not paid rent and thus are in process of getting evicted. On the positive side, I would say I have personally helped at least thirty tenants get rental assistance. I would give them the list and ask them to call the numbers, then help with their paperwork. We made it easy for them to get assistance.

When the moratorium expired in July 2021, Summerdale had 235 apartments occupied. Of these units, 180 tenants faithfully paid their rent monthly, but 55 were delinquent. Of these 55 delinquent tenants, 31 were behind one to three months, but they were paying current rent or complying with a payment plan and thus we worked with them. The remaining 24 tenants had an average delinquency of eight months and didn't pay anything, some owing more than $15,000. The State of Georgia was offering to pay up to 18 months' rent, and these tenants still would not respond. We had no choice but to file in the courts to start the eviction process. Adriane continued:

> Many of our tenants have paid nothing in rent during the pandemic. We know they got stimulus checks, and we know seventeen of the twenty-four evictions filed had jobs during the pandemic, but they just didn't pay rent. Many of these tenants bought new cars, had their nails done, their kids have new Jordan tennis shoes. Some even got the federal Paycheck Protection loans for their businesses, but still haven't paid rent.

The other apartment communities that we owned did not have the same delinquency issues. The properties we owned for years and that had developed strong community trust between ownership, tenants, and management had very little delinquency, even after the CDC eviction moratorium expired. Our Willow Branch apartment community in East Atlanta has filed only ONE eviction in ten years, including during the pandemic. We worked closely with our tenants to get rental assistance and they were grateful for the help. Unfortunately, this was not the case at Summerdale, which showed how much we needed to work to remove the blighted mentality and build community trust. These tenants didn't have the social capital or social emotional skills to advocate for themselves, despite the strong availability of resources, and were now facing eviction.

We used the Eviction Lab to launch the Star-C Eviction Relief Fund and raised almost $5 million by October 2020. The fund partners with landlords with qualified affordable apartment communities located near low-performing elementary schools. The qualified landlord nominates their tenants for a rent-matching scholarship up to 70 percent of the outstanding

> *rent due. We received another $4.3 million in the second round of federal relief. To date, the Star-C Eviction Relief Fund has more than 330 apartment communities registered representing 64,000 affordable apartment units. We have helped more than 4,500 families with rent relief, enabling them to avoid eviction and to keep their children in their schools, including families living at Summerdale Apartments.*

MEDICAL

We were very fortunate that Summerdale had no staff or tenant fatalities due to COVID-19. We put in place policies and procedures that limited exposure, and our residents were able to sequester in their apartments to protect themselves. Adriane said:

> We did have many tenants that had COVID including Ms. Humphries and one tenant in 604 was pregnant and had COVID twice during her pregnancy and she is fine now. She has six children ages thirteen to new-born and works at a restaurant in management. She worked through her entire pregnancy and had COVID and got behind in rent, but Star-C helped her pay her delinquency. When she was better, she went back to work. She was the only tenant who, when that first stimulus check hit, gave her whole income tax check to pay her back rent of almost $6,000. She paid every dime of her balance.

Dr. Payne saw the medical impact firsthand in Cleveland Avenue Elementary:

> We did have quite a few student family members affected and a few that are now deceased and passed from COVID. So, providing support to those students and make sure they are not displaced and they could stay in the area. But listening to a child say "my mom passed because of COVID," it's shocking and you have to take a step back. It hit home to see faces and know names of our parents who are no longer with us. And then this year, being face-to-face, we are definitely having more students diagnosed with COVID.

MS. HUMPHRIES

Despite being vaccinated, Ms. Humphries and her daughter Simona caught COVID and spent time in the hospital. At age eighty-six, Ms. Humphries survived but lost a lot of weight and had a slow recovery. Simona said:

> My grandchildren they stayed with my daughter and my niece son had COVID and they didn't know, and my daughter had all the kids that weekend. When they came back to us and we caught it. All of my family had it—my oldest daughter, my grandchildren, three sons, me, Momma, my sister, her friend, her old man, her fiancé, it just ran through. It was an experience.
>
> We caught COVID and believe me the symptoms is really true, and it is a real bad kind of feeling. When it hit us, it hit us so fast and I just started feeling so weak. It mess with your respiratory and by me having had open heart surgery, I had to hurry and get me something because it was hard to breathe. We went to the hospital but after treatment the doctor, she said you can go because your heartbeat and breathing level and everything is right on cue and then they released me. I sat in Momma's room 'til her doctor came in.
>
> Momma told us, "If He comes and gets me, I am ready because I made peace with it. I went over to the other side and seen it but then came back. We made it and he is a good God. I was scared because really, I am not afraid of death because death is coming, but you just don't know how, when it comes sudden like that, it kinda take you. We did good together, helping each other."
>
> I told her that they ain't ready for you and you were meant to be here. Now look at her. She has lost a lot of weight and we couldn't even get her to sit up but now she is eating good and her appetite back and she is start moving around taking her own bath. We got past it; we just kept praying and taking our medicine and we was good. They tested us again, and we are negative. Prayer just changes things.

CONSTRUCTION

On March 18, 2020, Atlanta Mayor Lance Bottoms shut down City Hall, completely disrupting municipal business operations including access to building inspections and permits. Summerdale Phase I was about 75 percent completed when the city shut down and businesses started lockdowns. But we were fortunate at Summerdale, because we had the permits to continue the renovation work while the city determined its next steps to safely continue operations. Literally billions of dollars in construction projects were in process in Atlanta at this time, adding pressure on the city to determine a safe and reasonable procedure to continue issuing permits and performing inspections. Jeff shared:

> Summerdale never experienced many delays or a labor shortage because the labor teams were in place and under contract before COVID hit. But starting around the beginning of April, the workers were nervous that the lockdown prevented them from traveling. They thought they would go to jail for being out on the road and working. I showed them the "essential worker" definition and had to give the guys a flyer in Spanish and English so that if they got pulled over, they could give to a police officer and not be jailed for violation of a lockdown period. At this time things were in "lockdown," but no one really knew what this meant. Sometimes it was called lockdown, stay-in-place orders, whatever, but it took me three weeks to convince the guys that they were not going to get in trouble for working with me. Once we got past that, the guys live paycheck-to-paycheck and don't want to stop working. So, I never really slowed down in terms of getting work done. We were able to access supplies despite the fact that supply stores would only let a limited number of people in the store at a time. I would wait in line, but maybe only thirty minutes.

By May, the city came up with protocol to continue operations and decided to outsource inspections to qualified third-parties including architects. However, the city still had to come up with the process to qualify them. Jeff added:

> To keep the job going, our architect Tim qualified to be a third-party inspector but he had to submit some paperwork to the city to get authorized and put on their improved vendor list. It took the city about a month to come up with the process to approve Tim, and then another month to come up with the process to actually accept an inspection performed by Tim, but

once we figured out this process, the process went much smoother. We had no more delays and hiccups dealing with city inspectors who kept changing the rules and making us remove things and then put them back and this was huge for me to get the job done!

As a licensed architect performing the inspections, Tim had his license on the line if anything went wrong, so he was strict in the inspection process and compliance with the rules. Of course, we had to make sure things were safe, but using Tim as a consistent inspector who understood the job greatly improved the efficiency in delivering the renovated units in a reasonable time frame.

By July, Summerdale received its final certificate of occupancy. We were thrilled to complete the process of moving in families in search of affordability. If it hadn't been for COVID and the city workers staying at home, we would have had probably had more delays finishing the project.

THE BRIGHT SIDE

By August 2021, the tenants and staff at Summerdale were starting to embrace the new normal of post-COVID-19. The office opened back up, requiring tenants to wear masks and encouraging them to get vaccinated. We reopened the Star-C program despite having lost Kristin, who resigned to pursue other job opportunities and get a PhD from Georgia State University. The Summerdale children returned to Dr. Payne and in-classroom learning at Cleveland Avenue Elementary, and many of our tenants reported back to work. Despite the disruption in so many aspects of Summerdale, some positive developments came out of COVID. Dr. Payne summarized:

Our children are more appreciative of school. We have not had discipline issues because they are so excited to be here and so engaged. They realize that school is what they enjoy and where they want to be, so it's nice having that renewed appreciation and interest for school. Our teachers are more developed when it comes to different strategies. They are more engaged and interactive and there are so many more sites and tools that they know how to use and integrate into the classroom. They are more tech savvy and have students work on multiple tasks. I would say working as a team and more collaboratively has been helpful. It has been a bright spot because teachers are tag teaming on lessons, resources or just pitching in and that has been a highlight—the collaboration of team members. One of the things I am grateful for besides health and safety of our students, is the academic progress. And one of things I attribute that to is Ms. Kristin who was the liaison between home and school. She was very integral; she would talk to the teachers what are some of the deficits and she would work with the students. We would provide her resources and strategies on how we teach our students. Ms. Kristin was very valuable because our students saw her as an extended teacher. My teacher at home so we knew there was a connection with grades. Normally when you talk about student growth it takes about three years, but with Ms. Kristin working at Summerdale and in Star-C partnering with us we were able to see some of those gains in a year and some of our students had higher performance. We were grateful not to just have a safe or clean environment but to know that Star-C was making an impact on our students academically is something you don't see in traditional partnerships. That is a testament to the work we have done in collaboration—ultimately increasing our student achievement.

CRIME

It was strange driving by the Exxon station at Cleveland Avenue and Old Hapeville Road and seeing it almost empty, but the pandemic put people indoors. Maybe even drug dealers and criminals didn't want to be exposed to a deadly virus and sequestered in their homes, at least initially. I checked in with Ski to see how his first year of COVID-19 went. He said:

I was so busy, I had to hire my mom to do my bookkeeping. It was a tremendous year last year. I ended up moving from the Summerdale precinct to precinct 6 and then head the City of Atlanta auto theft division . . . so you want to talk about busy—. We can prove up to 85 percent of auto thefts are due to people leaving the key in the fob or the car running. If people would just stop that we would have a big decrease in auto theft overnight. And all the homicides and aggregated assaults, it's just ridiculous but every city is experiencing this increase in crime. The good news is burglaries are down 30 percent."

We noticed that the loitering activity at the Exxon station was dramatically down at the beginning but then picked up. Recently the station sold to a new owner who renovated the building and put up new brick and bullet-proof glass. He took over and is trying to clean it up—there is not a lot of hanging out. However, the violence still did not completely disappear. There was a shooting a few weeks ago with someone killed along the street. We didn't know the details, but it looked to be drug-related. The dealers were slow in giving up their territory. In the summer of 2021, there was an active shooting during school hours, so Dr. Payne reached out to us to get assistance. We immediately scheduled a meeting with the new precinct captain who promised to take care of the matter, and he did. There have not been any active shooting incidents at Cleveland Avenue Elementary since this meeting.

Ski shared that the violent criminal activity moved west and the dealers are now about two miles away. He said, "You know that apartment community across the street from the Kroger? There were shootings there a few weeks ago. It's starting to get violent over there."

I understood all too well the challenges that lay ahead.

31

Solutions

Virginia and Ashley Humphries, Melinda Wyatt, James Wilkens, and other individuals and families portrayed in these pages are examples of neighbors who need our help. Housing is at the core of human stability. Human stability is at the core of community stability. High levels of tenant transiency at apartment properties throughout the United States is destroying schools and communities, creating a vicious cycle of poverty. In terms of schools, transiency, as discussed earlier, is the movement of children in and out of a school during the school year. This movement is common in blighted apartment communities or communities that are unstable due to high crime or large increases in rental rates. Families living in these unstable apartment communities are forced to move and take their children out of the school in search of safer neighborhoods. Research has proven that when a child moves schools, they lose approximately three months of learning, and this "churn" or school movement is a crisis hidden in plain sight. The high student transiency negatively impacts a school's performance hence reducing neighborhood desirability and home values.

I discussed transiency with Dr. Amanda Richie, principal at Brumby Elementary, a Title I school in north Atlanta. The very morning of our conversation, a single father enrolled his seven-year-old daughter in the second grade. Dr. Richie knew this young student from when she was enrolled in Brumby's kindergarten class two years earlier. From then to now, this child had moved five times and been enrolled in three different schools. The father was moving his daughter from apartment to apartment in search of safe, affordable housing. Maybe they had to move because of rent increases or maybe they moved to avoid crime. In any case, it was doubtful the daughter was current on her studies. This multiple moving is becoming the norm in public schools, specifically Title I schools, throughout the United States.

The problem is exacerbated by the "commodity" approach to apartment community ownership, where landlords singularly focus on raising rents to increase their profits. The resulting human and economic cost is significant. Commodity landlords purchase an apartment community, invest minimally in improving the structural environment, raise rents as quickly as possible, and sell the property at a large profit to the next purchaser, who repeats the cycle. The losers are the tenants, who endure dramatic monthly rent increases, eventually moving when they can no longer afford to stay, and the schools, who suffer increased transiency rates. For example, every time Dr. Richie and her staff receive a new student, considerable effort must be spent to evaluate the child's learning status and get her tutored to grade-level proficiency.

The TriStar Eduhousing model has demonstrated that housing stabilization reverberates positively through the community. Stabilized housing supports stabilized families, which in turn stabilizes schools, which in turn stabilizes communities. A child in consistent housing and in one school district has much better opportunity to thrive. In 2017–2018, the average "mobility rate" in Georgia public schools was 13.6 percent. The average mobility rate in Atlanta Public Schools for the same period was 25.4 percent. Some schools reported a mobility rate over 75 percent. Educators know the challenges of student transiency but I have found that very few landlords understand the critical role of housing and education. I have talked with dozens of school teachers who share stories of losing students mid-year, just when the student was showing promise and embracing his or her learning environment. These teachers invest in students only to have them disappear midterm, many as victims of their housing environment. One third-grade teacher in a Title I school shared:

> The successful teaching environment is so contingent on the connection between the student and teacher. I have wonderful young students who come alive when learning about certain math, reading or other topics, only to have them not show up one day for class—never to be seen again. I am truly invested in my students' success, and I can't help but worry about the children who disappear. I later learn that the student's family has withdrawn

them and we never learn what happened. Did they get another good teacher? Where they ever able to finish that math lesson? We never find out and its heart breaking. I never know what students are going to show up for class and by the end of the school year, I will only have less than half the students that were there on the first day of school but so many new faces. It can be very hard as educators to teach when you don't know if that student will be there tomorrow.

The resources to deliver equitable housing are available in every community, and the system can be designed so resources can be efficiently aligned when strategically invested in apartment communities. For example, educators, housing authorities, municipal leadership, nonprofits, banks, foundations, and medical providers are in business to provide their respective services, but if they cross-collaborate the impact of their services can have a multiplier effect. As mentioned in the opening of this book, educators focus on education, health care providers focus on healthcare, police departments focus on security, fire marshals and building departments focus on structure and safety, and nonprofits focus on their mission. However, if these resources collaborate in an aligned mission, a win-win can be created, to the benefit of the families and greater community, as demonstrated by Summerdale Apartments.

I came across a good example of a strong resource collaboration between two organizations with impressive results. Children's Healthcare realized that many of its young asthma patients were recurrent visitors to the emergency room. Many of these children lived in roach- or mold-infested housing. The dedicated doctors could treat the patient, only to have them return to their toxic housing environment. Children's Healthcare decided to partner with a nonprofit that provides free legal services to low-income families. Atlanta Legal Aid is now part of the emergency room intake process to assist the families of asthma patients dealing with substandard housing. Atlanta Legal Aid become involved as a tenant advocate to enforce the law and hold landlords accountable to provide clean, decent housing. The result was an improvement in home environments and a dramatic reduction in repeat visits by asthmatic patients.

Summerdale has been successful because the resources from multiple partners were aligned in the correct sequence that delivered stable students to Cleveland Avenue Elementary School. Summerdale houses approximately 20 percent of the school's students, and we know from the Georgia Milestone scores that our students were on par or outperformed their peers after just one year in the Star-C program. In turn, the success of local schools is a strong influencer of destination neighborhoods. Families look at schools when choosing neighborhoods in which to raise their families. Evidence is in a comparison of home prices near low-performing and high-performing elementary schools. In 2017, I surveyed the home prices of the five top-ranked and the five bottom-ranked elementary schools in Atlanta. The average home price in the zip codes with the top-ranked schools was $863,000, compared to the average home price of $51,900 in the zip codes with the bottom-ranked schools. Families are willing to pay a significant premium for homes in zip codes with top elementary schools. Hence there is a relationship between housing and education and the cycle of community success. Housing directly impacts school performance, and school performance directly impacts the demand for housing.

To repeat, resources that can be aligned to improve housing are available in every community. Resources from municipalities, federally qualified health clinics, churches, foundations, nonprofits, and other organizations are typically motivated to participate and contribute their resources to their communities. A general summary of these resources is below.

MUNICIPALITIES

Municipalities have a large toolbox to influence housing. Cities and counties have access to federal housing tax credits which can be used to deliver housing in both rural and metropolitan communities. We recently closed a federal tax credit housing bond through the Georgia Department of Community Affairs, which allowed our partnership to purchase twenty-five acres next to a low-performing elementary school in south Atlanta. The goal was to build 308 housing units affordable for families living on $49,000 or less per year. The majority of the students attending this particular elementary school live in marginalized housing in local trailer parks. Our new apartment community will offer rents lower than charged by our competitors, giving families a better housing option and access to free on-site after-school programs and summer camps. Our rents at this newly constructed apartment community average $925 monthly, or approximately $455 less than the competitive market rents of $1,380, converting more than $1.67 million per year in rental income into disposable income for our tenant families.

Another tool for municipalities is the Low-Income Housing Tax Credit (LIHTC). This is a federal program but issued through municipalities, many of whom don't have the staff to utilize it. I am looking for ways to partner with larger municipalities, and LIHTC could be a game-changer The U.S Department of Housing and Urban Development offers this insight:

> The Low-Income Housing Tax Credit (LIHTC) program is the most important resource for creating affordable housing in the United States today. Created by the Tax Reform Act of 1986, the LIHTC program gives State and local LIHTC-allocating agencies the equivalent of approximately $8 billion in annual budget authority to issue tax credits for the acquisition, rehabilitation, or new construction of rental housing targeted to lower-income households. An average of almost 1,400 projects and 106,400 units were placed in service annually between 1995 to 2018.
>
> HUD collects LIHTC data at the property level and the tenant level. The LIHTC database, created by HUD and available to the public since 1997, contains information on 48,672 projects and 3.23 million housing units placed in service between 1987 and 2018. Although some data about the program have been made available by various sources, HUD's database is the only complete national source of information on the size, unit mix, and location of individual projects. HUD also collects information on certain demographic and economic characteristics of households residing in LIHTC properties from state housing finance agencies that administer the LIHTC program. This page provides access to the property and tenant level data and also to data on Qualified Census Tracts and Difficult Development Areas designated by HUD.[78]

Public schools can reach out to apartment communities and develop working relationships with data sharing, after-school resources, and other programs. Eduhousing is a win-win partnership since the apartment community usually has the on-site community center building to host the program, and the children go from the school bus to the community center, freeing working parents from worrying about their child returning after school to an empty apartment. Our partnership with Drs. Carstarphen, Herring, and Payne with Atlanta Public Schools and other municipal school leadership is invaluable in maximizing student success. In turn, student success drives school performance.

After a presentation of our Eduhousing model, the CEO of a Fortune 100 company told me, "We adopted an Atlanta public school and invested $5 million in technology, personnel, and literacy programs over five years, and it did not improve the school performance one bit, so we stopped supporting the school. We want to make smart investments in our community and see results."

After meeting with this CEO, I checked the transiency of the elementary school he mentioned, and it was over 60 percent the previous year. No wonder the $5 million investment did not improve the school. The investment walked out the door whenever the family of a student moved. The odds of a student entering this elementary school in first grade and graduating after the fifth grade were lower than 10 percent. A $5 million investment in the local marginalized apartment communities would have more positive impact on the school.

A municipal city planning department can also greatly influence the delivery of affordable housing because it controls construction permitting, building code enforcement, and inspections. The leadership in this department in the City of Atlanta is very supportive of equitable housing. However, the city follows two different construction codes which creates a double administrative burden and confusion for developers and the city staff tasked with enforcing the codes. I've been a speaker at national conferences on equitable housing where several developers shared there is no affordable housing renovation development in their city, largely due to strict code requirements. While federal tax credits were available for the construction of new housing, the strict code rules made it cost prohibitive to renovate existing older apartment communities, which represent approximately 40 percent of all housing stock in the United States. Hence, the strict codes were making older housing functionally obsolete in communities which may have perfectly habitable housing stock that would support equitable rents.

Our renovation of Summerdale required a mind-boggling navigation of regulations, rules, code, and inspectors who kept changing the rules based on their interpretation. The Summerdale renovation was a smaller construction project—only ninety-two units—and we should have been able to complete the renovation in six months. Instead it took twenty months. The delays by the fire marshal, inspectors, and permit office added $2.4 million to our cost and $166 per month to the rental rates to cover these overages. We completely understand the desire for safe and secure housing. But many building departments create excessive burdens on housing projects, giving landlords no choice but to increase the monthly rents. The burdensome code compliance is being played out in many municipalities in the form of homelessness. As we noted earlier, research indicates that for every $100 increase in rent, homelessness increased 15 percent. Our experience at Summerdale supports this research. We had many tenants like Marilyn Moore, living on $12,084 per year, who said she would have no option but homelessness if we raised her rent $100 per month.[79] Fire marshals promote building codes in pursuit of zero fire casualties, however implementation of these strict codes is expensive, adding hundreds of dollars to monthly rent costs. It comes down to a social cost/benefit trade-off. In 2018, residential fires killed 2,720 civilians, of which 408 were in apartment communities.

Public safety is a large influencer in the stability and moral fabric of a community. The deficient community ecosystem allowed Anthony Fowler to thrive at Summerdale. With the dedicated resources of Officer Ski Pulaski at the Atlanta Police Department and the Atlanta Police Foundation, we were fortunate to eventually remove Fowler and his gang. But our toolbox for security is short-term. The judicial system did a poor job holding him accountable for his actions. In the future, we will build stronger data sharing with the police department. As a condition of Fowler's release, we were granted a restraining order to prevent him from returning to the property. That came in handy in the summer of 2020 when he was spotted at the property apparently setting up or grooming another young woman to be a phantom tenant to restart his business. I am forever learning from this model and every municipality is different; however, landlords need the criminal trespass tool as a tool to control criminals in its community. Landlords and their managers know the bad actors but unfortunately have to use expensive municipal tools like police and judicial resources to remove these actors. The criminal trespass citation would have helped punish these bad actors and moved them along—maybe even to a respectable business.

Fowler's illicit business attracted violent criminal activity which in turn traumatized the families and especially children living at Summerdale. Studies have clearly shown that community trauma influences brain development in children and we saw this first hand in the children living at Summerdale. Every one of the sixteen students who entered the initial Star-C program, were low readers. Many suffered from asthma and exhibited signs of severe trauma. The consequences of violent criminal behavior on the long-term success of children exposed to this violence is significant and should be part of the conversation if municipalities are serious about investing in housing and education of youth to be productive citizens as the future generation.

OTHER ORGANIZATIONS THAT CAN PROVIDE COMMUNITY RESOURCES

Municipalities are not the only resources universally available to apartment communities. Churches, nonprofit organizations like Girl Scouts, United Way, Salvation Army, and federally qualified health clinics can provide resources. Many family foundations reside in communities with some having a state-wide or national reach. The Coca-Cola, Chick-fil-A, and Woodruff foundations are based in Atlanta but provide grants beyond Atlanta.

Churches are a great resource for volunteers, prospective tenants and donations. Our church partnerships were valuable to securing books, school supplies and volunteers for many of our property programs. One of our properties averages over 7,500 volunteer hours a year for our after-school, summer camps and medical navigation events and many of these volunteer hours are from church partnerships. From these volunteers comes a better understanding and tolerance of our impoverished families and the community foot print. I tell my partners, investors and friends, if you need some good news, go visit the playground at our properties on a family day and see all the children and families come together in the spirit of community. You can't help but smile.

Nonprofits are an incredible resource for every facet of Summerdale. We partnered with Star-C who manages all the nonprofit relationships and operated the free on-site after school programs, summer camps and wellness events at the property. Dozens of nonprofits in communities operate after-school programs and are looking for partnerships. The efficiency offered by apartment communities is "location" and families that need services, wrapped up in convenience. Other nonprofits that can provide services include boys and girls scouting clubs, early learning programs, food banks, financial literacy programs (usually available through the local banks), United Way, senior programs and many others. If your property operates an after-school program, volunteers can be sourced through volunteer organizations like Hands On Atlanta, colleges, fraternities and civic organizations like garden clubs. Many high schools require a certain number of volunteer hours to graduate.

Federally qualified health clinics cover virtually every region of the United States. Summerdale and other apartment communities in our portfolio have partnered with Morehouse Medical and Medcura Medical to provide affordable medical services, health screenings and on-site insurance navigation for our families. Medcura Medical partnered with Star-C and we provided a "Back to School Readiness" event where the community children were transported to Medcura for on-site visits with a doctor, dentist, vision, and hearing specialist. Thirty-six children and their parents took advantage of this event, and free diapers, cleaning and personal products provided from a local garden club and church congregation were distributed. Tele-health is also becoming popular for families in equitable apartment communities—for ease and convenience. These federally qualified clinics are usually looking for partnerships and apartment communities can provide access to residents in need of services. Furthermore, developing a "medical home" relationship with people tends to keep them out of the local emergency room, which is much more expensive than a doctor's visit with the local clinic.

Family foundations can provide both donations to landlords and much needed low-cost capital to fund the acquisition and renovation. Foundations and family trusts are beginning to understand the process to loan money at low or zero interest rates to "mission based" landlords which in turn allows the landlord to offer lower rents for families in need.

In summary, every community has resources to assist landlords in the delivery of equitable housing. What is needed is the political will from the municipality, the community leadership, and landlord to braid these resources into a unified mission. Our mission is to provide equitable housing and improved educational outcomes for the families. We were able to access a wide swath of community partnerships and resources in the delivery of Summerdale. Specifically, this is why the Eduhousing model at Summerdale works:

First, Summerdale is located in the City of Atlanta which has the political will to provide resources to improve the community. These resources include:

• The Atlanta Police Department, which provided the manpower to address the community turbulence caused by the violent criminal network. This was a significant investment of resources by the APD, but it paid off handsomely in terms of the safety and stabilization required to begin building community capital and trust.

• The Atlanta Police Foundation which provided the avenue to purchase security cameras for the interior of Summerdale, allowing the APD to conduct stakeouts and eventually arrest the drug dealers. The cameras were not cheap—$45,000 for three—but they are routed directly to the APD central command center and give Summerdale permanent police surveillance into the future. Summerdale could easily have spent $45,000 per year on one full-time security person; we felt the investment in these cameras was a bargain.

• The Atlanta Public Schools and former Superintendent Dr. Meria Carstarphen and her successor, Dr. Lisa Herring, were a large supporter of our efforts to improve Cleveland Avenue Elementary School. Meria worked with us to obtain a "data sharing agreement" which allowed us access to the Georgia Milestones, report cards, and other data to monitor our student performance. She also supported Dr. Payne who has been a strong advocate of Summerdale, Star-C, and our efforts to improve the living conditions for her students. Summerdale and Dr. Payne developed a working relationship on multiple fronts. For example, if one of her student families has housing needs, she referred them to Summerdale. Many of her families could not pay their rent during COVID-19 and worked with the Star-C Eviction Relief Fund to get rent paid so children could stay enrolled, versus becoming another transiency casualty. Summerdale was fortunate to be in the Atlanta Public Schools district because APS was willing to partner with us. Surprisingly, we have worked with many school superintendents and educators who did not collaborate with TriStar apartment communities or Star-C, making the work more challenging.

• InvestAtlanta is the development arm of the City of Atlanta and is a powerful resource for equitable housing developers. In March 2017, the Atlanta City Council unanimously passed a $40 million initiative, the Housing Opportunity Bond, which funded affordable housing programs in the city including homeowner renovations, multifamily developer loans, down payment assistance, nonprofit development loans, and land assemblage for affordable and workforce housing development. This housing opportunity bond is managed through InvestAtlanta and provided Summerdale a $1.5 million loan at 1 percent interest for twenty years. This affordable capital directly impacted the rental rates we could charge, and in exchange we agreed to keep 20 percent of our rents affordable for families earning 60 percent of the area median income (or $44,520, which is 60 percent of $74,200) at the time we closed the loan in 2018. The bond was so successful, the City Council voted to issue a $100 million bond in 2021. Atlanta developers working on thousands of affordable housing communities have access to the affordable funding, allowing them to offer lower rents.

WE HAD OTHER COMMUNITY resources that allow us to help stabilize families.

• Morehouse Medical provided on-site medical services for Summerdale families. The COVID-19 pandemic paused those services, but we were able to do free on-site medical checks for our residents and have a local health clinic to refer for medical appointments.

• An anonymous Family Trust provided a $1.3 million interest-free loan to fund the acquisition and renovation of Summerdale. This low-cost capital allowed us to reduce our monthly rents by $35, which is important for low-income families.

• Renasant Bank. It took us many phone calls to find a bank interested in financing a blighted apartment community in a marginalized neighborhood, but Renasant Bank stepped up and agreed to be the lender for the property loaning us $4.9 million. It has been a good loan for them and helped Renasant meet its Community Reinvestment Act (CRA) credit.[80] I asked Chris Braun, our banker, why Renasant invested in Summerdale. He replied:

> Quite frankly, I am surprised that so many banks said "no." Not only did TriStar provide a fully underwritten business model, but the debt and equity stack made it very compelling to partner and to be a lender to the project. TriStar also brought the track record to the deal, which carries a lot of weight with Renasant. Overarching to the deal was the CRA opportunity that it presented to the bank, and CRA is something deeply engrained into the banks culture and our DNA. It is not only a box to check, or something we are obligated to do, but we wanted to do this. My CEO says community redevelopment precedes economic development. You have to have community development before economic development, which means certainly the idea that if the whole community doesn't benefit from economic development that bank loans bring, then it is not sustainable. It has to come from the ground up.

• Individual Impact Investors. We launched the TriStar Community Impact Fund in 2017 and raised more than $3 million to help fund the acquisition and renovation of Summerdale. The fund was designed based on the mission to invest in legacy apartment communities and improve educational outcomes through equitable rents. The term of the fund is ten years, and it pays a stepped interest rate starting at 2 percent the first year, 3 percent the second year, and 4 percent the third through tenth year. Many high-net worth individuals invested in this fund, including apartment developers, large commercial landlords, entrepreneurs, and family foundations.

This important low-cost impact investment fund enabled Summerdale to offer equitable rents for low-income families.

• The Atlanta Housing Authority. Summerdale came with seventy-four units under the Homeflex Program, a rental subsidy program funded by the U.S. Department of Housing and Urban Development and administered through Atlanta Housing. This program let us retain our long-term legacy tenants like Ms. Humphries and Ms. Moore and offer stability to their families. Under the Homeflex program, Ms. Humphries and Ms. Moore are able to stay in their homes and pay 30 percent of their gross income as rent; Atlanta Housing pays the remainder. Despite the administrative hurdles, we like this program because we control the apartment and rental process and relationship with the federal funding versus the Section 8 "tenant-based" voucher program where the tenant controls the relationship with the federal funding.

• Star-C. We signed a community program and lease agreement with Star-C, and Summerdale agreed to pay $3,000 per month plus a free two-bedroom apartment for the on-site program director and all utilities and costs associated with the community center. The Star-C director we recruited became a part of the community fabric. Star-C started operating once we deemed the property safer and provided the leadership to manage the community partnerships and braid resources. Star-C brought in KABOOM! playgrounds, the Georgia Power Home Energy Improvement Program (HEIP) to offer free energy efficiency upgrades, Morehouse Medical, Georgia Tech and United Way, Literacy Action, Trees Atlanta, and countless foundational grants, churches and volunteers. These community resources have been invaluable in elevating the community trust and capital created for our residents, Cleveland Avenue Elementary, and Summerdale Apartments.

• KABOOM!, a 501(c)(3) nonprofit, provided a great building event and united our community by delivering a dynamite play space for the Summerdale children and their families . KABOOM! worked with TI Asset Management to organize a two-day event where community volunteers came to Summerdale to construct a state-of-the art playground that was actually designed by the children in the Star-C program. More than 225 volunteers joined the two-day effort, including volunteers from the City of Atlanta, Atlanta Housing, city council members, judicial officials, local colleges, churches, businesses, other apartment communities, and families. The results were spectacular, and the KABOOM! playground is a popular amenity for the Summerdale families that sparks joy and fosters a sense of belonging for the children.

IN OUR EFFORT TO build "best practices" we should also look at opportunities for improvement in our model and from our partners:

• Criminal Trespass—the City of Atlanta adopted a criminal trespass citation, but then postponed our ability to use this valuable legal tool because of fear associated with a lawsuit in Florida that challenged the legal viability of the process. If landlords with properties in the City of Atlanta had this valuable tool to remove toxic characters like drug dealers, the violent criminal activity would never have escalated to the level that ravaged the trust needed for community safety. We could only sit by and patiently wait for APD to go through the long, expensive police process to eventually arrest the criminals who were operating in clear sight. Those arrested would back at Summerdale within a day, and there was little we could do to remove them without the criminal trespass citation. That tool could have given Summerdale control over criminal delinquents and removed the kingpin in a matter of days instead of months. We were fortunate that no one was killed or maimed by stray bullets while the long judicial process ensued.

• Permitting and the Department of Building and Planning. The City of Atlanta follows two permitting codes—the International Building Code (IBC) and the International Existing Building Code (IEBC)—that often contradict. Our contractor ended up using pieces of both codes, but the primary compliance was the IEBC. Summerdale must follow provisions of IBC, National Fire Protection Association (NFPA) 101, International Plumbing Code (IPC), International Mechanical Code (IMC), and National Electrical Code, or NFPA 70 (NEC). The IEBC references that if there are conflicting provisions between different codes, the IEBC takes precedence. But if not covered in IEBC, then the other codes can be enforced. Ultimately, how codes are enforced and interpreted is up to the Department of Building and Planning.

• Political Will. Summerdale works because we had the leadership and broad political will to develop the model. The low-cost investment capital necessary to fund the purchase and renovation of Summerdale allowed us to keep rents $200–$300 per month below market. Otherwise, we would have had to raise rents to cover our monthly loan costs, and many of our low-income tenants would have been forced to move. We also had the municipal leadership to provide resources needed to truly improve the educational outcomes and housing costs. Resources exist in every community that seeks to participate in solutions for families in need, and landlords are in a unique position to align these resources. One of the most rewarding aspects of Summerdale is the convergence of generous people, enthusiastic about participating in a mission-based community model which improves educational outcomes and delivers resources which equalize children with their wealthier peers. The evolution of "blighted" Summerdale to a successful community of choice involved tens of thousands of labor hours; some of those hours were a labor of love from a patient municipality and generous community.

EQUITABLE HOUSING IS A major problem in cities around the United States, and our Summerdale Eduhousing model is just one solution. Conscientious, devoted leadership in many communities have developed solutions unique for their families and within the framework of resources available. I urge you to get involved through means as simple as researching the web to find affordable housing solutions in your community. The Virginia Humphries, Marilyn Moores, and other neighbors in your community will be forever grateful.

Notes

1   *Eduhousing* is a "Marjy word"—I created it to explain our business concept, which has the mission of combining education and housing as a single property model.

2   US Census Demographic Profiles 2010, 2015 Estimates and 2020 Projection, Tetrad 10/29/2015.

3   Ibid.

4   Atlanta Regional Commission: "Metro Atlanta Added 89,000 people last year," March 29, 2018. See https//atlantaregional.org.

5   See: CoStar, AXIOMetrics, Cushman & Wakefield, Novogradac & Company Rent & Income Limit Calculator, Jan 2018.

6   See: Testscores: Georgia Department of Education Rankings. www.Schooldigger.com.

7   The National School Lunch Program (NSLP) established in 1946 reached 30.4 million children in 2016. Children from families with incomes at or below 130 percent of the Federal poverty level are eligible for free meals; those with family incomes between 130 and 185 percent of the Federal poverty level are eligible for reduced price meals. See https://www.fns.usda.gov for more information.

8   Governor's Office of Student Achievement, Georgia School Grades Report. See http://schoolgrades.georgia.gov.

9   In 1989, Congress established the National Commission on Severely Distressed Public Housing. Its 1992 final report led to enactment of the HOPE VI program enabling HUD grants to Public Housing Authorities for new construction and revitalization of existing properties. Over 15 years, HOPE VI grants were used to demolish 96,200 public housing units and produce 107,800 new or renovated housing units, of which 56,800 were to be affordable to the lowest-income households. The new and renovated units were mixed-income, less dense, and sought to attain better design and integration into the local neighborhoods. See en.wikipedia.org/Hope-VI.

10   Per the State of Georgia code, recommended capacity is two persons per bedroom.

11   City of Atlanta police records for 2017 documented 373 calls to 911 involving the Exxon station, including 52 for fighting (including with persons armed), 18 for drug activity, 21 for theft, and 32 for suspicious persons; an average of one 911 call per day. Source: Atlanta Police Department.

12   Section 26 USC-168(e)(2) of the Internal Revenue Service code.

13   $200,000 additional interest ÷ 244 units ÷12 months = $68 a month additional rent

14   The cost to operate an apartment community vary greatly based on location, age, and structural components. See National Apartment Association 2019 Survey on Operating Income and Expenses in Apartment Rental Communities.

15   The city of Atlanta has high water rates, starting at $12.27 per 748 gallons. Comparatively, New York City charges $4.30 per 748 gallons.

16   See https://blightedapts.org/wp-content/uploads/2022/09/Summerdale-Title
     -History.pdf.

17   "United States Residential Foreclosure Crisis: Ten Years Later," CoreLogics, March
     2017, pp. 4–5.

18   Fulton County Deed book 46750 page 663 and page 673 and 49866 page 591

19   See www.schooldigger.com for state rankings of U.S. elementary schools.

20   According to a June 4, 2004, letter from Hector Gomez to David L. Hammock of
     the Cobb County Attorney's Office, the owner spent $2,403,725 on repairs.

21   For an excellent research study on blight, please refer to Urban Land "Urban Blight
     and Public Health" by Erwin de Leon and Joseph Shilling, April 2017.

22   The "Distinguished Schools" program is designed to honor high-performing Title I
     schools that receive additional federal funding and services to support economically
     disadvantaged students.

23   Per the Office of Juvenile Justice and Delinquency Prevention. See OJJDP Statistical
     Briefing Book, released April 18, 2022.

24   In a traditional competitive market, sellers typically give a buyer approximately
     60–90 days to close a deal once a contract is signed

25   Fulton County records, deed book 58853, pp. 513, 535.

26   "Atlanta Mayor Unveils Ambitious Affordable Housing Plan for the City," J. Scott
     Trubey and Stephen Deere, *Atlanta Journal-Constitution*, June 29, 2019.

27   Balazs Szekely, Rent Cafe blog, November 1, 2018: The median household income
     for an Atlanta renter in 2017 was $38,556; see https://www.rentcafe.com/blog/rental
     -market/renters-median-income-accessibility-of-rental-stock/.

28   Kristal Dixon, "Affordable Housing Stock Shrinks Across Metro Atlanta," Axios.
     com, March 4, 2022.

29   One source (https://largest.org/misc/employers-usa/) names the largest employers in
     the United States as the U.S. government (2,700,000 employees at an average salary of
     $69,344 per year, https://www.federalpay.org/ employees/2017); Walmart (1,500,000 at
     an average salary of $12.78 per hour (careerstint.com/Walmart-employee-average
     -salary); McDonald's (420,000 at an average salary of $10.14 per hour, https://www
     .payscale.com/research/US/Employer=McDonald%27s_Corporation/Hourly_Rater);
     Kroger (400,000 at an average salary of $14 per hour, https://www.careerbliss.com
     /kroger/salaries/); IBM (377,757 at an average salary of $98,012 per year, https://www
     .payscale.com/research/US/Employer=International_Business_Machines_(IBM)
     _Corp./Salary); Home Depot (371,000 at an average salary of $12.55 per hour, https://
     www.payscale.com/research/US/Employer= The Home Depot Inc./Hourly Rate); UPS
     (362,000 at an average salary of $17.02 per hour, https://www.payscale.com/research/US/
     Employer=United_Parcel_Service_(UPS)%2C_Inc./Hourly_Rate); Target (371,000 at
     an average salary of $14 per hour https://www.careerbliss.com/target/salaries/.

30   The average wage of a domestic worker in 2017 was $12.01 per hour versus the aver-
     age wage of a general worker of $19.97 per hour. See www.epi.org. Victoria's net of
     $320 per week is the equivalent of $10.31 per hour in gross salary. The 2017 federal
     poverty level for a family of four was $24,600, or $12.06 per hour.

31 City of Atlanta police incident history notes recovery of nine stolen cars in 2016, seven of which were recorded at Summerdale; however, by our observation, the actual car theft activity was much more extensive. Source: Atlanta Police Department.

32 From the Georgia Apartment Association.

33 Landlords prefer tenants to have gross income of 2.5 times the monthly rent. Sharon's reported gross monthly income was $2,333 per month, or 3.6 times the advertised rent of $650 for Unit B-12. She would qualify for rent up to $700 per month.

34 Tenants can scam landlords by presenting false or stolen social security numbers or false identifications/passports. Landlords take extra screening precautions with applicants who have no credit history.

35 In the U.S. in 2017, 4.9 percent of workers and 5.3 percent of female workers held more than one job at the same time, U.S. Bureau of Labor Statistics, *Economics Daily*, July 19, 2018.

36 Key Substances Use and Mental Health Indicators in the United States: Results from the 2017 National Survey on Drug Use and Health, SAMHSA, September 2018.

37 Fowler did not respond to an interview request. His profile is based on records research, interviews with people at the property, and personal observations.

38 The cumulative Anthony Fowler arrest records can be found at http://justice .fultoncountyga.gov/Pajailmanager/jailingdetail.aspx?JailingID=1092401.

39 Recent surveys estimate that more than 50 percent of children and youth have experienced some level of community violence exposure. This experience has been shown to have a negative impact on development leading to increased emotional, social, and behavioral problems. A robust finding is the link between violence exposure and latter aggression and violence, referred to as the "cycle of violence." In other words, children who see or experience violence around them are more likely to use violence as they get older and into adulthood. The effects of violence exposure are particularly problematic for young children and have been shown to adversely impact brain development. Disruptions early in life can set in motion a physiological chain of development that becomes increasingly difficult to interrupt. In addition to higher levels of aggressive behavior, psychiatric disorders including depression, anxiety, and posttraumatic stress disorder (PTSD) are found at higher rates among youth exposed to community violence. Still, most youth who grow up in violent settings do not develop mental health or behavior problems, although more research is needed to understand specific processes of resilience. See: Nancy G. Guerra, Carly Dierkhising, "The Effects of Community Violence on Child Development," *Encyclopedia on Early Childhood Development,* November 2011.

40 See "Double Jeopardy: How Third Grade Reading Skills and Poverty Influence High School Graduation," the Annie E. Casey Foundation, January 1, 2012, www.aecf.org /resources/double-jeopardy/.

41 "Children in Poverty—Poverty and Its Effects on Children," All4Kids Newsblog, January 28, 2019.

42 "Adverse Childhood Experience and the Developing Brain," National Center For Mental Health, Elin Lewis, August 22, 2019.

43 Dr. Anne Fernald, Professor of Psychology at Stanford University American

Association for the Advancement of Sciences conference lecture "How Talking to Children Nurtures Language Development Across Socio-Economic Status and Culture.

44 "Tackling the "Vocabulary Gap" Between Rich and Poor Children, Christopher Bergland, February 16, 2014. *Psychology Today.*

45 Each state has a different method to report mobility rates. For Georgia's, visit https://gosa.georgia.gov/report-card-dashboards-data/downloadable-data and and scroll down to "Student Mobility Rates" by school and district. See also Sara Sparks, "Student Mobility: How It Affects Learning, *Education Week*, August 11, 2016.

46 The 2017 Poverty Guideline for a family of four was $24,600 or $11.83/hour for a full-time job.

47 Charles Basch, "Healthier Students Are Better Learners," *Journal of Health*, October 2011: "Children with asthma appear to be at a disadvantage for school readiness. They performed worse on tests of concentration and memory . . . Disparities among urban minority youth are outlined, along with the causal pathways through which each adversely affects academic achievement, including sensory perceptions, cognition, school connectedness, absenteeism, and dropping out. No matter how well teachers are prepared to teach, no matter what accountability measures are put in place, no matter what governing structures are established for schools, educational progress will be profoundly limited if students are not motivated and able to learn. Particular health problems play a major role in limiting the motivation and ability to learn of urban minority youth."

48 American Community Survey Five-Year Estimated, U.S. Census Bureau, September 18, 2017.

49 The calculation is $9,600,000 * 1 percent = $96,000 per year in interest divided by 244 apartment units = $393/year per unit in additional interest divided by 12 months = $33/month.

50 A sampling of the cost of evictions at Summerdale indicated $7,583–$8,185 per unit based on the timeframe to remove the tenant while they were not paying rent (usually four to five months) and the cost to clean, paint, repair and release the unit.

51 Will was interested in getting an official HVAC certification which requires the successful completion of several technical courses offered by the Atlanta Apartment Association. The starting hourly rate for an HVAC certified maintenance technician is $16–$18 per hour in Atlanta.

52 "Understanding Energy Burden and its Potential Solutions for Atlanta" (Colton, What is the Home Affordability Gap, 2017).

53 One of the planet's tallest mountain ranges.

54 According to the American College of Allergy, Asthma and Immunology, the saliva, feces, and shedding body parts of cockroaches can trigger both asthma and allergies. These allergens act like dust mites, aggravating symptoms when they are kicked up in the air. The National Pest Management Association reports that 63 percent of homes in the United States contain cockroach allergens. In urban areas, that number rises to between 78 percent and 98 percent of homes. Children from substandard housing are particularly vulnerable to asthma associated with roaches. See https://acaai.org/allergies/types/cockroach-allergy.

55 Access to these units was via a steep hill with a slope of 1:5 to 1:6, exceeding the maximum allowable running slope of 1:2 per UFAS. The compliance checklist is 46 single-spaced pages. See https://hud.gov and search for UFAS Checklist.

56 The U.S. Department of Housing created the 334-page Fair Housing Act Design Manual. See https://www.huduser.gov/portal/publications/pdf/fairhousing/fairfull.pdf.

57 To be protected by the ADA, one must have, or be perceived by others as having, a physical or mental impairment that substantially limits one or more major life activities. There were no public access accommodations in Phase I that required ADA compliance; however, since the management office and common areas were located in Phase II, Phase II was required to comply with ADA. See the 2010 ADA Standards for Accessible Design at https://www.ada.gov.

58 DCA is the Georgia Department of Community Affairs, providing local government assistance for economic development and helping communities meet housing needs. See https://www.dca.ga.gov.

59 For more information about Davis-Bacon, see https://www.dol.gov/agencies/whd/government-contracts/construction.

60 $482,000 at 4.5 percent interest came to $36,612 per year in mortgage payments, equaling $80.29 per month in additional rent for the 38 units required to have the tubs flipped. This is an example of how the regulatory environment increases rental costs with no particular benefit.

61 See the April 4, 2016, U.S. Department of Housing and Urban Development paper on fair housing and criminal history: "Office of General Counsel Guidance on Application of Fair Housing Act Standards to the Use of Criminal Records by Providers of Housing and Real Estate Related Transactions."

62 These would be tenants who no record of a tenant screening in their lease files. As noted earlier, there was evidence the previous management company did not do a formal credit or criminal background screening on several tenants. Per our records, 23 tenants had criminal histories from misdemeanors to felonies.

63 Fukuyama, Francis. *Trust: Social Virtues and the Creation of Prosperity.* (Simon and Schuster, 1996), 26, 104.

64 According to the Collaborative for Academic, Social and Emotional Learning, social emotional learning (SEL) is the process through which children and adults acquire and apply the knowledge, skills, and attitudes to develop healthy identities, manage emotions, set and achieve goals, feel and show empathy for others, establish and maintain positive relations, and make responsible decisions. See https://casel.org.

65 PACE (Positive and Adverse Childhood Experiences) measures the impact of trauma through a simple ACE Score. For an excellent website with community resources on the topic of childhood trauma, visit https://www.pacesconnection.com. Readers can take the ACE Quiz to determine their own personal scores at www.pacesconnection.com/blog/got-your-ace-resilience-scores.

66 *Atlanta Journal-Constitution,* October 20, 2015.

67 The cost to bring Sumerdale up to current fire code, including sprinklers, fire-rated walls, etc., was estimated at $30,000 per unit. At 5 percent interest to borrow the funds, that equaled $5.91/month in rental for each $1,000 spent, or a rent increase of $177.30 per month to pay for the code requirements. Building codes typically require

that a structure's walls, floors and roof be fire resistant in accordance with standards set by the International Building Code (IBC). A wall-rating indicates how long fire can be contained before it spreads to the next room. A 1-hour fire-rated wall is a ⅝-inch thickness of gypsum board to which noncombustible fibers have been added. Summerdale buildings A–D were constructed with ½-inch thick wallboard.

68   The City of Atlanta bills on a three-tiered water rate scale based on consumption of CCF (centum cubic feet or 100 cubic feet), from a low of $.0164 per gallon to a high of $.0292 per gallon. The average toilet requires 3.6 gallons, or, based on the tier, $0.06 to $0.11 per flush. The base CCF is calculated by multiplying the units in the apartment community times 3. Thus Summerdale Phase I should have a CCF base of 300 (100 units multiplied by 3); the actual CCF stated on our bill was 252 and we had that corrected to 300. The December 2018 bill for Phase II was $22,274 for 831,776 gallons of water consumed, or 1,112 CCF. The conversion of CCF to gallons is one CCF=748 gallons (831,776 gallons divided by 1,112 CCF). Under billing tier #1, the first 252 CCF (188,496 gallons) was billed at $12.32/CCF ($.0164/gallon). Under billing tier #2, the next 252 CCF was billed at $18.98/CCF ($.0253/gallon). Under billing tier #3, the next 252 CCF and above is billed at $21.85/CCF ($.0292/gallon). The average household uses 6,000 gallons per month or 8.02 CCF. The city's billing allows 2,244 gallons, or 3 CCF per month, per unit before reaching the next tier. The average American uses 17.2 gallons to shower, for which Atlanta charges $0.28 to $0.50 depending on the tier. The average older inefficient clothes washer uses 30–45 gallons, or $0.74 to $1.31 per load. The bottom line: water in Atlanta is expensive for low-income families. At 6,000 gallons per month, the bill will be $98.40 (at $0.0164/gallon) to $175.20 (at $0.0292/gallon).

69   The Georgia Tech students' research concluded that Summerdale used standard air filters with a MERV rating of 4 at an annual cost of $25; however, for $20 more per year we could offer a filter with a MERV rating of 11 or higher to capture more than 90 percent of large particles and 70–90 percent of small particles.

70   A Bloomberg analysis based on U.S. Census Bureau calculations and the distribution of household income ranks Atlanta as the most unequal large city in the United States in 2017 and the city's poverty rate sits at 24 percent or nearly one in four people. A child born poor in the Atlanta area is less likely to grow out of poverty than children in most other big U.S. Cities. See Fiza Pirani, *Bloomberg*, October 11, 2018.

71   A study by researcher Lin Cui of the University of Pittsburgh found that violent crime within 250 feet of a foreclosed home increased more than 15 percent once the foreclosed property became vacant ("Foreclosure, Vacancy and Crime," *Journal of Urban Economics*, 2015).

72   See "The Cost of Vacant and Blighted Properties in Atlanta: A Conservative Analysis of Service and Spillover Costs, Dan Immergluck, PhD, Prepared for the City of Atlanta and the Center for Community Progress, September 2015.

73    $166 per month in rent multiplied by 12 = $1,992 per year divided by 30% affordability factor = $6,640 per year. .

74   See "New Perspectives on Community-Level Determinants of Homelessness" by Thomas Byrne, Ellen A. Munley, Jamison D. Fargo, Ann E. Montgomery, Dennis P. Culhane. *Journal of Urban Affairs*, November 2012.

75 Final Report and Recommendations for King County, Washington, by the Regional Affordable Housing Taskforce, *Journal of Public Affairs*, December 2018, page 16.

76 For a great Podcast series on Evictions, visit WNYC studios On The Media, "The Scarlet E—Unmasking America's Eviction Crisis," June 6, 2019, hosted by Brooks Gladstone.

77 Anthony Fowler was also living in unit C-6.

78 For information on the Federal LIHTC program, see https://www.huduser.gov/portal /datasets/lihtc.html.

79 The Policy Advice report "The State of Homelessness in the US—2022" calculated that more than 552,830 people were living on the streets. Smiljanic Stasha, July 30, 2022.

80 The Community Reinvestment Act is a federal law enacted in 1977 to encourage depository institutions to meet the credit needs of low- and moderate-income neighborhoods. The CRA requires federal regulators to assess how well each bank fulfills its obligations to these communities. This score is used to evaluate applications for future approval of bank mergers, charters, acquisitions, branch openings, and deposit facilities.

Index

Names preceded by asterisks have been changed for privacy reasons.

Accu-credit 131
Accu-score 131, 134, 136, 140
Adverse Childhood Experiences Study 15
affordability (of housing) x–xi, 7–19,
    21–22, 27, 40–44, 45, 48, 52, 55–63, 66,
    110, 125, 148, 149, 154, 167, 169, 173, 179,
    181, 191, 205, 239, 252, 255, 258, 267, 293,
    309, 312, 314, 317, 328, 335, 338, 342, 345,
    348–350, 355, 359
*Allen, Sharon 79–85, 143, 212, 237, 275,
    293–295, 315, 318, 323
Americans with Disabilities Act (ADA) 165,
    179, 180, 181, 202, 220, 253, 254, 256,
    257, 271, 309
asthma 14, 88, 92, 111, 131, 137, 168, 186,
    200, 219, 225–226, 227, 283, 297, 301,
    315, 347, 352
Atlanta Community Food Bank xii, 42,
    330
Atlanta, Georgia
    and code enforcement 18, 29, 31, 244,
        246, 247, 248, 249, 250, 350, 358
    and developers 355
    city council of 279, 280, 283, 324, 355,
        357
    city planning 151, 251, 358
    Department of Records 141
    housing deficiency of 7
    population of 5, 6, 22, 116
Atlanta Housing Authority 179, 181, 191,
    193, 207, 212, 251, 257, 280, 357
Atlanta Legal Aid 15, 347
Atlanta Police Department 33, 95, 96, 117,
    148, 151, 158, 170–177, 235, 273, 324, 351,
    354
Atlanta Police Foundation 151, 159, 173,
    234, 320, 327, 351, 354

Atlanta Public Schools (APS) 7, 54, 57, 90,
    105–107, 110, 154, 219, 279, 295, 329, 334,
    346, 350, 354, 355
Atlanta Regional Housing Forum 42
Atlanta Technical College 284
Atlanta Volunteer Lawyers Foundation
    226
Avryn, Doug ix
Azar, Bernice 85

Bishop, Charles 178–182, 191
blight
    and communities 39, 45–54, 107,
        170–177, 183, 190
    and political will 35–44
    effects on tenants 86–93, 114–123,
        240–245
    science of 20–34
    solutions to 345–359
Bolling, Bill 42
Bottoms, Keisha Lance 56, 280, 329, 340
Braun, Chris 59, 356
Brumby Elementary School 29, 35–36,
    40–44, 218, 345
Buckhead Christian Ministries 317, 336,
    337
Bulldog (drug dealer) 74, 75, 78, 171

capital stack financing 55–63, 355
Capitol View Elementary School 106
Carstarphen, Meria 57, 279, 350, 354
Centers for Disease Control (CDC) 15,
    226, 335, 338
Children's Healthcare Atlanta 347
Chris 180 336
Civil Rights Acts of 1964, 1968 180

Cleveland Avenue Elementary School 7–8, 16, 33, 46, 54, 67, 104–113, 150, 259–261, 264–266, 268, 283, 288, 290, 294, 295, 298, 300, 302, 303–307, 312, 329–334, 339, 342, 344, 348, 354

Cleveland Avenue neighborhood 5–19
and blight 150
and social capital 149–150
demographics of 5–7

Cobb County, Georgia x, 21, 35–44, 57, 216, 361

Community Reinvestment Act (CRA) 59, 356

COVID-19 56, 328–344, 355

CRCP testing 40

credit history 39, 126, 131, 134, 212, 236

credit reports 29, 39, 81, 126, 127, 130, 131, 132, 134, 136, 145, 212, 236, 268, 316, 323

crime reports 85, 141, 145, 158

crime, violence 6–8, 9, 15, 16, 33, 50–53, 64, 66, 69, 99, 103, 107, 108, 114–119, 125, 132, 156, 157, 175, 194, 224, 234, 280, 306, 327, 332, 344, 352

criminal trespass 235, 276, 277, 323, 352, 358

Crystal Ball for Arthritis xii–xiv

Cushman & Wakefield 7, 56, 360

Davis-Bacon Act 167, 181, 272

DCA. See Georgia Department of Community Affairs

Decatur Cooperative Ministries 336

DeKalb County, Georgia ix, 21, 322

Destiny Church 40, 217, 218

Dickens, Andre 280, 324

Dressel, Donald 8, 32

drug kingpin. See *Fowler, Anthony

*Dummond, Shercia 144

Education for All Handicapped Children Act. See Individuals with Disabilities Education Act (IDEA)

Eduhousing 20, 36, 57, 59, 245, 346, 350, 354, 359

Epstein, Lianne 167, 182, 191

equitable housing 20, 347, 350, 354, 355, 359

evictions 226, 314–318, 338
and fees 82
and legal process 29, 83, 211, 235, 237, 268, 293, 298, 314, 338
and transiency 268
costs of 314, 318
in application forms 80
of Melinda Wyatt 196, 244, 268–271, 298
of problem tenants 195, 211, 235, 238, 277
of Sharon Allen 84–85, 237–239, 293
result of financial problems 28, 80, 150, 329, 337, 338

Exxon station 5, 10, 46, 71–72, 74, 92, 104, 118, 120, 175, 288, 289, 292, 297, 300, 343, 344

Fair Housing Act (FHA) 179–181, 202, 220, 309

Fair Housing Amendments Act 180

Fannie Mae 32

Federal Fair Housing Act (FFHA) 165, 166, 271, 310, 311

Fort Valley State University 227

*Fowler, Anthony 15, 49, 74–78, 98–103, 145, 149, 170–177, 212–213, 234, 236–237, 275–276, 315, 318, 322, 323, 325, 327, 351

Fulton County, Georgia 18, 328
courthouse of 69, 268, 276
courts of 95, 99, 114, 211, 235, 236, 237, 274, 293, 318, 321, 325
district attorney of 235, 274, 277, 324
extension services of 316
jail of 19, 98
judicial system of 9
property records of 10, 32, 33
sheriff's department of 69, 100, 117, 284

*Galindo, Maya 48, 69, 70, 81–85, 91, 102, 128–129, 132–139, 142–144, 147, 197, 313
Georgia Apartment Association 82
Georgia Department of Community Affairs (DCA) 181
Georgia Department of Education 40, 109
Georgia Milestone Test 109, 110, 111, 282, 299, 334, 348, 357
Georgia Power 82, 357
Georgia Southern University 105
Georgia State University x, 237, 342
Georgia Tech 153, 162, 279, 283, 299, 308, 357
Gideons Elementary School 106
Girl Scouts 352
*Glover, Benny 134, 136, 137, 138, 139, 142, 159, 160, 200
Grady Memorial Hospital 6, 71, 239

Hamby, Lucy 20, 134, 155–169, 171, 172, 174, 191, 192, 195–203, 207–213, 214, 221, 223, 226, 227–232, 233–244, 260, 267–269, 273–277, 281, 293, 314, 321–322, 325
Hammer, Eli 57
Hands On Atlanta 353
*Harris, Evan 195, 196, 203, 227, 228, 229, 230, 231, 240, 241, 244
Hartsfield-Jackson International Airport 6, 52
*Mr. Hayes (security) 124, 128, 132, 135, 137, 142–144, 155, 157–159, 163–164, 171, 175, 195, 197, 235
healthcare x, xi, 14, 19, 56, 150, 154, 347, 353
Hemingway, Kristin 40, 201, 214–219, 224–225, 243, 259–266, 291, 299–303, 305, 306, 328, 330, 333, 342
Herring, Lisa 350, 354
Home Energy Improvement Program 357
Homeflex 165, 166, 179, 181, 191, 207, 210, 254, 260, 293, 310, 317, 318, 337, 357

HOPE scholarships 105
HOPE VI grants 8, 10
housekeeping classes 232, 241, 244
housekeeping issues 14, 16, 29, 141, 142, 147, 161, 162, 168, 186, 196, 227, 231–232, 240–245, 268–269, 289, 295, 297, 304, 315, 318
Housing Opportunity Bond 355
"human school bus" 73, 120
*Humphries, Virginia, and family 64–78, 114–123, 148, 162, 221–226, 283, 284, 289, 290, 312, 330, 339, 340, 345, 357

Individuals with Disabilities Education Act (IDEA) 180
International Building Code 252, 254, 358
International Existing Building Code (IEBC) 358
International Mechanical Code 358
International Plumbing Code (IPC) 358
InvestAtlanta 57, 60, 355

Jackson, Omari 79
*Jackson, Reginald 74–78
Jackson, Shawn 134, 143
*Jennings, Robert 134, 138, 141, 143, 159, 160, 194, 312
Journal of Public Affairs 366

KABOOM! playgrounds 188, 279–280, 289, 299, 328, 357
Keane, Tim 251, 253, 255
Kirk, Cassandra 274
*Kirk, Kandice 207–208, 212, 213, 337
Klementich, Eloisa 57

legacy housing x
Lennon, Christine xiii
Literacy Action 357
Long Middle School 7, 8, 90

Madison Hills Apartments x, 21, 35–44, 57, 61, 216, 218–219

MARTA. See Metro Atlanta Rapid Transit Authority (MARTA)

Massey Services Pest Control 169, 195, 227, 229, 240, 241

Medcura Medical 353

Mercer University 107

Metro Atlanta Rapid Transit Authority (MARTA) 86, 292

Milestone Test. See Georgia Milestone Test

Miller, Jeff 20, 152–154, 164–167, 178–182, 191, 192, 193, 202–206, 213, 216, 220, 228, 238, 241–245, 246–258, 267, 270, 275, 278, 308, 311, 321, 328, 341–342

mold 14, 23, 29, 30, 35, 37, 82, 111, 124, 147, 159, 160, 162, 186, 219, 226, 252, 253, 260, 306, 347. See also asthma

*Moore, Marilyn 137, 139, 160, 194, 200, 223, 289, 312, 330, 351, 357

Morehouse College 281, 298

Morehouse Healthcare 154, 329, 353, 355, 357

Morehouse Medical. See Morehouse Healthcare

Morehouse School of Medicine 154

"$99 Move-In Special" 28

Mt. Carmel Baptist Church 65, 70

National Fire Protection Association (NFPA) 358

Old Hapeville Road 4, 5, 8, 32, 46, 49, 52, 53, 71, 74, 86, 104, 112, 120, 143, 155, 172, 192, 193, 246, 259, 260, 283, 343

Operation Shield 173, 174

Ott, Robert 35, 36

Parker, Angie 274, 276, 277, 323

Payne, Anyeé 73, 92, 104–113, 119, 120, 174, 175, 215, 219, 264, 265, 280, 283, 290, 292, 295, 298, 303–307, 330, 331–333, 339, 342, 344, 350, 354

PCCI 336, 337

permitting process 18, 153, 201, 250–258, 288, 307, 309, 350, 358

pest infestations, control 14, 51, 90, 91, 111, 137, 141, 160, 169, 195, 196, 201, 202, 219, 227–232, 260, 264, 270, 315

phantom tenants 30, 79–85, 100–101, 172, 236, 237, 275, 289, 294, 317, 318, 352

political will 21, 57, 61, 354, 359

Project Open Doors 336

Pulaski, Joe "Ski" 94–103, 173, 175, 176, 194, 205, 235–236, 276–278, 280, 288, 293, 303, 318–321, 325–327, 343–344, 351

Rehabilitation Act of 1973. See Uniform Federal Accessibility Standards (UFAS)

Renasant Bank 59, 356

ResidentCheck 81, 82, 145

Richie, Amanda 29, 36, 41, 42, 43, 345, 346

roaches 14, 26, 29, 87, 90, 91, 111, 129, 136, 141, 147, 161, 168, 169, 194, 195–196, 200, 202, 209, 227–232, 241–245, 264, 294, 297, 306. See also pest infestations, control; See also asthma

Salvation Army 352

Shepherd, Denise 135, 136, 283

Simmons, Betty 37

social capital xi, xv, 9, 17, 20, 39, 40, 42, 54, 77, 101, 126, 127, 147, 148, 149, 150, 174, 209, 234, 302, 306, 338

social hierarchy 16, 17, 149

South Atlanta High School 8, 334

Stagmeier, John xii

Stagmeier, Margaret "Marjy"
    and capital for real estate investments 55–63
    and charitable fundraising xii–xiv
    and chasing criminals 277

and Madison Hills Apartments 35–39, 42
and Summerdale Apartments 190
and TI Asset Management 39
and TriStar 9–21, 24, 29
as "community" vs. "commodity" investor 125
as fashion-setter in blighted neighborhood 52
as mission-based optimist xiv, 52, 149–150, 285
background of ix–x, xii–xiii
Star-C afterschool program 9, 15, 40, 55, 56, 149, 153–154, 173, 174, 189, 201, 204, 214–219, 225, 231, 243, 254, 259–266, 279–282, 290–293, 296, 299–307, 312, 328–331, 333, 335–338, 342, 348, 352, 353, 355, 357
Star-C Eviction Relief Fund 338, 339, 355
Stone Mountain, Georgia ix, xiii
Summerdale Apartments
and church and foundation partnerships 352
and COVID-19 pandemic 188, 328–344
and crime, violence 9, 187
and drug dealing 143, 170–177, 233–239, 272–278
and evictions 267–271
and government regulations 16, 18, 165, 166, 167, 178–191, 185, 246–258, 351
and pest control 186, 227–232
history of 8, 23–24, 32–34, 46, 70, 183
management office of 192–206
pre-purchase inspections 124–147
rebuilding social capital of 149, 184, 279–287
renovation of 188, 189, 351, 359
Tenant Association of 281, 284–287, 288, 316, 328, 329
tenants' views of 220–226
toxic culture of 207–213
TriStar's purchase of 9–10, 148–154
Summerdale Commons Apartments 32
Summerdale Partners 32

Summerdale Tenant Association 281, 284, 285, 316, 328, 329

tax credits 348, 349, 350
tele-health 353
Thompson, Adriane 172, 181, 207–213, 237, 238, 242, 281–287, 312, 316–318, 324–325, 328, 330, 333–339
TI Asset Management (TIAM) 39, 151, 158, 169, 272, 279, 357
Title I x, 40, 42, 43, 345, 361
transiency 11–13, 22, 29, 31, 36, 38, 43, 44, 110, 149, 150, 196, 243, 260, 268, 304, 314, 332, 345–346, 350, 355
Trees Atlanta 357
TriStar
and education 13, 15, 41, 173, 214, 268, 346, 355
and Eduhousing 57
and Summerdale purchase 10, 16–19, 21–34, 124–147
business model of 45, 56, 149–150, 173, 179, 210, 214, 315, 356. See also Summerdale Apartments: TriStar's purchase of
mission of 9, 20, 43, 59, 125, 147, 173, 209, 314, 354
Summerdale operations of 158–169, 174
TriStar Community Impact Fund 59, 356

Uniform Federal Accessibility Standards (UFAS) 165–166, 179, 179–181, 180, 191, 192, 196, 202, 203, 220, 228, 241, 242, 243, 270, 271, 309, 310, 311, 312
United Way 329, 336, 352, 353, 357
U.S. Census 5, 21
U.S. Department of Housing and Urban Development 8, 56, 181, 254, 349, 357, 360

vagrants 30, 34, 51, 124, 147, 152, 234, 251, 305

vandalism 20, 29, 37, 42, 51, 81, 146, 184,
254, 301, 307, 311

*Walker, Janet 325
water consumption, leaks 17, 25, 29, 129,
134, 160, 167, 267, 314
Waters Road 34, 53, 107, 324
*Webster, William 70, 77, 83, 90, 99, 137,
159, 160–163, 260
*Webster, Andre 84
*Wilkens, James 130, 148, 289, 316, 345
*Williams, Dane 144
*Wyatt, Melinda 86–93, 160, 171, 191,
195, 202, 228–232, 240–245, 267–271,
295–298, 315, 345
family members of 86, 88–89, 91–92,
295

*Young, Sammy 47, 48, 49, 50, 51, 52, 77,
78, 128, 129, 138, 142, 145, 146, 147, 162,
200

Z Summerdale LLC 32, 33